Contents

v

The CAULDRON of ETHNICITY in the MODERN WORLD

The CAULDRON of ETHNICITY in the MODERN WORLD

Manning Nash

The University of Chicago Press
Chicago and London

MANNING NASH is professor and chair of the Department of
Anthropology at the University of Chicago. He is the author of
many books, including *Machine Age Maya* and *The Golden
Road to Modernity*, both published by the University of
Chicago Press, and *Unfinished Agenda: The Dynamics of
Modernization in the Developing Nation*.

The University of Chicago Press, Chicago 60637
The University of Chicago Press, Ltd., London
© 1989 by The University of Chicago
All rights reserved. Published 1989
Printed in the United States of America

98 97 96 95 94 93 92 91 90 89   5 4 3 2 1

LIBRARY OF CONGRESS CATALOGING-IN-PUBLICATION DATA

Nash, Manning.
    The cauldron of ethnicity in the modern world / Manning Nash.
        p.   cm.
    Includes bibliographical references and index.
    ISBN 0-226-56866-0:   ISBN 0-226-56867-9 (pbk.)
    1. Ethnicity.   2. Social change.   I. Title.
GN495.6.N37   1989
305.8—dc19   88-29522
                                                       CIP

∞ The paper used in this publication meets
the minimum requirements of the American National
Standard for Information Sciences—Permanence of
Paper for Printed Library Materials, ANSI Z39.48-1984.

Preface

This book is part of a continuing concern with social change in the modern world, particularly those parts of it popularly and mistakenly called the Third World. An earlier work, Unfinished Agenda: The Dynamics of Modernization in Developing Nations (1984), attempted to give an account of social change since the retreat of empire and the birth of new nations in old societies. The notion of "modernization" had (and may still have) evolutionary, ethnocentric, and teleological overtones as well as ideological resonance. In my usage, I have tried to free it from those elements, none of which I subscribe to, nor do I believe a reasonable, useful, and empirically relevant notion of social change can be built on those discredited overtones of the misplaced polarity of "tradition—modernity." But like all mythological dragons, even when slain they continue to writhe and may have the ability to grow another shape from the severed and hacked pieces.

This work looks to an even less global level—the problems of ethnicity in the nation-states of the world, both old and new. Ethnicity again has all sorts of unwanted ideological and evolutionary accretions, and again I have tried to scrape the barnacles from the concept and make it clear in my usage and as a tool in the analysis of changing societies and cultures. I hope my conceptual labors prove not to be Sisyphisian but rather more like Daedalus. Time, however, is the final judge of such things.

In this book, like others I have written, I have used as an empirical base chiefly my own fieldwork, supplemented by other material I consider reliable or at least comprehensive, coherent, and more or less complete. With these strictures on data and observation, coupled with the predilection for closely viewed crucial instances rather than statistical or cross-cultural nets, much of the world enters only by implication of contrast and control. The large area of the Soviet world and Eastern Europe, with their special interests in "nationalities" (whether or not according to the policies first laid down by Stalin), is not here touched; nor is the relations of the Han people of China to the more than 65 million "minorities" seriously treated. Old European conflicts like the Flemings and the Walloons or the Basque and others also are not analyzed. Much of the world, and some of the ideas needed to handle ethnicity, remains outside of the ken of this book.

What I have endeavored to build are some "islands" of firm data and useful theory from which greater land masses may be constructed until the world of time and space is encompassed. I am not so much interested in forging a theory of magnificent generality, enduring for decades, as I am in the quest for scale and durability. In the human sciences, it is systematic understanding with diagnostic tools applicable to real societies in time and space which I take, at this point in time, to be the glowing achievement of social science. To these ends this book is, I hope, a contribution. And as such, may it help ease the pains of transition for those who bear in their lives and bodies the costs and blessings of social change.

1
Ethnicity: Meanings and Vicissitudes

"Ethnic," "ethnicity," "ethnic group" are words and ideas that seem to have a clear and solid meaning, a referent in the world, and to be the sort of self-evident social reality that needs no other explication. But "ethnicity" and "ethnic group" are among the most complicated, volatile, and emotionally charged words and ideas in the lexicon of social science. And this is the case for good and sufficient historical and theoretical reasons.

The modern world, that system of cultures and societies fashioned since about the 1500s, is in large part the struggle among nations, peoples, and ethnic groups. The nation-state, itself a product and agent of the process of modernization, is responsible for the rise and definition of social entities that are currently called "ethnic groups." Before the rise of the nation-state, there were, of course, different cultures, political levels of organization, civilizations, and other forms of cultural and social diversity.

But the nation-state, over the last five centuries, has emerged as the most potent, maximal, and perduring form of social and political organization. As a historical phenomena, the nation-state (whose vicissitudes through a long and complicated history is well-documented and need not be a major concern of an anthropologist, no matter how infinitely interesting to historians and political scientists) grew out of the wreck of empires, the breakup of civilizational blocks of cultures, and the absorption and transformation of "peoples" within and without the hegemony of either encompassing political structures or cultural patterns of civilizational complexity.

1

The nation-state hence often had more than a single "people" within its borders, and often it had much cultural diversity within its political boundaries. The modern nation-state is founded on the idea of citizenship (another interesting idea born in city-states and transformed in the process of modernization into current meaning), which has overtones of voluntary allegiance, loyalty, and of exclusivity. Those people who were not politically dominant in the nation-state and who still had significant cultural markers of difference and sufficient social cleavage from the dominant political majority were "ethnic" groups. The ethnicity was sometimes viewed in romantic terms like a "volk," a vestigial, colorful remnant of earlier times, soon to be swamped by the inexorable tide of the nation-state, that most rational, efficient, modern, and natural form of social and cultural being. At other times, the ethnic group was viewed as a "minority" people whose every aspect, except political self-determination, was to be granted full scope by the nation-state or, more accurately the state made up of nations. And sometimes the ethnic group had aspirations toward nation-state status itself and thus became a militant minority. In the nineteenth century, German romanticism gave rise to the notion of every people in its own national entity, what A. D. Smith (1981) has righly called the "ethnic revival." And in the twentieth century, with the end of the imperial system of states and colonies, the drive toward national sovereignity was given renewed impetus, which still continues in wars of national liberation even when colonial entities have long ceased to exist. The historical context in which "ethnicity" is studied has every bearing on the meaning of the term or concept.

That which is universal, timeless, or ahistorical about the relations among peoples or groups exists at a level of abstraction that is either unproductive of further knowledge or verges on a tautology. One of the chief hindrances in the understanding of ethnicity has been the premature drive to forge a general, all-encompassing theory. This could not be done, and cannot be done, without a more general theory of social, cultural, and psychological systems. The later trinity of theories, or a general all-inclusive social science, does not yet, and may never, exist. The useful, sensible path of procedure is to form partial theories responsible to bodies of observation and fact and testable on further observation and further fact. This is the sort of program or plea often heard in social science. It requires a considered movement between local and temporal structures in a never-ending attempt to transcend them. This program of comparison and contrast aims at empirical generalizations, but it is comfortable with the polythetic framework in which different instances mutually enrich understanding of each other. It uses concepts diagnostically. From its general budget of analytical ideas it draws on those in an order that seems to fit the historical, structural, and cultural dimensions of the case at hand. But it is one that may result in the dredging up of islands of knowledge from the seas of speculative ignorance. Something like this use of concepts was recommended by Wittgenstein, and something akin to this method of comparison was part of Franz Boas's anthropological agenda.

Clearly, a major defense against a spectral universalism is the historical specification of limited segments of human history. The segment long enough to have distinct pattern and more or less agreed-upon trajectory in time is the last 500 or so years—the emergence, spread, and dominance of modern social and cultural systems. This worldwide process of modernization has had as a major component the "nation-state," and it is the nation-state in which ethnic groups have the standing and conceptual meaning used throughout this work.

Differences between groups, collectivities, and societies have existed since the beginnings of the archeological record in human history. What this "we-they" difference meant then is probably not recoverable, as is the case with so many things in the incompleteness of the archeological record. And what group difference meant in the early civilizations, the early empires and the imperial and colonial systems, is much more accessible and of some import to the inquiry here. But no one system of concepts or generalizations will explain all of this panorama of human cultural variety and its meanings to the carriers of the varied cultural and social systems.

What seems to unite all of these historically and socially disparate situations is some underlying social psychology of interpretation of group differences. But even this phrasing of the search for universals in group loyalties and boundary-maintaining mechanisms is difficult to spin into empirically relevant sentences. Ethnic ties have been bundled together with other kinds of deep, core, and primary bonds suffused with affect into a category of "primordial" ties. Primordial ties lie at the core of the person. They form the basic identity, and they are the markers of humanity that come to the person at the earliest periods of socialization, before there is a filter of rejection and acceptance. Primordial ties are thus the social expression of the psychological basis of identity, selfhood, and of others who are like the self, and yet others who are different from the self.

There is an immediate appeal in the utility of the idea of primordial ties. In the modern world of rootlessness, deracination, alienation, and the twin search for meaning and a usable past, the idea of a discoverable, fixed, comfortable, and historically continuous identity is highly charged with psychic rewards and appeal. Finally, the self has a home, with a past, a present, and a future transcending the fragile biological vessel that is its container.

Whatever the subjective utility of primordial ties may be, the cold social fact is that primordial ties are like any other set of bonds, forged in the process of historical time, subject to shifts in meaning, ambiguities of reference, political manipulation, and vicissitudes of honor and obliquy. The reality of ethnic identity, its content, and its boundary lines—being a historical product and thus subject to change, redefinition, and varied salience in the lives of members of the group—does not overcome the insight that the *building blocks of ethnicity,* defined as the self-conscious group within a nation-state, are virtually the same over time. It is this confusion between the relatively unchanging building blocks of ethnicity and the permanence of the ethnic group, its boundaries, content, and social and personal salience, that make the use of "primordial" so problematic and resistant to further elaboration as a powerful and productive concept. Which building blocks of ethnicity are invoked to construct a category and what boundary forged to set the category off from others is historically specific, structurally constrained by the economic and political power differentials among the groups, and conditioned by the cultural images of the past and future and the strategies the groups try to enact in view of their divergent agendas.

The building blocks of ethnicity have been the *body* (a biological component expressed as blood, genes, bone, flesh, or other common "substance" shared among group members), a *language* (some spoken and written forms of communication that are thought to contain modes of communication, meanings, essences, and stylistic elements unavailable in other languages), a *shared history and origins* (this gives the sense of shared struggles, shared fate, common purpose, and the implication that personal and group fate are one and the same thing, with personal fate being itself dependent on group survival), *religion* (the set of beliefs and practices that purport to relate a group in a special way to the supernatural; often the divide is between religions calling themselves different, but other times the differences lie in the interpretation of what is ostensibily the same religion), *nationality* (this is the right to a territory, an equality with the most powerful other nations, and all the symbolic and political accoutrements of a sovereign and independent people).

These elements are woven together in various ways to form the kaleidoscope of ethnicity now and over time. Woven together is not the proper metaphor, for the elements are organically interactive and take different shapes according to historical and political circumstance. Smith (1978) and Isaacs (1975) have traced the historical amalgams of the elements of ethnicity to show the bewildering variety of combination. This historical variety has, in part, contributed to the difficulty of defining ethnicity, or even identifying its elements and components.

Not only is time or history a confounding feature in ethnicity, the continuum between cultural—political, or cultural—natural elements in the idea of ethnicity is a further source of problems and unclarity. Language seems straightforwardly a piece of culture. But on reflection it is clear that language is often a political fact, at least as much as it is a cultural one. It has been said that "language is a dialect with an army and a navy." And what official or recognized languages are in any given instance is often the result of politics and power interplays. Similarly, the body aspect is not straightforwardly biological or physical. What is noticed, classified, and socially relevant is rarely brute biological fact (whatever that may be) but a cultural perception sometimes rooted in body imagery or physically available markers of bodily aspect. No amount of physical observation could have produced the elaborate "casta" distinctions of the Spanish empire in the New World, ending the list of supposed physical types with one called, "well there you have it," exhibiting cultural fatigue in classification.

Thus the study of ethnicity needs to be rooted in a

definite time period, with an eye to the malleability of the combination of elements that go into its construction at different times and places, all this with a sensitivity to the continuum of cultural-political-natural which also has a dynamic shaped by history, circumstance, politics, and economics. In a sense, the study of ethnicity is the attempt to study all of social science under that single rubric. The reason that ethnic studies have had no more than limited success or more perduring generalizations results largely from overlooking that fact. Ethnic studies depend upon a general social and cultural theory, and also upon a powerful social psychological base. They cannot be successfully prosecuted without that underpinning. And of course such studies, like all macrosocial inquiries, rest on the historical dimension which alone provides the arena of social change and allows the separation of the superficial from the basic in understanding group persistence and cultural dynamics.

Studies like that of Edmund Leach (1954) among the Kachins of highland Burma exhibit the interplay between general social and cultural theory and ethnic studies. The findings of Leach that the social system of the Kachin oscillated between an equalitarian organization and a hierarchical order using different arrangements of the same cultural features was, at the time, striking enough. But the fact that the hierarchical form of Kachin could move into the Shan configuration—including language, religion, dress, and other "primordial" features—came like a relevation in Southeast Asian studies and caused fundamental reorientations in social and cultural theory. Chiefly, the empiricist notion of social structure as a thing was the victim of Leach's work, and competing concepts of social structure have been vying for theoretical dominance ever since. Also, cultural indices, or group boundary markers, came to be seen as much more fluid, malleable, subject to rapid change, and even manipulation. Moerman (1965), in his work on the Lue in northern Thailand, showed the situational bases of ethnicity and the strategies of choice for economic advantage by a tribal people who could be Thai when the need, opportunity, and advantage arose.

In the light of these studies (and many more worldwide, emphasizing the historical, the contingent, and shifting theoretical bases for the study of ethnicity), another effort cannot be lightly undertaken. Any addition must stipulate reasons for the choice of historical trajectory, make clear theoretical commitments: why particular cases are examined, what partial hypotheses are strengthened, which are weakened or rejected. The "moral" and "value" components of the study of ethnicity and ethnic groups cannot be totally ignored. Much of the previous work on ethnicity has had its focus on problems of cultural and political survival in terms of a vision of justice, decency, and human worth. A good part of the history of the modern world is involved with the clash of ethnicities and the national politics of ethnicity (Worsley 1984). It is probably of little use to elaborate a moral position on the issues, since such a position can only be assented to or denied.

My own commitments are partially derived from anthropology (human variety, cultural and otherwise, is probably a good thing in itself for a variety of reasons), from a reading of history (ethnic conflict tends toward bloodshed and resolves nothing), and a general sense that human social and cultural differences are persistent, necessary, valuable, and that the problem lies not in ethnicity but in the political, economic, and human worth conflicts that get entangled with or use ethnicity as a rallying point.

I am not sure the world can be made better with honest facts and new ideas, but I am certain that it can (and has) been made worse by lies and falsehoods. In that spirit, I will explore three instances of ethnicity in the modern world.

The cultural dimension of groups, ethnic and other, is largely taken up by a set of symbols that define and mark off the group from other groups. The chief symbolic marker is

a name, and names exist in a system of names. The system
of names must be acknowledged across the group boundaries, but self-names need not be isomorphic with other
group namings of it. This is akin to all linguistic symbolism:
a system-wide set of differentiations but lodged in different
social settings, and with only partial overlap from social
setting to social setting, from group lexicon to group lexicon. Names not only mark group boundaries, they also
implicate relations of super- and subordination, relative
power, status, economic, and moral worth positions of the
different entities. These relative status and power dimensions among named groups, like other symbols, need not
be fully consensual, symmetrical, or isomorphic. The mapping of group names, the spelling out of the rules of difference among them, and their placement in a series of relative power and worth among the cultural hierarchies is the
first and most important task in the systematic study of
ethnicity.

The mapping of named categories, or the discovery of
the vocabulary of group differences in a given lexicon of a
culture, may not describe actually existing groups. Many
studies in both anthropology and sociology have com-
piled racial and ethnic taxonomies, which have limited
social referents and no or few consequences in the everyday life of the society. Cultural categories (ethnic or
otherwise) may exist without group referents, just as animal names exist in culture but not in nature, as in the case
of the unicorn versus the lion, or the metaphor of the
phoenix, the powers of the griffin, or the evil of the dragon.
The cultural system of names, however, has a meaning,
and that meaning lies in the pattern of the names and the
meanings associated with them. Much valuable social information is constructed through the mapping of ethnic
categories, the modes of boundary maintenance, the various hierarchies in which the names are ranked. What
groups call themselves and what they call others is both

the language of esteem and language of insult. Names condense the relevant cultural information into handy social and psychological packages for easy self and other identification which can set off a behavioral repetory associated with the symbols of group identification. I will eschew the anecdotal citation of some patterns of group names on the grounds that anybody can, from his own experience, validate the existence of ethnic group labels and their systematicity in terms of differentiation, ranking, and implied social response.

Cultural categories with social and group referents are the focus of ethnic inquiry. Where there is a group, there is some sort of boundary, and where there are boundaries, there are mechanisms to maintain them. These boundary mechanisms are cultural markers of difference. The differences among groups are index features. The index features must be easily seen, grasped, understood, and reacted to in social situations. The index features implicate or summarize less visible, less socially apparent aspects of the group. These boundary-marking features say who is a member of what group and what minimal cultural items are involved in membership. Like all things at boundaries, these index features must be visible to members of the group as well as to nonmembers. The meanings associated with the boundary differences among groups need not be, and most frequently are not, isomorphic. Valued insider aspects of culture may be comic or derided by outsiders, and caricature and exaggeration frequently mark outsiders' depiction of boundary mechanisms. Stereotyping is a form of caricature of cultural, index features of group differentiation; an emphasis and ranking of features that in itself helps mark the boundaries among different groups.

The most common ethnic boundary markers, in the ethnographic record, and the most pervasive, in any system of ethnic differentiation, are *kinship,* that is, the presumed biological and descent unity of the group implying a stuff or substance continuity each group member has and outsiders do not; *commensality,* the propriety of eating together indicating a kind of equality, peership, and the promise of further kinship links stemming from the intimate acts of dining together, only one step removed from the intimacy of bedding together; and a *common cult,* implicating a value system beyond time and empirical circumstance, sacred symbols and attachments coming from *illo tempore.*

These cultural markers of kinship, commensuality, and religious cult are, from the point of view of the analyst, a *single recursive metaphor.* This metaphor of blood, substance, and deity symbolize the existence of the group while at the same time they constitute the group. If these boundary mechanisms were breached with regularity, the group as a differentiated entity would also cease to exist. And, indeed, history is littered with group names for which there are no contemporary groups, or even claimants to affiliation to vanished entities. Both the durability and the ephemerality of ethnic groups are cultural and social enigmas of the first magnitude.

This trinity of boundary markers and mechanisms is the deep or basic structure of ethnic group differentiation. It is the presence of cultural markers of blood, substance, and cult that separates ethnic groupings from other kinds of social aggregates, groups, and entities. But sometimes the members' basic symbols of ethnicity are not visible, graspable, or available in social interaction, and hence other surface features stand for the index features. These are, more or less, secondary to the basic recursive metaphor of ethnicity, and hence more mutable over time and less psychologically central to group identity.

These surface pointers make recognition at a distance, or in a fleeting instance, possible, and as such are in themselves often barriers to more intimate contact in much the same way as the core trinity of ethnicity.

The frequent surface pointers include dress, language, and (culturally denoted) physical features. To this secondary trinity a host of subsidiary indices of separateness can be layered on: house architecture and interior arrangments, ritual calenders, specific taboos in joint social participation, special medical practices, special economic practices, and a host of other secondary and tertiary markers of differentiation. All of them take their force of separating groups and persons only if they are linked to the core features of differences. Differences in dress, from whole costumes to single items of apparel, serve as surface markers of group differences. These items of apparel best serve when visible and public, but items of dress may reinforce group boundaries even if not visible, like the underwear of Sikhs, or the undergarment of pious Jews. The meaning of dress codes in ethnic boundary identification is a branch of semiotics until it is tied to the core elements of social differentiation.

Language is a marker akin to dress. A different language, or a series of public utterances far from the norms of communication, may mark off an ethnic group as does dress. And some language usage is akin to Sikh or Jewish hidden apparel; it serves an internal reminder of difference. Language as group marker has more social and psychological weight than dress does. Successful mastery of language implies learning it from birth, in the context of the kinship or primary group. Learning a language as an adult or as a later-in-life accomplishment is not the same as being a "native" speaker of the language. I leave the problem of "true" bilingualism to the linguists and the psychologists, while noting that culturally such a speaker is an ethnic anomaly.

Physical features are also secondary cultural markers, because what is relevant for social differentiation is not given in the body form of persons but in the cultural attention and stipulation of aspects of that body form. Again, body form has the Möbius band dimensions of inside and outside which form a continuous surface. Physical elements may include skin color, hair form, height, density, eye shape, or whatever superficial things the culture stipulates as making for essential difference. But it must also include the less visible physical features, some of which are internal to the group, like body mutiliation (circumcision, scarification, or tattooing).

All of the secondary surface and tertiary indices of group differences must be related in determinate ways to the basic or core elements of ethnic group formation. Physical features, language, dress, and the others must stand for and imply differences in blood, substance, and cult and hence to the building blocks of ethnicity. If the social markers do not relate to the structure of the building blocks, they are forms of social differentiation of the sort that mark off lodges like the Elks from Masons, boy scouts from sea scouts, or other superficial and transient social identities. These transient social identities are often voluntary, in that they can be volitionally assumed or cast off. Some aspects of ethnicity are also voluntary in that sense, and the balance between voluntary social groups and involuntary elements in social groups is of foremost interest in the study of ethnic groups in modern societies. The ideas of assimilation, integration, fusion, and pluralism have in large measure to do with the mix of voluntary-involuntary aspects of ethnicity as that is defined by the social system and internally in the groups constituting that social and cultural system. The choice of "cauldron" in the title of this work indicates my conviction that assimilation or total erasure of ethnic groups and differences is less likely than a pluralism resembling a sometimes calm, sometimes boiling pot more than it does either a melting pot or a pressure cooker, to borrow common images.

While ethnic differences and group identities have a history and a historical dimension, as noted in restricting the use of ethnicity *sensu stricto* to the historical time of the rise and spread of nation-states and to kinds of social and cultural orders called modern, there is a kind of time, or most exactly temporality, that is a cultural construct rather than a chronological record of time and events as they actually passed—if that sequence could be recovered and its facticity agreed upon. This temporal aspect of culture is grasped in the concept of "tradition."

Tradition is the past of a culture, as that past is thought to have continuity, a presence, and a future. These features of tradition bestow upon the past a weight of authority; the very fact of survival, pastness, and continuity give an aura of authority, legitimacy, and rightness to cultural beliefs and practices. The phrases common to most cultures— such as "time honored," "the way of the elders," "in the eyes of the ancestors," "as our fathers before us," and "the way it was always done"—indicate the reverence and authority for the pastness of things. That things and practices have traditional warrant makes for a linkage over generations, thus bestowing upon even the most humble member of the group a pedigree, allowing him to identify with heroic times, great deeds, and a genealogy to the beginning of things human, cultural, and spiritual. Max Weber has written extensively on some of these aspects of tradition as has E. A. Shils, but since they were chiefly concerned with tradition as a form of authority neither did much to tie tradition to the pedigree of the dispossessed, the formerly "historyless" and the newly arrived on the world scene.

Tradition, while chiefly concerned with the past and hence backward looking, has a forward, future dimension. The preservation and the continuity of tradition is enjoined on its carriers. The social-psychological meaning of this forward orientation binds the individual fate of group members to the fate of the future of the group. This set of attitudes tries to merge the life trajectory of persons with the trajectory of the group, positing the two as indissoluble.

The group has strengths from the evident fact of its survival, and that strength is augmented if individual survival is but a link in group survival. In the forward motion of tradition the elements of blood, commensality, and cult are those most emphasized through their symbolic markers. In brief, an identity is fashioned by name and symbol. A recursive metaphor of social differentiation is constituted, and tradition is enshrined. Group and individual survival meld into a personal identity. These are the basic features when the differences between groups are of the sort called "ethnic" and when this ethnicity take place in a system of such differences in the political organization of a nation-state.

Category and name, boundary, and survival deal with two-thirds of the true theoretical interest in ethnicity; the last third is the action aspect of ethnic groupings. Do such groups have political, economic, cultural, or expansionist or exterminationist agendas? These groups, then, may have action consequences amounting to agendas or more inchoate social activities and strivings.

The minimal action aspect of ethnicity (less than this amount makes it an etiolated entity bordering upon voluntary organizations like the country club) is the formal celebration of difference. The action can be as minimal as a national day of songs and costumes and then a disappearance of the social relevance of the ethnic group for another year or so (St. Andrews day and Von Steuben day parades approach this action minimum for Scots and Germans in New York). The other pole of ethnic activity is the total domination of social and cultural life by ethnic considerations, as in the bloodier clashes of the twentieth-century wars on ethnic or racial lines. Most of ethnically oriented action lies, in the nature of the case, between the ends of the continuum. Mere symbolic recognition of ethnicity indicates a spectral and Cheshire cat–like existence of group difference, while total absorption with ethnicity in political and social life indicates an unstable state of crises (the root of the crisis does not have to be, and frequently is not, itself, ethnic).

The action aspect of ethnicity inherently involves symbolic claims to social parity or superiority vis-à-vis other groups in the nation-state. (I know of no action programs by ethnic groups insisting upon inferior status. The closest is to entirely opt out of the prevailing rank system, like the Black Muslims in the United States, or to declare all systems of group rank to be invalid, as in the teachings of many religions and secular brotherhood movements.) The claims to status are closely linked to the minimal-maximal action line. The claim to status involves an insistence on the "rightful place" of an ethnic group. This rightful place, as a minimum, takes the form of being allowed to practice the group's way in peace without hindrance or molestation. The maximalist insistence goes toward conferral of most of the valued items on a single group in disproportiate measure, or even the denial of social value to some ethnic groups. These action aspects make for the conflict among ethnic groups within a social system. The conflict-accommodation relations among ethnic groups rest on some sort of "bargain" among groups as to both the division of socially valued things and symbols and the speed and directions of modification of perceived unjust disparities. Social bargains sometimes include rank concession, in which the subordinate group accepts its subordination and tries to modify its social differences along the axis set by the superordinate groups, or else individuals move, where possible, from the less privileged to the more privileged groups, leaving the less privileged groups so depopulated that they collapse and disappear. Social bargains as to relative group worth are clearly historical products and shift with the tectonic drift of ideology or the more accelerated motion of political and economic upheaval.

There is one further continuum to take into account: the strength-weakness of the nation-state vis-à-vis ethnic,

regional, or other subnational groups. It is nearly taut-
ological, but not quite, that ethnic power is inversely
related to state power, or that ethnic power is strong only
when supported by state power, or that state power is
strong only when supported by major ethnic groups. This
complicated interaction of state-ethnic power is obviously
the stuff of political science, but it bears on anthropology in
the area of trust in social life. Trust, in social life, rests upon
the ability to get redress in a breach of contract of implied
and expected social behavior. The ethnic group, with its
notion of identity and the merging of individuals, is the
group where redress can be exacted from members, or
used as a group against outsiders, making it very costly to
harm, cheat, or menace members of the ethnic group. And
the less impersonal, fair, and swift in redress, the more
important is the ethnic group. This function of trust is a sort
of insurance mechanism that ethnic groups are able to fill
in the presence of weak, venal, or ethnically dominated
states. This interplay between state and ethnic groupings
in terms of trust as that bears on redress and the insurance
of equitable social chances is most tragically enacted in
contemporary Lebanon, once thought of as the most remarkable of social bargains since the Swiss cantonal
arrangement.

This partial conceptual and theoretical approach to
ethnicity in the modern world needs, as stated earlier, both
temporal and typological limitations. The historical segment has been limited to the rise and spread of modern
social and cultural systems, roughly the development of
the nation-state and capitalism and its penetration into
Asia and Africa and Latin America. This appears to form
both a manageable and a coherent slice of human history.
But within this 500-year segment of history not all cases of
the phenomena of ethnicity can be handled. Capacity and
common sense dictate a more selective sort of comparison. There are many modes of comparison in contem-

porary anthropology, including the view that none is possible.

Between the single instance well analyzed (a la Durkheim, for example) and the global, statistical comparison of all known, recorded instances, I have chosen to concentrate on three instances I claim illuminate the phenomena and nearly exhaust among them the crucial variables involved in the explanation of ethnicity in the modern world. These are not case studies meant to support or refute some hypothesis or generalization, nor are they exemplars of typicality. These instances are meant to chart, map, order, and provide the basis for the understanding and perhaps eventual explanation of the course of ethnicity in the modern world, and as earlier said to be a form of polythetic comparison in the spirit of both Boaz and Wittgenstein.

The three instances chosen are Mayan Indian–Ladino in the highlands of Guatemala, Malay-Chinese in Peninsular Malaysia, and Jews in Modern America. The Mayan instance came into being with the spread of the Spanish Empire to the New World, and it developed over the past 500 years as that royal mercantile system moved to capitalist nation-states. In Guatemala, the conquered Indian moved into the submerged citizenry in an estate-like position in the total social structure, but each muncipal variety of Indian culture and community retained cultural and social distinctiveness. The Indians are at least, and possibly more, than 50% of the population. This situation represents one where a small conquering group places itself at the top of an indigenous hierarchy and over time develops various ethnic categories to account for the division of labor, status, political power, and definition of the nation. Now this historical instance is in a phase of crisis, which from time to time is inevitable in this sort of ethnic system.

The Malay-Chinese ethnic situation in the peninsula arose from the late expansion of capitalism into a tropical dependency. The extractive and export industries of tin mining and rubber plantation required a large and fairly docile labor force, quickly assembled. And in the British empire, three "races" always moved together in Asia—the British, the Chinese, and the Indians. Into Malaysia, Chinese miners and laborers and Indian rubber plantation workers came to live with the rural rice-growing Malays. The economic division of labor, the ensuing political arrangements, and the rise of Malay nationalism and its Muslim components are the chief ingredients in this on-going drama. The population is about even between Chinese and Malays (there is a large Indian population I do not extensively analyze) with a slight percentage in favor of the number of Malays.

Jews in contemporary America are a small group of about 6 million in a population of more than 240 million. They are immigrants who came in several waves from Europe—an early German wave, a later Eastern European wave, and now a small Soviet and Israeli wave of immigrants. In American society they have been socially mobile and are now chiefly middle class and upward in social scale, and chiefly urban dwellers. The intermarriage rate between Jews and non-Jews fluctuates but approaches 30 percent of marriages in some periods. The Jewish community is divided by different places on the continuum of piety to secular indifference, but it is still a community in times of perceived crises, now chiefly centered on events in Israel. As a small successful minority in a society dedicated to pluralism, the Jews are a test case of assimilation, voluntary ethnicism, or the tendency for nativistic revival movements in times of crises.

These thumbnail sketches of the three instances in this work are, at this point in the study, merely meant to illustrate the range of things to be later spelled out and analyzed. The more important methodological point is that the instances permit the deployment of a range of variables useful for the construction of explanatory hypothesis. The variables are present in different values in each case. It is the different *values* of features that make them variables. This point is often not acknowledged or understood in anthropology, where items, present or absent, strong or weak, seem to be the limit of methodological wisdom and sophistication. These variables must be combined with other concepts (the definitions and ostensive meanings of ethnic, index features, secondary markers, and boundary mechanisms, etc.) in order for analysis and synthetic interpretations to take place. The variables of demography, historical conjuncture, kind of nation-state, development of economy, economic competition among groups, and others will be developed as the exposition progresses.

There is, at least, one fortuitous factor in the selection of Mayans, Malays, and American Jews for the subjects of this study. I have lived and worked in all three of these societies. My years of work in Guatemala and Mexico, in Kelantan and Malaysia, plus being a native American informant, give a "feel" for the data, the way it can be used, what it will support, and where it is thick and where it is thin, that no amount of scouring and pouring over alien monographs can match.

2

Ethnicity in Peninsular Malaysia: The Idiom of Communalism, Confrontation, and Cooperation

In the postcolonial world of old societies and new states, the facts of cultural, social, economic, and above all ethnic diversity in the internal structure of the new states loom large. Ethnicity and its role in the future of the nation-state are seen as problematical, and often of the first magnitude of urgency for the continuing integration and national solidarity of the political order. Ethnicity may be seen as a barrier to civil politics (Geertz 1963), or as a constituent in a pluralist society, or as a basis for an ethnic revival and rise to dominance of a new form of nationally oriented ethnicity.

All of these visions of the proper role of ethnicity—the hegemonic of a dominant ethnicity, the liberal view of the irrelevance of ethnicity, and the pluralist view of several ethnicities accommodating in an overarching citizen image—have spokesmen and adherents in the new nations, including Malaysia. All of these views have limited merit, for they only partially confront and encompass the social and cultural problems and tasks of the recently formed nations like Malaysia.

New nations do have immense problems overcoming "primordial" ties (Shils 1957). Old claims to autonomy and sovereignty suppressed under colonial regimes may surface as political demands and movements with the advent of independence. Radical and socialist movements may call for the restructuring of society which ignores ethnicity and rearranges class power, and new political parties may compete for power using the appeals of ethnic ideology and solidarity. All of these possibilities are products of the actual history of ethnic blocs as they are formed and dissolved in social processes of the formation of basic identity and social and cultural differentiation.

Malaysia offers an embarrassment of riches for the analysis of one form of development of ethnicity and its interaction with other forms of social and cultural loyalties and groupings. There exists a good historical record of more than 100 years on the changing kaleidoscope of the ethnic elements on the peninsula; there is an abundance of good fieldwork, sophisticated economic and political analysis as well as the self-conscious reflections and analyses by local scholars and intellectuals.

It is customary, indeed even obligatory, to talk of the "three" major ethnic blocs or groups or populations that make up Malaysia. The Malays, the Chinese, and the Indians seem to be self-evident components of the nation of Malaysia, and these groups seem to have a solidity, permanence, and historical basis that is beyond cavil. They are, it is often maintained, the self-evident, basic, and irreducible categories for the further analysis of any social process in Malaysia. This view, superficially adequate to a first approximation of a description of contemporary Malaysia, overlooks or ignores the fact that ethnicity, in its modern sense, is a historical process. Ethnic groups get their significance in a political system. Ethnicity requires the nation-state for its political salience, for its meaning depends upon the overlapping or noncongruence between the categories of citizen with that of a people, a volk, a race, or some other prenational, noninstrumental, and cultural category for sorting human beings. The categories also require cultural markers, boundary mechanisms, albeit these in fact are porous and ambiguous. Finally, ethnicity needs a charter of authenticity moving the origin of the ethnic group beyond historical ken, often into the misty realms of the "natural" divisions of mankind. Along with the charter is a social psychological commitment to an identity in the deep sense of shared pasts, current predicaments, and common futures. Ethnicity is a supplier of answers to the questions: Where are we from? How are we different? What must we do?

If this view of ethnicity approximates the social, cultural, and psychological dimensions of that phenomena, the processes of formation, maintenance, growth and decay, and revival of ethnicity are the most interesting aspects of that phenomena, and Malaysia is an excellent locale for shedding light on a common (to much of Southeast Asia) but not universal process of ethnic interactions in the framework of new nations in a world of competing nation-states in the shadow of the superpowers.

Malaysia was absorbed into the British empire in bits and pieces and almost, it seems, in a state of absentmindedness as the British kept India, the jewel in the crown, at the center of the imperial network. The history, military and diplomatic, of the British expansion into Malaya, Borneo, and Burma is well and widely chronicled. First the settlements of Singapore, Malacca, and Penang formed the Straits Settlements. Then the territories of the West coast of the peninsula became the Federated Malay States, with the Eastern portion being the Unfederated Malay States, and then the Malaya Federation. Finally independence after World War II and the emergency operation against communist guerrillas, and then the formation of Malaysia with the inclusion of Sabah and Sarawak into Malaysia. Singapore was for a brief period part of Malaysia before it became the Republic of Singapore.

When the British began the imperial expansion into Malaya, the chief occupants of the peninsula were Malays. There were some Chinese, some Indians, some Orang Asli (the now official name for shifting cultivators and the seminomadic groups), some Thai, and some "others," all of whom are still in the census as categories of the population. The Malays were thought of by the British as the indigenous people of the peninsula, and in some sense the rightful owners and rulers of the territory, with all other people or groups as something of guests or immigrants, even those of long-standing and possibly predating the migrations of the Malays, as the Orang Asli were alleged to have done.

Who and what is a Malay? The question seems superfluous, but its answer requires an evaluation of ethnological, historical, sociological, and even religious dimensions. In the ethnological literature and anthropological tradition, Malay refers to peoples and cultures of archipelagic Southeast Asia, from the Isthmus of Kra to the Sulu Seas. This was a melange of cultures and languages broadly belonging to Malayo-Polynesian language phyla, and sharing a village agricultural life-style based on wet-rice agriculture, welded together from time to time into maritime states or land-based sacred *negara* (the realm, or political dimension of sacred kingship). In this ethnological sense, some of the inhabitants of the peninsula are certainly Malay—whether of the proto-deutero or other dubious migration waves that ethnologists assert peopled the peninsula several thousand years ago. These ethnological categories did not, and indeed in the nature of the case cannot, have a social coherence and cultural community. The peninsular Malays are part of this grouping. They are the descendants of migrants from the North, as those groups were augmented from time to time by migrants from other parts of the archipelagic cultural area. The Bugis were migrants to Selangor, the Minangkabau settled what is now Negri Sembilan, and other groups from Java all have become over time the contemporary Malay. The subdivisions of Kelantanese, or other regional variants of Malay, are only relevant within the category of Malay when that designation is used in contrast to other categories of the same national level of social organization—like Chinese or Indian or Thai. The point is that Malay as it is now constituted is a category built up over time from groups in interaction, and the current definition took its major contours during colonial days and even more so during the political processes of postindependence party maneuvering for running the political system (Ali 1981).

Similarly, the other ethnic categories are of national reference in a framework of contrast to each other and the Malay. The Chinese arose from seven or so language groups from various parts of the mainland and adjoining islands to become on the peninsula the ethnic category they are today. The Indians have become an ethnic counter in the same crucible of politics. They include Tamils from Tamilnad; Jaffna Tamils, Sikhs, and other Hindus from parts of India; and Muslims and Hindus from what is now Pakistan. Even with the categories of amalgamation, the fusing into ethnic blocs by time and politics, reality remains refractory, and people escape from the census containers of ethnicity, so terms like *Bhumi putera* are coined to include the Dyaks and others in Borneo who do not fit the definition of census Malay. Even the constitutional definition of a Malay as "a person who professes the Muslim religion, habitually speaks Malay, conforms to Malay custom," and who was born before independence or who had parents who had those characteristics before *Merdeka,* is becoming more and more ambiguous. With conversions to Islam, and with the spread of *bahasa Melayu* (the official name for the national language), just who is a Malay is becoming problematic and is often context sensitive in places like cosmopolitan Penang (Nagata 1974) rather than a reflex of easily observed personal traits and conduct. No longer is the mere conversion of a person to Islam said to make that person *masok Melayu,* to become a Malay. Now conversion means to *masok Islam,* to become a Muslim, as Malays recognize that religion and ethnicity are not isomorphic, and even that most Muslims in the world are not Malay speakers, nor do they follow *adat* (Malay custom).

From about 1820 to 1920 was a period of relatively free immigration into parts of British Malaya. The discovery of tin in abundance in the 1850s and the growth of world demand spurred by the American Civil War for food packaged in "tin" cans required a large labor force for the mines. Chinese labor was the chief human element in tin mining, for the agricultural Malay was uninterested in such labor at such low wages. The Chinese poured into the West Coast of Malaya under British aegis and were largely self-governed by "Captains China," local overlords and labor recruiters. In the 1870s rubber seedlings were transported to Malaya where they prospered, and the demand for rubber on the international market sharply increased in the wake of the automobile and its need for rubber tires. For this work on the rubber estates of the plantation economy, Indian labor was imported. The Indians were brought to Malaya with the assistance of the colonial government and with the aid of private capitalists (Parmer 1960). Most of the workers on the plantation frontier were Tamils, and, unlike the Chinese in the mines, there were many women rubber workers and in the early stages much more of a family life on the plantations (Jain 1970). The plantation isolation of the Indian labor force and the urban clustering of the Chinese miners still play a part in the contemporary life of Malaysia. Of course other Indians worked on the railroads, as clerks, and as police, and as businessmen, while there were (and are) Chinese farmers, businessmen, and professionals.

It is clear that the present population of peninsular Malaysia grew up in the wake of the expansion of capitalist enterprise under the protection of the colonial government of the British empire. While there was some division of labor along ethnic lines, there did not evolve the classic plural society (Freedman 1960) that Furnivall (1948) describes for Burma and Indonesia. The division of labor did not follow strict ethnic lines; although Chinese were predominant in the mines and Indians in the plantations, there were Malay rubber tappers, some Malay miners, and Malay minor bureaucrats and professionals. Partly the multiethnic society was kept from being the Furnivall plural model because of the special position the British, from the beginning of the "connection," granted to the Malays. The British gave protection to Malay custom and culture and special place to the Malay aristocracy, whom they considered the rightful and traditional rulers of the various peoples and parts of the peninsula. In this arrangement the Malay population was largely indifferent to the influx of Chinese and Indians, who in some sense came to an economic and geographic frontier in which the padi farming peasant and the Malay aristocrat had little interest. The three major populations did not compete economically (Sundaram 1986), did not mingle much socially, and in the colonial setup did not contest for political power. The British and Malays (especially the protected nobility, whose guaranteed social position tempered the winds of economic assault on their class position), when they thought about it, considered that the Chinese sojourners would come for economic reasons and would leave when their economic ends were met. Indians lived largely self-contained lives in the near total institutions of the rubber plantations, and it was unclear whether or not they intended to return to India, but the question of identification with "Malaya" did not arise from the Tamil point of view. Malaya was a mere administrative division within the British domain.

After the 1920s there were sizable increases by birth and by immigration in both the Chinese and Indian populations, but the relations among the groups to each other and to the colonial regime remained about the same during the depression years. The depression slowed down world demand for Malay produce and slowed the influx of foreign labor; it also saw the first stirrings of a belated Malay nationalism (Roff 1967). More historical work on this period will no doubt show the roots of class, ethnic, and political consciousness (Ali 1984).

But the years just prior to World War II and up to independence in 1957 is the era marked by crucial shifts in relations among the different populations and underlies the formation of the contemporary communal life and politics of Malaysia. It became clearer that the bulk of the Chinese were not going to return to an unstable and war-torn mainland. Furthermore, there were significant numbers of Malaya-born Chinese, raising problems of the application of *jus soli* for citizenship status. In addition, the Chinese had diversified from being mainly tin miners to filling most commercial middlemen positions in the economy as well as some of the larger capitalist roles, also becoming professionals and other sorts of urban proletarians. Due to the postwar "emergency," as the twelve-year insurrection (a war fought by British troops in combination with the Malay troops and constabulary against Communist-led guerrillas, most of whom were Chinese) was locally called, almost all of the Chinese became urban as they were moved for security and military reasons from the countryside. Chinese also became active in political participation. Just as the Malays began to realize that they were underrepresented in the commercial and industrial sectors of the modern economy, the Chinese began to be aware they lacked power and organization in the political realm. Indians also began to have a group consciousness of being underrepresented in the sphere of politics. So the major communal perceptions began to form and to take the crystallized shape that has dominated Malaysian social life since the middle 1950s. The Malays came to see themselves as rightfully politically dominant but economically at a disadvantage in their "own" land; Chinese came to see themselves as the modern economic sector with the dynamic for growth if they could hold their own in the political arena and obtain their full rights, while Indians moved from the plantation frontier into Southeast Asia's largest labor organization and also sought political power and citizenship protection.

The demographics of peninsular Malaysia (1980 census) show Malays 55% (includes 100,000 Orang Asli), Chinese 34%, Indians 10%, and others 2%, as the visible cleavages to which people respond and census takers can ennumerate, but this masks some important distributional facts about the 12 million or so people of the peninsula. The Chinese are heavily settled on the West Coast of the peninsula, are majority populations in Kuala Lumpur, Ipoh, and Penang, and as remarked earlier tend to be urban or town based. So that even on the East Coast, where the Chinese are small populations (for example, under 6% in Kelantan), they reside in urban conglomerates like Kota Bharu, or Kuantan in Pahang. And in the towns they tend to live in residentially distinct areas. Indians also tend to cluster in the West Coast, but beside cities they are still heavily resident on the rubber estates of the region. In the middle of the urban Chinese are stretches of padi-farming Malays like those in the Krian district, but on the whole the Malay are clustered in the rice-growing regions of the East Coast— Trennganau and Kelantan—and the rice areas of the North—Kedah, Perlis, and Perak—and in Johore and Negri Sembilan. There is no neat, clean, or easy way to shuffle the populations into separate compartments, even if someone thought that desirable (as no responsible policymaker in Malaysia does).

This is, then, the setting for the modern period of ethnic relations. The modern period is conveniently divided into two subperiods based on climactic political events which restructured communal relations. The first subperiod is from 1952 to 1969, beginning with the "bargain" of the Alliance and ending with the riots of 13 May in Kuala Lumpur. The second period is from 1969 to 1983 (and apparently still continues in large measure), from the reconstitution of the parlimentary system to the new ascendancy of Malay right and culture. Broadly characterizing the subperiods— the first period was marked by intercommunal cooperation with periods of confrontation and a breakdown of accommodation in 1969. Since 1969 there is a time of ethnic cooperation and accommodation on the new basis of accepting greater Malay cultural dominance and at least a willingness to level up the poor, paying special attention to the majority of the poor who are rural farming, fishing, and artisanal Malays.

Cooperation, accommodation, and confrontation among the communal groups and the individuals who compose these categories take place at three analytically distinct levels: the political, the economic, and the world of ordinary, daily interaction. These are analytical levels, and the separation is a construct of the observer or the analyst, for political symbols and acts may suffuse daily life, and economic considerations and activities deeply involve the flow of daily life and often form the stuff of politics and other kinds of social and cultural activities. Nonetheless, analytical levels are a useful way to begin to understand ethnicity, which in Malaysia comes near to what Mauss called a "total" social fact, in that its strands lead into all of social life. The "daily life" descriptions are based mainly on monographic material as that was reported chiefly by anthropologists from largely Malay villages and from a Malay viewpoint. Urban "race relations" (Rabushka 1973) also have been partly described, and Chinese- and Thai-centered reports exist in the literature too; the Malay locus and the Malay focus is predominant in the social science literature on peninsular Malaysia.

In daily life, Malays, Chinese, and Indians interact in all

the public spheres of exchange of goods and services, in the schools, on the sports fields, the coffee shops, on the buses, in the clinics, and in all the open and public locales. This is true of the cities, the towns, the kampongs, and all the social spaces in between. In the kampongs in East Coast Malaysia, there may be no Chinese or Indians resident. In the market towns and in the cities, however—in the presence of government officials, police, teachers, traveling pitchmen, and on the radio and via the televisions—the presence and nearness of different sorts of persons, cultures, beliefs, and conduct systems are omnipresent. People may not be intimate, but culturally different people are neither exotic nor remote. This public interaction is generally nonhostile among individuals and shows no marked signs of hierarchy, class, status distinction, or any form of disdain. These categories of human variety, whatever they are, are not racial in the conventional Euro-American sense, sensitivity, or sensation.

For Malays, as for everybody else, they are first cultural categories, then quasi-legal or constitutional categories, then conduct categories, and then categories of ancestry and of origin. In Kelantan, as in other heavily Malay dominated rice-growing regions, who is who is not a problem. The prefix of orang (persons) with its modifier—Melayu, China, India—covers the three main divisions of encountered humanity. Other kinds of orang-like orang puteh (literally white man, but meaning European) or orang asli (literally original man but meaning the non-Malay indigenous peoples of inland river, mountain, and forest) may be encountered, and these are the chief kinds of *bangsa* groupings of persons in the world by culture and ancestry. Orang as a prefix can mark other lesser divisions—*sukubangsa*—varieties of persons whose ancestry is thought to be in some sense immediate or traceable, somewhere between the bangsa generality and the genealogical *kelawarga,* or family. Orang can also mark purely social distinctions—*orang besar,* the big man of power; or *orang kaya,* the rich; or *orang kenamaan,* a notable. But the use of orang (X) as a spoken designation is usual only in reply to a question (usually by an anthropologist or other outsider who may be in doubt about someone's bangsa or for some reason wants to classify a person in the tripartate scheme), like in Who is that person? the answer can be: That is orang (X), bukan orang (Y). That is an Indian, not a Malay. But as earlier remarked, that question does not arise at the level of local, day-to-day ordinary social interaction. The cultural markers are, first of all, so visible, distinct, and obvious that the questions Who are you? Where are you form? and What is your line? rarely need speech to be answered. The answers are open to a casual inspection (this and the fact that the weather is uniform from season to season, and sports of no great moment in the countryside, limits "small talk" to gossip and to politics). Extensive knowledge of one's neighbors, and the prevailing belief that politics is *main kotor* (a rough and dirty game), make gossip and political talk lively and interesting.

A person is an Orang Melayu (in everyday definition, by cultural account, in the folk sense, not at law or in the constitution nor in the canons of ethnology or physical anthropology) whose first (and most often, only) language is *bahasa Melayu* which is the Malay spoken locally. For a Kelantanese it is the Kelantan variety of Malay, as it is for other regional dialects (they are mutually intelligible, but one must pay close attention, and often a Johore dialect Malay may not listen closely to a Kelantan Malay and say the latter's speech is unintelligible, which it is not). Now the term "bahasa Melayu" means the national, official language. Formerly that was called *Bahasa Kebangsaan* (national language), but since being made mandatory as the school and official language, the national language is called Melayu, as part of the more general stress on Malay symbols as national symbols.

In addition to Melayu as a mother tongue, a style of comportment, called *halus* (refined), is alleged to be Malay. This halus style is seen in polite social interaction, a consciouness of deference to age, status, piety, and other socially valued personal characteristics. Halus behavior is thought to be part of being a Malay, but not all Malays exhibit it, nor even is it exhibited in all Malay interactions between and among Malays who know the halus code. But halus serves as a cultural marker in contrast to behavior of Chinese and Indians who are thought to be, on the whole, *kasar,* or rough in social interaction as compared to the usually smooth and gentle style of the Malays. Halus goes along with following customary law (adat). This is chiefly the rules of domestic and personal life. Who are kinsmen, who inherits, how small disputes are composed, and other domestic and personal relations form a loose code of adat. Adat comes in two major forms, the patrilineal adat of most Malays, and the matrilineal adat of the Minangabau (the chief population of Negri Sembilan and migrants from the Sumatra home of these people), but it is still, in both varieties, a differentiating feature between Malays and others.

Another part of the categorical definition of Malay is religion. A Malay is a Muslim, of the Sunni sect. (But Shia were never socially or linguistically recognized until the rise of the Ayatollah in the Iranian revolution. Shia as a sect is still of little social significance in Malaysia. What import it has derives from its militant assertion of Islam as a *din,* a way of life. Some Malay Muslims admire this, many deplore it, and most have no strong position on it). Muslims of other sorts exist in Malaysia—Bengali and other Indian, Pakistani, Arab, Pathan Muslims are found scattered throughout the peninsula. They are not usually considered Malay, but they do, sometimes, intermarry with Malays, and the children become *peranakan* (children of the country rather than immigrants) and could pass into the Malay category, depending on what they are culturally on the axes of the previous markers of category. Chinese who become Muslim through conversion do not become Malay. Chinese children who are adopted and brought up in a Malay family as Muslims are Malays. Offspring of converted Chinese and Malays need at least one generation to become Malay.

This question of ancestry is clearly a cultural marker, but in the hierarchy of markers it is fourth. It is rarely invoked, since the other three cultural markers subsume it in most instances, and ancestry is, in itself, relevant chiefly in the sphere of politics and granting of citizenship. What is clear is that ancestry—traceable sukubangsa, or imputed bangsa—does not have Nurenburg grandfather connotations, nor the outmoded southern United States notion of "one drop of blood" that assigns one to being a categorical Negro. The culture/nature relationship in Malay culture is different from the substance/conduct metaphors of Euro-American construction of racial and ethnic categories.

These categories of kinds (*jenis*) of ethnically defined persons in the world take their measure from the notions in the category of Malay. That category is the benchmark (not the keystone) from which cultural variations along the axes of significant markers is calibrated. The other "categories" are basically residuals by their distance from Malay. They are negatively posed in this categorical system. When the other categories are filled in by informants, at least in Kelantan (Nash 1974), they are a mix of the cultural markers of language, custom, religion, and ancestry plus imputed essences or behavioral complexes that usually form the stuff of stereotypes. Stereotypes condense cultural markers and conflate them with imputed traits, essences, and behaviors. Stereotypes serve as reflexive, unthinking means of taking account of cultural and ethnic diversity. Sometimes they actually govern social interaction. In the interpersonal sphere Malays, Chinese, and Indians (the major categories) pay much attention to actual characteristics of persons, but in thnking about the abstract dynamics of social and political life the stereotype is frequently invoked. Stereotypes flourish in remote and impersonal power and economic contexts, where knowledge, information, and control are scarce items for the ordinary people of society, and images serve the media and elites better than reasoned catalogs of the world.

These categories approximate social divisions and spheres of social intimacy by a series of boundary-maintaining mechanisms. The differences between cultural markers (signs of and symbols marking differences) and boundary mechanisms (devices serving to socially separate cultural difference) are plain and easy to comprehend, but they are subtle to use analytically and often slippery in theoretical or practical arguments and programs. The first boundary-maintaining mechanism is the virtual absence of intermarriage among the categorical groups. Malays can only marry Muslims and other people of the "Book." Christians and Jews are said by Muslims to have earlier versions of scripture, of which the Koran is the final "Book." In Malay sacred books are Kitab, secular books are "buku" from the English word rather than the Arabic. But Christians are usually not Malay on the other cultural markers, are few in number, and not really available as marriage partners for Malays in Malaysia. Jews in Malaysia are virtually a mystical category, belonging either to biblical times or to the turmoil in the Middle East involving Israel-Arab wars and disputes. They also are not real marriage partners in Malaysia. A Chinese can become a Muslim like anyone else by reciting in good faith the creedal *dua kelima* which acknowledges a single deity and Mohammed as his final prophet. As a Muslim, the Chinese (male) can now marry a Malay (female conversion is so rare as to be almost a nonevent). But conversion to Islam (whether to marry or for other reasons ranging from conviction to economic advan-

tage) is a total, wrenching cultural and social transformation for a Chinese. First, the convert must abjure Chinese
cuisine, since Chinese food preparation involves the use of
forbidden pork, improperly slaughtered animals, and other
foods or food items (like hunted game, snake, dog, etc.)
forbidden to Muslims. Also, the use of alcohol is *haram* to
Muslims, while its ceremonial and personal use is an inte-
gral part of Chinese ceremonial life. Conversion means
using Malay as the daily (and often only language) medium
of communication. It severs a Chinese from intimate social
interaction in the Chinese community, both because Muslims are not found there and because the Chinese tend to
look askance at converts, or even hold them in mild con-
tempt. On the whole, conversion seems rare for Chinese
because of the high social and cultural costs and disloca-
tions it entails.

Along with the boundary mechanism of endogamy
among categories is the virtual bar to commensality. Eating
together is the closest form of interpersonal intimacy and
is often a metaphor for connubium, common substance,
and common origin. Of course, the Muslim code of *halal-
haram* separates Chinese from Malay, and sometimes from
Hindu Indians. Apart from the heavy meanings of gustatory
delight and aesthetic sensibilities involved in dining, this
code prohibits so many of the ordinary foods of the Chinese
that Malays cannot dine in a Chinese home or restaurant.
Chinese restaurants (or Indian for that matter) must post
halal signs if they seek Malay custom. In Kelantan, Chinese
restaurants do not serve pork; even if the full halal code is
not observed, acceptable items can be ordered by Malays.
Chinese, of course, can eat anywhere, since their only food
taboo is "not eating anything whose back is not toward
heaven," presumably an injunction against cannibalism,
since Chinese are reputed to eat monkeys, which are often
upright creatures. The difficulties in interdining prevent, or
minimize, occasions for intimate interaction. An absence of

intimate interaction makes the kind of personal knowledge involved in forming marriage alliances less likely and is thus an added buttress to the walls of ethnic separation. Such interdining as does occur is in ritual, ceremonial, and public occasions, underlying the lack of intimacy among categories.

Religion both as a belief system and as an institutional complex underlines as well as creates differences among ethnic categories and elevates these differences to visible social and cultural gulfs. Muslims, Chinese Taoist-Buddhist, and Indian Hindus do not engage in comparative religion exercises in Malaysia. Knowledge of the tenets and practices of another's religion is vague and sketchy. Malays call Chinese religion *kaffir,* roughly, unbeliever, heathen, non-Islam. Chinese when pressed say they believe in "anything good," and an observing anthropologist would emphasize the ancestor memorial cults, the temple worship of several traditional deities, and the stress on omens, divination, trance, and propiation. There are, however, all the visible differences that summarize the underlying separations in belief and practice among the various religions.

Speech habits among pious Malays include the frequent interjection of phrases tied to Islam—"inch' Allah" (God willing), "Allah Akbar" (God is Great), and "May he rest in peace" after the name of the prophet—and other sorts of Islamic tag lines pepper the speech of Malays and Muslims setting them off in these small ways from non-Muslims. The architecture of both sacred and profane places mark the differences in religious identifications. The Malay house is quite distinct from the Chinese house— either in the rural areas or in the towns and cities—in its layout, its room plan, its interior design, its ornamentation, and its furnishings, and often in its orientation to the cardinal points of the compass. And no one could confuse a Chinese house with a Malay dwelling or the mosque with a Chinese temple or a Hindu temple.

In the daily round, the weekly cycle, and the annual rotation, secular time is structured and punctuated by sacred events, rituals, and observances that constitute gulfs between the categories. Even the mundane calendars of the communities differ—Muslims on "After the Haj" time live in a different year than Chinese and Indians, who may use Gregorian time or other calendar counts, and the year of the rat, dog, or other dominant influence is different from the astrology of the Hindu, or the anniversary counts of the Malays. Every day the five prayer calls for Muslims sound the tocsin of difference from non-Muslim; even if the Muslim does not heed the calls to pray, he and others are aware of the injunctions to sacralize each day by the prayers. Once a week, on Fridays, Muslim males are enjoined to engage in congregational prayer at a mosque (or a local chapel, *surau,* if nothing as grand as a mosque is available). The streams of men in their Hari Juma'at finery streaming toward mosque and chapel on Friday afternoon as work stops for Malays is like a rivulet separating different belief islands. Other major Malay holidays and festivals—Hari Raya Puasa, celebrating the end of the fasting month of Ramadam is but the most conspicuous annual rite—that chop up the year into the Muslim calendar make up a separate sacred year. On the Chinese side, the firecrackers of New Year's day, the ancestral candles, the homage to the kitchen god, and the exchange of *ang paw* packets demarcate a different sacral year, as do the spectacular rites of Hindu rituals and fulfillment of vows. Religion is, then, a pervasive marker of categories in peninsular Malaysia.

These boundary-maintaining mechanisms enclose cultural differences that are historically created and variable over time—as witness the decreasing salience of Malay language as a marker and the shifting role of Islam as a definer of Malay. The boundary mechanisms of bed, board, and cult are a recursive metaphor underlying self-other in terms of substance, behavior, and belief. They may not be, as isolating mechanisms, perfectly isomorphic, since they too grow historically and change circumstantially, but they communicate, create, and constitute the socially important aspect of persons as members of collectivities thought to differ in human substance (like kinship and lineage), in conduct (their histories and aims are different), and in purpose and destiny (their implicit dominant ontologies are different and irreconcilable). All of this is socialized in individuals as a particularly precious heritage, as a personal identity, and in the conditions of contemporary Malaysia as somewhat in peril, in a state of siege against hegemonic cultural and religious others.

In social structure, there are sets of enduring relations generated by differences in economic, political, expressive, and other domains of life that make for patterns of roles whose shape and order are only partially in the consciousness (native model) of actors, and which must be constructed by the observing social scientist. Cultural categories may find only partial social expression.

Due to the play of historical circumstance as colonial extractive industry and capitalism came more and more to dominate the economy of the peninsula, the Chinese, Malay, and Indians came to have different positions in occupational life, resulting in wealth differences and in class or stratification nearly coinciding with ethnic category. The best census and survey data and statistical interpretations of that data (Snodgrass 1980; Anand 1983) agree on the gross facts of the economic and occupational structure of peninsular Malaysia, whatever the discord is on the more subtle dimension of class—as that has political, consciousness, and activist dimensions. Defining poverty at $25 (ringgit) per capita (a reasonable level based upon several dimensions of customary expenditure for minimal levels of subsistence and fitting ethnographic reportage— my ethnographic experiences and the reports of other ethnographers), about 40% of all households fall below this poverty line. In estimates by number of persons in ethnic categories, Malays are 56%, Chinese are 18%, and Indians are 33% of the poor. Chinese income on the average is about 2.44 times that of Malays, while Indians are about 1.77 times that of Malays. The poverty profiles in peninsular Malaysia can be summarized under these seven topics (the interpretation of this summary is of course not a problem for social science alone, but is the stuff of policy, politics, ideology, and ethnic strife and cooperations):

1. Of the poor households, 78% are Malay. The Malays are overrepresented in poverty by a 1 : 41 ratio.

2. Poverty is rural. More than 87% of poor households are rural.

3. Farmers as household heads are 62% in poverty.

4. The agricultural sector holds 75% of the poor.

5. Persons whose schooling does not extend beyond primary school are 93% of the poor households.

6. The poor are in Kelantan, Trengganu, Perlis, and Kedah, the rice bowls of delta padi production, a rural Malay occupation.

7. The rich are in Johore, Penang, Perak, and Selangor where the modern economic sector is found, as are the cities, the Chinese, and the middle and upper echelons of Malays and Indians.

These distributional facts are obvious. How they came about and why they persist is far from obvious. As Snodgrass (1980) and others note, classic economic theory gets nowhere in accounting for origins and persistence. And the theory of legal and social discrimination fares little better, since income differences (but not asset or wealth differences, a much more difficult magnitude to discern) and its meaning depend largely upon what measure of inequality are used. When the populations of the peninsula are compared on a generational background of variables, differences are accounted for by education, place of residence, occupation, and parent's occupation, all highly intercorrelated measures. The outstanding fact is that the Chinese are economically modern, better educated, and receivers of higher incomes than are the Malays. Indians approximate the Chinese distributions. There are poor, rich, and medium in all ethnic categories, and ethnicity plays a minor role (statisically, at least) in placement in the social structure.

But in the folk version of the social structure, at least in the Malay naive or native model of wealth, Malays are poor, Chinese are rich, and this economic fact is one and the same thing. Malay poverty and Chinese wealth are the same social fact. Curbing Chinese wealth will promote Malay income; redistributing wealth and opportunity to Malays will "level up" the Malays to a position competitive with the Chinese. Malay privilege in the law (what in the United States is called affirmative action) will redress past imbalances and prevent the deepening of the economic gulf between Malays and Chinese. Indians are in the folk version along with "others and orang Asli" residual in this program of changing the Malay economic position and hence altering the social structure.

This folk version is the stuff of politics among rural Malays. It is less subscribed to by Malay elites and Malays in the modern economic sector, but it is nowhere repudiated by Malay politicians. In fact, the trend of politics among Malays as part of national politics may be viewed as an oscillation between the populist demands of greater and greater Malay privilege (both cultural and economic) and the needs of the Malay segment of the elite to accommodate the Chinese and Indians in order to win elections and hence to govern within the constraints of a parlimentary system. This tension in the political system was born before independence and has been constant in the political life of Malaysia, with accommodation, confrontation, and cooperation having turns at salience, but still in dynamic unease. This management of irreducible tension has so far steered a course between an embattled dictatorship, Lebanese-like communal warfare, and a communally based parlimentary system with representative institutions, what in looser terms is usually called a working democracy. Gyroscopic management is a feat in the world of politics with ethnic blocs, and something of a heroic feat when the populations are in such near numerical parity, but spinning out of control would lead to civil strife of horrendous proportions. The balance between the politics of terror and the politics of bribery for the regime of civil politics is one whose formula (if it exists) is elusive, and much depends on the art and skill of the politicians as well as *tasamuh* (mutual respect) of the ethnic or communal groups for each other.

The political process in Malaysia has been, and still is, rooted in communalism (Ratnam 1965)—the local concept for politics based on ethnic identification and appeals to voters on supposed communal, cultural, and common economic predicament grounds. Also, there has been a note of nondirect competition among ethnic blocs forming communal-based parties. There have been, and are, noncommunal parties—that is, those basing their appeal on class position, nonethnic ideology, and supranational images, but they have never gained significant power, except intermittently at local levels. The politics of Malaysia is in some sense "overdocumented" in the political science literature in terms of constituency politics, voter swings, party platforms, and other usual rubrics of mainstream political science analysis. What is lacking, or slighted, is some deeper understanding of what ethnicity is in the social sense and the way that cultural meaning enters into politics and defines what is being contested and who the contestants are. In some sense, Malaysia is as much a politics of culture, a calculus of meaning, as it is a politics of power or a calculus of advantage and self-interest.

Preindependence politics was a mixture of class and ethnic interests as the British sought to disentangle themselves from empire (Funston 1980), and the elites of the various ethnic groups sought to find a way to govern this multiethnic and stratified society. In 1952, after a series of local electoral problems and the rejection of some British formulas, including the Malayan Union, and the failure of noncommunal political initiatives to gain wide support, the coalition arrangement was devised. This coalition ruled Malaysia from independence to 1969. This Alliance, as the coalition came to be called throughout its dominance of Malaysian politics, was based on the successful formula of a mayoralty election in which the Malays would run Malay in strong Malay areas, and the Chinese and Indians would do the same. It would be noncompetitive politics among communities at the local and state levels and ethnic cooperation at the national level. This Alliance of blocs into a single national coalition indicates the ever present tensions of balance. Malays were not dominant in national politics, merely the major partner in the coalition of ethnic blocs. This accommodation was worked out at the elite level of the three communities, with the bulk of the electorate voting in a bloc manner, along strictly, or almost strictly, communal lines. This arrangement of hierarchy and populism rested upon the absence of class identification as contrasted with ethnic loyalties. The elites of each community made what has been called the "bargain" or compact of the Alliance. The understanding was that Malays would be politically dominant—the chief posts, the symbolically important political roles, would be in the hands of Malays and filled by Malays, especially those of the prime minister and the deputy prime minister. Malays would be granted privileges in education, jobs, land holding, and government service. But the basic economic position of the Chinese and Indians would not be hampered by restrictive economic legislation or confiscatory activities. Apparently this bargain, struck among the United Malays National Organization (UMNO), the Malayan Chinese Association (MCA), and the Malayan Indian Congress (MIC) appealed to the voters, at least it held while the economy continued to grow at a socially satisfactory rate. Alliance handily won control, again and again, in open and free elections.

There was a scattering of opposition parties to the Alliance, but only the Pan-Malaysian Islamic Party (PMIP in its English acronym, or PAS, Parti Islam se Malaysia, sometimes glossed Party Islam in English accounts) was of significant and enduring challenge to the Alliance from 1959 to 1969. The more left-oriented younger group of the MCA and a more nationalist component of MCA along with the leftish elements and communal elements of the MIC did not surface politically till the events of 13 May 1969. At any rate, from the point of cultural and social analysis the PAS, its symbols, structure, and constituency is the most important and paradigmatic for the future development of Malay ethnic and political interaction.

PAS politics is instructive for understanding how ethnicity mobilizes or fails to mobilize political activity in social circumstances like those of peninsular Malaysia. The chief constituency of PAS were the padi farmers, fishermen, and artisans of East Coast Malaysia. The party opposed itself to the town-based, salaried, and commercial Malays. These Malays and their bureaucratic and political leaders had made a pact with the Chinese and the Indians, and that pact would keep the East Coast Malays and others like them locked into the lower spaces of the economy, bereft of political power, without dignity in a land owned by strangers and run by doubtful Muslims.

The condensed slogan of PAS, *bangsa* (race or ethnicity) *ugama* (a fundamental Islam calling for society to be more closely modeled on Koranic and Hadith codes and injunctions) and *tanah ayer* (ownership of land and natural resources by Malays only), articulated real economic, class, and cultural grievances of East Coast Malays as Kessler (1978) and I both noted (Nash 1974), but we disagree on the dynamics of the political system, as will become clear subsequently. The appeal is directed by Malays whose situation is that of poverty, piety, and powerlessness, the position of the East Coast peasant when compared to Chinese and Indians, on one hand, and the town-based "salariat" of UMNO Malays, on the other. It is not only an economic and political grievance, it is a statement of a moral case in terms of the code of Muslims and the culture and ideology of the kampong Malay. Thus it is ethnicity of a particular sort—the basic, the true, the real Malay as against the Chinese, Indians, Thais, and sophisticated, urban, commercial, and accommodating Malay. This moral case is underlined by the PAS rejection of obvious economic blandishment by the UMNO. The ruling coalition dangled bridges, building programs, mosques, and schools before the Kelantanese if they would abandon the PAS and vote UMNO. The lures were rejected. In a situation where not much can be gained by the individual peasant by backing UMNO, nor can much be lost economically by backing PAS, the romantic, religious, communal cast of real political and economic grievances can mobilize peasants.

But peasants, fishermen, artisans, the denizens of the kampongs can be mobilized only through some sort of leadership and party structure. The leadership of the PAS was provided by a local literati, a traditional class of intellectuals and educators skilled in the symbolic currency of Islam and local Malay culture. This literati is the refined, authoritative repository and exponent of the great tradition of Islam, on the one hand, and the little tradition of Malay kampong life and culture on the other. Also, the literati is in great danger of being expelled, swamped, or ignored by the expanding educational and bureaucratic apparatus of the national state. The literati or traditional class is, in almost textbook fashion, made up of two wings— the educators (the uztazes and religious teachers), and the religious experts (the Imams, pondok heads, lebais, and Koranic teachers). The waves of social change from the expanding economy and the secular-bureaucratic state pound unceasingly upon this traditional elite, and they appeal to the peasant masses who have real economic and political grievances. They are united in a demand of justice in the moral terms of Islam and Malay culture. This combination was viable in the East Coast of Malaya (and in other heavily Malay padi areas like Krian on the West Coast) because it harnessed powerful symbols and deep identity feelings to a team of threats to the elite as cultural leaders and to the peasants as powerless and oppressed. The growth of a radical definition of the peasant's plight was inhibited by the experience of the emergency struggle against "communist terrorists" of the past twelve years and the identification of socialism with aliens and with anti-Islamic sentiments and groups. Uneven social change, a differential modernization, had made the East Coast— peasants and elite—ripe for the organization of communal politicals of the PAS variety.

While PAS continued to ply its oppositional politics on the East Coast and in selected areas of the West Coast, the Alliance coalition creaked along. The breakup of the hegemony of the Alliance did not come directly from pressures of the PAS, although that party's insistence on Malay culture, Malay privilege, and Malay political dominance kept forcing UMNO to take stronger and stronger Malay favored positions. Still, the rampant "cultural-nationalism" mix of PAS did not much transcend the peasantry and its embattled traditional literati. And PAS failed to establish, at this juncture, viable, meaningful international links. PAS was sympathetic to greater "Malaysia" notions of Indonesia's Sukarno, and did not side with the UMNO in its opposition to the "confrontasi" war between Indonesia and Malaysia. PAS skirted with "treasonable" behavior in some of its leaders open and active support of "greater Malaysia" visions of Indonesia. But a viable nationalism and Malay internationalism did not emerge. Majorities, however slight, do not and cannot undertake separatist movements. The path of Sri Lanka is instructive as a contrast, where the Tamil separatist movement in part depends on the international connections with Tamil Nad across the narrow water to the mainland of India (Tambiah 1986). The 1969 riots of Malaysia, while bloody and disastrous, turned out to be an interregnum in democracy rather than what may turn out to be a dismantling in the Sri Lanka situation.

The 1969 riots occurred, in the first instance, because of pressures on the UMNO from its ultra-Malay wing, and from unexpected defections from the Alliance in general and gains by opposition parties. The event-by-event accounts of the killings, burnings, and lootings (Slimming 1969; Tunku Abdul 1969, and National Operations Council 1969) show how little things escalated into large disturbances, and how civil and military authority failed to react intelligently, swiftly, and impartially. The deeper structural impetus to the riots lay, however, in the changing constellation of political forces, and the growth in Malay demands among the younger elements in UMNO coupled with a different set of demands among the youth of MCA. This violent eruption of political pressures was symptomatic of the undermining of a fragile communal consensus. It was dramatic notice that the "pact" among the elites and their constituents was in immediate need of renegotiation. That bloodshed was virtually confined to Kuala Lumpur was an indication of urban impersonality and hyperpolitical organization of the capital as well as the network of ties that Chinese and Malays had in places like

Kelantan (Winzler 1985). Communal tension always has the potential to erupt in riot and violence, but the potential is politically activated, while the extent of violence is a direct function of the use or misuse of police and military power by the authorities. Enough political pressure and sufficient bias in the use of military and police power can lead to festering and revolutionary unrest which, when coupled to separatist ideologies and receiving the sanction or blessing of extranational powers or movements, can lead to civil war of the Sri Lankan, North Irish, Turk-Cypriot, and Lebanon tragedies.

Fortunately (for Malaysia), the events of 1969 stopped short of such confrontation among the communal groups. The upper echelons of the political groups in the Alliance formed the National Operations Council, a governing group which played a holding action until parlimentary processes could again be organized. The National Operations Council held the public arena while a new compact was worked out. The new compact is exemplified in the Third Malaysia Plan (Snodgrass 1980) on its economic side and the emergence of the Barisan Nasional (United National Front) on its political side (Mauzy 1983). Between the plans of the technocrats and the coalitions of the politicians, the ideology of communal life in peninsular Malaysia may be triangulated.

This third economic plan aims to eliminate poverty (as defined above) among all groups but to pay special attention to the Malay poor, since that segment is overrepresented among the poor. The plan hopes to do this by a combination of stressing development (a rising tide raises all bottoms) and redistributions of Malay quotas (minima) in hiring, in company equity share ownership, in preferential university admissions, and in government land redistribution program.

The political expression of the new compact welded a more militant UMNO (led by former ultras who displaced the conservative and aristocratic leadership), a more compliant MCA and MIC, and even co-opted the PAS for a while. This United Front handily won every election since its foundation and only showed some signs of creaking in 1986. That this political arrangement of ethnicity works is partly due to a displacement outward of some hostility in the look "East" campaign that blames the "West" for slowed economic growth, and partly to some of the (as yet small) effects of the new politics and economics on the daily life in the society.

Economically, more and more Malays are moving into urban areas and into urban (and hence modern, and usually higher paying than padi farming) occupations. Factories in areas like Petaling Jaya and other suburbs of Kuala Lumpur begin to show the direct implementation of Malay quotas. New universities like the National Malay University and the National Religious University, as well as quotas at University of Malaya and Sains University at Penang, bring many more Malays into higher education and begin forming a Malay intelligentsia with a program of Malay cultural development and spread. The use of Malay only as the medium of instruction in the national schools, and the spread of the use of Malay in business and in government, also is part of the cultural policy of the Barisan, and in part this makes for a more genial view of some cultural differences.

The Chinese, while resentful of Malay educational opportunities, or more accurately at the entailed Chinese restrictions on educational access at the University level, seem less exercised by the economic consequences of the Third Malaysian Plan. They feel no immediate threat of deprivation or confiscation of assets. The delicate balance between Malay advancement and Chinese resentment (or deprivation) is still being negotiated.

The stress on *muhibbah,* goodwill among ethnic groups, is still part of national policy. The emergence of something called "national" culture or Malaysian culture (as against Malay, Chinese, Indian, or Western adaptations) is still merely an item of discussion among some intellectuals and not a program of the government, even if such efforts are notoriously doomed.

Though this ethnic accommodation, in both cultural and economic aspects, works in the political and economic spheres, there are clouds on the horizon. The clouds are political dissent with tendencies to stronger Malay dominance (a revived and impatient PAS) and anticapitalist, nonethnic sentiments in other parties. These political parameters will always exist around the "center" of accommodation and cooperation in the Malay context. But there are more possibly disturbing possibilities—the call of fundamental Islam or the lure of revolutionary communism. Of the two, only militant Islam seems of any social relevance at this point in time.

In the last twelve years or so, fundamentalist movements have arisen in peninsular Malaysia. Locally they are grouped under the rubric *dakwah,* and that term is fairly but partially descriptive of their collective aims and impetus. Dakwah is the Malay language version of the Arabic *da'wa.* Da'wa means call or invitation to Islam, what in the West is called missionary or evangelical activity (a somewhat ethnocentric parallel). But contemporary dakwah is more than the older Malaysian Muslim Welfare Organization (Pertubohan Keb Ajikan Islam Malaysia Perkim) which trained missionaries (*muballigh*) to seek converts to Islam. This dakwah movement is aimed at people who are already Muslims. It seeks to purify religion by harking back to the beliefs and practices thought to exist at the time of Mohammed and his companions. It seeks to establish a total way of life, a *din,* based exclusively on the Koran, Hadith, and the law code in Shar'ia. In anthropological terms, Malaysian dakwah is a nativistic movement seeking to establish or reestablish an idealized past in order to condemn or indict a corrupt present and to avoid a bleak and meaningless future.

On the international scene (a strong reminder that analysis moves from the local, to the regional, to the national, to the international and to the world system as the questions demand and as relevance requires), two events of the 1970s sparked renewed Islamic political activity. The oil boom was taken in Malaysia as a sign of Islam's validity, since worldly success was always a sign of Allah's grace. Some Arab oil revenues flowed into Malaysia to subsidize some elements of the dakwah revitalization. In the latter part of the decade, the rise of the charismatic Iman Khomeni as the leader of the Iranian revolution caught the popular imagination. In Malaysia, as elsewhere, it was noted that Khomeni, like Mohammed, rose to political and worldly power on faith alone. Furthermore, oil was discovered in offshore Malaysia, fulfilling the folk wisdom about the divinely ordained distribution of good things in this world. According to folk accounts of the world's bounties, Euro-America received science and technology; the Jews intelligence, acumen, and solidarity; the Chinese diligence and business sense; but the Malays received Islam and now oil, reserved for the Muslim peoples of the world.

Other immediate national and local political events spurred on the birth and survival of dakwah moments. The breakdown of civil order and the suspension of the democratic regime (in the 13 May 1969 riots and the National Operations Council governance) indicated the lability of politics in this world, and the formation of the Barisan Nasional with the co-option of the PAS left the religious issue without a political voice. The religious issue—the Muslim moral claim to a just society—was left to the dakwah groups.

When the notion of "religious issue" is raised, it is a shorthand for the dialectal tensions and contradictions in

Malaysian society that also fuel the dakwah movement (Lyon 1979). Malyasia is a secular state with Islam as its official religion. For many Muslims this is an oxymoron, and the proper relationship between Islam and State has yet to be achieved. It does not comfort the *lebai,* the pious, and other traditional literati of the sacred that other societies with majority Muslim populations have similar problems and ambiguities about Islam and the State. In some sense, multiple pulls on basic identity are built into Islam-State relations as the complexities of *Watan,* (modern state), *Qaum* fellow tribesman, the Arabs, and the *Umma* (the worldwide community of believers) show in other Islam-state contexts. In Malaysia, the social organization of Islam also produces tensions. Beside the National Religious Organization, each of the Malay states (those headed by Sultan) has its own *Majilis Ugama* (religious council). Friction may then arise among the several states and between a state and the federal juridsiction. Muslims see this as a barely tolerable state of affairs that needs to be set right.

The final tensions have to do with modernization in the form of the expansion of the economic frontier for Malays and the resulting class and life-style differences that seem to violate the basic fraternity or equality of believers. With modernization and economic development have come— as elsewhere in the developing world—occupational, status, and class differences among Malays, even in the backwaters of the East Coast. The once simple tripartite division of Malays into aristocrats, peasants, and town civil servants has been complicated by the emergence of a commercial middle class, numerous professionals, and an urban proletariat in the new factories and assembly plants of Malaysia. The strain is heaviest on the new middle class, that group formed by the recent economic expansion. This recent and distinct new middle class of commercial sector bureaucrats, officials, and professionals is the most pre-

carious, both economically and in terms of status and
accepted ways of living. Many of the new middle class find
the urban life-style, the need for Western sophistication,
and the continual interethnic tolerance threatening to their
core values. Dakwah is often a fitting and welcome relief
and retreat.

The events, reasons, and contradictions that I have
adduced as making a viable environment for the rise and
spread of dakwah in Malaysia provide a social science perspective. From the point of view of the people in the
dakwah movements, their joining is a biographical fact in
historical circumstance perceived as making that choice
moral and necessary. This decision to abandon the ordinary life of the larger society has the shape outsiders would
call a conversion experience. For whatever precipitating
reason, the person sees the hollowness, the meaness, the
purposelessness of ordinary life and opts for the full meaningful life oriented to salvation and heaven after the day of
judgment. The hundred or so members of the dakwah I
came to know well in Kelantan made this nativistic-rejec-
tionist decision because the immediate truths of Islam as a
total way of life convincingly overwhelmed them. For the
outsider it is a conversion experience; for the convert it is
the realization of truth.

The social composition of this dakwah and its ideology
is described elsewhere (Nash 1984a), and there are strong
resemblances to the Al-Ikwan of Egypt's Al-Azhar or the
Jama'at Islam in Pakistan or even the seminary students at
Qum in Iran. It is a volatile mix of anti-Western modernity,
youthful radicalism, and Islamic affirmation, espoused by
middle-class, educated, and youthful Malays. What becomes of this (and similar movements in Malaysia) depends not on religious or Islamic innovation but on the
complex interaction of the members of this movement with
the pressures from the nation-state, the continuing Wester-

nization and modernization, and the social status of the Malay community in the political struggles of this multiple society.

Islam is a reservoir for turbulence. In times of sharpening social contradictions, economic regression, and poli-,tical competition, Islam provides vocabulary, values, identities, and organization to some believers as possible responses and resolutions. Islam does not provide blueprints for a new social order, nor does it guarantee political victory or religious renaissance to its Malay or other adherents.

To rise slightly above the descriptive level, where so far I have been "hovering" close among the facts in Baconian style, is to strip some of the circumstantiality and particularity from Malaysian fact to make it comparable to other situations of multiethnic states in Southeast Asia or elsewhere. Just what dimensions of comparability with what specific societies awaits the conclusion of this essay with its descriptions and analyses of two other social configurations.

Contemporary Malaysia indicates the fluctuating role of ethnicity in new nations as they come out of the colonial period into the world of political and economic relations among unequally potent national structures. At the local, immediate, and personal level, ethnicity is a salient social fact. Human beings come in the varieties of Orang Melayu, Orang China, and Orang India, to stick to the major categories. These human beings have index features like language, dress, religion, or custom and cuisine which make them easily identifiable without interrogation or close personal inspection. Ethnic category is a part of cultural classification of human beings, and the social boundary mechanisms operate to keep the categories fairly distinct. The recursive metaphor of bed, blood, and cult all emphasize the reality of the category in the peopled world of Malays, Chinese, and Indians in the peninsula, though the presentation here takes the Malay baseline and assesses cultural categories from that perspective, possibly overemphasizing cult in the meaning of ethnic category. These ethnic categories may or may not form in social groups; may or may not be relevant or pertinent in social interaction, and may or may not be important in all dimensions of self. No actual social group includes all the members of the ethnic category. Such groupings as there are based on ethnic criteria may (or may not) have social, economic, and political consequences. This careful (and boring but necessary) spelling out of ethnicity stresses the socially contingent nature of what on the peninsula is considered a "natural" fact.

The extent to which ethnicity is used as a counter and resource in political and social competition is a function of the way that political arenas, state and national, are structured. The clearer, more impersonal, and legally governed political relations and coalitions are, the less use is the organization of political action based on ethnicity. So the current paradox: Since Malays have increased privileges, quotas, and advantages built into the legal and constitutional structure, Malay ethnicity is less politically relevant. In the absence of confrontation, Chinese ethnicity becomes less relevant as an organized entity.

Too much cannot be made of the analytical distinctions between category and identity dimensions of ethnicity as against politically organized and economically competitive aspects of ethnicity. They are dialectically related: organization is not possible without identity commitments; and successful organization increases identity commitment; very successful organization decreases the need for ethnic appeal, and as that wanes the political utility of ethnic identity may weaken.

This dialectical relationship of ethnicity and political organization takes place within a structure of political and economic relations which is only partly constituted by ethnic or communal meanings and groupings. The elite/non-elite, the urban/rural, the modern/traditional, the highly educated/just literate, and the fundamentalist/modernist Muslim cut across the ethnic identity vector at the local and national levels.

On the basis of Malaysian data and experience, some tentative generalizations, possibly adequate for much of archipelagic Southeast Asia may be hazarded. I am much encouraged in offering these as hostage to an uncertain future by the success of forecasts made in 1974 (Nash 1974) where I correctly (or luckily) forecast the general tenor of Malaysian politics for the coming decade against a set of equally likely, but in the event nonhistorical, possibilities.

The nation-state was won and run by elites, a coalition of communal groups. Each communal grouping relied on ethnic appeals to build mass bases in the political arena. Citizen was a category that captured only a sliver of personal identity: people came not as Malaysians (the citizens) but as Malays, Chinese, Indians, Thais, and others as citizen-ethnic contenders. In new nations, where the nation-state is both an elite and imported concept, building citizens from peasants (the mass of humanity in the new states of Southeast Asia) is a chancy political and economic endeavor. At the heart of the process of partial transformation (since ethnic identity will endure and citizen is rarely a category exhaustive of all dimensions of personal identity in political relevance), are the forging of new relations or extension to new persons of old ones. Making peasants into citizens requires relations of equity, trust, insurance, and justice, to be institutionalized in the central loci of power and come to embrace the bulk of the population.

The social consequences of these large and abstract notions are seen in the everyday actions of Malays, Chinese, and Indians. Above the local level, relations of trust are fragile. From a peasant's point of view, trust is lodged in his family, next in the kampong which is assimilated to the familial idiom, and beyond that to the ethnic category which is also absorbed in the idiom of brotherhood. This movement from kelawarga to kampong to sukubangsa can be paralleled in different terms and slightly different social spans among Chinese and Indians in the countryside and small towns of the peninsula. Trust then rests on twin pillars: partial identity and equality, and the ability to bring to account those who violate the norms of trustworthiness. The ethnic category is already stretching the familial idiom to its limit, for that category also contains social class, occupation difference, urban residence, and educational differences which strain or violate the notion of family.

Trust is important not only for the personal security it entails but also for the insurance functions implied in equality and brotherhood. Old age, sickness, incapacity, sudden loss, drastic and possibly catastrophic change are never far from the ordinary peasant's horizon. The time-honored way to guard against these ever present threats is to be involved in the life cycle networks of trust. At the peak of life, one supports both the young and old. As one moves from productive middle years to less productive older years, the middle generation can be trusted to transfer resources of support to the elder generation. Under normal, slowly changing peasant social organization, the elders are repositories of knowledge, wisdom, and religious lore. They exchange the services of adjudication, interpretation, and insurance of cultural continuity for support, deference, and a chance to pursue and exemplify the ultimate goals of the ideal person.

But with the advent of the nation-state, resources and opportunities appear beyond the local level and beyond the levels of ethnic trust with its norms of insurance, mutual help, and generational interdependence. In order to participate in the new structure peasants utilize what they have at hand—familial and ethnic resources. These norms can be expected to operate, even if weakened, over a long period of interaction between the older peasant structure and the newer nation-state. States, new and old, are subject to the misuse of power, venality, coercion, the granting of special privileges to selected persons and groups. Ethnicity is a way of dealing with the vagaries in the use of power by the bureaucratically organized nation-state. Ethnicity organized politically may be the most effective way to deal with the imperfections of the political structure and at the same time to express a basic concern for the community and a moral world.

As the state becomes more and more powerful, both in accumulating and disbursing resources and in its coercive power, it becomes the custodian of equity. In Malaysia, as elsewhere, the nation-state has the task of creating insuring equity (how this became a vital function of the state is one of the principal themes in modern Western history and in the diffusion of capitalism and its associated social organization to the non-Western world). This expectation of the nation-state means the political apparatus must do something about income and wealth distributions, economic and educational opportunities, and about the politics of meaning and culture. This is what the people of the new state demand, while the state itself has built in dynamics for increasing rationality and efficiency (what is loosely called in some social science literature the scientific-welfare state; the name is revealing in itself). Everybody gets into the political arena, and ethnicity is a variably useful resource in that arena. The state must remain sensitive to demands for equity and justice. The ability of the state to contain and define competition and confrontation determines its viability, and economic growth or the promise of economic growth in believably near terms is a condition for the survival of a more or less competitive society. (Thoroughgoing repressive societies are a limit, on one end, and "thugocracies" of competing gangs the limit on the other end, of the continuum of organized threat and use of force that underlies all state structures.)

Ethnicity, however, may run deep, both socially and personally. The greater the congruence on the blood, bed, and belief dimensions and the more effective the boundary mechanisms enclosing social groups, the more likely ethnicity is to appear in the political arena as a consciously organized effort with a vision and ideology. Islam, as it now exists in the world and in Malaysia, is said to have a blueprint for all the activities of man and all of his social relations, to model a perfect society, and to be able to bring about a moral life in conformity with Koran and hadith. Of course, neither Islam nor any other religion has this detailed a design for living in the conditions of the twentieth-century world. But many Muslims (and one might add Christians and Jews outside of the Southeast Asian context) fervently believe such a ground plan exists, and moreover, it can be implemented in the here and now (notwithstanding the agonies of Pakistan in attempting to define and build the Islamic state and society for which it came into being, or the historical record of the Iranian theocracy). So Islam, in its dakwah form, poses an ever present threat to the secular state's promises and performances. The state must continue to perform economically, provide public services with competence, and regulate educational opportunity and occupational placement within competing demands and definitions of equity and justice.

The largest generalization (that can be unblushingly offered as faithful to, and encompassing and surpassing fact and history) is that ethnicity is part of the political process, and that the role of ethnicity in social life can only be gauged by the dialectical interplay of local identity and supralocal politics. The stronger and more competent the state, the less relevant are ethnic factors to the political process; the weaker and more incompetent the state, the more politically relevant are ethnic movements.

This is a large generalization set among many other things being equal (which they never are): such things as international events and political connections, since national societies are not a closed system; the art and skill of local leaders and politicians at any critical juncture; and the general dynamics involved in economic growth, cultural change, and symbolic and scientific reformulation and discovery and invention. Knowledge, the only sure guide, is not a crystal ball foreteller of the future.

Pluralism in the Land of Plenty:
Jews in America

The saga and historical vicissitudes of the Jews since the destruction of the second temple in A.D. 70 is one of the most instructive and poignant cases of ethnicity in the civilizational matrix of the *oikemene* and its Western civilizational descendants and offshoots. But what is of concern in this essay is the more recent history of the Jews, the history in the context of the national state structures and the mass migration to the United States. The modern history of the Jews is often dated from a series of events both internal and external to the people themselves. All dates and important events in Jewish history since the Diaspora have the Janus character of inward and outward facing from the point of view of cultural and physical continuity and survival of the Jews.

Modern history begins with the *haskalah* (enlightment) period of Europe when citizenship rather than confessional adherence became the major marker of membership in the recently powerful secular national entities. For many Jews, this meant the opportunity to move into the mainstream of European culture and society, with whatever disabilities and social stress being both a Jew and a citizen of a nation-state entailed. Modifications within the Jewish communities of Europe, especially France and Germany, followed on this wave of secular citizenship, and the Jew in the great world, as a citizen of a national entity, rather than an enclave or protected minority or pariah people emerged. Internally, reactions against the monumental trauma of Shabbetai Zvi, the false messiah, who dashed the hopes of the severely oppressed masses of Eastern Europe, and the emergence of the Baal Shem Tov as leader of a revitalization movement of the pious Hasids against the establishment of rabbinical Judaism, further differentiated and broke the Jews of Europe into sometimes bitter factions.

In the "backward" states of Russia and Poland, however, official discrimination against Jews, coupled with a long tradition of violent anti-Semitism in those societies, continued to make life miserable and hazardous for Jews. The Cossack rampages, the officially sanctioned pogroms, the threat of long and arduous military service coupled with conversion, and the barriers to participation in full civil and economic life caused a massive outpouring of Jews from Europe (along with other Europeans who suffered from lack of economic opportunity, the rigid class system, and often ethnic hostility).

The United States was a natural magnet for immigrants. The first new nation had a nearly insatiable appetite for labor in its burgeoning economy, and it had the democratic, open, and tolerant traditions summed up in what has been called the "American Creed." The economic, cultural, social, and demographic aspects of the United States from about 1880 to 1924 made it the "land of gold" for Jewish immigrants, despite the hardships, prejudices, and low social status that most Eastern European Jews encountered upon arrival in the United States. Jewish immigration surged in 1881, peaked at the turn of the century, slowed considerably after the restrictive laws of 1924, trickled from the 1930s to the end of World War II, and showed a small continuing flow from the 1950s onward. With only sizable Jewish populations in Russia, South Africa, and parts of South America, and with Israel as a competing destination for these Jews, the migration history of the Jews in America is largely of the past. The

challenge of modernity, the generational differences, and
the pressures of assimilation to the larger cultural identities, coupled with the revival and rediscovery of Jewish
ethnicity, are continuing themes in the drama of Jews in
America. For the analytical purposes of this book, the
American Jews represent a minority in a relatively open
society, where ethnicity is tolerated and even celebrated,
but where this plurality is to be encompassed within the
overarching unity of American identity and culture. E plu-
ribus unum is not only a political stance of the United
States against local governments, it is in large measure a
statement about the relations of subnational groups to the
national culture. And like all such tensions of center-pe-
riphery and majority-minority, it changes intensity and
direction, meaning and salience, but it is never resolved,
for that is what the society and culture _is_: an articulation
of levels of politics, styles of life, and ethnic identifications. The articulation is never in doubt, but its terms,
content, and form are endlessly produced and reproduced
by the changing meaning of equality, dignity, and abundance in the democratic process.

The quantitative and qualitative aspects of American
Jewish life have been well documented, debated, and discussed, both within the Jewish community and among
social scientists seeking an understanding of the dynamics
of ethnic life in the United States. The basic facts on the
transformation of the Jews in America (Goldscheider and
Zuckerman 1984; Cohen 1983; Glazer and Moynihan 1975;
and Waxman 1983 are summaries of much research, while
Silberman 1985 is an able journalistic and readable summary of the status of Jews) are not in dispute. Trends,
forecasts, and futures are in some doubt and debate, although much of that uncertainty and ambiguity stems from
different value premises as much as it does from different
observations and facts.

The American Jewish population has stabilized at just

above 6 million. After a 100-fold increase in the past century, the Jewish population has just about reached zero
population growth. Consequently, most Jews have small
families, with an average of two offspring per family (this
is the same thing, obviously as zero population growth, or
reproductive maintenance). The exception to the small
family are those religiously segregated communities of
the Hasidim, with an average of four children per family
(the segregation is physical, and largely voluntary, and
from other more secular Jews as well as non-Jews). The
norms of endogamy are changing. They are now at a high
of the cycle of intermarriage: about 30-plus percent of all
marriages of Jews are with non-Jews. Just what the demographic consequences of this intermarriage rate are for
the Jewish population as a whole are unclear since many
non-Jews convert after intermarriage, and many of the offspring of mixed marriages are reared as Jews. Emigration
hardly matters in the demographics of American Jews, for
only 341 migrated to Israel in 1982, and of the several
thousand who went to Israel from 1967 to 1973, the high
watermark of emigration, 30%–40% have returned to the
United States. For better or worse, the major locale of the
American Jew is likely to continue to be the United States.
The memories of the charnel house of Europe, the rigors
and uncertainties of life in Israel, and the positive appeals
and commitment to the culture, ideals, and life opportunities of the open, plural, and democratic United States
combine to make America the home of its Jews.

In occupational and educational structure, Jews have
been in the forefront of the vast changes in social structure
and the American ethos of the past quarter-century. The
largest single shift in the value structure of the United
States in the last twenty-five years has been the implementation of the long held doctrine of equality, while the
economy has been shifting jobs into the tertiary sector.
What has been called the "civil rights" revolution has been

a change in the legal and cultural pattern of the United States that has opened up the whole society to all of its members, irrespective of the particularistic traits of any of its members. This vision of America still lacks full implementation and full social reality, especially for those groups who are "racial" in the idiom of American classification of persons and groups. But the movement toward a fully open society of equal opportunity and of equity in the distribution of rewards and benefits, however uneven, appears as an irreversible trend. (Where and when it will peak, as all social movements and trends do, is an extremely important and interesting political issue. Will it be the pressures of "special" groups like feminists, homosexuals, or antievolutionists to wear the mantle of ethnic or racial group insistence on rights, or overzealous demands to right historical wrongs againt ethnic and racial categories that will trigger a new cycle? Whatever happens, the new cycle will start on the higher ground of the achievements of the past quarter-century.)

By generation there has been a steady growth in the level of education and of social mobility among American Jews. The last twenty-five years have seen a dizzying increase in these trends in the wake of the greater openness of the larger society. Jews have been occupationally reconcentrated in white-collar, professional, and managerial roles. Nearly all Jews of college age attend college. The income of Jews matches that of Episcopalians. Jews are almost all in the middle and upper-middle class (however that is defined: status, occupation, income, education, or life-style), and many have joined the elite as senators, heads of Fortune 500 corporations, and directors of major American colleges and foundations. The mobility and status of American Jews is not in doubt, whatever argument exists over the "causes" of that mobility. (Family structure, achievement motivation, a tradition of learning and literacy, marginality, and group solidarity have all been candidates for the efficient engine. From the perspective of this book, the dialectical interplay between cultural aspects, time, opportunity, and the structure and culture of the larger social system is where the real answer lies, rather than in the superficial correlations of economists, survey sociologists, and trait psychologists.)

This mobility has all but obliterated important characteristics of earlier generations. The working class and socialist orientations of American Jews is severely attenuated and replaced by a liberal-humanitarian stance as the dominant political value system. The questions of German versus Eastern Europe origins, once of significance for status, has faded into oblivion. And many of the earlier markers of Jewish ethnicity like language, dress, and knowledge of the liturgical tradition spread along a continuum of relative presence.

American Jews, organizationally and theologically (although theology is not and never has been a important category or preoccupation), have differentiated into four major religious arrangements. These institutional loci are defined by different sorts of rabbis and their training, while those affiliated with one or another kind of Judaism have markedly different behavioral repertories and life-styles. The large segment of "unaffiliated" Jews (about 42%) who are not members of a defined congregation, *shul,* or temple usually observe one or another of the major religious ritual days (holidays in the American idiom of secular usage rather than holy days) in one of the four congregational styles. Freethinkers, agnostics, and outright atheists have long been part of the Jewish community, even if their number at any time has, perforce, been small.

Each of the four major movements in American Judaism has its own seminaries, standards for ordination, and differing emphases on religious texts, philosophy and practices expected of its rabbis and congregants. Reconstructionist Judaism (the smallest of the major branches) was founded in America by Rabbi Mordechai Kaplan. The Reconstructionist Rabbinical College in Philadelphia follows the teachings of the founder. The major tenet is that Judaism is an evolving religious civilization, and the idea that Jews are a chosen people, a light unto the nations, and as priests to non-Jews is rejected. Reform Judaism, the largest component of American Jewry (about 1.3 million members in 791 synagogues), trains its rabbis at Hebrew Union College in New York, Cincinnati, Los Angeles, and Jerusalem. A year of residence in Israel is also required. After graduation, the Central Conference of American Rabbis votes whether or not to accept the new rabbi into the organization. Reform Judaism believes that the traditions of the Jews (still a Chosen People) changes with every era, and hence practice and interpretation of text and law move with time and changing historical circumstance. Conservative Judaism (about 1.25 million members in 825 synagogues) believes that Jewish law (*halacha*) is divinely inspired, but its meaning may change to meet changing times. It trains rabbis at the Jewish Theological Seminary in Manhattan. A year of residence in Israel is also required. Rabbis enter the Rabbinical Assembly. The Orthodox (about 1.2 million members in about 1,800 congregations) is, of course, the oldest form in the United States in both its Sephardic and Ashkenazic versions. The large number of congregations maintains an older tradition of local worship, often without a paid rabbi or any official rabbi at all, since many of the orthodox were learned enough not to need the services of a religious specialist. They are united in the belief that the halacha is unchangeable and was given by God for all eternity. Their major seminary is at the Yeshiva University in New York, and their graduates become members of the Rabbinical Council of America. Within the Orthodox are the Hasidim, who are more traditional in style than the non-Hasidic Orthodox, and who add many boundary markers of dress, language, and near endogamy within a particular Hasidic community to set themselves off from the "modern" Orthodox and the Jews of other movements. The Hasids combine orthodoxy (a set of beliefs and religious practices) with orthopraxy (narrow and strict interpretation of halacha) to exhibit a distinct community.

The differences among American Jews turns on the meaning and implementation of halacha. The legal code is the heart of Rabbinic Judaism as that has evolved since the Diaspora (Epstein 1959; Neusner 1983); that code based on Torah (the first five books of the Bible, the Pentateuch), the Talmud, (the centuries of commentary on the Torah and its legal implications), and *aggada* (the lore, or oral tradition) together with congregational worship has defined the Jewish community since A.D. 70. So the behavioral implications of a given interpretation of halacha is, in the first instance, what defines who is a Jew. In the second place, the larger non-Jewish society has its category of who is a Jew. Finally, there is the matter of self-identification. This triparte social identification of who is a Jew depends upon which of the rabbinic authorities are interpreting and applying halacha, what the larger political and social entity considers a Jew to be, and who is self-identified as being a Jew. Usually this triangulation is isomorphic and hence unproblematic; who is a Jew is not an issue most of the time for Jews or non-Jews, but recently, with the emergence of the State of Israel, there has come some competition among rabbinic authorities as to who is a Jew, especially in the matter of conversions and in the strictness of the rule of matrilineal descent. In America, too, the problem of intermarriage and the definition of the offspring of such nonendogamous unions has also raised the issue of who, exactly, is a Jew. As always, it is the practicalities of life in a non-Jewish world of secular national states that raises the issue of who is a Jew rather than the abstract argument about the boundaries of the category. The argument itself may be seen, from the point of view of an analyst, as a sort of luxury product. When Jewish authorities and populations do not have the deep and dangerous problems of survival and continuity, the issue of who is a Jew surfaces. It is an argument of secular success rather than of legal crisis, while the debate over ordaining female rabbis (fait accompli in Reform and Reconstructionist Judaism) and the mixing of women with men in services and other ritual contexts still agitates some movements in America.

Nonetheless, the behavioral implications of halacha— literally, the way—define for themselves and others who is a Jew, even if the differences in the interpretations do not amount to what Rabbi Irving Greenberg of the National Jewish Center for Learning and Leadership in New York has called a "civil war." If the conflict between the ultra-orthodox-orthoprax (about 7% of American Jews) and the rest of American Jews may not be a harbinger of a permanent schism, it is a serious problem at the political level in the State of Israel. The behavioral implications of halacha, called more colloquially "observances" in America usage have been scaled by survey studies in Boston (and elsewhere) into indices of "identification." Cohen's (1983) listing of observances, their frequency by generation, and their weighting in importance (to self and others) for Jewish identification is a good springboard for a more cultural analysis of the meaning of some boundary markers and how they serve both as a "fence" between Jews and non-Jews and as validations of self-identity as a Jew in America. These are the selected measures of Jewish identification and social participation on which there is good survey information, and obviously these measures were in part selected because they are easily amenable to the questionnaire format of survey research, at least as much as their theoretical or deeper meanings. People were asked: Do you keep kosher (kashrut), light sabbath candles, have a *mezuzah* on your doorpost, fast on Yom Kippur, get rid of *chometz* (forbidden wheat products) for Passover, attend a Seder, go to services, are you a synagogue member, do you belong to a Jewish organization, do you contribute to Jewish charities, and are all or most of your friends Jewish, and, finally, are you married to a non-Jew? This list of features are certainly the "face-sheet" facts of Jewish identity in America. Interestingly, they show that the Seder meal on Passover is the most common aspect of Jewish identity, with about 85% of third-generation American Jews still practicing this ritual which was nearly universal among those of the first generation. Keeping the dietary rules at home is only practiced by 9% of the third generation, while it was practiced by nearly 61% of the first generation in 1965. Other interesting results of the surveys are reported by Cohen, some of them unexpected, like the constancy of synagogue affiliation over the generations, and the increase in membership in Jewish organizations by length of time in America and by generation.

Kashrut (the dietary laws of orthodox Judaism) plays a particularly salient role in the understanding of the Jews as a people in history, and as an ethnic group anywhere, especially in the United States. "Kashrut" is an adjective in Hebrew meaning ritually appropriate food, called "kosher" in English, and often confused with the noun "kosher," which means fitness, capacity, or faculty. Whatever the niceties of the Hebrew, the ideas of fit and ability are closed linked in the notion of qualified and able in the root of kosher. The rules of proper diet are but a set of rules, injunctions, observances, and laws that distinguish Jews from other people, and in fact constitute what a Jew is. The basis of the constitution of Jews as a people is of course the Torah and the Talmud, but the rule of law and of contract play a special role in the social constitution of Jews. The analysis of the role of kashrut (and hence of the law) in forming and defining Jews is done from an anthropological perspective. That stance requires the interpretation of the relevant texts (both written and acted) first from the point of view of the actors, and then from the analyst's angle of trying to impose system, comparison, and perhaps explanation on the insider's web of meanings. The difficulties involved in this sort of enterprise are, obviously, enormous. The insiders view is polysemic, speaking in many voices and inflections at any one time and in a bewildering array of claims to authenticity of meaning over time. Not only as chorus that verges on cacaphony, but there is a clamorous tradition of expert disputation, virtuoso attribution of meaning, and a sacred and secular literature displaying and arguing a range of positions that in their variety and contrariety could, and has, exhausted the finest of intellects and the keenest of scholars. Add to this the vagaries of anthropological theory (what the analyst uses to impose system, to make comparison, and to offer explanation), and the possibilities of error and plain wrongheadedness are staggering. But the challenge of the task outweighs the risks, and so the task proceeds in the teeth of the learned sharks and the talons of the self-righteous.

Earlier the metaphor of bed, board, and cult was described as a recursive statement of the boundaries among groups, and coupled with origin traditions and a sense of community and historical destiny offered as the meaning of the concept ethnic group. The laws of kashrut are a textbook example of the validity and utility of phrasing the ethnic dimension in those terms. Food plays an important part in any culture, and anthropologists and others have used the food and culinary habits of a people as a template for the ethos and worldview of many cultures (Forster and Ranum 1979; Arnott 1976; Douglas 1966; Firth 1973; Levi-Strauss 1964–71; Young 1971; and Feely-Harnik 1981, to mention a few of the more recent works). The dietary laws of ancient and modern Jews have been codified, interpreted, and much commented on (Soler 1979; Dresner 1982; Morgan 1984; Levin and Boyden 1940; and Shenker 1979, to again touch on a vast literature).

Since the "Law" is central to the idea of the Jews as a people, in fact they come into being as a function of a legal contract, the covenant between God and Man, and the law refers to the distinctiveness of the Jews and the observances that make them distinct, among them food usages. Kashrut may be taken as a condensation of the Law in practice and as a further distillation of the relations among the Jewish trinity: God :: Man as mediated by Law (or the Torah, or the covenant, or the Word). God asks man to sacralize custom and behavior so that man can be an instrument of God. It is the Law (Word) that mediates between the perfection of God and the imperfection of Man. Adherence to the Law means submission to God, and submission to God yields fecundity, continuity, land, prosperity, and victory over enemies. This convenant is first sealed between Abraham and God and has to do with the sacrifice, and hence food, and it reaches its final form with Moses and the separation of clean and unclean food, which is but an aspect of the setting off of the Jews from other people. Food and worship are but aspects of the separation, the cutting off of the Jews from other people by the erecting of boundary mechanisms. Jews come into being by boundaries—a triple cutting off—worship, food, and circumsion are all cuts that mark the special relation between God :: Man as mediated by the Law. Where Jews lived in encapsulated worlds boundaries are not problematic, for there is little or no choice. When Jews come in larger state structures with citizenship potentials, dietary laws (like other boundary mechanisms) become a problem, and the laws of food stand for the whole law. In the Diaspora, the Seder, with its special food usages and its recounting of the birth of the people and the facts that the word of the Lord coupled with observance and faith lead to redemption and the promise of redemption—over and over again—is the ritual most observed by Jews. This ubiquity of observance in the Diaspora is tied to the place of a meal among kinsmen who have made a covenant with God and will preserve their special practices for the everlasting promise of redemption. In this context, kashrut is the law, and the Seder is the meal of the reenactment of the nuclear experience of Jewish peoplehood.

In fact, the Jewish Scriptures span a long time period, and come in various redactions (from the Babylonian Exile in the mid-sixth century B.C.) when the Pentateuch and Deuteronomic books took nearly final form and other writings composed during the early postexilic period became canonical. I do not want to use the phrase "the Old Testament," since this implies a Christian view of these writings, nor does the Hebrew Bible quite describe this body of writing called Jewish scripture. The literature on the Bible is also vast. I have used chiefly modern English-language sources, and I hope I have committed no egregious errors, since I have no historical or theological axe to grind or perspective to urge. I write as an anthropologist, somewhat committed to the activity of making sense of the near historical *bricolage* of the writers and interpreters of the Bible.

Apparently there are three dietary epochs in the Jewish Scriptures (Torah). In Genesis God gave Adam all the fruit to eat, except that of the tree of knowledge. So paradise was a vegetarian regime. After the floods, Noah was told that he could eat all things of the earth, so that meat and plants were allowed. But with Moses came the specific dietary codes of the Jews. As the Jews were made a separate people, their food habits were also made separate from other people. The dietary laws in Genesis, Deuteronomy, and especially Leviticus are the Torah basis of distinction, and these regulations were supplemented by the Mishna and Gemara (together these laws and commentaries are the Talmud) to make the extensive and complex code of Jewish dietary laws. The making of a separate people, a separate diet, and a separate cult is not easy. It took forty years, two generations, before the old notions of people, food, and cult were extripated. (Forty, the number itself is often a metaphor for infinity, or without number, or forever in the Middle East. Ali Baba and the forty thieves, the forty posts of the Chehel Sutun in Isfahan, and the rains of forty days and forty nights as well as the forty-day period of recall after death are current instances of the use of forty to mean near-infinity.)

There are further complications underlying the dietary laws. God is in charge of life and death; life and death are intimately involved in food; God provides food, and hence people live or die by God's will and bounty. But since men kill animals to eat them, God only demands the "vital" principle that the animal be returned to him. The vital principle is found in the blood. In the times of the Temple blood, was sacrificed as an offering to God. In the Diaspora, meat is treated so that it is as nearly bloodless as man can make it, thereby keeping the separation of God from man, and Jew from other, intact.

The dietary code has, of course, evolved over time—witness the bare injunction not to seethe a kid in its mother's milk being elaborated into the whole business of separation of milk and meat products—and is still open to interpretation and elaboration. The rise of *glatt kosher* in the United States is an example of modern emphasis in the dietary restrictions. Originally glatt (meaning smooth) had to do with the inspection of the lungs of animals to see if they had a blemish that made them unfit for Jewish consumption. This notion of glatt is a function of affluence coupled with the display of piety. Only a rich person who wants to show his piety would call for the secondary exam of fitness involved in glatt. But with the rise of affluence in the United States and the division between the mere Orthodox and the ultra Orthodox, glatt has a new role to play, and hence the superkosher public eating place and product has come into being. The signs in a system of signification, like the kashrut code, are symbolically arbitrary, constrained only by the operation of the system as whole, but social usage stresses the employment and salience of certain signs within the symbolic system.

What the whole system is about, as is the whole Law, is of course the making of a special people by separation. The logic of the system is the making of categories, so that Jews are categorically set off from others. The making of categories has an intrinsic logic, but it also arises from historical circumstance, and the logic of classification is never perfect, although there is a strain toward consistency (especially as religious experts debate and define the categories and what shall be included and excluded in them). The categories have, on the surface, to do with "clean" and "unclean" foods or, as said earlier, fit or unfit food. Clean and unclean have nothing to do with health or hygiene (as folk wisdom often contends) but with the proper intake of a people made holy by the Law. Since life is the province of God, and blood is the vital principle wherein life is manifest, a holy people may not take life. Animals that take life as a rule are on these grounds forbidden. Vegetarian animals are permitted, if the blood is drained from their meat in the act of proper slaughtering and proper preparation for cooking. Animals who are ruminants are vegetarian, hence those who chew the cud (the mark of the ruminant stomach) are permitted animals. Domestic animals can be clearly observed and put into proper categories. But some animals are anomalies. (Given the imperatives to clean boundary categories, the anomaly is anathema. Douglas's (1966) Venn diagrams are a recognition of the status of anomalies in the dietary laws of what she quaintly calls the ancient Israelities.) The anomaly is the animal who chews the cud, but it may also be omnivorous, like the pig. To the stomach is added the fact of the hoof. A hoofed animal cannot seize prey, like an animal with claws. Hence the carnivorous animals of prey (from the taloned eagle to the clawed felines) are barred, as well as the pig who has a cloven hoof, and is unclear in its ability to seize, but is barred because of this very unclarity. The cloven hoof is the norm of the domestic animal, but it eliminates other domestic animals like the horse, the ass, and the camel (all beasts of burden and not raised for food in the first instance).

Clean and unclean are categories having to do with life and death, and hence with closeness to God. Perfect and imperfect are further categories of an approach to God, and the notion of the "blemish" separates the perfect from the imperfect, man from God. Imperfect animals (and men) are blemished and hence unclean. Offerings to God must be without blemish; both the animals in sacrifice and the priests who offer the sacrifice must not be anomalies. This notion of the perfect, the ideal, the categorical as fit underlies all the other food tabus and practices in the code, and it also forms the basis for the continued decisions upon kashrut. Thus the animals of the realms of water, air, and earth must conform to the type, the norm. So birds fly, fish swim, and animals walk in their proper medium of water, air, and land. Any deviation is a blemish, a failure to conform to type (and the Creator's original intention), and hence an anomaly, unclean and unfit for a people consecrated to holiness, whose custom and life must, everyday, remind them (how easy it is to fall away into the flesh pots of Egypt or the arms of willing women) of their dedication to holiness. The fish without fins or scales, birds with wings that do not fly, or birds that spend most of their time in the water, or animals at home in two elements are all in virtue of category violations, unclean. These ideas are expanded to the Passover ritual, to fermentation, and other contexts in a paper by Soler (1979), thus showing the underlying system to the whole structure of kashrut.

The six recognized divisions of the kashrut code (at least since the sixteenth-Century codification in the authorative Shulchan 'Aruch) are but detailed steps in observing the categorical imperatives of boundary maintenance. These divisions—the laws of (1) slaughtering, (2) trayfus (blemishes), (3) milk and meat cooking, (4) blood, (5) fats, (6) soaking and salting (koshering)—are guides to the laity and authorities regarding the observance of kashrut. The involved code of food selection, food preparation, and food serving gives rise first to a host of specialized purveyors, preparers, and certifiers of kosher food. Obviously, at the public level, it prevents Jews who are observant of the code (*frum* in Yiddish, *dati* in Hebrew, and now as a group name *Harid* in Israel) from public interdining, erecting that barrier against intimacy. At home keeping a kosher table requires large expenditures of time, money, and attention, serving, as was intended, to turn the mundane into the special and the profane into the sacred.

In theory, any rabbi is able to certify products and foods and their ingredients as kosher or trayf, but in kashrut specialized agencies and experts have developed. The "big four" of certification, as Shenker (1979) calls them, are in New York, and they are the center of the national system. Two of the major Jewish movements, Orthodox and Conservative, have experts and boards of kosher certification, and they are also in New York. The Reform rabbis are not concerned with this, and their congregants are free to ignore or observe the laws of kashrut, as are the Reconstructionists. The Union of Orthodox Jewish Congregations has a kashrut division dating from the 1920s. When I interviewed Rabbi Menachem Genack, rabbinic coordinator of the kashrut department, he stressed that the kashrut division grew up as a service, a demand for certification from the laity, and the division sees itself doing a public service, as being concerned with the public weal and preventing the practice of fraud in claims of kashrut. They do not seek out companies, clients, or cases. Firms come to them to seek the imprimatur of the OU stamp of kosher approval. There is a fee charged for this service, and the Union publishes a kosher directory listing the firms and products that have passed muster as kosher, according to the on-site inspections of an approved Orthodox rabbi, even to providing a *mashgiach* (watchman) who will stay in the producing plant throughout the whole process to see that the laws and injunctions of kashrut are duly observed. Kashrut cases come up from people where there are zones of ambiguity from new products and new technologies—like the dishwasher and the mix or separation of dishes used for milk products and for meat products, or whether glycerine is kosher, or using sugar from corn during passover, and other such problems as may arise among the observant. Cases also come from excessive zeal in observing kashrut. The rabbi recounted a request for koshering water from a fresh mountain spring. The request borders on the ridiculous, but does reflect the doubts of orthodox American Jews living in a world of both tradition and of novelty. Orthodox belief is, of course, that the laws of kashrut are divine injunctions, and that observance is a form of discipline, and that discipline and piety leads to the sacrilization of daily life. The making sacred of daily life is what separates Jews from others, and from other living things, human and animal. The Law constitutes the category of Jews, observance makes a person a Jew, and being a Jew is being set apart from a mere biological existence, on one hand, and from others who are not Jews, on the other. This is the paradigm of Orthodox Judaism, and kashrut is part of that logic. The Laws are eternal, unchanging, inflexible, and must be followed. What is subjected to interpretation is novelty of product, of process, and of technology involved in food. The kashrut department reaches its decisions, and the new products and processes enter the proper category, or are modified until their inclusion or exclusion is clear. The problems are not great for the learned, and consensus is easily reached. Differences with Orthodox rabbis who may rule otherwise is a condition with which the conscience of the congregant has to deal. This has always been so in Judaism, where learned men disagree and where the less learned seek rulings. Without a true hierarchy of clerical statuses, rabbis differ from each other by their reputation as to knowledge and wisdom, and there is fairly wide agreement as to the standing of rabbis in the world of those who make such judgments and to whom such judgments are important. Since the Orthodox observers of kashrut are about 8% of American Jews (with a variable of 2%–10% of other Jews being variably observant of kashrut), the problem does not exist beyond the bounds of a fairly recognizable community whose adherence to kashrut is likely to be largely self-enforcing, with recourse to rabbis only in special and puzzling instances.

The other major Jewish movement involved in kashrut definitions and demands on its members is the Conservative branch of Judaism. The views on Conservative stands on kashrut presented here derive chiefly from an interview with Rabbi David Pollock, a member of the faculty of the Conservative seminary in New York. Rabbi Pollock is also with the Jewish Community Relations Center, an umbrella organization dealing with public and private agencies of the larger community. The Conservatives do not make kosher certifications, leaving that activity to the OU or to other rabbis.

The Conservative notions of kashrut differ in minor details from the usage of the Orthodox. The differences have to do with things like rennet—an extract derived from the stomach of animals and used in making cheese, in certain jellies, in Jell-o and some other gelatins. Orthodox usage is that the extract must be taken from animals that have been ex ante certified as kosher. The Conservatives, while conceding that rennet must come from kosher animals, define it as pareve—neutral, so that it can be used with either milk or meat—while Orthodox kosher status makes it a meat by-product and hence affects serving certain sorts of packaged desserts with milk meals. The two branches of Judaism also differ on the status of wine. For the Orthodox anything squeezed from the grape has the status of wine, and wine cannot be prepared by, handled by, served by, or drunk with non-Jews. Obviously this is a strict extension of commensality—drinking with non-Jews may lead to intoxication, intoxication may lead to intimacy, intimacy may lead to sexual relations, sexual relations will lead to a violation of endogamy, and breaching endogamy violates the boundary of integrity of the Jews. This long chain to reasoning from event to remote consequence is part of the style of relentless logic taught and practiced in the study of Talmud in the major seminaries of the Orthodox and the Conservatives, but it is also a style of discourse highly valued among Jews at the same time as it is slightly mocked as *pilpul,* the making of endless fine distinctions with little or no consequence in the world of activity. Apart from their differences on who makes wine or the status of grape juice, the Conservatives differ from the Orthodox in allowing swordfish and "monkfish" into kosher diet. The argument here is whether the swordfish has scales or not. The Conservatives say both the swordfish and the monkfish have scales. The Orthodox say who knows, it looks like skin—and hence according to the rule of the anomaly of sea dwellers without scales and fins (and who walk rather than swim) the swordfish and monkfish are prohibited to kosher Jews by the Orthodox.

Even if the Conservatives and the Orthodox differ on technical details of the observance of kashrut, they hold it in the same esteem for the same reasons. Rabbi Pollock says Jews are enjoined to observe kashrut because:

1. Jews must seek those aspects of tradition and of law that promote continuity and are unifying forces in the Jewish community (what I have earlier called the constitution of people through the Word, Covenant, Logos, or Law). Kashrut is part of the making of the Jewish people.

2. It is humanistic. The attention to how animals are treated and slaughtered promotes a general sensitivity to living things.

3. It sacralizes biological activities like eating, and hence invokes a daily consciousness of God and of the community.

4. It is normative and reminds the observant that they are governed by laws, not by whims.

These are, of course, good functionalist explanations (even if, like most functionalist explanations of social practice, the empirical consequences are not what is deduced from the implications of the norm). The meanings of kashrut, its imputed consequences, and its internal cohesion as expounded by Rabbi Pollock shows the strong tendency to rationalism and legal forms of reasoning long cultivated by the "people of the Book."

An article by an orthodox rabbi, Rabbi I. Greenberg (cited earlier as head of the National Jewish Center for Learning and Leadership in New York, and who graciously took time from a busy schedule to be interviewed by me), on the "kosher pig" makes the points about the increasingly symbolic nature of dietary rules, and the ever more conscious knowledge of the symbolism and its role in defining social groups among both rabbis and many other Jews. (Again life imitates science. As functional explanations move from the unaware to the level of consciousness, what earlier functionalist anthropologists called the manifest and latent consequences or functions of norms and practice, adherence to norms becomes more and more voluntaristic as a form of making a statement about group membership and identity.) The *babirusa* is an Indonesian animal, a member of the pig family reported to have a ruminant stomach, thereby making the split-hooved babirusa a sort of kosher pig by the injunctions in Leviticus 2.7. Is the babirusa permitted? Rabbi Greenberg sees the question as largely irrelevant, and the species identification of academic biology largely irrelevant to the problem. He holds that the Laws of Kashrut, like the Law in general, have to do with the moral conditions of Jews, the status of a holy people, or a people in search of holiness. Eating, as other life experiences, should be directed in a conscious way toward holiness. The Law and kashrut are ways of consecrating life. Here the symbolic meaning of kashrut is acknowledged by an Orthodox rabbi, the notion of food observance is spread to a life of awareness, and separation is extended to the idea of distinctness.

This discussion of kashrut and its interpretation by experts turns on the role of Law in the constitution and life of the Jews. Even if many, or most, American Jews do not fully observe the Law of kashrut (or other parts of the law, ritual, and practice as laid down in what I have called the Jewish Scriptures), there is a widespread understanding that the Law is the basis of the specialness of the Jewish people. In the circumstances of modernity, and especially American modernity, only a small segment of Jews observe the dietary (and other) laws, but this centrality, in the historical and symbolic sense, is never denied. Differentiation and diversity mark the American Jewish community (as evidenced by the different movement, practices, observances, and levels of religious commitment), but this diversity does not equal either disappearance, denial, or demise of the cultural community. Boundaries of blood, food, and cult may be (and are) permeable, but the boundaries exist and are manifest in a ritual context that stresses what I have earlier called the recursive metaphor of ethnicity, and they add the all-important dimension of tradition to that symbol system.

The Seder (order) ceremony at Passover is the central ritual of identity in American Jewry. And according to the theory here developed, that is not an accident but an expectable consequence of the behavior of the system of symbols in new contexts. A symbol system—when transplanted to a new setting, or under conditions of rapid social change occasioned by modernity and the residential and social mobility involved along with the ontological uncertainty implied by the rise of science as the norm of knowledge in modern industrial society— does not disappear all at once. There is a pattern of change involving the shearing off of peripheral symbols, the reinterpretation of existing symbols, and the innovation of new symbols. This has happened to the symbol system of Judaism in America—in the development of the different movements, in the rise of secularism, and in the modes of accommodation of Jews to the larger society and the larger society to Jews.

Symbol systems disappear when the population carrying them disappears, and demographically American Jews are at a replacement level. Since the symbol system has not uniformly changed for all segments of Jews, there exists realistic possibilities for nativistic movements, revitalization movements, and the spread of more (or less) traditional aspects of the symbol system to other kinds of Jews. The evidence for the reservoirs of Jewish vitality are fairly obvious. The various Hasidic movements (as described by Liz Harris) are a continuing source of Orthodox energy, and they even set forth to proselytize other Jews in their mobile *mitzvah* vans. The rise of study groups (*chavurah*) not associated with denominations or even synagogues and current search for roots (Cowan 1982) are other sources for Jewish renewal. At any rate, Jewish life in America, contrary to the expectations of some and the hopes of others, both Jewish and non-Jewish, is not about to disappear, nor is that larger society committed to a policy of *ethnoktonos* (cultural elimination), nor is the specter of genocide other than a remembered historical nightmare. Anti-Semitism lives on (as a small disprized social attitude in about 20% of Americans, as annual surveys of the Anti-Defamation League show. This seems an irreducible minimum; at least it has been constant for decades, only its incidence by social class has changed—generally down the social and educational scale. Neither social disability nor government policy flows from attitudes among the few and the least powerful in society, and these attitudes of anti-Semitism may sour the core of the holders rather than poison the civility of daily life.

But to return to the Seder—which according to the account developed here is the locus of the reinterpretation, reincorporation, and innovation of the Jewish symbol system in American society and culture. The fact that about 85% of American Jews participate in the Seder meal at Passover gives it a social centrality matching its symbolic importance. The Seder is a ritual of didactic intentions. It tells of the central, nuclear experience of the formation of the Jews under the Law of God; it recalls that experience; and it makes that experience relevant to contemporary life. Like all rituals and myths, its content is overdetermined (historically, psychologically, and functionally) and the statement is redundant, both in the oral presentation and in the different media in which it is expressed. The story is told in words, mimed in icons on the Seder plate, and reprised in the questions asked by the youngest of the participants (Fredman 1981). The purpose of the meal is explicitly didactic, and the instructional theme is struck over and over again during the course of the ceremony. Furthermore, to the message is added the idea of generational transmission. The Seder is chiefly for children, for the reproduction of the symbol system constituting the distinctiveness of Jews.

Historical levels of meanings and symbols coexist in the Seder meal. The items placed on the Seder plate constitue a mini-history of the special events in the Jewish recall of history. The egg represents the Temple, the shankbone refers to the sacrifice of the lamb, the bitter herbs recall the times of slavery in Egypt, the *maror* (a soft vegetal mixture) stands for the mortar used in the bricks when Jews toiled to build for the Pharaohs, the wine glass is for Elijah who will announce the coming of the Messiah. And of course the unleavened bread is for the flight from Egypt, the provision of manna in the dessert, and the close relation between food and the word of God, between the faith of Jews in the mission God has assigned them and the duty of God to make that mission possible. These meanings lie at the surface of the meal: they are part of the ceremony, explicitly set forth in the Haggadah (the textual basis of the Seder), and they further the purpose of instruction and remembrance.

Modern American Seders, as did past ones, reflect historical currents. In modern services, readings from the diary of Anne Frank, selections from speeches of Martin Luther King, writings from the Warsaw Ghetto uprising are likely to be added to (or be part of) the time-tested traditions. These usages are less likely to be found in Orthodox Seders, but it can be confidently predicted that a few Warsaw Ghetto excerpts will find their way into even Orthodox Seders. What the Seder is then is a dramatic ritual presentation of the central core of Jewish peoplehood: the special relations between God and Man mediated by the Word. God is "other" and ever powerful, mysterious, watchful, wrathful, but ultimately tied to the protection of the Jews by the promises exchanged between God and Jews. Man is bound to God by the same Laws that bind God to Man, and it is the Law given by God

to Moses (the deliverer, he who drew forth) that encapsu-
lates this relationship. The Word is the Law; the law is
manifest in those things that make Jews distinct; what
makes Jews distinct is summed up in the Seder, and the
food provisions of the Seder and Passover emphasize that
God is the provider of sustenance (food) in his manner,
and man the receiver of food in accordance with the conditions God sets forth. This is what the Seder says and
what Jews enact when they perform the ritual. Other practices, like keeping kosher all the time, observing Sabbath,
the high holidays, or items of dress and personal adorn-
ment are derivative from the ideas of distinctiveness, or
are in the language of social anthropology secondary
boundary markers.

The addition of specific American items to the Seder,
like the singing of "God Bless America" along with such
traditional songs as "Dayenu" (Enough, in the sense that
anything the Lord has done is sufficent, but he continues to
shower blessings, as he did in the past), or "Who Knows
One" show the process of incorporation at work. Reinterpretation and innovation in a tradition shows its vitality
rather than its imminent demise (Scheingold 1982).

Of Jewish religious and ritual observances, the Seder is
the one that non-Jews are most likely to be invited to attend. Partly this is due to the central role of feasting in
American society, and partly because of the role of religion
in the larger social system. Religion in American culture is,
in itself, a good thing. It is better to have a religion than not,
although the views of agnostics, atheists, and secular hu-
manists find a place in the spectrum of views about religion. But what is universal is that religions should avoid
public confrontation. Each has its message, its believers,
and its style. They should try to "get along" rather than
contend for position or urge the exclusiveness of their
views. In a sense, they are "civil" religions, domesticated to
living in a secular order where tolerance and diversity are

fundamental. Of course, the fundamentalists of the mainstream religions (Protestant, Catholic, and Jew) are
uncomfortable with a civil religious view, and the civil majority is uncomfortable with fundamentalists (as well as the
sects, cults, and other religious expressions like the
Krishnas, Scientology, and I Am, which follow a long American tradition of giving birth to new religions). Some attain
mainstream status, like the Mormons and the Christian Scientists, after long histories of persecution or persecution
and ridicule). But religion in a modern United States is
largely concerned with private fates (with personal salvation), is civil in character (acknowledges what is God's and
what is Caesar's) and tolerant of a plurality of creeds (di-
alogic rather than confrontationist). The central symbolic
rites of American society are largely secular, or if religious
only vaguely so under "God," as in ceremonies for the
Fourth of July or Memorial Day, or the feast of Thanksgiving
which from its inception had "heathens" and nonconfor-
mists as celebrants and as guests.

Other symbols and organizations provide bonds
among American Jews. The mitzvah of charity (*tzadaka* or
sedaka, depending on phonetic convention) takes a special place among the 613 *mitzvahot* enjoined on Jews
(many of these good and blessed deeds are connected
with the Temple and cannot be done under existing circumstances). Giving—first to the needs of the community
(its poor, destitute, unfortunate, synagogues, schools,
hospitals, and welfare services) and then to the State of
Israel, and then to the needs of the larger society, and
more recently the cultural aspects of life—is a basis for
much of the organization of Jewish life. The organizations
that raise and distribute tzadaka and culture involve many
more Jews than do the strictly religious organizations.
Giving is tied in some ways to the overwhelmingly liberal
politics of American Jews as well as to the long traditions
of compassion and good deeds.

Currently, American Jews tend to be "liberal" in politics, and this is manifest by an adherence in a numerical
majority to the Democratic party, the traditional locus of a
liberal-humanitarian politics. Jewish radicals and Jewish
rightists, of course, do exist, from anarchists to right-wing
Republicans, although the emergence of overtly fascist
parties and leaders has not occured. But these are in numerical (but not insignificant) minorities. The politics of
American Jews is tied into the longstanding notion of social
justice for fellow human beings and also to the openness
and tolerance associated with the liberal-humanitarian
left. The politics of Jewish self-defense and self-insurance
still play a role in America, but the organizations of burial
societies, *landsmanschaften,* workers' schools, the Jewish
press, and other similar responses to a new environment
are fading into the memories of the immigrant past. Giving
to and supporting the State of Israel is now an important
part of American Jewish identification. Jews are pro-Israel
rather than pro-Zionist. They do not migrate in large numbers to Israel, and of those who go about 30%–40% return
within five years. The support of Israel accords with current American foreign policy which sees Israel as an ally in
the Middle East and maintains a special relationship with
that ally. But, if this avoids a conflict of conscience, it is not
the basis for support of the State of Israel. That support is
rooted in the current meaning of being a Jew in America.
Support is rooted in compassion, pride, historical promise,
and the fact that a state is part of the apparatus of a people,
and in the subliminal sense of a haven in a ever chancy
world.

The bonds of organization and the symbols of difference that make the Jewish community in America stem
not only from its internal dynamics but are rooted in the
larger social and cultural system. Whatever else the
United States may be, it is a modern industrial society, the
world's first "new nation," and a world power still fashion-

ing its identity and trying to find its role in the scheme of things. America is modern (for a more extended account of the major tendencies of modernity, see Nash 1984b) in the core sense of being committed to ontological uncertainty, that the final truths are not yet fashioned, and different confessional groups may all have a part of the truth, as its dominant philosophical world view. That phrasing of its implicit dominant ontology is an analyst's abstraction and labeling (this analyst, with whom others might disagree). Ontological uncertainty implies an open and changing universe only partly known by men. What is known is known through the agency of "science," a public methodology of systematic doubt and revision. Hence belief systems, in the nature of the case, cannot be final. Being tentative, competing views can and must coexist. Religious diversity is a corollary of this ontology, as is an accent on novelty, search, and tolerance for difference and dissent. (Modernity also implies social and spatial mobility with social rewards going to producers and achievers, which of course has historically aided each immigrant wave to move toward the American mythos where everybody is middle class.) The ontology is politically enshrined in what has been called the "American Creed." This ideology of America is expressed in two of the documents that constructed the United States—the Declaration of Independence and the Constitution, nearly sacred embodiments of the openness, the tolerance, and the expected diversity of American culture and society. True, there have been (and are) glaring deviations from the ideology (chiefly in the peculiar institution of slavery, the late extension of civil rights throughout the social order, or the aberration of the internment of Japanese during World War II), but these are recognized as deviations and as troubling to America's self-image until they are righted or compensated for. This creed and the important places where it is institutionalized (courts, laws, historical documents, drama, school systems, etc) are the warrant for religious and ethnic diversity within the over-arching state as secular guardian of "inalienable" rights. The advent of modernity does not mean, in the American context, secularization so much as a civil religion and the status of believers in traditional religions as a cognitive minority.

On the social side, the legacy of dissent and diversity (and the immigrant past) has not meant the disappearance of ethnicity but rather its weaving into a mosaic under the same overarching secular state. Ethnicity is, in fact, the refuge of the individual in the increasingly impersonal and bureaucratic state, as a metaphor for the scattered kins-men that a mobile society develops. Ethnicity is all the pedigree of the common man. It is the heritage of the ordinary democratic citizen when asked who he is and who his ancestors might have been. Ethnicity makes real people with imputed pasts and diffuse bonds of solidarity in the context of a modern state that demands performance, pro-ductivity, and patriotism.

These assertions about ethnicity in general, the Jews in particular, and the American context in which modern eth-nicity takes place needs some further comparison. But the voluntaristic, emblematic, and identity aspects of contem-porary ethnicity are manifest in most of the social science studies on the topic (the literature is vast, and much of it has a not-so-hidden value agenda). The modes of accom-modation of the "new" immigrants from Asia and Latin America are the crucial tests of the views set up here. The special fate of the American blacks is equally central to understanding both modern American society and the role of ethnicity as against (or combined with) race.

The study of the major urban centers is obviously the locale where these social dynamics will take place, but the typical community locus of the anthropologists cannot be ignored. I would recommend Cleveland as the place to observe the finer dynamics of American Jewish ethnicity, along with places like New York City; Skokie and Park Forest, Illinois; or Newburyport, Massachusetts, which have been the usual loci of reportage. This report (like all studies interested in real events in time and real space) is but an interim report on the continuing saga of Jews in America.

4

The Maya: Persistence of a People

The Maya are endlessly appealing to anthropologists, archeologists, and cultural historians of civilizations. Currently, there are more than 3 million Mayan Indians living nearly in the same locales as they did at the time of the Spanish Conquest, nearly 500 years ago, and virtually in the same regions of southern Mexico, Guatemala, the Peten, the Yucatan peninsula, and parts of Honduras, where their civilization developed and decayed. Since the Maya are the only people to found a civilization in the tropical jungle lowlands, they provide an abiding puzzle to cultural historians and those who place great stress on environmental limitations on cultural evolution and development. And, further, since the Maya civilizations seem to have been built without the technological benefit of the wheel, iron or bronze metallurgy, beasts of burden and other domesticated animals of the old world, their development is a challenge to technological determinists and an anomaly to cultural materialists. For social and cultural anthropologists, the 500-year persistence of a cultural tradition under adverse pressures from the Euro-American world clamors for a tidy explanation.

The Maya (a place-name taken by the Spanish for the Yucatec people and generalized by anthropologists for all of the speakers of the related family of languages grouped as Mayan) are among the original "others." When the Spanish conquistadores came to the New World, the people they encountered posed for them severe ontological problems. What manner of men were these? Were they to be included in the human species, and if so in what category of humanity? And depending on the category, What were the rights and duties of the Spanish vis-à-vis these men, already miscalled Indians? The battle of symbols, meanings, and political and cultural interpretations is well documented by Todorov's (1984) careful reading of the texts. That the Spanish could not grasp Indian culture nor plumb the depth of the complicated cosmologies of the Indian civilizations is no surprise. That the Indian became the "other" seems a political and economic inevitability given the clash of interests and worldviews. The first contact with the Indians of the New World has bequeathed to Euro-America the persisting problem of what to make of and to do with others. Equal but different? Different but lesser? Equal but similar? And through all the possible combinations, the world has not yet decided on equality, difference, and brotherhood, and it may never reach that anthropologically sound but politically and economically difficult set of equivalences.

When the Spanish conquered the Indians of the New World, and the Maya among them, they wrought cataclysmic changes in the culture and social structures of the Maya. The conquest, bloodier in some parts of the Maya world than in others (the river that runs by Quezaltenango is still called the "River of Blood" in memory of the slaughters of Alverado in that region), decapitated the Mayan social order, substituting Spaniards at the top of the social order in place of the native nobility. At the same time, a new dominant ontology of peninsular Catholicism was made mandatory and the Indian religion, its deities, rituals, books, and calendar consigned to the devil and prohibited. Along with saints and steel, the Spanish introduced a host of new crops, new animals, new technology, and new forms of social organization to make the colony both governable and economically profitable, at least to the crown and the colonists and conquistadores if not the Maya. The trauma of the conquest in some areas of the Maya region resulted in sporadic attempts to evade the Spanish yoke—rebellions in the highlands of Chiapas, the war of the castes in the Yucatan peninsula—but on the whole the conquest was the basic, unalterable fact of the foundation of the contemporary Indian societies and cultures of the Maya.

The Indians, who were rural, living in agricultural settlements around the temple centers which housed the priests and the nobility, were brought under the "sound of the bells" by the decrees of aggregation, and they were apportioned as laborers and tribute payers by the Spanish devices of the *encomienda* and the *repartimiento*. The settlements were laid out according to the Roman camp plan of the central plaza that the Spanish had found so useful in the recent *reconquista* of the Iberian peninsula from the Moors. So the Spanish imposed a "Conquest" culture on the Maya, and the Indians began a long process of adaptation and culture change that has resulted in the "heritage of conquest" that is metaphorically the panorama of Mayan life today.

The various stages of interaction among the cultural traditions and the emerging nation-states with local societies was first sketched by La Farge (1940) and brought up to date by Beals (1967). This periodization has served as the skeletal frame for the culture history of the Maya. But whatever the fine details of social change in the region are, the major processes and products of the change are fairly evident. The Indians were transformed into a series of rural settlements around town centers. Many of these are still the contemporary vacant towns, similar in residence pattern to the preconquest temple centers. But now the Indians were subordinate to the colonists and later were the representatives of the new nations of Mexico and Guatemala (later Belize and Honduras, as well).

This fracturing of the principalities or realms of the preconquest Maya reduced these political entities to the municipal level, a local society without much attachment or consciousness of social bonds with larger Indian units. As an entity, "Quiche" refers to a language grouping, not a socially conscious unit or a single demarcated cultural tradition. As elsewhere, race, language, culture, and social organization may be but usually are not closely bound or indissolubly linked. Tax's classic paper (1937) recognizes that the ethnology of the Maya must proceed from the ineluctable fact that the *municipio* is the unit from which all further research must begin—it is the starting point but not necessarily the terminus of investigation. The locus of investigation must not be confused with the focus of investigation. And attempts to see the larger social and cultural system of which the Maya form but a part like my own Multiple Society formulation (1957) or Colby and Van den Berge's work (1969) on the Ixil do not violate the ethnological integrity of the municipio as they go beyond it to consider problems of the national and supranational levels of social organization and cultural processes. Hawkins in *Inverse Images* (1984) challenges the notions of two cultural traditions interacting over the time since conquest and sees the cultural and social variation in the region as a single continuum marked by status and locality differences. This notion's applicability and consequences I have evaluated in my foreward to Hawkins's book, and that argument is probably of chief interest to specialists in the region, but here I stay with the modified concepts of the municipio and the developments of located social units as being most useful for the understanding of social and cultural change in the region.

South of a line formed by the Grijalva river in Mexico and throughout the whole of that part of Mesoamerica, there are virtually only two kinds of people—Ladinos and Indians. Ladinos are the people of the national culture, those in the Spanish version of Euro-American culture; and Indians are those who are in the tradition of the Mayan

Indians. Ladinos speak Spanish, wear European-style clothing, are Christians in a recognizable Catholic or Protestant idiom, have social classes, and are members of and participants in the modern world culture and society of the industrialized Western world (at whatever level of competence or comprehension they in fact exhibit). They are Guatemalans and Mexicans, not Indians residing in Guatemala or Mexico without the worldview of the other Mexicans or Guatemalans. The situation on the ground is (as is always the case in ethnographic description) more complicated. Ladinos, besides rustic and class designations, also include representatives of other cultural traditions—Turcos, Chinos, Gauchepines, etc.—but in general this may be glossed as non-Indian. Indians may be called *Indios, naturales, muchachos, tontos,* etc. and this may be glossed as not a Ladino. At any rate the Ladino-Indian division, with whatever linguistic marker or sociolinguistic status and deference usage, like the *vos* pronoun from Ladino to Indian or the Don-Doña from Indian to Ladino, is the cleavage line between kind of persons. This line is almost wholly culturally defined. True, there are physical features thought to be Indian, but they are subordinate to the cultural markers of dress, language, occupation, wealth, place of residence, and other social and cultural aspects of being a Ladino. As such, the movement from Indian to Ladino is a process of cultural change, an individual becoming a Ladino through a process of Ladinoization—that is, the acquiring of cultural features and a social identity of self and validation by others of being a Ladino. In this view of the matter, Ladinoization is a matter of detachment of individuals from Indian societies and their transformation (or their descendants' transformation) into Ladinos. Whole communities of Indians do not become Ladinos, whatever the level and rate of absorption of traits or features of national or world culture. Acculturation, if it means the gradual bombardments of the little tradition with cultural traits from the superordinate great tradition until identity or fusion takes place, never happens in Mesoamerica (and as some anthropologists hold, never happens anywhere at anytime). Ladinoization is a process of individual detachment from an Indian society, and if enough persons are detached or abandon that society it collapses. Disappearance comes through demographic depletion, and that depletion is caused by individuals who are one by one giving up or repudiating a cultural tradition. Of course, the larger forces that affect the rate of demographic devolution must be understood, but it cannot be overstressed that it is individual detachment from an organized social group that is the efficient motor of ethnic change and demise, not the spectral bombardment of cultural traits from one society to another.

The persistence of any people and their distinctive cultures and social arrangements is, of course, a precipitate of history. History in Guatemala, and in the Maya area, shows varying degrees of "pressures" on the Maya. That is, the national or colonial societies exerted over time various degrees of force attempting to change, absorb, or eliminate Indian culture and society. The adaptive responses of the Indians, of course, varied over time and according to circumstance. But the Indian communities of today are formed largely by the pressures during the first and second republican periods, as those are in Guatemala defined by Goubaud (1951) and by Beals (1951) for Mexico. The history of attention, inattention, pressure, and neglect by national governments, and the Indian location near Ladino and national centers of commerce and administration have resulted in a variety of different sorts of Indian communities. Typologies are notorious for the suppression of important social fact and process, but their undoubted heuristic utility in reducing a welter of fact to manageable proportions cannot be denied. Hence, they continue to proliferate, and classifcations change at the adding of new ethnographic observation and at the whim of new theory. Some of the most useful typologies are noted later on.

Time as caught in history is an obvious and important variable, as is space as defined in ecology in the persistence of people and culture. The bulk of the modern Maya have always lived and now live in the altos of the region—the Western Highlands of Guatemala, and the highlands of Chiapas Mexico (with considerable Maya in Yucatan and Belize). The highlands were, before the advent of roads and motor transport and the airplane, difficult of access and rather remote from the Ladino centers of power and wealth. Their mountain fastness, their relative inaccessibility, served to shield Indians from direct intervention and from the movement of large populations of Ladinos into Indian municipios. Even today Ladinos are relatively few in Indian-populated highland municipios, and *los altos* are still in a meaningful sense "Indian country." Another aspect of ecology is that until the nineteenth century there was no economic incentive for Ladinos to covet Indian land or to compete in agricultural or extractive industries with the economies of the Indians (Nash, 1970). In the first half of the nineteenth century, the national elements were concerned with throwing off the Spanish yoke and building new and republican nations. Indians were only marginally concerned in these struggles, and they were left much to their own devices. In the latter half of the nineteenth century, the export-plantation economy was developed, and the Indian became a valuable resource for labor on the coastal and piedmont plantations producing coffee and other products for international markets. The prevailing ethos of the national society was laissez-faire capitalism, driving the weakest, in this case the Indian, to the wall (along with many campesino Mexicans and Guatemalans). Land, under the liberal view of markets, made state policy by the Ley Lerdo in Mexico and the Barrios reforms in Guatemala, became a commodity.

There then ensued an attack on Indian holdings. The up-shot of the liberal and brutal laissez-faire regime was the growth of the minifundia among Indians and severe land pressures on the municipios. Part of the defensive Indian response was a growth in specialization and in trade and commerce, on the scale Tax has aptly called Penny Capitalism. The social defense against the encroachment of the national economy (with its tendency toward impoverishment and the national polity with its tendency to subordination) was the growth of the "corporate" Indian community.

The Spanish during the colonial period had established "republicas Indias," largely self-governing local Indian governments within the hierarchy of the viceroyalty. These Indian republics were to take care of their civil and religious affairs and have representatives who would deal with the outside powers, whether crown or republic. Of course, the constitution or formal charter of the republicas worked out over time to be something other than was planned, but this structure formed the basis of the "corporate" community, a defensive organization against the pressures of the larger and more powerful society and a repository of Mayan values and *costumbre*. This corporate community also has been called "traditional" as against "modified" or "centrifugal" as against "centripetal" (Camara 1952), or "open" as against "closed." All these stress a historical entity somewhat embattled against national society in a defensive posture guarding against the erosion of personnel, land, social structure, and cultural pattern.

The social structural basis of community defensive reaction was the civil-religious hierarchy. In one form or another this basic institutional mechanism protected Indian communities, but it has undergone change, and in some parts of the region has disappeared entirely. In constructing a model of the civil-religious hierarchy, it is methodologically important to play down such important social factors as the size of the population and its settlement pattern, the presence and number of resident Ladinos, the number of foreign Indians, the presence or absence of political factions in the local community, and other circumstances like the recent social unrest, the presence or absence of guerrilla warfare, the influence of Protestants, or the army's attempt to set up "safe villages." These other factors are, of course, the variables that are causing, and have caused, along with shifting economic fortunes and the international climate of the cold-hot war, the social and cultural changes in the Indian communities and in the relations of the different segments of the multiple society. This model is built from those features that historical and ethnographic studies indicate were once the most general and fundamental social structures in the altos of Indian country.

Typically, Indians organize local communal life around a series of ranked offices. These offices form two ladders, one a ladder of religious posts and the other of civil posts. The two ladders, however, are tied together by common symbols and because office holders alternate between posts in each of the ladders. The difference between the two ladders is conceptual. Indians tend to think of them as one system. The term civil-religious hierarchy recognizes this fact of interrelation. (Emic is the designation of significant features marked by native speakers of a language. By extension it is applied to other cultural domains). From the point of view of an Indian in a local society, the hierarchy represents fixed tasks of communal service to which he must devote a number of years from his adult life. Each man who serves in an office is in reality, above the very lowest rung, a representative of a family. So that it is family units, rather than individuals, that pass through the cycle of public service. A male enters service at about sixteen or seventeen years of age, at one of the lower posts in the hierarchy. After a year of service, there is a rest period between posts, running from three to four years. He then assumes the post on the opposite ladder, one rung higher. The crossing from religious to civil office back and forth up the hierarchy is usual, but a fixed order with regular alternation is not essential. The offices are unpaid and take up, depending upon the task, from half to all of an individual's working time. As such the posts are called *cargos,* and they are in a literal sense burdens, since a family loses work time and spends assets in performing the duties of office. Usually taking on the post is a ritual occasion requiring a stipulated cash outlay for liquor, food, and other items like rockets and firecrackers. During the term of office, expenses in the worship of the saint, of paying for masses, buying candles and incense, hiring marimba bands, and other similar activities use up current income and personal savings. In view of this drain on personal resources, there is some reluctance to accept offices in the hierarchy, but public opinion (and sometimes public coercion, like jailing, until the post is accepted) and personal rewards of honor and deference offset this current. Individuals subscribe to the value of the hierarchy, and the community rewards them for service. Families with long faithful service are known to be good persons, having demonstrated their moral worth publicly. They are usually given deferential greetings in public, funerals of their family members are heavily attended, and their advice is sought and valued. After service in one or another of the top offices in either wing of the hierarchy, an individual "retires" from public service and becomes one of the elders, usually called a *principal.* Principales are those who make the decisions for the group, serve as its judges in disputes, and have coercive power to see that younger individuals serve in the hierarchy paying the same costs as they paid during their previous years of service. In some communities, the elders and civil-religious hierarchy still perform annual world-renewal rites to set the sun in its course of rising and setting and the moon in its place in the night sky as they play father and mother to daughter earth. From the perspective, then, of the families participating in the system, the civil-religious hierarchy is a system of interrelated, ranked-office service which is obligatory as a public duty and costly in terms of family resources. The life cycle of the family in an Indian community is a continuous alternation between civil and religious offices, whereby families grow older, more prestigious, and wiser in a socially fixed rhythm (to see variations on this model and some of the recent changes in Guatemalan local systems, see Cancian 1967; Adams 1957).

The ordinary operation of the civil-religious hierarchy defines the limits and membership of the local society. A person is a Panachjeleño, or a Chimalteco, or a Cantelense, or a Maxeño, only insofar as he is eligible for and participates in the hierarchy. (Indian communities have a "first" name of a saint and a second "place" name, and sometimes the first name designates community members, and sometimes the second name fills that function. For example, Sto. Tomás Chichicastenango is the full name of what is called by all Chichicastenango, but its inhabitants are called Maxeños in the Indian version of Tomás.) Ladinos in any community may fill with regularity the top posts of the hierarchy (like secretary or alcalde), but they do it for pay or for political reasons and are hence outside of the cargo system. Foreign Indians (residents born in another municipio and who therefore do not know local costumbre and are not under the aegis of the local patron saint) do not enter into the system. There is a folk belief in culture being attached to a people who are territorially and physically distinct and hence by blood, cult, and place alien if they do not reside in the place of their people. I have known three-generation residents in an Indian municipio still called by the name of their natal muncipio and still wearing the costume of that group. The hierarchy is virtually the entire social structure of an Indian municipio. At the most general level of social integration, this structure does for Guatemalan Indians what kinship and clanship does for African societies like the Tallensi, or what social class does for Ladino society.

Looked at from the point of view of the total society, the civil-religious hierarchy is the means by which all the families of the municipio are tied together in a single social structure. It is a boundary-maintaining mechanism against outsiders, Indian and non-Indian alike, whether or not the local Indian organizations are usefully viewed as ethnic units. All of the families are age-graded according to which rung in the ladder they have reached, and at the same time they fill a general position of respect due to past service given. The carrying out of duties entailed in the various offices is how the public business of the community is performed. Cooperative work tasks, like clearing the cemetery or repairing roads, are done at the behest of the principales acting through the officers of the hierarchy. Justice is dispensed by the top Indian alcalde (judical assessor), as the national law is interpreted in the local situation. Disputes between relatives or arguments over property rights, unpaid bills, and slanderous allegations are settled by recourse to the officials of the hierarchy. The hierarchy is the mechanism for tabulating community opinion and sentiment. At open meetings, the principales along with officials of the hierarchy decide upon activities using communal resources and local personnel. For the Indian it is the way public order is kept and regulated and the channel through which group decisions are made and ratified.

The religious or sacred aspects of the hierarchy relate the entire community, through its chosen representatives, to the supernatural. By filling an office in a religious post, the individual acts for the whole community in maintaining the society's relations with the supernatural, caring for the physical plant of the church and fulfilling the proper cere-monies of the saints and the fiestas of the religious calen-der. The hierarchy organizes the communal fiestas, from the celebration of the patron saint through whatever spe-cial days of worship are marked in the religious and ceremonial calendar. The secular tenor of daily life of Indi-an societies appears to stem from the fact that it is the burden of officials rather than private individuals to care for and to keep connections with, and propitiate super-nature. The prevailing matter-of-factness in ordinary problem solving of these deeply religious communities is probably likewise due to this structural arrangement, as I have elsewhere argued (Nash 1979).

In addition to the consequences described, there are other important effects stemming from the ordinary opera-tion of the hierarchy. These tend to be harder to apprehend and sometimes not known to, or consciously intended by, the community. The hierarchy serves as a leveling mecha-nism in terms of curbing the extreme skewing of wealth distribution and as a channel for the socially controlled modes of personal display. No aspect of the hierarchy has been so misunderstood as the leveling mechanism. Under the proper demographic, economic, and political condi-tions, the leveling mechanism breaks down, and wealth classes and prestige or power lineages may emerge in Indi-an communities. But the understanding of this phenomena requires a prior analysis of the leveling mechanism and the step-by-step erosion of it so that wealth and power cleav-ages may emerge (see Cancian 1965 for an analysis of how the leveling mechanism was transformed in Chiapas). By using income and resources of families and of the commu-nity, the hierarchy keeps any one family from accumulating very much cash or property. This communal call on per-sonal wealth—coupled with the inheritance system and the low level of technology and marginal land and a small enough population so that most families proceed through the system—keeps a class of wealthy families from developing and perpetuating themselves over time. These are precisely the conditions which, when all changes in the direction of limiting access of the poorer families, results in the system's operation as Cancian describes it, or as it operates in Chichicastenango. The rich, in local terms, cannot use their wealth for personal aggrandizement nor can they comfortably build houses patently superior to the ordinary, average dwelling. They may, of course, move through the hierarchy more rapidly than the poor (the poor may never reach the top posts) since they can afford to take their offices in sequence. Thus the well-to-do may, and usually do, become principales at a younger age than the less affluent. But the hierarchy is usually effective in keeping a social class distinction from crystallizing and in blocking the polarization of wealth from generation to generation. It is an efficient device for keeping a community more or less homogeneous, and marking clearly the paths and methods for achieving respect and political say in a local society. The importance of equality and the absence of hard-and-fast class lines is crucial in enabling the community to present a united and granite-like face to the outside world.

The hierarchy is the link between the local community and the supralocal institutions with which the members of the local society must deal. It mediates between a local society and the nation, on the one hand, and between a local worldview and religion and the Catholic Church, on the other. Since its beginning, the hierarchy has played the role of organizing the local community, while at the same time articulating it as a corporate entity with wider networks of social relations and encompassing social systems. The representatives of the national institutions, culturally apart and socially superordinate to Indians, do not deal directly with Indians as individuals. Contacts between Indians and Ladinos are of short duration, impersonal, and usually of a commerical nature. These superficial relations exclude the widespread phenomenon of *compadrazgo* (ritual coparenthood) where Indians often seek Ladino compadres for the economic, political, and social advantages such ties may bring. Commands, laws, requests, and demands by the agents of the nation are made to the officials of the hierarchy. The hierarchy is often an imperfect agency, and this stems from its Janus-like structural pose. On the one side it organizes and defines the local community, on the other it acts as an extension of the political apparatus of the nation. Frequently, the demands made on the hierarchy from within the local society and those from without are not easily compatible. National pressures and decrees are translated necessarily into some sort of conformity with local conditions, often making Indian officials seem stubborn and uncooperative to Ladinos or traitorous and pliable to fellow Indians.

In the political role of the hierarchy, two major social conditions appear necessary. First, the officers of the hierarchy act in the name of the community and remain passive agents of the nation; and second, the nation does not bypass the hierarchy by direct appeal to individual Indians. These conditions have characterized Guatemala for a long time and formerly were the usual case in prerevolutionary Mexico. It is this combination—the Indian community as a corporate, local, defense organization in a nation that finds it convenient or advantageous to deal with Indians indirectly—that has accounted for the persistence of the Indian communities and their local social and cultural bases. When the national society seriously tries to "incorporate" Indians, on whatever terms, into national society, or radical and revolutionary elements strive to make supporters or guerrillas of the Indians, or romantic intellectuals seek to restore an idealized Indian heritage, the local community, its culture, and its personnel are under pressure, and attacks and crises of continuity and cultural integrity arise.

The universalistic tendencies of the Catholic Church (in an assault on Indian belief systems begun in the early days of the conquest) are also muted or overcome by the particularistic operation of the civil-religious hierarchy. In religious life, the symbols of the universalistic faith are given local meanings, and it is the *cofradía* (the religious brotherhood dedicated to the saints, or the Virgin, or Jesus) rather than the priest that is the center of sacred organization. The religious brotherhoods deal with the Church and its representatives in the name of the community, translating and reinterpreting religious edict and symbol to meet local conditions and understanding. Sometimes the Church has organized its own groups, like *Acción Catolica* to win support away from folk organizations, but making Indians members of the Catholic community in orthodox terms is just as difficult as making a member of the nation in participant citizen terms. Both are transformations or conversions away from one set of values tied to friends, neighbors, and kin to another set of values bound up with strangers, far-off unseen persons, and nonrelatives. Evangelical Protestantism is an increasingly important force. In the nature of the case, conversion to Protestantism detaches an Indian from the community, bars him from service in the hierarchy, and starts him on the road to membership in the national or international society and culture. Protestantism stems from North American efforts and missionary activities, but there are now established Guatemalan churches and sects, both among Ladinos and Indians. These sorts of induced changes set a recurrent problem in the "community-nation" of "ethnic-civil" relations—identity and diffuse solidarity verus impersonal rules of procedure untempered by kin and kith.

A fourth cluster of variables (or factors) involved in the survival and continuity of Maya is the dominant worldview. In talking about "Maya" worldview, abstraction is made from the reported cultures of some forty Maya communities in the ethnographies over the past half-century. This abstraction, perforce, only deals with a small segment of the ontology of the Maya, as that bears on the facts of persistence. This abstraction, while it transcends any particular occasion of occurrence, can be broken down into real components in actually existing (or formerly so) societies. Hence, it is not a flight of fancy, like a Benedictine borrowing from Nietzsche, or a construct embraced for its logical and philosophical niceties. The important axis of this worldview, in relation to persons and culture, is that Maya Indians see cultural difference as "natural." Cultural variety is a fact of nature. Different customs are both characteristic and appropriate for different people. These cultural differences are tied to both "blood" and "territory" and to the different inherent features of the patron saint of the people. Cultural differences are like differences among individuals: natural, inevitable, tied to birth, to place, and to cult. Furthermore, these cultural differences all exist at the same level of human validity. They are not ranked. Differences are neither better nor worse—just different. They are in the scheme of things, not to be obliterated, overcome, or discarded. That one group of Indians wears short skirts, another wears wool jackets, while yet another wears striped trousers is noted but not ranked or considered remarkable. This indigenous cultural relativism goes for all aspects of culture—language, saints, occupation, and food preparation as well as dress. This kind of worldview, seeing variety as natural, unranked, and stemming from the deepest aspects of persons and groups, is true of all Mayan Indian communities—at least the 67% of Indians who live in the altos where the "traditional" and "adaptative" types are found (other Indian types are Modified and

Ladinoized, according to Early's (1982) empirical categories based on census, survey, and monographic materials. The differences among his four types rest on dress variations, degree of dominance of subsistence occupation, functional civil-religious hierarchy, national Catholic dominance over folk organization of religion, and presence and salience of Protestants. This is obviously a rough sort, but it shows the continuum of Indian communities and the range of culture that is still identifiably Indian. (My only caveat is that it still accepts the outmoded idea of acculturation where communities disappear, with the implicit notion that beyond Ladinoized is full Ladino.)

This Indian worldview contrasts sharply with a Ladino worldview, in which cultures are ranked from clear superiority to inferiority, and the most important social dynamic is the drive toward social mobility leading to the precious possession of the valued, civilized, high-status culture of the *gente decente, los correctos, catrines,* or whatever term is used at the proper class level for civilized persons against "naturales."

These worldviews are incompatible, as are the Indian expectations that their ways of life will continue (with whatever changes are made) from generation to generation, and the Ladino certainties that some variant of national culture (itself a variant of Euro-American culture) will come to characterize the whole people of Guatemala and Mexico, only marked by differences in rural-urban, rich-poor, and class and cultural refinement. It occurs neither to Indians nor Ladinos that some variant of Mayan culture will someday come to be the dominant element in, say, Guatemala or Chiapas.

From the vantage of Indian-national relations, social change in Guatemala passed a watershed in the advent of the 1944–54 revolutionary decade when serious efforts were made to build a democratic and pluralist social order, and then a reaction-holding period from Castillo-Armas to

Rios-Montt where army regime after regime sought to pacify guerrilla movements and limit political protest in the national sector. Now, as a civilian government currently holds the reins, Indians are uncertain as to what government policy will be about land, about military incursions, about civil rights, and about cultural autonomy. National society holds its breath while a shaky representative regime tries to contain politics to civil dimensions, under the wary eye of a military ever ready to intervene.

A detailed review of recent Guatemalan (or Mexican) history would serve little purpose. The continual dramas of Indian-national interaction go on in varying levels of conflict, accommodation, intrusion, and neglect. The larger questions remain. Will Indians be seen as full members of the national state while they keep their valued culture? Will civil institutions allow Guatemala to develop a stronger set of representative devices including civil rights and parliamentary procedures? Only time can say, and no formula is apt to bring desired results.

The Maya are still (despite the variety of community organizational forms and the continuing process of Ladinoization) basically local communities, with local cultural variants of a tradition distinct from Ladino culture. As the national government reaches into Indian communities (to make them into "safe" hamlets, or interdict guerrilla havens), disruption of lives and communities takes place, and there is a stream of refugees into Mexico and even entering the United States. Under pressure, and sometimes attack, Indians have the options of fleeing, withdrawing, or giving surface acquiescence to demands they cannot resist. But they have not yet become an "ethnic" group in the sense of a larger Indian solidarity vis-à-vis Ladinos. They are still, in day-to-day life, localized, rooted, territorially attached members of relatively distinct and bounded communities. Becoming an "ethnic" group in the sense of wider ties of identity, organization, and common action and purpose is possible, and is more likely than becoming part of the revolutionary peasantry envisioned by radical Marxist groups.

But whatever turns time and circumstance bring to the Maya, their social organization, their worldview of cultural differences, their unwillingness to concede superiority to other ways of life, and their sheer abilities to live in the face of adversity and to continue to find meaning in daily life provide shields against disappearance and paths toward persistence and continuity. Culture, worldview, and identity commitment may be the weapons of the weak, but they have staying power beyond the momentary glories of both empires and nations.

5

Ethnicity: Reservoir of Turmoil and Refuge for the Embattled

Describing and analyzing three historically and structurally dissimilar ethnic-national situations was a deliberate strategy, reflecting a methodological and theoretical set of preferences. There is, in all my work, a marked tendency to select a "crucial" or telling instance, or a few cases brought to bear on some limited set of assertions, or, more elegantly, hypotheses or sentences in the fund of common wisdom. This is in contrast to a way of work that is statistically cross-cultural, on the one hand, or deeply descriptive, on the other. Careful description of a case or cases is, of course, essential before all else, but analysis cannot stop at description (and it really never does, since even the merest description entails some commitment to concepts and theory). I aim at "empirical generalizations" lodged in a set of concepts that are diagnostic and hence more than local. They need not be universal, as I think ethnicity was not omnipresent over all time and space. They should be general enough to cover more than a single instance and be the scaffold for forming generalizations. These sentences should exhibit the virtues of being falsifiable and at the same time able to be linked to other sentences at the same level of abstraction, with similar grounding in the ethnographic record. But beyond the hypotheses or generalizations generated by these procedures of comparison and contrast, there is the mutual enrichment of understanding of each case through the reflexivity of instance upon instance. This "polythetic" comparison, an often used but seldom named manner of comparison, is in some contrast to the more positivistic modes. And understanding ethnicity in three widely separated and diverse contexts is no mean thing in itself, I do not have a name for these procedures (methodology and conceptual apparatus seem too grand and too awesome for what is actually proffered). I would offer "creative eclecticism" as a first approximation, if that did not have overtones of being an oxymoron. The features of the three cases described and analyzed in the second, third, and fourth chapters are an introduction of the way of work exemplified in this book. They demonstrate the use of some general ideas on the basis of fieldwork-generated data, combined with historical and regional context. The chief theoretical novelty, in addition to the way of work displayed, is the selection of the three instances. The "cases" were selected because they highlight different aspects of the multifacted phenomena of ethnicity. They show that the kind of social structures preceding either colonial, conquest, or revolutionary-immigrant formation of the basis for the national state, and hence the ethnic groups composing it, were crucial in the formation of ethnicity, as was the interaction with the subsequent social and cultural structures. The point is that ethnicity was built over time, and it was built of disparate parts, in fluctuating and uncertain circumstances, but still there are some commanalities over the instances. So the cases were first selected because they showed differences in initial social structures, historical trajectories, and differential outcomes. The historical, structural, and cultural differences and contrasts were stressed to approximate the range of variability within the common domain of the formation and operation of ethnic groups within different forms of the nation-state. The axes of structural, cultural, and historical variation used in selecting and comparing the three instances may be viewed as a three-dimensional grid with many blank spaces. The blank spaces could conceivably accommodate other instances of ethnicity in the context of the nation-state.

The commonalities among the cases stem from the struggles within the nation-states over the values of political power, economic reward, and prestige and deference. The struggle over power, prestige, and economic reward is first set by the special position of the "indigenous" group. In a colonial situation, if the indigenous group is granted special status, they then become the politically dominant group in the new state. The other ethnic groups either enter in political contest to protect citizen rights, ask for autonomy, or mount a secession movement. The actual course taken depends on the demographics and the organization differences among the groups. Political power is closely related to economic reward but can vary fairly independently, as it did in Malaysia. The government, however, has great impact on wealth and income distributions, and part of the political jockeying is tied to attempts to monitor and influence income redistribution. The different political strategies followed by the Chinese in Malaya, the Jews in America, and the virtual absence of strategy of the Maya are in large part reflexes of the economic and political resources available to each ethnic group vis-à-vis each other and vis-à-vis the state apparatus. There is also the interaction of power, wealth, and prestige. Prestige has a dual component. It is made up of rank in scale of values more or less across the whole social system, and an internal group evaluation of its worth in a generalized human scale. The first component of rank is expressed in social demeanor and public deference, while the second component is that of identity—identity in the sense of that part of the self that is defined as being inextricably wound up with the ethnic group. The question of "Who am I?" is usually not a problem outside of ethnic interaction, but in a ranked situation, where there is some possibility of mobility between groups and up the status ladder, the question may be salient. And when it becomes acute, the question becomes who am I "really."

This question of "authenticity" comes about in situations of possible movement between ethnic groups and where parity is being approached in power wealth and rank concession. The Jews in America are faced with this question; the Chinese in Malaya are not; and the Maya are faced as individuals with an option to abandon Indian identity in some instances. The subjective, self-related notion of identity is best viewed somewhat like an onion, peeling off layers. So some of the boundary mechanism is at the surface of the person, and others are deeper and deeper toward the core of identity. But like an onion when all the layers are peeled away, nothing remains. At the core, ethnicity is a consciousness of belonging to a group with whom one's humanity is inextricably intertwined. The operation and formation of ethnic identity, at the psychological and social psychological levels, is carefully explored in the papers edited by De Vos and Romanucci-Ross (1975). And even the pathologies of "ethnic" identity are explored in their hostile and possibly paranoid manifestations.

Ethnic identity involves the use of "strategies" at the level of interpersonal interaction as well as at the structural level and at the symbolic levels. What in daily life constitutes ethnicity, what aspects of the person are relevant to ethnic identification, and what is presented in what sort of social situations is in part negotiated within the structural and cultural constraints. The choice of strategies, their situational determinants, and the persisting or evanescent aspects of identity are summarized and analyzed by Royce (1982).

Whether or not my instances run a reliable chain and compass along the frontier of "ethnicity" studies (at least those oriented to the social and cultural dimensions to a greater degree than the self-identity psychological aspects of ethnicity), I strongly believe this is the path to further research and further knowledge. Growth comes from having something to argue about, a strong making of a position that requires much work to demolish. My summary shows how the axes of selection may be used among the three cases as contrasting (particularizing) and comparatively (generalizing). Some other instances of ethnicity in the nation-state are also assimilated to this perspective of contrast and comparison, and presumably other cases and data could be so treated. The limits of this procedure needs further empirical and theoretical stipulation.

Malaysia was a British colony, and the Malays were chiefly a people engaged in riverine and coastal traffic, fishing, and padi farming. As Malaya moved into the sphere of international commerce, Chinese and Indians were imported as workers, clerks, and in the middle echelons of the emerging export economy. Malays became officials or stayed in the primary sectors. As immigration increased, the Chinese became nearly demographically equal in size to the Malays, and the Indians became a sizable population. These peoples are permanent elements of the Malaysian nation. This is truly a multiethnic nation, and accommodation and interaction among "communal" groups will be a long time, if not eternal, aspect of the national life, even if a national culture evolves over time. The major problems of Malaysia are fairly apparent: (1) the Malays must be leveled up by distributing them throughout the whole economy and reducing the disparities of income among the ethnic groups (although each group has a significant number throughout the income and occupational distributions), and (2) a political balance must be achieved and perpetuated that gives the Malays predominance but does not penalize the Chinese or Indians. Minimally this requires a growing economy (redistribution needs something to redistribute) and a commitment to the parlimentary form of government. So far the Malaysians have shot the rapids of communal rioting and emergency government without capsizing the democratic ship of state. With the present constellation of political and economic forces, the nation seems able to continue to navigate in these highly perilous waters. They are perilous because of what is happening in Southeast Asia as well as other parts of the world. Sri Lanka, long an exemplar of ethnic harmony based on an economy, polity, and colonial and postcolonial heritage similar to that of Malaysia, has exploded into fierce, murderous communal warfare. Tamils battle Sinhalese, and terrorists and soldiers clash over the bodies of innocent victims. Sri Lanka has developed a mythology (Tambiah 1986) about its ethnic heritage and about its early history. The myth is powerful and is what I have called an ideology—defining what the world is, a program to change it, and a goal of an ideal future. The Tamil tigers and the Sinhalese nationalists have the further complication of a large nation serving as a refuge and base. Tamilnad in India is identified with the Tamils of the Jaffna peninsula, and the Sinhalese may call on Pakistan for military aid.

Even where there seems to be no real basis for communal strife, it breaks out. The recent coup and rioting on Fiji is a case in point. What all these ethnic conflicts have in common is a large immigrant population—occupationally and economically differentiated by culture and religion and set off from the large "indigenous" population—and crucially the emergence of a national state from a colonial past. The national state has things to confer and withhold: the suspicion (or reality) of the state being ethnically biased is ever present, and the ethnic groups want parity, opportunity, recognition, and power. The national state, under these conditions, cannot be neutral. In Malaysia, it is dedicated to "Malay privileges" as defined in the constitution, and this form of "affirmative action" is aimed at overcoming the disparities of the past. There is always the

"ultra" wing asking for more privileges or downright confiscation of "immigrant" wealth and power, and the moder-
ates have to deal with their "ultras." On the Chinese side,
the "ultras" demand greater equality or more radical policies, and the centrists must handle that.

On the international scene, the "ultras" among the Malays are attracted by the slogans and political maneuvers of
fundamentalist Islam. The theocracy of the Imam Khomeni
in Iran, or the militant Muslims of the Middle East, or the
Islamic parties of nearby Indonesia offer models for emula-
tion. Chinese ultras have, or had, the example of the
People's Republic of China and the radical teachers of the
Middle East to learn from and model themselves after. In a
violent and unstable political contest among nations near
and far, it is difficult for leaders to offer a counsel of sanity
and restraint. Passion and ideology as well as the internal
struggle for power at home between the haves and the
have-nots, between the ins and the outs, and between the
young and the old and the very process of struggle toward
national and communal viability are more likely to fill the
air of campaigns. In a world of superpowers who are often
menacing and with titanic internal challenges, Malaysia
cannot rely on experts to provide safe charts or easy formulas. In this volatile world, poverty is possible, and
powerlessness is always a threat. Politicians can usually
rely on the valued cultural heritage, the unique cast of
human possibility exemplified by constituents to have real
appeal and to represent the special graces of a people.
Tradition, however modified and whatever the social costs,
is not only stressed by the elite, believed by a sizable
number, and taught in the intimate confines of the family
and kampong (or urban neighborhood for the Chinese or
laborers' lines for the Indian plantation workers), it is a real
motivating and legitimating political and economic force.
This a social situation where all political and economic
decisions have an inevitable ethnic dimension.

The Jews in the United States are among the most successful Jews in the Diaspora. They came in immigration waves from a Europe that grew ever more inhospitable and finally murderous toward its Jewish populations. Jews came to the United States for the same reasons as other Europeans, Africans, or Asians who came voluntarily. (That means, not bound in slave ships or forceably transported to the New World. Voluntary is always a socially defined state of possibilities, not the pure exercise of free will.) Jews had the added incentive of grave physical danger or harm in the pogroms of Eastern Europe, and the larger movement from 1904 to the closing of the gates of entry in 1924 was largely powered by physical and mortal danger from pogroms or life service in the czar's military.

At birth, as the first "new nation," the United States reflected the best ideas of the enlightenment in its Constitution and its Declaration of Independence. These two documents (and their interpretation over time) represent the official ideology of the United States. They are the basis of its political culture, and they are what is aptly called the "American Creed." This creed—life, liberty, the pursuit of happiness in a republic of civil rights and representative institutions among legal equals in a secular state—has not always been, and is not quite now, the social fact, the economic and political reality described in the official ideology. But American history on the whole, with fits and starts, has been a movement toward the social, political, and economic realization of the revolutionary creed.

What the creed meant for immigrants, Jews among them, has likewise varied over time. The Protestant Ascendancy of first Americans assumed that their culture and worldview represented the best efforts of mankind to date, and they expected new immigrants to emulate, learn, absorb, and become like them. This notion of the melting pot saw successive waves of immigrants move from ghettos and foreign languages, strange dress and custom into the

American "mainstream" to become, if not WASPs, at least WASP-like. But there always was a traditional remnant that clung to valued "Old World" ways, and fresh waves of immigrants reinforced the cultural variety of the United States. The melting pot was more like a pressure cooker, if one reads about the struggles of immigrants and the costs borne by the generation that became "Americanized." This movement from immigrant to hyphenated American to plain American to generations without memory of past cultural heritages encompassed most immigrants, so that the phrase "We are a nation of immigrants" means our forebears were different but we are all as American as apple pie, baseball, the Fourth of July, and those first immigrants on Plymouth Rock. The melting pot and pressure cooker worked its alchemy on wave after wave of immigrants— Irish, Italian, Central European, Jew and Catholic alike. Only the blacks, here since before Independence, were not much affected by the absorption process. Perhaps the uniform of color, or the persisting racist ideology, or the clustering at the bottom of the economic heap or the paternal government measures are all responsible for the special instance of American blacks. Even in black-white relations it is possible to see a declining importance to physical features alone. There seems to be a movement from race to ethnic status. They are socially not fully distinct. But the emphasis is different, even if both are social constructions. Ethnic has a lesser sense of the inevitability of social separation and more attention to class than race or continued status as an inferior estate-like order.

American Jews, as noted in the chapter dealing with their experience differentiated into religious varieties, spread among the social classes and over time moved into almost all of the open, and not so open, spaces in contemporary society. But anti-Semitism is not wholly gone from the American scene. Annual surveys conducted by the Anti-Defamation League shows a persisting 20% of anti-

Semitic attitudes among Americans. What shifts is the incidence of who holds these attitudes. Anti-Semitism almost
disappears as people move up the educational and class
hierarchy. Government bodies no longer condone or support anti-Semitism even in the private sector, and its
display in public is either a crime or at least a solecism.
Anti-Semitism has been reduced to a crank view of the
world, along with the Vatican conspiracy and the gnomes
of Zurich.

American culture in the domain of ethnicity has moved
from melting pot to tolerance and on to "consensual pluralism," where cultural difference in ethnic modes is
positively valued. Ethnicity is seen as the legitimate expression of identity, with political claims, and rituals and
customs not to be either interfered with or suppressed. But
the pluralism is under the overarching notion of citizen-
American which encompasses a wide variety of ethnic
modes. Ethnic categories, groups, or organizations are encouraged to make public displays—Puerto Rican Pride
Day, St. Patrick's Day parade, Columbus Day, Israel Independence Day, Von Steuben Day parade, St. Andrew's
Marching and Chowder Society, and a host of others. These
displays are not seen as the exclusive province of an ethnic
category or group—all can participate and are welcomed
to do so—come to the Cinco de Mayo celebration, march in
Black is Beautiful parades, and dance a polka in honor of
Polish nationalism or have an extra egg roll on Double 10 or
Chinese New Year.

Among Jews, however, there seems to be a sense of
urgency to preserve a cultural heritage, a religious viewpoint, and ethnic viability probably stemming from thousands of years as a pariah people, the recent memories of
the Holocaust, and the precariousness of a secure position
depending upon secular democracy, itself a labile structure.

These are separable elements, although they are often

fused in the same person or within a single organization. The religious, Orthodox Jews have the most impenetrable boundary mechanisms. Entry can only come through conversion by Orthodox rabbis, and a way of life with food taboos, dress codes, and language barriers along with residential segregation keep these communities distinct. Other American Jews have become "returners" to religion or to tradition in the wake of the discovery of "consensual pluralism" and that others are proud of ethnic heritages, and many people are engaged in the search for "roots" or a usable past or a basis for pride and dignity, whatever the current circumstances may in fact be. Nonetheless, the intermarriage rate among American Jews hovers around 30%, and it is not known how many remain Jews or rear their children as Jews (although there are about 12,000 conversions to Judaism yearly in the United States, almost all performed by Reform rabbis, possibly raising problems in Israel where only Orthodox conversions are recognized). But since ethnicity is now a social good, and having a religion continues to be a social good, the disappearance of American Jews by attrition is not likely. Nor are they migrating to Israel in any numbers. So few go, and of those who go so few remain, that Israel does not even publish figures on American and Canadian migrants. American Jews remain in the category of American. There is strong support for Israel, increasing public identification as Jews, and the proliferation of organizations. In an increasingly meaningful sense, Jewishness and the degree of Jewish identification is becoming more and more of a voluntary act, like joining and maintaining membership in any special club or group. Whether or not to call this "secondary ethnicity" is a matter of semantic nicety, adding little to understanding.

In the open social structure of a culture dedicated to pluralism in an affluent society with a secular and democratic state, American Jews have flourished (as have other immigrant groups) and have differentiated into varieties with the majority being "Reform" or "secular" Jews. Only a small segment cherishes the Hebrew Bible notions of "a light unto the nations," while most American Jews settle for a social conscience that has *tzadaka* charity and compassion at its core of values.

The Maya, unlike the Malay-Chinese new nation or the American Jews as immigrants in a land of opportunity, were a civilization decayed into principalities and subjugated by conquerors. Used throughout the colonial period nearly as a natural resource, they developed defensive organizations, and in the national period they were either ignored or abused and exploited. The gulf between Ladinos and Indians is marked by ecology, social organization, and worldview. The Indians believe in cultural variability as a fact of nature tied to a people united by blood and custom on their own territory. Ladinos share the arrogance of early European culture that civilization is a European monopoly and that there are lesser breeds before the law that need the missionizing zeal of a superior human set of arrangements. The Maya, when they become Ladinos, do so by defection, by leaving or being detached from their society and culture. But they are not disappearing. There are millions of Maya, and they and their cultures appear to be viable in every sense of the word. They may be subjected to harassment by the state or by guerrillas, terrorized by rogue military units, or preached at by missionaries, but they have the mechanisms and capacities to endure, as demonstrated by five centuries of handling adversity through cycles of conquest and repression. What the future of the Maya, or of Central America for that matter, will look like requires a crystal ball, but that Maya Indians will be where they now are is highly likely, and whether they will become an ethnic group in the sense of the Chinese or the Jews is an open question, although the North American Indians have been moving along the contiuum from tribal to pan-Indian and may foreshadow developments in Maya land.

The three cases of ethnicity in this book demonstrate the historical, structural, and cultural variability in the formation of ethnic groups within the encompassing form of the nation-state. The question, Are nations or ethnic groups "modern" or "primordial?" as posed by some sociologists and historians (Smith 1987) is one of these provocative but essentially falsely posed dichotomies. Clearly nations and ethnic groups are built out of social elements like those cited in the recursive metaphor of blood, bed, and cult, and these elements are, well, elemental, if not primordial in social life. But they need to be fused with a belief in a shared past and a common destiny for the *ethnie* to appear and, when the ethnic group seeks political status and even sovereignty, then a state may emerge, and the nation-state (with or without ethnic groups or nationalities) may also emerge. All the elements of ethnicity are implicit in social life; what transforms them into a social fact of ethnicity or of a nation or a nation-state is historical process. The historical process of making nations the dominant form of political aggregation is a late, modern European development, arising from the forms of human association of the Middle Ages, where the embryonic state was submerged in other forms of association (Bloch 1981). Smith, in his two useful and penetrating reviews of the sociological and historical evidence on ethnic revivals and the ethnic elements in the formation of nations, amply documents the terse summary above (1981, 1987), and there is no need to cover ground already so ably tilled (although I think he finds ethnicity too easily and too early in the historical record).

The processes of the formation of ethnic groups are historically varied and fortuitous, and here I have explored three different temporal and structural trajectories of ethnic formation within the political category of the nation-state, the predominant modern mode in which ethnicity exists, and where it takes its social and cultural meaning. Polyethnicity within a single political order appears to be the norm (in a frequency and perduring sense of norm) for most of the human community since the rise of the first city-states and civilizations. There has been, and now in some places continues to be, an ideology of homogeneous "peoples" or "nations" or "ethnic" groups with jurisdiction in their own territory. There was the classic Greek ideology of a heroic and homogenous citizenry in city-states with imperial hinterlands (from which slaves were recruited so the theory class could have leisure to philosophize). But McNeill (1986) has shown how time bound and evanescent this ideal was. Nineteenth-century romantic nationalism harked back to this anachronistic ideal and talked about the national sovereignty of a homogenous ethnic group. And the echoes of that rang through the aftermath of the First World War, when "national" self-determination was one of the aims of the victorious allies. The truly barbaric notion of "one people, one state, and one leader," to which nationalism degenerated in Nazi Germany, shows the extremes of inhumanity to which the idea of nationalism can be pushed when coupled to a biological theory and hitched to superman ideas of leaders over docile masses.

The concepts of "ethnic," "nation," "class," "race," and "state" are closely linked in content, sometimes in fact, and sometimes historically fused. What they "really" mean is a bootless exercise in definitional imperialism. Meanings can be assigned by a given scholar (within the cultural boundaries of understanding in the time-space continuum where the writer defines), and only two things can truly be asked of a set of definitions: first, that they are logical and clear and have the possibility of empirical reference; and, second, that they maintain the same meanings throughout the length of discourse where they are employed. Beyond these two requirements is the hazier one of being more "productive," but that is so largely subjective that it is hard to employ, no matter how much one likes productivity, elegance, and simplicity. This latter requirement appears to me to be aesthetic rather than scientific, though beauty is not to be scorned. They are, despite Keats, not the same.

Whole libraries have been written about ethnicity and its relations to state, nation, class, identity, and culture. Bentley's 1981 bibliographic guide lists 300 annotated major items and more than 2,000 additional items, and similar guides exist as well as special journals devoted solely to the topics associated with ethnicity and its near synonyms. Theories, from all of the social sciences, compete for recognition and dominance, and the descriptive and historical literature continues to proliferate. The following sources nearly exhaust among them the regnant ideas in anthropology, sociology, and political science on ethnicity (Anderson 1983; Barth 1969; Brass 1985; Banton 1983; Enloe 1973; Epstein 1978; Gellner 1983; Kedourie 1960; Keyes 1981; Maybury-Lewis 1984; Reminick 1983, and Rothschild 1981; Warner 1953). These titles are a sampler, but if one reads on in the literature, a certain repetitiveness appears, and the issues become more and more minor and of small detail, so that only someone with a particular topical or regional or historical interest would need to read beyond this sample to feel well informed about the state of knowledge and speculation in the area of ethnicity and its conceptual relatives. My citing of the literature is more heavily oriented to the structural and cultural than to the psychological dimensions of ethnicity, leaning perhaps on my technical competence. Similarly, the literary and biographical richness of the many works on ethnicity have not played as large a role as they should in contemporary anthropology, and they remain a resource to be mined for both insight and data. Reviewing the positions of the nineteenth-century giants (and their epigoni), like Marx, Weber, Vico, Herder, Pareto, and Durkheim, is a theoretical exer-

cise most useful for a history of theory rather than development of newer components, and so I eschew that exercise.

What then can be said that is fresh, novel, significant,
and possibly of reasonable validity and generality about
ethnicity? The inferences based on the case material in this
book have some of those qualities. They hold that ethnicity
is formed over time by historical processes based on pre-
existing elements of society and culture but fused into a
recursive metaphor of blood, bed, and cult and tied to what
Anderson (1983) has called an "imagined" community of a
shared past and a common future. Ethnicity becomes a call
to action when such a group organizes for political and
economic ends. The struggle for a state, or a state based on
a nation (the ethnic group in search of sovereignty), leads
to political battling within the confines of existing states or
against the definitions of existing states. When economic
ends are sought (opportunity, wealth and income redistribution, or claims to ownership of a national patri-
mony), the ethnic group may approximate a political class
and exhibit a form of the class struggle powered by an
ethnic ideology, not a false consciousness but often a true
appreciation of the existing state of economic affairs. When
the ethnic group seeks to express its cult and belief system
in a hostile setting, the struggle is about culture—or those
domains that define a meaningful world and a valuable life.
So ethnicity as forged in the crucible of modern and mod-
ernizing nations may be political, economic, or cultural in
its struggles and conflicts, or all of them at one time. The
struggle may move from the literary, romantic, and nostal-
gic to violent guerrilla tactic and terrorist or civil war
activities. Ethnicity is a reservoir for turbulence in a world
where power, wealth, and dignity are unevenly and il-
legitimately distributed within and among nations. Ethnicity is a resource in political, economic, and cultural struggle. It is not likely to disappear so long as there are nations,
inequality, and perceived injustice in the way the good

things of the world are distributed among the peoples of the world.

Ethnicity, then, is clearly related to politics, to class, to economics, and to culture and ethos. Just exactly how and when ethnicity gets to be part of other struggles is a historical outcome, neither fully determined by structure nor purely aleatory. Ethnicity has a deep personal component—it is often at the core of personal identity, either as membership in an embattled ethnic group or in a dominant one with the attributes of nationalism. Neither the sociologists who talk of the fusing of elements, the anthropologists who discuss the invention of tradition, the political scientists who remind us of imagined communities, nor the economists who note the costs of nationalism seem able to override the sentiments of ethnicity and nationalism as they are lodged in the personal identity of social actors. Real people die for king and country, for irredenta, and for hopes of national liberation. The daily examples in the struggles of Sikhs in India, Tamils in Sri Lanka, Catholics in North Ireland, Palestinians in the Middle East, Revolutionary Guards in Iran, Turks and Greeks in Cyprus, Afgans, and others in a long and melancholy list attest to the power of ethnicity as it is coupled with politics, economics, class, and religion. The identity dimension of ethnicity (whatever its deep psychological roots) rests on the fact that fellow members of the ethnic group are thought to be "human" and trustworthy in ways that outsiders are not. The ethnic group provides a refuge against a hostile, uncaring world. Like a family, it has a continuing claim on loyalty and sacrifice, and it has its sagas of heroes, martyrs, victims, and victors. The idea of refuge, the place where one is fully human, whatever failure or success happens in the larger world, is the cement and power of ethnic membership and continuity. Until all men are brothers, brotherhood exists chiefy in the ethnic group or the nation. The nightmare of the modern man is to be deracinated, to be without papers, stateless, alone, alienated, and adrift in a world of organized others.

If the social and psychological aspects adduced above have validity, then ethnicity is not likely to soon disappear from this world—not until liberty, equality, and fraternity have in fact become social realities for the bulk of humanity. The one-worlders, the dedicated internationalists, are the modern romantics of political organization, and as noble as the ideas are their realization or political fruition remains only a utopian dream. The individual rejection of the bonds of nation and ethnicity is likely to remain a heroic but individual act. James Joyce's non-serviam: I will not serve that which I no longer believe; Mother, Country, God. It can be lived by as Joyce did, but it means a life of exile and wandering. The struggle between community and state, between human compassion and impersonal power, between explicit and cold contracts and warm and diffuse loyalties is likely to continue as the world of inequality organized in nation-states is likely to continue, even as it forms an interacting world system beyond the control of any nation-state or any coalition of nation states.

The movement toward liberty, equality, and fraternity can be charted on the global scene of politics, economics, and culture, and even more tellingly monitored in the writings of those undergoing these processes of change—in biographies, paintings, sculptures, and novels of the gifted and sensitive observer. The mass media of motion pictures, television, and music as the bearers of popular culture also tell us social scientists where it is at and what it signifies. Ethnicity is likely to remain a cauldron of seething elements rather than a smooth mixture of benign diversity in the world as it is presently constituted.

References

Adams, R. N., comp. 1957. *Political Changes in Guatemalan Indian Communities: A Symposium*. Publication 24. Tulane: Middle American Research Institute.

_____. 1979. *Crucifixion by Power*. Austin: University of Texas Press.

Ali, Husin S. 1981. *The Malays: Their Problems and Future*. Singapore: Heinamann.

_____. 1984. *Ethnicity, Class and Development*. Malaysia: Universiti Malaysia. (Kuala Lumpur: Kaum, Kelasdan Penibangunan).

Anand, S. 1983. *Inequality and Poverty in Malaysia: Measurement and Decomposition*. Oxford: Oxford University Press.

Anderson, Benedict. 1983. *Imagined Communities: Reflections on the Origin and Spread of Nationalism*. London: Verso.

Arnott, M. L., ed. 1976. *Gastronomy: The Anthropology of Food and Food Habits*. Chicago: Aldine.

Banton, Michael. 1983. *Racial and Ethnic Competition*. Cambridge: Cambridge University Press.

Barth, F. 1969. *Ethnic Groups and Boundaries*. Boston: Little, Brown.

Beals, R. L. 1951. "The History of Acculturation in Mexico." Pp. 73–82 in *Homenaje al Doctor Alfonso Caso*. Mexico.

_____. 1967. "Acculturation." *Social Anthropology, Handbook of Middle American Indians* 6:449–68.

Bentley, G. Carter. 1981. *Ethnicity and Nationality: A Bibliographic Guide*. St. Louis: University of Washington Press.

Bloch, M. L. B. 1981. *Feudal Society*. Chicago: University of Chicago Press.

Brass, P., ed. 1985. *Ethnic Groups and the State*. London: Croom Helm.

Camara, F. 1952. "Religious and Political Organization." Pp. 142–73 in *Heritage of Conquest*, ed. S. Tax. Glencoe, Ill.: Free Press.

REFERENCES

Cancian, Frank. 1965. *Economics and Prestige in a Maya Community: The Religious Cargo System in Zinacantan.* Stanford: Stanford University Press.

———. 1967. "Political and Religious Organization." *Social Anthropology, Handbook of Middle American Indians* 6:293–98.

Cohen, S. M. 1983. *American Modernity and Jewish Identity.* London: Tavestock.

Colby, B. N., and P. L. Van den Berghe. 1969. *Ixil Country: A Plural Society in Highland Guatemala.* Berkeley: University of California Press.

Cowan, P. 1982. *An Orphan in History.* New York: Doubleday.

De La Fuente, Julio. 1967. "Ethnic Relationships." *Social Anthropology, Handbook of Middle American Indians* 6:432–48.

De Vos, G., and L. Romanucci-Ross, eds. 1975. *Ethnic Identity: Cultural Continuities and Change.* Palo Alto: Mayfield Publishing Co.

Douglas, M. 1966. *Purity and Danger: An Analysis of Concepts of Polution and Taboo.* London: Routledge and Kegan Paul.

Dresner, S. H. 1982. *The Jewish Dietary Laws.* New York: Rabbinical Assembly of America.

Dresner, Samuel H., and Seymour Siegel. 1959. *The Jewish Dietary Laws.* New York: Burning Bush Press.

Early, J. D. 1982. "A Demographic Survey of Contemporary Guatemalan Maya: Some Methodological Implications for Anthropological Research." Pp. 73–89 in *Heritage of Conquest: Thirty Years Later,* ed. C. Kendall, J. Hawkins and L. Bosser. Albuquerque: University of New Mexico Press.

Enloe, Cynthia H. 1973. *Ethnic Conflict and Political Development.* Boston: Little, Brown.

Epstein, A. L. 1978. *Ethos and Identity.* London: Tavestock.

Epstein, I. 1959. *Judaism: A Historical Presentation.* Baltimore: Penguin Books.

Feeley-Harnik, Gillian. 1981. *The Lord's Table: Eucharist and Passover in Early Christianity.* Philadelphia: University of Pennsylvania Press.

Firth, R. 1973. *Symbols, Public and Private.* Ithaca: Cornell University Press.

Forster, Robert, and Orest Ranum, eds. 1979. *Food and Drink in History: Selections from the Annales.* Vol. 5. Baltimore: Johns Hopkins University Press.

References

Fredman, R. G. 1981. *The Passover Seder.* Philadelphia: University of Pennsylvania Press.

Freedman, M. 1960. "The Growth of Plural Society in Malaya." *Pacific Affairs* 33:158–68.

Funston, J. 1980. *Malay Politics in Malaysia: A Study of UMNO & PAS.* Kuala Lumpur: Heinemann.

Furnivall, John S. 1948. *Colonial Policy and Practice: A Comparative Study of Burma and Netherlands India.* Cambridge: Cambridge University Press.

Geertz, C. 1963. "The Integrative Revolution." In *Old Societies and New States: The Quest for Modernity in Asia and Africa,* ed. C. Geertz. New York: Free Press.

Gellner, Ernest. 1983. *Nations and Nationalism.* Ithaca: Cornell University Press.

Glazer, N., and D. P. Moynihan. 1975. *Ethnicity, Theory and Experience.* Cambridge, Mass.: Harvard University Press.

Goldscheider, C., and A. S. Zuckerman. 1984. *The Transformation of the Jews.* Chicago: University of Chicago Press.

Goubaud, Carrera A. 1951. "Indian Adjustments to Modern National Culture." Pp. 244–48 in *Acculturation in the Americas,* ed. S. Tax. Chicago: University of Chicago Press.

Harris, L. 1985. "Holy Days." *New Yorker Magazine* (Sept. 16, 23, 30): 41–101, 57–100, 73–110.

Hawkins, J. P. 1984. *Inverse Images: The Meaning of Culture, Ethnicity and Family in Post Colonial Guatemalan Society.* Albuquerque: University of New Mexico Press.

Hinshaw, Robert. 1975. *Panajachel: A Guatemalan Town in Thirty-Year Perspective.* Pittsburgh: University of Pittsburgh Press.

Isaacs, H. R. 1975. *Idols of the Tribe: Group Identity and Political Change.* New York: Harper & Row.

Jain, R. K. 1970. *South Indians on the Plantation Frontier in Malaya.* New Haven: Yale University Press.

Kedourie, E. 1960. *Nationalism.* London: Hutchinson.

Kendall, C., J. Hawkins, and L. Bossen, eds. 1983. *Heritage of Conquest Thirty Years Later.* Albuquerque: University of New Mexico Press.

Kessler, C. S. 1978. *Islam and Politics in a Malay State: Kelantan 1938–1969.* Ithaca: Cornell University Press.

Keyes, Charles F. 1981. *Ethnic Change.* Seattle: University of Washington Press.

REFERENCES

Leach, E. 1954. *Political System of Highland Burma*. London: G. Bell.

La Farge, O. 1940. "Maya Ethology: The Sequence of Cultures." Pp. 281–91 in *The Maya and Their Neighbors*. New York: Appleton-Century.

Levin, S. I., and E. A. Boyden. 1940. *Shulkhan Aruch: The Kosher Code of the Orthodox Jew*. Minneapolis: University of Minnesota Press.

Levi-Strauss, C. 1964–71. *Mythologiques*. 4 vols. Paris: Plan.

Lyon, M. L. 1979. "The Dakwah Movement in Malaysia." *Review of Indonesia and Malaysian Affairs* 13, no. 2:34–45.

McNeill, W. H. 1986. *Poly-ethnicity and National Unity in World History*. Toronto: University of Toronto Press.

Mauzy, D. K. 1983. *Barisan Nasional Coalition Government in Malaysia*. Kuda Lumpur: Morican.

Maybury-Lewis, D., ed. 1984. *The Prospects for Plural Societies*. Proceedings of the American Ethnological Society, 1982, Washington, D.C.

Milne, R. S., and D. K. Mauzy. 1986. *Malaysia: Tradition, Modernity, and Islam*. Boulder: Westview Press.

Moerman, M. 1964. "Ethnic Identification in a Complex Society: Who are the Lue?" *American Anthropologist* 67:1215–30.

Morgan, M. 1984. *A Guide to the Laws of Kashrus*. Brooklyn.

Nagata, Judith A. 1974. "What is a Malay? Situational Selection of Ethnic Identity in a Plural Society." *American Ethnologist* 1, no. 2 (May): 331–50.

————. 1979. *Malaysian Mosaic Perspectives from a Poly-Ethnic Society*. Vancouver: University of British Columbia Press.

Nash, Manning. 1957. "The Multiple Society in Economic Development: Mexico and Guatemala." *American Anthropologist*, no. 59, pp. 823–36.

————. 1958. *Machine Age Maya*. American Anthropological Association Memoir, no. 87, Menusha, Wis.

————. 1970. "The Impact of Mid-Nineteenth Century Economic Change upon the Indians of Middle America." Pp. 170–83 in *Race and Class in Latin America*, ed. M. Mörner. New York: Columbia University Press.

————. 1974. *Peasant Citizens: Politics, Religion, and Modernization in Kelantan, Malaysia*. Athens: Ohio University Press.

————. 1979. "World View and Social Relations: An Extension of

References

Tax's Analysis." Pp. 95–102 in *Currents in Anthropology: Essays in Honor of Sol Tax,* ed. R. Hinshaw. The Hague: Mouton.

_____. 1984a. "Fundamentalist Islam: Reservoir for Turbulence." *Journal of Asian and African Studies* 19, nos. 1–2:73–79.

_____. 1984b. *Unfinished Agenda: The Dynamics of Modernization in Developing Nations.* Boulder: Westview Press.

National Operations Council. 1969. "The May 13 Tragedy." A report, Kuala Lumpur.

Neusner, J. 1983. *Judaism in Society: The Evidence of the Yerushalmi.* Chicago: University of Chicago Press.

Parmer, J. N. 1960. *Colonial Labour Policy and Administration: A History of Labour in the Rubber Plantation Industry in Malaya.* Ann Arbor: Monograph of Association of Asian Studies.

_____. 1983. *1980 Population and Housing Census of Malaysia: General Report of the Population Census,* pp. 17. Malaysia Department of Statistics, Kuala Lumpur.

Rabushka, A. 1973. *Race and Politics in Urban Malaya.* Stanford, Calif.: Hoover Institution Press, Stanford University.

Ratnam, K. J. 1965. *Communalism and the Political Process in Malaya.* Kuala Lumpur: University of Malaya.

Reminick, Ronald A. 1983. *Theory of Ethnicity: An Anthropologist's Perspective.* Lanham, Md.: University Press of America.

Roff, Wm. R. 1967. *The Origins of Malay Nationalism.* New Haven: Yale University Press.

Rothschild, Joseph. 1981. *Ethnopolitics: A Conceptual Framework.* New York: Columbia University Press.

Royce, A. P. 1982. *Ethnic Identity: Strategies of Diversity.* Bloomington: Indiana University Press.

Scheingold, C. 1982. *New Pockets of Jewish Energy.* New York: American Jewish Committee.

Shenker, I. 1979. "With Them, It's Always Strictly Kosher." *New York Times Magazine* (April 15): 37–42.

Shils, E. 1957. "Primordial, Personal, Sacred and Civil Ties." *British Journal of Sociology* 7:13–145.

Silberman, C. E. 1985. *A Certain People: American Jews and Their Lives Today.* New York: Summit Books.

Slimming, J. 1969. *Malaysia: Death of a Democracy.* London: John Murray.

Smith, A. D. 1981. *The Ethnic Revival in the Modern World.* Cambridge: Cambridge University Press.

REFERENCES

_____. 1987. *The Ethnic Origins of Nations.* New York: Basil Blackwell.

Smith, W. R. 1977. *The Fiesta System and Economic Change.* New York: Columbia University Press.

Snodgrass, D. R. 1980. *Inequality and Economic Development in Malaysia.* New York: Oxford University Press.

Soler, Jean. 1979. "The Semiotics of Food in the Bible." Pp. 126–30 in *Food and Drink in History: Selection from the Annales, Vol. 5,* ed. R. Foster and O. Ranum. Baltimore: Johns Hopkins University Press.

Sundaram, Jomo Kwame. 1986. *A Question of Class Capital, the State, and Uneven Development in Malaya.* Oxford: Oxford University Press.

Tambiah, S. J. 1986. *Sri Lanka: Ethnic Fratricide and the Dismantling of Democracy.* Chicago: University of Chicago Press.

Tax, Sol. 1937. "The Municipios of the Midwestern Highlands of Guatemala." *American Anthropologist* 39:423–44.

_____. 1952. *Heritage of Conquest: The Ethnology of Middle America.* Glencoe, Ill.: Free Press.

Todorov, T. 1984. *The Conquest of America.* New York: Harper & Row.

Tunku Abdul, Rahman. 1969. *May 13: Before and After.* Kuala Lumpur: Utusan Melaya Press.

Warner, W. L. 1953. *American Life: Dream and Reality.* Chicago: University of Chicago Press.

Waxman, C. I. 1983. *American Jews in Transition.* Philadelphia: Temple University.

Winzler, Robert L. 1985. *Ethnic Relations in Kelantan: A Study of the Chinese and Thai as Ethnic Minorities in a Malay State.* Oxford: Oxford University Press.

Worsley, P. 1984. *The Three Worlds: Culture and World Development.* Chicago: University of Chicago Press.

Young, M. W. 1971. *Fighting with Food: Leadership, Values and Social Control in a Massin Society.* Cambridge: Cambridge University Press.

Index

adat (customary law in Malaysia), 33
affirmative action, in Malaysia, 41, 117
altos, los, 98
American blacks, special instance as ethnic group, 119–20
American creed, 62; nature of deviations from, 89; meaning for immigrants, 119–20
American Jewish community, diversity within, 82
American Jews, 61–91; as an ethnic group in a pluralistic society, 63; as successful immigrants, 119; stable population of, 64; socioeconomic attainments of, 65; organizational and theological divisions of, 66; ethnic self-identification of, 68; liberal political tradition of, 87–88; desire to preserve separate culture, 121
Ancestry as a cult marker in Malaysia, 33–34
Anti-Semitism: as a factor in immigration of Eastern European Jews, 62; in Amer-

ica today, 84, 120–21
Arts, as a record of ethnicity, 129
Authenticity in ethnic self-identification, 115
Axes of identity, applications to future work, 116

Baal Shem Tov, 62
Biological component of ethnic identity, 5
Boundary markers of ethnic groups, 8–11

Cargos (communal responsibilities of Maya), 101–2
Case study method, used in this book, 113–14
Catholicism: among Maya, 105, 107, 109; in Ladinoization, 96–97; role in Spanish conquest, 93
Charity, as a central cultural symbol of American Jews, 87. *See also* Tzadaka
Circumcision as a marker of ethnicity, 13, 72
Citizenship, 2, 28–29, 56, 121
Civil-religious hierarchy of Maya, 99–100; social function of, 103; religious as-

KILLER
PANCAKE

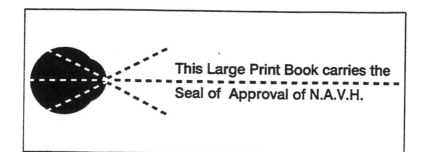

This Large Print Book carries the
Seal of Approval of N.A.V.H.

KILLER PANCAKE

DIANE M●TT DAVIDSON

Thorndike Press • Thorndike, Maine

Published in 1996 by arrangement with Bantam Books,
a division of Bantam Doubleday Dell Publishing Group, Inc.

Thorndike Large Print ® Cloak & Dagger Series.

The tree indicium is a trademark of Thorndike Press.

The text of this Large Print edition is unabridged.
Other aspects of the book may vary from the original edition.

Set in 16 pt. News Plantin by Juanita Macdonald.

Printed in the United States on permanent paper.

Library of Congress Cataloging in Publication Data

Davidson, Diane Mott.
   Killer pancake / Diane Mott Davidson.
     p.   cm.
   ISBN 0-7862-0635-7 (lg. print : hc)
   1. Bear, Goldy (Fictitious character) — Fiction.
  2. Women in the food industry — Colorado — Fiction.
  3. Caterers and catering — Colorado — Fiction.
  4. Women detectives — Colorado — Fiction.
  5. Large type books. I. Title.
  [PS3554.A925K5 1996]
  813'.54—dc20   95-47311

For my sisters and brother
Lucy, Sally, and Billy

Huckabucka beanstalk, Chumley!
And don't forget the raft for
Allenhurst, Looie and Sal!

O vraiment marâtre Nature,
Puisqu'une telle fleur ne dure
Que du matin jusques au soir!

(Truly, Nature is a cruel stepmother
Not to allow such a flower to live
Even from morning until evening.)

— from "Ode à Cassandre" by
PIERRE DE RONSARD

Acknowledgments

The author wishes to thank the following people: Jim Davidson, Jeffrey Davidson, J. Z. Davidson, and Joseph Davidson, for their neverending love and support, and special thanks to Joe, who came up with the title; Sandra Dijkstra, for being an unbeatably enthusiastic agent; Kate Miciak, for being the phenomenally hardworking and brilliant editor she is; Katherine Goodwin Saideman and Deidre Elliott, for their insightful reading of the manuscript and their helpful suggestions; Mark D. Wittry, M.D., Assistant Professor of Internal Medicine, St. Louis University Health Sciences Center, for the extraordinary amount of time he took to share information as well as read and comment on the manuscript; Heather Kathleen Delzell, makeup artist, for introducing the author to the world of cosmetics and answering many questions; Pete Moogk of The Ground Up Espresso Bar, Evergreen, Colorado, for giving the author space and electricity; John W. Dudek, Divisional Loss Prevention Manager, Payless Shoes, for painstakingly sharing information about his field of expertise; Nancy

Reichert, Ph.D., Mississippi State University, for providing much-needed scientific data; Tom Schantz of the Rue Morgue Bookstore, Boulder, Colorado, for sharing horticultural background; Lee Karr and the group that assembles at her home, for their helpful comments; Carol Devine Rusley, for great weekly conversations; Karen Johnson and John Schenk of J. William's Catering, Bergen Park, Colorado, for insights into catering; William Weston, M.D., for information on dermatology; and as ever, Investigator Richard Millsapps of the Jefferson County Sheriff's Department, for providing valuable expertise, assistance, ideas, and insights.

FALL INTO COLOR WITH MIGNON COSMETICS!

Lowfat Luncheon Banquet
Wednesday, July 1
Hot Tin Roof club, Westside Mall,
Furman County, Colorado

Crudités with lowfat dips

*Turkey with hoisin sauce and
pine nuts in lettuce cups*

Creamed cold asparagus soup

*Steamed sole with
spa-style hollandaise sauce*

*Grilled mushroom and
Japanese eggplant on field greens with
red pepper sherry miso dressing*

*Corn rolls, breadsticks, and
Grand Marnier cranberry muffins*

Nonfat chocolate torte

1

I was in caterers' hell.

I groaned and surveyed the spread of crudités on my kitchen counter. *If looks could kill,* I asked myself, *would this tray of cauliflower do the trick?* Actually, the crisp cauliflowerets, delicate buds of broccoli, slender asparagus spears, and bias-cut squash, celery, and carrots looked appealing enough. So did rows of crunchy brussels sprouts, bright-red cherry tomatoes, and small, musky-tasting mushrooms. But there wasn't a drop of rich, homemade mayonnaise, not a puff of whipped cream, not a slice of tangy cheese in sight. And forget dimpled pats of sweet, unsalted butter or luscious dollops of sour cream. Behind the vegetables stood imposing jars of low-calorie dips with horrid colors like pink (raspberry) and orange (carrot). I dipped a spoon into the raspberry, tasted it, and shuddered. Made according to the client's recipe, it was too thin and had the metallic taste of saccharine. A similar foray into the carrot spread revealed a chunky concoction that kindergartners might make for a project on vitamin A.

In other words: hell.

I steeled myself as I washed the last flecks of broccoli off my fingers. Sometimes the proprietor of a catering business has to give herself a pep talk. As the owner of Goldilocks' Catering, Where Everything Is Just Right! I was no exception. Beauty is in the eye of the beholder, I observed as I wiped my hands on my apron. I'd seen enough clients drool over six-layer fudge cake to know that folks eat with their eyes before the food ever reaches their tongues. But *eating with the eyes* was a concept I associated with *chocolatey, creamy,* and *calories.* Or perhaps *flaky, fudgy,* and *fattening.* Disheartened, I stepped away from the sink and cast another look at the entire first course to be served at that afternoon's banquet.

"It looks great," I reassured myself aloud, ". . . if you're a rabbit."

So much for the pep talk. Why on earth had I agreed to cater the July banquet introducing the fall line of Mignon Cosmetics? My irritation blossomed to frustration, a frequent occurrence when the rationale for taking a job melted away. The weather — cool in the beginning of June, when I'd agreed to cater the banquet — was now, at the beginning of July, unbearably hot. In the flat stretch of land that abutted the foothills west of Denver, the thermometer had topped 105 for the past three days. Although the mercury in our mountain town of Aspen Meadow, forty miles west of Denver, had fluctuated only in the upper nineties, that was still unseasonably warm. *Definitely* too hot, I had discovered, to be mucking around in the kitchen taste-testing food made with buttermilk and nonfat sour cream.

Not only that, but I had my doubts about the Mignon Cosmetics people, the same people who had provided the dip recipes. I mean, did they really think the cowboy-worshipping folk of Furman County, Colorado, longed for a lipstick named *Fudge Royale*? A blush named *Lust*? Could people truly be enticed to spend a hundred dollars an ounce for anti-aging cream fortified with kelp and placenta? Whose placenta, I wanted to ask rod-thin, pale-haired Harriet Wells, the senior sales associate who'd hired me to do the banquet. I agreed with Harriet that the more sophisticated, well-heeled customers would enjoy making their purchases in the magnificently refurbished department store of a remodeled mall, where the effects of aging, at least on a building, had been painstakingly eradicated. But structures, I pointed out to Harriet, could be restored. People are another matter.

On the other hand, maybe I was wrong. *Women,* Harriet Wells told me, *crave the* idea

13

of fudge on their lips. And, she went on, *the word* lust *makes them at least* think *of blushing.* What was worse, my thirteen-year-old son Arch had recently watched a television special on advertising. To my dismay, he had dutifully reported back an ad maven's statement: *Make a woman insecure enough, and you can sell her anything.*

Well. I must have made Harriet Wells and the Mignon Cosmetics Company feel pretty insecure, because I was catering their banquet at an enormous premium over my cost. The high compensation I would receive had been a compromise over their strict lowfat requirement, and the fact that, over my objections, they'd supplied half the recipes for what they wanted, including the two horrid dips. For their requests for an unusual appetizer, an array of breads, and a chocolate dessert, I'd developed new recipes. At that, however, I'd put my foot down: No mashed lentils, no margarine, no egg substitute. To my delight, the appetizer and the muffin recipes I'd come up with were quite delicious, especially if no one mentioned they were lowfat. But the dessert effort had demanded a serious undermining of my cooking standards. I'd gone through seven dozen egg whites trying to develop a recipe for chocolate torte with no butter.

Perhaps *hell* was not strong enough.

14

"Goldy, it *does* look great," said Julian Teller, my assistant. Wallowing in fat-free self-pity, I had been oblivious of his entrance. Julian marched briskly toward the counter, dipped a spatula into the shocking-pink dip, leaned his broad shoulders and blond, sides-shaven head downward, and sniffed. The "mmm-mmm" noise he made deep in his throat was unconvincingly ecstatic. Compact and muscled from a stint on his school swimming team, nineteen-year-old Julian did not look like someone with his heart set on becoming a vegetarian caterer. Yet he was. Luckily for Goldilocks' Catering, he wasn't one of those fanatics who give you a dirty look if you don't put grated carrots and soy flour in everything. Julian loved cheese, butter, and eggs as much as any traditional chef.

I let out an agonized sigh.

"It's going to be fabulous," Julian reassured me with mischievous eyes and an enthusiastic lift of the dark eyebrows that he had not bleached to match the hair on his scalp. He'd recently had his bright hair trimmed in a bowl shape to replace his old mohawk-style haircut. Now, instead of resembling a Native American albino, he looked like an ad for Dutch Boy paints. Ready to fulfill his function as server today, Julian wore a neat white collarless shirt and baggy black pants. The shirt had been

15

a gift from me. The bagginess of the pants might have been thought stylish by those who did not know Julian had haggled for them, as usual, at Aspen Meadow's secondhand store.

"Goldy," he declared, "the Mignon salespeople are going to love you." He grinned. "And better yet, they're going to love *me*. Correction: *One* of them is going to love me."

"Yeah, yeah, yeah. Let's sauté the turkey."

As mounds of ground turkey began to sizzle in wide frying pans, the scent of Thanksgiving filled my summery kitchen. I opened the first jar of hoisin sauce and took a greedy whiff. Like most people, I'd first encountered the dark, pungent stuff in a Chinese restaurant and fallen in love with it. Hoisin served a double purpose in the recipe I'd developed for the banquet appetizer: Its spicy taste and velvety texture would add richness without fat. I handed the jar to Julian, who energetically ladled it along with the contents of the other sauce jars and a mountain of cooked wild rice into a mixing bowl. I opened the oven and shook the large pan of roasting, golden pine nuts that was inside. At least *this* was food, I thought grimly.

"Hey, boss?" Julian's blue eyes sparkled. "If lowfat is what these folks want" — he gestured at the dips — "then give it to them!

16

Claire says the diet stuff will be a huge hit. And it looks fabulous. Be happy. You're going to make money! Go buy a vat of bittersweet chocolate! Buy ten pounds of macadamia nuts! Buy six kilos of —"

"Lie, lie, lie," I replied. "*You* said these saleswomen subsist on a steady diet of caffeine, nicotine, and chocolate." Which didn't sound too bad, actually, if you took out the nicotine.

Julian shrugged dramatically and drained the turkey, then deftly stirred it into the hoisin and wild rice. Although he had been living with Arch and me for just over a year, I never tired of watching Julian cook. He was attentive without being fussy, and his ardor in food preparation was unmatched.

"Okay, okay," he admitted as he stirred. Now the sharp smell of hoisin mingled appetizingly with the scent of sautéed turkey and buttery roasted pine nuts. "So say, today, the saleswomen slug down coffee with their chocolate torte, then step outside for a smoke. You still get paid, don't you? Aren't you always saying to me, what's the bottom line here?"

"Chocolate torte? Chocolate *torte?*" I cried, gesturing in the direction of the desserts. "Who are you kidding? Ninety-nine percent fat-free chocolate-flavored *air* is more like it. I mean, what's the point? I'm going to pack

17

up the grilled vegetables. Want to start on the muffins?"

Julian's high-top black sneakers squeaked across the vinyl as he energetically nipped past the counters and clattered in the cooler for the cranberries we'd chopped the night before. Unlike me, Julian was in a very good mood. And it wasn't because he — again unlike me — enjoyed the challenge of preparing a lowfat menu. It was not even remotely likely that Julian's good humor came from working with roughage and ricotta; he was hardly conversant with nonfat milk solids. As he folded the cranberries into the delectable Grand Marnier-flavored muffin batter, I recalled how he generally lavished dollops of creamy-anything on every dish he prepared. No, it wasn't the food. This budding vegetarian cook, now ladling spoonfuls of cranberry-studded dough into muffin cups, would have been excited today if we'd been serving steak tartare. Julian was in love.

The current object of Julian's affection, Claire Satterfield, Mignon sales associate *extraordinaire*, was due at our door any minute. Julian had assured me that Claire would have no trouble finding her way from Denver to our place off Main Street in Aspen Meadow. Claire was intelligent, Julian maintained, in unnecessary defense of this woman who was

HOISIN TURKEY WITH ROASTED PINE NUTS IN LETTUCE CUPS

½ cup pine nuts
1 pound ground turkey
1 teaspoon cornstarch
7 ounces hoisin sauce
2½ cups cooked wild rice
8 iceberg lettuce leaves

Preheat the oven to 400°. On a rimmed cookie sheet, toast the pine nuts for 5 to 10 minutes or until golden brown. Set aside.

In a large skillet, sauté the ground turkey over medium-high heat, stirring, until it changes color and is cooked through. Drain well and return to the pan. Stir in the cornstarch and hoisin sauce. Heat and stir over medium heat until bubbly. Add the pine nuts and the rice and stir until heated through.

Spoon ⅓ cup of the hot turkey mixture onto each lettuce leaf.

Serves 8 as an appetizer

three years his senior and who had opted out of a university education to work for Mignon Cosmetics. I certainly hoped her intelligence extended to geography. Claire had arrived from Australia with her work visa only nine months before, and during that time she'd lived in downtown Denver. The mile-high city was probably not that different from Sydney, as large urban environments go. But once you get off the interstate and head for Aspen Meadow, the roads become curvy and complicated. So much so, in fact, that the best-selling map book of our area is entitled *You Use'ta Couldn't Get There from Here.* Did they have mountains in Australia? I couldn't remember.

There was a muffled banging on the front door.

"It's me, it's me! Hallo! I got here! Where am I, the Himalayas? Let me in, I gotta use the facilities!"

Julian heaved the muffin tins into the oven, flipped on the full wattage of his smile, and strode in the direction of the banging. Leaving him to play host, I closed the box of vegetables and turned back to the dieters' delight. There is a reason why weight-loss cookbooks have you serve everything dripping with hot mustard, streaked with Tabasco sauce, or speckled with chopped peppers or red pepper flakes.

20

GRAND MARNIER
CRANBERRY MUFFINS

1¼ cups orange juice
¼ cup Grand Marnier liqueur
¾ cup canola oil
2 cups chopped cranberries
2½ cups all-purpose flour
1 cup whole-wheat flour
1½ cups sugar
2 tablespoons baking powder
½ teaspoon salt
1½ tablespoons chopped orange zest
4 egg whites

Preheat the oven to 400°. Combine the orange juice, the Grand Marnier, and the oil; set aside while you prepare the batter. In a large bowl, combine the all-purpose flour, whole-wheat flour, sugar, baking powder, salt, and orange zest. In another large bowl, beat the egg whites until frothy. Combine the juice mixture with the beaten egg whites. Add the egg mixture and the cranberries to the flour mixture, stirring just until moist. Using a ¼-cup measure, divide the batter among 24 muffin cups that have been fitted with paper liners. Bake for 25 minutes or until golden brown and puffed.

Makes 24

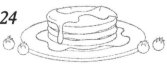

They want to convince you you're actually eating something. *Forget your appetite, see if this doesn't make fire come out of your ears!* Of course no one can consume much of these spicy lowcal concoctions. Why willingly engage in electroshock therapy for the mouth?

In any event, I had my own Macho Jalapeño Theory of Lowfat. Men heartily dislike diet food, but will eagerly engage in I-can-eat-hotter-stuff-than-you contests. No wonder diet experts recommend spicy foodstuffs when women are trying to wean their menfolk from their beloved meat and potatoes. On the other hand, nobody cared about my philosophy, and I was defying my own jalapeño theory today by offering classic cuisine to the Mignon Cosmetics people. But the recipes they had supplied left much to be desired. So now I was having second thoughts. I groaned again.

I decided to stash two dozen individual peach cobblers and an equivalent number of chocolate-chip-dotted brownies into zippered bags underneath the corn rolls made with — *forgive me, Escoffier* — nonfat sour cream. After giving me instructions about the banquet, Harriet Wells had had the guts — skinny, washboard-ab guts — to give me her lowfat muffin recipe. I had ignored it because it called for okra. The emergency supply of brownies and cobblers was an insurance policy, I reflected, in case someone came up to me today and demanded real, honest-to-goodness comfort food.

"This is Goldy!" a smiling Julian announced as he held the door open for Claire Satterfield to step haltingly into my kitchen.

For someone who had thumped so vigorously to herald her arrival, Claire, suddenly demure, sidestepped uncertainly toward the counter. Although I'd heard a great deal about her, I'd never actually met this wonder. So I was unprepared for what I saw. Claire Satterfield was surely the most gorgeous creature on the planet. Or at least, she was the loveliest female I had ever seen. About four inches taller than Julian, the girl was svelte yet shapely, in a way reminiscent of Marilyn Monroe. Her black hair was arranged in long, shiny ringlets that brushed her tanned shoulders. Bangs framed a striking face that featured breathtaking cheekbones. With her dewy skin, irresistible face, and glossy hair, this vision resembled a landlocked mermaid. She gave me a frightened glance and mutely opened her mouth.

"And this is Claire," added Julian, blushing. Blushing, I imagined, with *lust*.

"Pleased to meet you," I said, and meant it. Claire had been the one who had recommended me to the Mignon folks as their banquet caterer. Even though the food preparation for the event had been a mixed blessing, I very much wanted Julian to be happy. My young friend had made several false starts in the social-life department, including one with a Mignon sales associate who lived down the street. But now he had settled on Claire. Actually, he had not so much settled as fallen for her, the way a Rocky Mountain skier can plummet into an oncoming avalanche and try to swim with the wave. And I had enjoyed watching this loveswept delirium. Despite Julian's planned departure this fall for Cornell, I fantasized about becoming the catering-trainer-landlady-of-the-groom after he got his degree. To my amazement, I had become something of a marriage booster. Maybe I'd even cater their reception.

"Pleased t'meet you," Claire said demurely. The Australian accent hung heavily over her high, babyish voice, a voice that did not go with her sophisticated image.

While Julian and Claire conversed in low tones, I whisked together the sherry and miso for the grilled vegetable dressing. Sometimes you can put unusual ingredients together, and they work. That was certainly true for me. At age thirty-two, I had remarried just over two months ago. My new relationship was as good as my first marriage — begun at age

24

nineteen and ended at twenty-seven — had been dreadful. So I'd decided the first time around had been an aberration. Marriage was great, I'd proclaimed. Just like stopping smoking, *everyone* should do it. This analogy had not gone over in a big way with my new husband, Tom Schulz. In fact, while he was trying to refurbish my hopeless garden, Tom wore a custom-made T-shirt that read: BETTER THAN A CIGARETTE.

I set aside the salad and smiled. Now that Tom and I were wed and Julian and Claire were enjoying each other's company, the idea of romantic harmony sweeping our little household was extremely appealing. Certainly more attractive than an endless buffet table of food without fat. . . .

"I need to talk to you about parking," Claire announced loudly and without preamble. It took me a second to realize she was talking to me.

"Parking?" I echoed. I heaved a vat of chilled asparagus soup out of the walk-in refrigerator. "I'll be parking by the nightclub."

"The nightclub?" Julian sounded confused. While he was good with the cooking for these affairs, and he was a whiz in the classroom, the logistic details of catered events frequently escaped him.

I said, "This luncheon buffet is at the Hot Tin Roof Club." Julian frowned, still not understanding. I explained, "It's unusual to have a nightclub in a mall, but that was the only bid the mall owners got for the old Xerxes' Magic Shop. Anyway, the Hot Tin Roof Club is geared to upper-crust single types. Since it's not nighttime," I continued with unswerving logic as I turned to Claire, "there shouldn't be a parking problem."

"Sorry." Claire's frowning lips were colored a purplish-tan. I wondered what color the Mignon folks had christened it: Passion Plum? or Torrid Tan? "Expecting a bit of trouble, I'm afraid."

"A bit of trouble?" I shifted the vat uncomfortably. "Parking trouble? Or some other kind of trouble? And who exactly is doing the expecting?"

Claire closed her eyes. Her lids were shaded in a pure powdery wave of purple and brown. I was in awe. One moment she looked and sounded like a girl, the next she was a sensuous woman. "Right. See this color?" She pointed.

"Yes." I shot a glance at Julian. He wrinkled his nose and shook his head. The connection between parking problems and eyeshadow eluded him too.

Claire opened her eyes wide. Her irises were

dark violet. I wondered how many males besides Julian had gotten lost in their mesmerizing depths. "Right. According to the most recent *Beastly Bulletin*, Mignon Cosmetics blinded albino rabbits testing Sensual Midnight eyeshadow."

"*Beastly Bulletin?*" I said faintly.

"Animal rights newsletter," Claire announced crisply. "So the way we heard it, the *BB* folks have organized a task force. They're starting a protest against Mignon." She shrugged. A shiver went down her exposed shoulders and through her short-skirted black sheath, the kind of dress not usually seen at luncheons, the kind of dress I haven't had the figure for since I was sixteen. "Word from store security is, they might be causing problems at the banquet. Sorry 'bout that," she added with a nod at all the vegetables.

"Causing problems? Demonstrators? Because of albino rabbits?" I was still trying to get my footing in the cosmetics universe. "These people are protesting at today's banquet?"

"Yeh, we think so. Their campaign's called Spare the Hares." As this came out *speh the hehs*, it took me a few beats to translate. "Yesterday," she went on, "the animal rights people were outside the department store. Demonstrating. Y'know, Prince & Grogan

27

carries Mignon exclusively in the Denver area. So we're the target." *We'h the ta-get.* "The demonstrators even had a picket line. Today we heard they might be made up as freaks. They could be swinging rabbit carcasses at each person who comes in —"

"Oh, for crying out loud!" I shrieked. I banged the vat down on the counter. "I give to the Sierra Club! I give to the National Wildlife Federation! I don't even wear eyeshadow! Can't I get some kind of safe passage or something?"

"Y'don't know the kind of person y'dealin' with here," Claire observed. Her slender body slid over in the direction of the steamer. "They see you carrying in that fish over there? They'll mark you as the enemy. A fish murderess. They'll scatter your food trays from here to kingdom come. All for rabbits." She giggled. "Rabbits — the scourge of Australia! My folks wouldn't believe this one, I can tell you that."

"Just tell us where to park," Julian interjected placatingly before I could erupt again. "We're not into carcasses."

"Okay." She puckered her painted lips. "You know where the entrance to the garage is?" We nodded. "The mall has that above-ground parking garage," Claire explained, "and the entrance to the Hot Tin Roof Club is on the first level. There's a glass door at the entrance, but we're supposed to ignore that. The club's *service* entrance is an unmarked door inside, next to Stephen's Shoes. You walk through the shoe store, then come into the club."

. I had the sinking feeling I should be writing all this down. The *Beastly Bulletin*. The service entrance by the shoe store. A picket line. Carcasses.

"Prince & Grogan's head of security," Claire was saying, "has told all the Mignon people *not* to park by the department store or the nightclub, because of the demonstrators. We're supposed to scatter our vehicles, but not to use the garage roof, because they're getting ready for the food fair. Y'know. What's it called?"

"A Taste of Furman County," I replied dully. Starting day after tomorrow, I was supposed to be at that food fair. Starting day after tomorrow, I prayed the demonstrators would *not* be at that food fair.

"We just park and come into the club through the service entrance next to the shoe store," Claire concluded triumphantly. The maneuvers in this particular war appeared to please her immensely. "The head of security will be in the garage. Name's Nick. He told us they've called the police in. Just in case

29

things get messy."

So that was where Tom was going today. Although his official title was Homicide Investigator, there weren't enough homicides in Furman County to occupy my new husband full-time. So he was kept more than busy analyzing robberies and assaults and going out on special assignments, like today. When I'd asked what today's assignment was, he'd answered mischievously, "Shopping." And more than that he wouldn't say. He didn't want me to worry, and I didn't want to be intrusive. In the two months of figuring out what it meant to be married after extended periods of being single, we were both treading carefully around each other's privacy. But honestly, the man was impossible. We could have planned a late lunch. Real lunch too, with vichyssoise and pâté, maybe a little hasenpfeffer . . .

"Goldy?" queried Julian. "Are you going to steam that sole up here or down there?"

"I'm going to start it here and finish it there," I said. "It's the last thing I have to do." The steamer was full of water. I flipped on the burners, lowered the vat of asparagus soup into a box, and packed up the crudités. Within moments, steam bloomed plentifully and I laid the sole fillets close together on a rack above the bubbling water. When I turned around, Julian and Claire had disappeared. "What the —"

I knew Julian couldn't, *wouldn't* leave without helping me pack the supplies into the van. Buffet for forty was still just that, and it was not possible for one caterer to do all the hauling, setting up, and serving. But, I reminded myself as I vaulted out the back door to check the van, love had made Julian forgetful in the past few weeks. First he'd neglected to bring two out of three desserts to a fund-raising picnic for the ACLU. As a result, I'd survived endless jokes about no freedom of choice and had given the ACLU a hefty discount on their final tab. Julian, embarrassed, had offered to take the docked pay off his own. Of course I wasn't heartless enough to do that. The kid was saving money to take to college. But I did promise him the next time he screwed up for the ACLU, I'd punish him with a John Birch Society barbecue.

I checked inside my detached garage. Julian's Range Rover — inherited from former employers — sat stolidly next to my van, but neither Julian nor Claire was in evidence. I peeked around the back of the garage and remembered another example of Julian's recent spaciness. Just last week he had managed to get into a car accident with a new client, Babs Braithwaite. Three days after Babs had

31

booked me for her Fourth of July party, she and Julian had crashed into each other. Usually a careful driver, Julian had managed to be rear-ended by Babs in her Mercedes 560SEC. Babs said he'd stopped in the middle of an intersection. Julian said he thought he had his turn signal on. He admitted he'd been only half watching though, because moments before the collision, a giggling Claire had tried to cool off by putting her shapely feet out the window of the Rover. But it had been no joke when Julian had been judged at fault. The Mercedes had sustained a thousand dollars worth of damage, and Julian's savings would be sorely depleted paying the deductible. It seemed that even when I tried to save him money, he ended up losing it anyway.

I touched the Rover's bruised bumper, left the garage, and stepped onto a new flagstone path laid down by Tom. Even if finances were a little tight for proud, independent Julian, he would manage. He was rich in love, I reflected as I walked down the path. It led through a lush garden of perennials that Tom was somehow managing to coax out of what had been my barren yard. Julian had enthusiastically helped Tom compost, rototill, and plant. And owing to relentless spring snow, we were having a one-in-ten growing season. The magnificent show of yellow columbine, tiny blossoms of white arabis, and sky-blue bellflower campanula were Tom's pride. But at the moment it was a floral display empty of Claire and Julian.

I pushed through my back door and ran upstairs. Julian really wouldn't have brought Claire to his room, would he? I knocked gently and then peeked into the boys' bedroom. Empty. Where in the world were they? I felt sweat bead my brow. Julian was becoming so forgetful that I was considering reneging on my promise to let him take over the catering business for the next few days while I prepared for and ran the booth at the food fair. But if Julian continued to mess up bookings, the catering business would be kaput. And I'd worked too hard for financial autonomy to allow my business to be threatened. No matter how blissful we were as newlyweds, I was not about to start depending on Tom's paycheck. I clattered back down the staircase, removed the steamer cover, and turned off the burners. The sole had just begun to change color, but was not yet done. I headed down the front hall.

Julian and Claire were entwined on the living room couch. They were wrapped in a deep, silent kiss. Longer and leggier than Julian, Claire did not so much hug him as drape herself around his body. Embarrassed to be witnessing such passion, I hastily retreated to the kitchen.

"Okay!" I hollered diplomatically once I'd lifted out the steamer basket filled with sole fillets. "Let's get this stuff into the van and see if we can avoid *Speh the Hehs!*"

After a moment the lovelorn pair sheepishly reappeared. Claire's makeup, I observed, was miraculously intact, although Julian looked a trifle rumpled. He handed Claire a covered bowl of (lowfat) hollandaise, then hoisted the first box containing the soup. I suppressed a grin and picked up the container of turkey with hoisin. Ten minutes later the three of us started out for the forty-minute trip to glorious, newly refurbished Westside Mall, *still nestled,* as the recent advertisements relentlessly screamed, *at the foot of the Rockies!*

Children were already out riding their mountain bikes and kicking soccer balls against the curbs when our vehicles chugged out of my driveway. When we reached Aspen Meadow's Main Street, windblown dust shimmered in the morning light, forming a translucent veil between the town and the peaks of the Aspen Meadow Wildlife Preserve. The snow on the mountaintops had shrunk to uneven gray caps that would not completely melt over the summer. As Julian and I followed Claire's white Peugeot in the direction of Interstate 70, we passed stores whose entrances were clogged with summer tourists seeking Aspen Meadow's higher altitude, cooler temperatures, and claim to quaintness. Enterprising merchants had landscaped the area between the sidewalks and the street with a tangle of dianthus, daylilies, and bleeding heart. Below the stores' intentionally rustic signs swayed hanging baskets of white petunias, red ivy geranium, and delicate asparagus fern. Nearby Vail had used this Garden-in-Disneyland-type decoration to great effect in attracting tourists, and our little burg was following suit. The Chamber of Commerce seemed to feel that the less our place looked like a real town, the less tourists would feel they were spending real money. Still, it was home, and I loved it. I usually do not enjoy heading "down the mountain," which is how Aspen Meadow folk refer to the physical and spiritual descent into Denver and environs.

As the van lumbered eastward behind Claire's little Peugeot, a Flight-for-Life helicopter thundered overhead going west, toward Aspen Meadow. I braked automatically and pulled into the right lane in front of a pickup truck. The driver had to swerve to avoid me. Julian and I exchanged a glance. Paranoid, overprotective mother that I was, I felt my heart race as I mentally placed Arch.

My son had spent the night at a friend's house. He was due back home this morning. As soon as we arrived I would call from Hot Tin Roof and make certain he was all right.

Forcing my mind off the helicopter and its rescue mission, I sped up again and imagined all the gorgeous women who would be attending the day's banquet. The nightclub would be filled to bursting with blondes, brunettes, and redheads. All would be impossibly thin, impeccably made up, and fashionably dressed in suits with skirts shorter than what I used to wear when I played tennis, back when I was a doctor's wife. Thinking of my caterer's uniform and scrubbed face, I had a sudden attack of feeling inappropriate. Was that the real reason I resented doing this banquet — there would be all those stunning women, and then there would be *me?*

Disheartened, I glanced in the van mirror and gave myself another pep talk. The helicopter had droned away and was no longer visible. The pickup driver had changed lanes. My own face looked the same as always, my uniform, equally drab but serviceable. Later, I realized I'd made a mistake by not checking my reflection more closely. But at the time I was saying to myself: *Relax. Nobody ever notices the caterer.*

Also a mistaken assumption.

2

"So are we supposed to follow her, or not?" I asked Julian as Claire's car spewed a cloud of inky exhaust while passing the silvery-gray marble exterior of the Prince & Grogan store building. No demonstrators stood outside the entrance to the upscale department store. I hoped this was a good sign.

The Peugeot darted into Westside Mall's parking garage. Julian craned his neck to see where Claire had gone. "Let's stay separated, the way she said. In case the activists are waiting at any one place. The salespeople aren't even supposed to wear their Mignon Cosmetics uniforms. Claire's going to park by the crêpe place because she has some stuff to bring in. She told us to go on over by Stephen's Shoes. She'll take her things in while we start to unload."

I wheeled the van past the majestic hemlocks and short, lush aspens that formed the mainstay of the expensive new mall landscaping. After a moment of confusion, I headed into the far end of bottom-level parking spaces. Hopefully we were going in the direction of empty parking spots near the chrome-and-

37

glass garage entrance to the mall near Prince & Grogan. The space inhabited by the department store, as opulent and inviting a shopping environment as one could ever hope for, had formerly housed a Montgomery Ward. I'd come to know Montgomery Ward well during my lean divorce years, but the refurbishment and enlargement of Westside Mall had been so ambitiously undertaken that at the moment I felt completely turned around.

Not so Julian, who pointed to the garage entrance to the mall. I strained to catch a glimpse of police cars or activists waving signs, rabbits, or Lord knew what-all. I saw only gaggles of gorgeous women, presumably the sales associates and top customers who'd been invited. They threaded through the rows of cars on their way to the Hot Tin Roof Club. Near us, a stunning hermaphroditic blonde dressed in blistering lemon yellow strutted alongside a Porsche with an empty parking place on the row just behind it. Beyond that line of cars glowed the neon sign for Stephen's Shoes. I waited for the woman in yellow to move away, then quickly swung the van past Prince & Grogan, around the end of the row, and into the vacated spot. I checked my watch. So far we were exactly on schedule.

Guarding the doors to this level's impressive glass-prismed mall entrance was an older-looking man in the process of instructing a couple of muscular fellows sporting slicked-back hair, matching charcoal suits, and gleaming black shoes with pointed toes. The muscular two stood nervously, feet braced, hands clasped behind their backs. As the older fellow addressed them, they rolled their massive shoulders and tilted their heads over-attentively. I was pretty sure the three weren't policemen. For the threat of riots, the Furman County Sheriff's Department would certainly send officers in plainclothes as well as uniforms. But no matter what they were wearing, sheriff's department deputies never acted so obviously like hired goons.

I glanced at my watch again: ten-thirty. "The mall's open, right?"

Julian's cap of blond hair fell sideways as he tilted his head to get a better look at the suits. "Actually, yeah. It opens at ten usually, but earlier day after tomorrow because of the food fair. Most of the stores don't get busy until the afternoon, Claire says. Those dudes look like they're from Mignon Cosmetics or Prince & Grogan. Or maybe they're from some private security company."

"I guess they're supposed to look tough." I turned off the ignition and pulled up the parking brake. "Maybe they figure they'll be a deterrent if they act like they're wearing shoulder holsters. That ought to tick off the *Beastly Bulletin* folks." I couldn't remember what the law regarding carrying a concealed weapon was in this gun-loving part of the country. Coloradans don't like to conceal their weapons. In fact, they seize every opportunity to be exhibitionistic about them.

Outside the van, the foul, overheated garage air hit us like a slap. We'd have to hustle to get the food into a cool spot. In this heat, anything could wilt or grow bacteria. I opened the van doors, surveyed the undisturbed array of spa dishes, and wondered if the muscle-bound security men in the matching suits would go for the roast hot pepper, if I laid a few jalapeños on top and sprinkled them with cayenne.

As we began to unload the vegetables, shouts erupted from near the garage entrance to the mall. Julian and I exchanged a worried glance, hoisted our loads, and began to walk rapidly toward Stephen's Shoes. Twenty feet away, the security guys were hollering at several demonstrators who had suddenly appeared, waving large placards. Laden with trays of broccoli, I couldn't see if the activists were carrying anything else. From my vantage point, the demonstrators' ages and gender were indeterminate. They uniformly sported long, unkempt nests of hair above their logo'd

T-shirts, torn blue-jeans, and sandals. I couldn't hear what everyone was yelling, but I could guess it had to do with preserving small gnawing mammals with cute tails.

"Feel all right?" Julian murmured as he whacked open the service-entrance door with his sneaker and held it for me to pass through.

"Yes," I said uncertainly. The shouts had increased in volume. "Maybe the security guys, or whoever they are, can run interference while we bring in the supplies." I tried to sound more confident than I felt.

Julian moved to the shoe-store door and opened it wide. We quickly carried our culinary burdens past rows of brightly colored pumps and air-cushioned cross-trainers. Curious customers and gaping store employees allowed boxes of sandals and sailboat shoes to drop from their hands as we hustled past. They acted as if they'd never seen a catering duo lugging eighty pounds of food past them before.

The store manager, a tall fellow with sandy-red hair, came to our side quickly and murmured conspiratorially, "I know about the routing for the banquet."

I wondered if he was going to ask for the password to cross enemy lines. "Sorry," I whispered from behind the broccoli. "This'll just take a few minutes."

41

As the manager moved across the store's carpeted floor to reassure his customers, Julian said, "I don't know if those security guys will be able to protect us going back and forth." He glanced back at the garage. "Just for safety, we'd better make all our runs in tandem instead of alternating." He nodded knowingly to show how much he was learning about food service.

I didn't return the nod. It looked as if more people had joined the altercation outside. Julian was right, though. When two caterers work an event, one usually hovers over the delivered food while the other brings in the rest of the supplies. If you leave platters out *anywhere* before serving time, people will take the mere presence of edibles as a sign it's time to start consuming them, no matter how impenetrably the food is wrapped. Perhaps there would be a bar at the nightclub where we could stash all the courses below eye level.

We came out the main entrance of the shoe store and turned to enter the august beauty of the renovated main hall of Westside Mall. In the late sixties, when it opened, Westside had been a splashy, hugely successful shopping center. But Westside Mall had gone bankrupt like an F. Scott Fitzgerald hero: gradually and then suddenly. The Denver papers had been full of accounts about stores going out of business during the first phase of the oil recession. It wasn't long before the whole mall ended up repossessed as part of the savings-and-loan mess. After several years of vacancy, the management of Prince & Grogan, a department store chain with its headquarters in Albuquerque, had agreed to provide the anchor for a redone, upscale mall. A complete face-lift of the old shopping center and construction of the multilayered garage had transformed the former shopping haven into a glitzy series of fancy stores and chic boutiques.

But Arch had mourned the loss of the old Xerxes' Magic Shop. As I stepped across the threshold of the Hot Tin Roof Club, I imagined my son would be awed at the unquestionably magical transformation of the old store he'd loved so much. Gone were the rows of masks, the shelves of top hats, the glass counters filled with tricks. The walls of the enlarged space were painted silver and black. Under high-intensity spotlights, chrome buttons and table edges glistened. An array of overstuffed furniture had been upholstered in black leather. A slender woman with elaborately teased hair and a sheath as diminutive as Claire's nodded in our direction and motioned us past the hostess stand.

We moved uncertainly out of the service entry and through the new foyer. Despite the fact that it wasn't quite eleven in the morning, a palpable air of excitement filled the place. Lively music pumped out of overhead speakers. About thirty women had already arrived and were bustling about. One was setting up a slide projector. Another pulled down a screen. Two more checked on the audio system and the podium. Whether the high-pitched voices and feverish rushing around were the result of nervousness over the upcoming event — the unveiling of their fall line — or the presence of the demonstrators outside was impossible to determine. I saw Claire briefly. She seemed to have forgotten us as she giggled and squealed and moved from group to group of chattering females. On one long table, three rows of brightly colored corsages were arrayed. Some women already had them on. Others were in the act of pinning them to their stylish outfits. My guess was that the flowers had something to do with the fall colors we were about to see. I wouldn't have minded having a corsage, I thought absentmindedly as I moved toward the bar with the heavy tray of broccoli. On the other hand, was there such a thing as a bittersweet-chocolate-colored orchid? With raspberry-colored roses to complement it? Probably not.

A sudden banging and shouting outside caused a momentary hush to fall on the bevy of scattered women. Launching into a new song, the music from the speakers blasted into the silence, overwhelming any sounds of a disturbance. I cursed silently when I thought of all the food Julian and I still needed to bring in past whatever had erupted outside.

Julian read my mind. "Stay put," he ordered firmly. "I'm making another trip."

"No, let me do it. I'm used to moving around with heavy containers of food."

"No, no, I'm much faster than you," he replied without apology. "If some demonstrator started yelling at you, you'd get into a big argument, the way you always do. You want the food in here fast? Let me get it."

"Well," I said reluctantly, "why don't you see if you can get those security guys to help you?"

But Julian was already moving away. "If they're not busy," he replied over his shoulder. If he heard my call to be careful, he gave no sign.

I used the phone at the bar to call Arch's friend, Todd Druckman. Todd's mother told me the two of them were sitting in front of the television eating Cocoa Puffs and Pop-Tarts. Did I want to talk to Arch? I laughed and declined, then hung up and washed my hands in the bar sink, grateful that my concerns about my son were needless. And Arch loved eating at Todd's; it meant he didn't have to taste-test a single nonfat roll or experimental curry.

I poured the dips into the hollowed-out cabbages, then checked the trays. The rows of vegetables had become only slightly disheveled. I lifted the plastic wrap and reached in to straighten them.

"Oh my God, Harriet, they're stunning!" exclaimed a low, fruity voice from the other side of the oblong granite bar. "Diamond-cluster earrings? That must have set Mignon back a pretty penny!" It was a voice I recognized. I looked up to see big-bodied, big-haired, big-moneyed Babs Braithwaite standing next to Harriet Wells.

"Top producer for May," Harriet announced smugly.

"Wait a minute," commanded Babs as she put a hand on Harriet's forearm. Then she steered Harriet in my direction, and addressed me. "Goldy? You're doing this banquet too? Are you ready for Charles's and my party?" Without waiting for a reply, she rushed on. "Harriet, do you know Goldy of Goldilocks' Catering in Aspen Meadow? Isn't that a cute little name? She didn't always do catering. She used to be married to a *gorgeous* doctor."

Well, now, wasn't this nice. I stared at Babs Meredith Braithwaite and tried to think of something to say. Babs was about fifty, although the heavy makeup she wore over pockmarked skin made her look older. Charles Braithwaite, her reclusive microbiologist husband, was younger than his wife and reportedly quite handsome, but he hadn't inherited a fortune from the family butter company. With her bags of bucks, Babs spared no expense on decking herself out. Her large features were accented with masklike foundation and powder, dark smears of blush, black eyeliner, and long, false eyelashes. Her elaborately frosted hair was wildly poufed, and her expensive-looking dark silk dress was adorned with a fat corsage of pink roses and baby's breath. She looked like the mother of a Barbie doll. I was again conscious of my plain apron and unstylishly curly hair, worn Shirley Temple-style.

"What was his name," Babs continued, tapping her bottom lip with a plump finger. "Well, of course. Korman! *Doctor* Korman."

"No," said Harriet sadly. "I didn't know."

Incredible, really. Someone, it always seemed, was still dying to share the news now five years old. It had been that long since I divorced John Richard Korman, whose initials made up his oh-so-appropriate nickname, the Jerk. People could never understand why I'd

47

let such a good-looking and wealthy guy get away. They just didn't know about the violence. My descent into food service was observed with a pitying sneer. I was already working for Harriet's company. I'd be doing Babs's party in three days. Wasn't that enough? Why bother with the history? *Because people can't resist being bitchy,* Marla Korman, my best friend and the other ex-wife of Dr. Gorgeous, was fond of pointing out. Marla had recommended my business to Babs, so I kept mum and summoned a flat smile.

"Goldy has garnered quite a reputation in Aspen Meadow," said Babs with a wide, explanatory sweep of her bejeweled hand, "for the success of her little business."

"Yes." Harriet's saccharine tone was hard to decipher. Also around fifty, Harriet was as slender, petite, and understated as Babs was expansive. Her beehive of golden hair, impeccable makeup, and short, slender fingers with their manicured nails paired perfectly with her flared Chinese-style royal blue silk pants and matching sleeveless top. "Goldy and I have had many discussions about the lowfat food for our banquet. She was the one who pointed out that when people have fish for a main course, they always want chocolate for dessert! We're lucky she was able to come all the way down here."

"I come to Denver all the time," I said, trying not to sound defensive. "I'm doing the food fair too."

"You're doing the food fair? You shouldn't," Babs reprimanded. "You might just be overburdening yourself."

Did I look as if I wanted advice from Babs Braithwaite? I scanned the room for Julian. Maybe if I appeared busy, these women would leave me alone.

"Of course," Babs continued, "all the major food people in Denver will be here. The food fair is one of our benefits. Playhouse Southwest, do you know the group? We used to be called the Furman County Dramatic Auxiliary. We just did *The Taming of the Shrew.* Sound familiar? Didn't I tell you about it?"

I nodded vapidly. Actually, I'd talked to Babs Braithwaite on the phone only about the Fourth. We'd seen each other briefly after her car hit Julian's. I bit my lip. Don't say anything, I reminded myself. At least not anything nasty. *The Taming of the Shrew. Sound familiar?* Actually, no. Knee-deep in nonfat ingredients, I hadn't caught any plays lately. Then again, her little auxiliary might want to have a catered function sometime in the future. If I could do John Birch Beef, I could do Shakespeare shashlik. I gave Babs what I hoped was an ingratiating grin.

"Yes. Let's see, Dr. John Richard Korman," she mused throatily as she touched a sapphire necklace. "*Up and Coming in Denver* did an article on our most recent production. You must have seen that issue, there was also an article on Dr. John Richard Korman. So —"

"I'm sorry, Babs," I interrupted. Anything to get off the subject of the Jerk. "What's your connection to Mignon Cosmetics?"

"Ooh!" She chuckled and gave Harriet a flirtatious look. "I'm *such* a good customer, they invited me. Oh, there's Tiffany Barnes . . ."

And off she sailed. Man, I couldn't *wait* to ask Marla about that piece of work. I put Babs Braithwaite out of my mind and set about carefully unwrapping the lettuce leaves that would form the containers for the hoisin turkey.

Claire trotted over to me. Her comely brow was wrinkled with frustration. But before she could explain, something across the room caught her attention. I looked in that direction and saw only a group of beautifully groomed chattering women, all wearing corsages. "Oh my God," Claire groaned.

"What?"

"Nothing . . . Look, Goldy, I'm in trouble," she announced. "I . . . forgot the damn dec-

50

orations. They're Mignon bags we stuff with colored tissue paper. We call them exploding bags. Y'know? I need to go to my car and get them. Come with me? I don't want to go out there alone." She looked desperate. Considering the swelling group of protesters I'd seen outside, I felt a pang of sympathy for her. I wasn't too eager to face that indignant group alone either.

"Of course I'll come with you," I assured her. "I might as well bring in the sole and get the steamer going, anyway. We need to make it quick, though," I added. I lifted the trays of vegetables and hid them on a shelf under the bar. I had the feeling we were being watched, so I grabbed a spare tablecloth, unfurled it, and placed it over the wrapped food while Claire tapped her foot. I ignored her impatience. I would be damned before I came back to picked-over trays.

At the service door we met Julian. He was laden down with Nonfat Chocolate Tortes.

"Where do you two think you're going?" he demanded as soon as he saw us approaching. "It's a zoo out there. I couldn't find one of those suits to help me —"

"We'll be fine," Claire cooed as she kissed her index finger and planted it on his nose. She swept past him in a flurry of dark ringlets and black sheath. "Just going to pick up some bags. Back in a jif." Mimicking her touch on the nose, I followed on her heels.

The demonstrators had become a jeering, sign-waving horde. A few uniformed members of the Furman County Sheriff's Department were attempting crowd control. I didn't see Tom. Claire and I decided to pick up our respective bundles and meet at the column nearest the mall entrance. I made off for the van, fumbled with the keys, and rummaged around in the dark interior, looking for the steamer. At last I found it underneath the container of roasted vegetables. If I loaded myself up, this would be the last trip out to the van. Another roar went up from the angry demonstrators. I quickly surveyed all the remaining food and decided it was worth the hassle. Balancing the bowl of vegetables on top of the plastic container of greens, I picked up the steamer, then carefully made my way toward the appointed column. With the hubbub all around, I desperately wanted to look inconspicuous. Or as inconspicuous as a woman toting forty pounds of fish and vegetables can be.

Over the rumble of the demonstrators, I heard a revving engine. It was closer to me than to the cops and the crowd, and getting closer by the moment. I craned my neck around. There was no car in sight. Neither the crowd nor the cops seemed to take any notice of me, so I continued to meander through vehicles on my way to the entrance, my attention on the triple deck of supplies I was balancing. There was another shout from the crowd and behind me, a squeal of tires.

I heard the scream first, then a horrid, sickening thud. The scream echoed from the concrete walls all around. Then the engine roared again and the tires screeched. Far over at the entrance, two uniformed cops started running in the direction of the scream. I willed myself to start breathing again, and looked around for Claire. Where was she? Had she seen what happened? My skin prickled. After being momentarily stilled, the demonstrators started up again with their "hoo-ha!" shouts that sounded like an ominous pep rally.

When Claire did not appear I whacked the steamer, the bowl, and the vegetables down on the hood of a nearby Jeep. Unencumbered, I started briskly off in the area where I thought Claire had parked her Peugeot.

I saw the policemen first. One was talking into his radio. The other knelt on the pavement. A woman was lying at his feet. Had she passed out? As I came closer, I realized the body could not have landed in that contorted way from a faint.

The kneeling policeman looked up and saw

me. "Get back!" he yelled. "We need to clear this area!"

But I took no heed. Blood pooled on the cement near the inert body. The woman on the pavement was Claire.

3

I'm going to be ill. My mouth opened but no
sound emerged. A car drove slowly by behind
me. In one of its windows, children's faces
gawked at the policemen. I lurched forward
through a shock wave of car exhaust. Had
Claire been struck by a car? But of course,
that was the only explanation. *There has to
be some way I can help.* Where was that vehicle
I'd heard screeching through the garage? What
were the two cops doing? Why wasn't someone else coming? I knew I would regret walking closer, but I kept moving forward anyway.
My footsteps gritted loudly. *Please let her be
all right.*

"Go back," said the policeman again, this
time in my face. His wide shoulders and deeply
lined face loomed in front of me. He was not
someone I knew. I murmured Claire's name
and felt my knees buckle. Then the policeman
seemed to change his mind. "Wait." His powerful hand gripped my elbow. "Did you see
what happened? Do you know this woman?
Were you with her?"

"No. I mean, yes." It came out a croak.
"I only . . ." What? My face was wet. Tears.

When had I started to cry?

The policeman's gruff voice insisted: "The woman who was hit — you knew her or not?" So Claire had been hit. Of course. The policeman's eyes bored into mine. Surely he didn't think I was responsible? "Her name?" he demanded.

My mouth fumbled around Claire's name. I did not know her address. Julian would. Oh, God. Julian.

Behind us people began to gather. The policeman sharply ordered them to stay back, then continued with curt questions: What exactly had I seen? Had I observed any vehicles before I heard the scream? Why was Claire in the garage? Not far away, the other uniformed cop continued to speak urgently into his radio. There was no movement from the twisted body on the pavement.

The man questioning me took his fierce eyes off my face and looked over my shoulder. "Oh, good. Schulz," he murmured. I turned to see my husband walking swiftly toward us between parked cars. Relief rushed through me. Over his street clothes, Tom wore a raid jacket, a gray windbreaker with the Furman County Sheriff's Department logo emblazoned on the left pocket. The jacket was what the plainclothes police put on when they needed to distinguish themselves from regular folks.

But distinguishing Tom Schulz from regular folks was not now, nor had it ever been, difficult.

He did not see me at first. I wiped my cheeks hard and watched him stride toward the uniformed officer with the radio, who was again kneeling on the garage floor. Tom wore his purposeful, commanding look, a look that I knew both comforted and cowed those who worked for him. It was also an expression that cut like a cleaver into a suspect's babbling. Tom dropped to one knee to talk to the cop with the radio. The officer motioned in our direction. Tom glanced over, gave a brief, puzzled shake of the head when he saw me, then turned back to Claire.

I shivered, coughed again, and clasped my arms. I felt ridiculous in the double-breasted chef's jacket and apron. The blood in my ears pounded as worries about Claire and Julian crowded my mind. Tom took the radio and talked into it. The policeman beside me seemed to sense there was no point in continuing his interrogation. Tom would join us momentarily and take over. An approaching siren wailed. Too soon, I thought. But of course — the new hospital was right across the street from the mall. Suddenly the red, white, and gold EMS truck careened around a cement column, then screeched to a halt and disgorged two paramedics. They ran over to Claire's dreadfully inert body. Tom straightened and walked over to us. His face was grim.

"This is —" began the uniformed cop.

"Yeah, okay, I know who she is. Go help Rick with those demonstrators."

The uniformed cop trotted away. Tom gave me the full benefit of his green eyes.

To my dismay, I began to cry again. "It's Julian's girlfriend . . . you know . . . Claire. Is she alive? Is she going to be okay?"

"No, she isn't." He put his arms around me. "I swear, Goldy, what are you doing out here in the garage?" When I didn't answer, he held me closer and murmured, "She probably didn't suffer much. Looks like she died on impact." He released me and narrowed his eyes. They were filled with seriousness and pain. "Goldy, try to pull yourself together for a minute. Did you see it?"

I brushed the tears from my cheeks and took a shuddery breath. "No."

"Where's Julian?"

"Inside that nightclub. Hot Tin . . . you know, where they're having . . . he was catering with me." I tried to think. "What should we do, tell him? Or wait? Did the person who hit her not stop?"

"Hit-and-run. State patrol will handle it. You know, they do traffic. And yes, you and

I should go find Julian. Let's not tell anybody else, though, we don't want a general panic. Plus we need to follow procedure here, find the next of kin. . . . How long have you been here? You said you didn't see this accident. What did you hear, anything?"

Haltingly, I told Tom that Claire and I had come out to get supplies from our vehicles about ten minutes before. I had not seen Claire after I got to the van. I'd loaded up and only moments later heard the growl of an engine, squealing, and the horrible thump as metal hit flesh. I pointed in the direction of the van, then remembered slapping down the fish and vegetables on the hood of a nearby car. "I guess I better go get my stuff," I said lamely.

"Hold on." He brought his bushy eyebrows down into a V. "The car you heard, did it honk? This squealing, was it like tires or brakes? Was it the sound of a car going around a corner?"

I chewed the inside of my cheek, trying to clear what felt like cotton in my head. "No horn. The sound was like someone going around a corner. I guess."

Two light beige Colorado state trooper patrol cars pulled up. Tom held up a hand for them to wait. Then he pointed at the shoe-store entrance. "Get your stuff and meet me over there, would you?"

"Get my stuff?" I was incredulous. "You mean you think I still should do this stupid banquet when one of the company employees has just been killed?"

"Please. Goldy, we can't tell her employers or coworkers yet. We're going to have to take care of Julian. If you don't do the banquet, the word will get out and then the journalists will make a mess —"

"Okay, okay."

"We'll go in to see Julian together. Avoid the demonstrators." Then he strode off to deal with the troopers while I struggled to get my bearings. After a few shaky breaths, I turned to backtrack toward the Jeep, then turned back. Tom and the two troopers were crouched near the garage floor. Beyond them, the paramedics had hooked Claire's body up to their telemetric equipment. Tom and the troopers were pointing at something on the asphalt.

I surveyed the garage and shivered. Could Claire really be dead? I had just talked to her, been with her, less than half an hour ago. I started to walk, then suddenly felt dizzy and reached out for one of the cement columns. How am I ever going to break this to Julian? What could I have done differently? What? *Get a grip,* I ordered myself. I stepped on something and stared down at the asphalt.

Under my foot was the stem of a rose. At first I thought the fluorescent light of the garage must be playing tricks on me, or maybe stress arising from what I'd just witnessed clouded my vision. The rose seemed to be blue. Its closed petals were blue as a robin's egg, blue as the color of the Colorado sky in the early days of autumn.

Without thinking I reached down for the blossom I'd crushed beneath my heel. Immediately I was rewarded with a thorn in my right index finger. Well, Tom the garden man would be interested in seeing it anyway, I thought absurdly. I held the flower up to my eyes, still unable to determine how its unique color had been applied. I turned back to see what Tom was doing. He was deep in conversation with the troopers. Twenty feet away, the ambulance, its sirens off, moved slowly out of the garage.

I walked holding the rose by its stem until my steamer and bowls were in front of me, on the Jeep hood. I put the rose on top of the salad greens, picked up the food, and started walking toward Stephen's Shoes. Where had Tom said to meet him? Oh yes, by the entrance. Well, he'd have to come find me. He was remarkably good at that.

As I lugged the food toward the shoe store, a voice screeched.

"Hey! You! You're one of them! You're serving the animal-killer fascists!"

The man who accosted me was short, with a thin face framed by tightly curled black hair tucked into a small ponytail, and a wiry beard. A gold earring adorned one ear. He put his hands on his waist, cocked one hip, and glared. I made him out to be in his late twenties. He was very attractive in addition to being diminutive, but neither quality quite went with the fury emanating in my direction. Crossing his arms, he yelled, "You're either for us or against us, you know!" His black eyes blazed. "Do you care if innocent albino rabbits are tortured for makeup? Do you? Do you think you could see if you'd had a Draize test?" He folded his arms and pushed his body forward. Taking another step, he chest-bumped the steamer and bowls I carried. "Do you *care* about animals or not?" he demanded.

My skin prickled hot with rage. After all I'd seen today, I was in no mood for this.

"So do you care about animals or not, bitch?" he shrilled.

I announced loudly: "I'm going to pour forty pounds of vegetables on the ass in front of me if he doesn't move."

The demonstrator's mouth dropped open. Unfortunately, he quickly recovered. "You don't know about the rabbit body-count,

62

then? Is that why you're serving the fascists?"

I began, "You don't know what I've just seen —"

"Hey, lady! Do you think I care —"

"Excuse me," said a familiar voice behind me.

The demonstrator's Adam's apple bobbed as he fell silent and looked Tom over. His glance stopped on Tom's jacket logo. "What's this? The storm troopers protecting capitalists?" He turned his glare back to me. "You got a vested interest in being a fascist? You think eyeshadow's going to help your looks, Ms. Plump? Take the attention away from your blond afro?" He rolled his shoulders in a muscular, he-man sort of way. Then he reared back and once again chest-bumped the food in my hands. "Guess what?" he yelled. "I'm not going to let you go in there!"

I hauled back and thrust the full weight of myself, the vegetables, and the steamed fish into him. Too late, Tom realized what I was doing and launched himself at us. Tom's wide hands managed to catch the steamer, a heavy metal rectangle with a rigid plastic top. The covered bowl of salad greens skittered across the garage floor. No such luck with the container of vegetables. My ponytailed irritant lay at my feet decorated with roasted red peppers, thick slices of grilled mushroom, chunks

63

of charred onion, and blobs of cooked tomato.

"Man, lady, what is your *problem?*" he
shrieked from the floor. "Did you see that,
Officer? Wasn't that assault? I'm going to
press charges!"

Tom handed me the steamer. His face was
impassive. "Do not let go of this," he ordered
in that voice of his. "Get up, you," he commanded the demonstrator. "Go on over there
with your anti-fascist friends. Don't let me
see your face by this door again. Hear?"

"You *pig!*" the demonstrator screamed as
he scrambled to his feet and brushed off vegetables. I noticed with satisfaction that the tomatoes had left long red smears on his SPARE
THE HARES T-shirt. "I'll show my face by any
door I want!"

Tom Schulz loomed over him. "You want
to go to jail, Jack? Try blocking public entrances again."

"What the *hell* do I pay taxes for?" the demonstrator barked over his shoulder as he scurried back to his buddies.

Tom Schulz retrieved the covered bowl of
greens from the garage floor and shot me a
look. "You just can't help yourself, can you?"
he asked. He didn't wait for an answer.
"Where'd this come from?" He was staring
at the rose that had miraculously stayed with

64

the bowl of greens on its bounce across the asphalt.

"From the floor near where Claire" — I gestured — "over by that column. It's probably been sprayed —"

"What column?"

I pointed.

"You found this fifteen, twenty feet from the body? And you picked it up?" he said, trying to clarify.

"I'm sorry. She was hit by . . . a vehicle, and I just saw the flower there on the floor —"

"Okay, wait a minute, let me go put it in an evidence bag."

He strode away holding the flower delicately by its stem. When he returned, he said, "Goldy — no more violent encounters with the demonstrators, okay?"

"Look, I hit that guy with the food only because he was threatening me and he wouldn't get out of my way. That's justified, isn't it? Oh, Lord." I teetered backward. What did I care about some demonstrator?

Tom took hold of my shoulders, steadied me, and shook his head. "Goldy, I know you've taken a lot of crap in your life and now you don't take crap anymore. Good for you. But don't make more work for me than I already have. Next time hit the guy with your pepper spray, not an entire meal. Please? We've got big problems here, and we need to go take care of Julian. Let me get the door."

Inside the club, rock music still throbbed against the black walls. People were gathering, expecting food. After what we'd just gone through, the shock of business as usual felt disorienting. In my absence, Julian had laid out the crudités and dips next to a stack of glass plates, and served up glass bowls of asparagus soup. The buffet line was progressing smoothly; it looked as if about half of the forty women had moved through and were seated. Julian was managing to keep the platters filled and neat as he served, smiled, and answered questions. The women giggled coyly at him, and I could guess at their whispered questions: *Isn't he cute? How long do you suppose he's been doing this?* As we entered, Julian's eyes darted toward us. I knew we weren't who he was looking for.

Tom took the bowl and steamer from my hands. "Just let's put the food down. Tell him to come outside," he murmured. "If these folks see me, they might know something's wrong. I don't want to start or to deal with a general frenzy."

I moved across to the bar. Julian's face creased in alarm when I asked him to come outside. As we moved toward the door, the women seemed to take no notice of us leaving.

Outside, Julian immediately demanded, "Where's Claire?"

For a moment, neither Tom nor I spoke. Then Tom sighed. He said bluntly, "There's been a hit-and-run accident. Claire was hit. I'm sorry, Julian, but she's . . . she's dead."

Julian clutched Tom's jacket. He cried, "What? What? What are you telling me? I don't get it. You're wrong. You must be wrong." I felt my throat tighten as I put my arms around him. His hands dropped from Tom's jacket and his muscled body started to shake. One hand slammed the wall. "Huh?" he cried. "What?" Sweat glistened over his pale skin. His eyes were wild. Shoppers from the mall stopped and stared.

"Oh, bad sign. He's going into shock," Tom told me. "He needs medical attention right away." As Tom barked into the walkie-talkie that we needed another ambulance, I fumbled to undo the top button of Julian's shirt so he could breathe more easily. I'd graduated from Med Wives 101 and knew all about shock.

At that moment the service entrance to the nightclub opened and the woman in yellow poked her head out. Her blond hair looked oily under the fluorescent lights of the hallway, and her thick makeup seemed to add years to her age. Her jet-black eyebrows gave her a menacing aspect, like Tallulah Bankhead on a bad day.

"What the hell is going on out here?" she demanded in a throaty falsetto. The mall shoppers turned their stare on her. "Where are the exploding bags? Where is Claire Satterfield?"

Tom Schulz ignored her barrage of questions. "Get back, please, ma'am. Leave us alone."

"Oh, gawd . . . I suppose." With a huge sigh and bang of the door, she disappeared. Julian slumped against the wall.

"Takes all kinds," observed Tom as he lifted one of Julian's eyelids to check on his state of consciousness.

Thirty seconds later the door opened again, this time revealing Harriet Wells. We were a long way from our conversation about muffins with okra and how much Mignon would pay for the banquet. Harriet looked with genuine alarm at Julian.

"Can I help?" she asked us. Her intelligent blue eyes were full of concern. She looked from Tom to me, trying to ascertain who was in charge. "Can you tell me what's going on? Will we be one server short for the banquet?"

Julian slumped forward and began to sob. "I'll be there to serve the food in just a minute," I snapped as I clutched him. Harriet Wells tilted her head at me skeptically. Clearly, my tear-streaked face and smeared apron did not inspire confidence. Tom once again talked into his radio. The smell of cooking hamburgers from a mall restaurant unexpectedly wafted over us. *Julian, Julian,* I prayed, *pull yourself together. Please.*

"Can you tell me what is going on out here?" Harriet asked.

My throat closed in panic. I coughed and began to say, "You see, there's been —"

Tom put away his radio and interrupted. "We have a crisis. Thanks for your patience. Your caterer will be there momentarily."

"I certainly hope so," was Harriet Wells's parting comment as she quietly closed the nightclub door.

Julian's face was distorted, as if he'd swallowed something and then choked on it. He pulled himself away from me, gasping for breath.

"Where should we take him?" I asked Tom. "Couldn't you even tell that woman what happened to Claire?"

Unexpectedly, Julian reeled in Tom's direction. Tom snagged him as the group of spectators shrieked.

"Lower him to the floor," Tom ordered tersely. "Slowly, very slowly. Don't hurt yourself."

Together, we grasped Julian and helped him down. Before we had him stretched out on the floor, a shaggy-haired policeman rushed up to tell Tom a second ambulance had arrived from the hospital across the street.

"I'm okay, I'm okay," gagged a still-shivering Julian. "I want to get up. Don't make me stay down here."

Tom ordered the cop to get a stretcher in. Two more paramedics appeared and lifted Julian, moaning, to a stretcher. As they moved off, I felt suddenly bereft.

"Where are you going?" I called after them. "When will I hear if he's okay?"

Tom was at their heels. "Across the street, Southwest Hospital. Don't tell anybody what happened. I'll call you later." And he was gone.

The next two hours passed in a fog. I barely noticed the women I served. I found I could block out the day's events by focusing, focusing, and focusing again on the food, on the job at hand.

Mercifully, the steamer had stayed closed when I'd heaved it at the angry demonstrator. The bowl of greens was also intact. Without the roast vegetables to garnish and dress the salad, I thinned out the carrot dip with olive oil and balsamic vinegar. The resulting dressing was delicious. I had the ridiculous thought that I should have written down how I'd done it. It was such a trivial thing after what had happened to Claire. *Hit-and-run.* I wondered who would contact her parents in Australia.

I knew Tom was right, that he could not make a public announcement of Claire's death to her coworkers at Mignon. Since Julian was the closest American to Claire, Tom was duty-bound to inform him. But Tom had to keep news of the death under wraps in the hope that Claire's family could be notified by the authorities rather than a journalist in search of a juicy story. The sheriff's department had a hierarchy of people to notify in the event of sudden death, and they stuck to it. The only folks who managed to screw this up were from the media. One of Arch's young friends had heard over the radio of his father's death in a plane crash. The poor child had immediately gone into shock.

Speaking of which, I couldn't bear recalling Julian's disbelieving face and his stricken *What? What?* I felt his absence by the extra amount of work I had to do: clearing dishes, refilling platters, wiping spills off the granite bar. Sometimes engaging in a load of work heals the heart. In this case, it didn't.

4

The lunch took an eternity. When it was almost over, a slender, elegant woman with long raven-black hair that contrasted with her sleek beige dress and pale orchid corsage got to her feet. Sending a twinkly smile in the direction of the guests, she announced breathlessly that Mignon was going to show slides of the new line of cosmetics for autumn, and then we would have dessert. The spotlights dimmed, and soon we were looking at the luminous, enlarged faces of stunning women. Then we saw the same lovely females with their fingers caressing suggestively shaped plastic bottles. The bottles were filled with stuff you were supposed to put on your face: Magic Pore-closing Toner with Mediterranean Sea Kelp. Extra-rich Alpine Nighttime Replacement Moisturizer with Goat Placenta. Ultragentle Eye Cream Smoother with Swiss Herbs. It sounded like makeup by Heidi. Then we saw the same dramatically made-up women modeling colors of foundation, blush, lipstick, eyeshadow, and mascara. Strawberry Sundae lipstick. Hot Date blush. Foreplay eyeshadow. S'More mascara. The models' eyes were half closed and their lips were pursed, as if they were trying to kiss the air, or at least seduce it. When it came time for the lipstick, out came the models' tongues, just touching the tops of their mouths. The message wasn't exactly subliminal: *Buy these cosmetics and you will get sex.* When the slides were over and the lights came up, there was so much clapping, you would have thought they'd just announced the Nobel for Makeup.

I wondered how Julian was doing. I wondered what phase of the investigation the police were in now. Tom had said the state patrol handled traffic, which included hit-and-run. I wondered if the driver who had struck Claire had turned himself in. I tried to imagine where Tom was, what he was dealing with. . . .

"Okay, girls," announced the black-haired woman, who had left her table and was standing in front of the slide screen, "that was for *you!*" She put her hands on her hips and wiggled them provocatively. There was more uproarious clapping. She quieted the group with a restrained Queen Elizabeth-style wave. "We've got the best products and the hottest line," she continued authoritatively. "*Everyone* is going to be copying us — but we've got the jump on them because we've got the *best* sales associates and the *best* customers!" More thunderous applause. "And you're going to take us into the *future!*" From her jacket pocket she whipped out a pair of sunglasses and put them on. This was some kind of cue, because from her table, half a dozen other women quickly donned sunglasses. "So look out, everybody!" she cried. "The future of Mignon Cosmetics is so bright you're going to have to pull out those shades!" And then there was final, furious clapping from the audience as the black-haired woman strutted back to her seat. Wearing sunglasses, she had a hard time finding it, but someone finally took her hand and guided her back to her spot.

Out of place. That was what Tom always said he looked for, something out of place. And that was what appeared at exactly that moment: a person who didn't fit. Someone who was usually a slob. Someone who didn't wear lipstick or blush or face powder — ever. Someone who, as far as I knew, owned nothing but an ancient, too-large black trench coat and a ratty pair of sneakers held together with duct tape.

"Frances?" I asked tentatively as I doled out pieces of nonfat chocolate torte to the women in line. "Frances Markasian?"

She smiled broadly at me and winked, then put her finger to her lips. But I was having none of it.

"Why are you here?" I demanded of

Frances Markasian, a reporter from Aspen Meadow's small weekly newspaper, the *Mountain Journal*. Had the *Mountain Journal* even run one article on fashion and makeup? The only piece I remembered seeing was on hunters wearing camouflage blackface when they went looking for elk.

Frances Markasian arched one freshly plucked eyebrow at the superbly groomed women who surrounded her, and grinned broadly. She patted her dark dreadlocked hair, now pinned into a thick, frizzy bun, then wiggled fingers at the women as they surveyed her. I itched to tell them that Frances Markasian wearing sling-back heels and a spangled St. John's knit dress was about as rare a sight as a red-tailed fox at a country club tea. But I kept mum.

As the women wandered back to their tables bearing their plates of Nonfat Chocolate Torte, I hissed, "How could you possibly have heard already?"

Frances picked at crumbs on the torte plate at the bar. "Heard what?"

Doggone it. When she finally raised her trying-to-look-innocent black eyes at me, I said evenly, "About the demonstrators. One of them tried to block the door and I whacked him."

"You whacked him? With what? A knife

75

or a chocolate torte pan?"

"A tray of vegetables."

The sleek black-haired woman had taken off her sunglasses and was making a concluding announcement. The Mignon luncheon was finally breaking up. I tried to make my tone to Frances conciliatory. "Why don't you tell me why you're here? In fact, why don't you help me pack up my stuff while you're spilling your guts?"

"Do you have any *real* food? I'm still hungry."

I sighed. "Peach cobbler or brownies?"

Before Frances could reply, a short, slightly plump young woman with dyed orange-blond hair cut in a brushed-forward pixie style appeared at the bar. Dusty Routt, unlike journalist Frances Markasian, was not out of place at this perfumed, stylish lunch. Dusty lived just down the street from us in a house built by Aspen Meadow's branch of the charitable group Habitat for Humanity. For a time she'd gone to prep school with Julian, but had been mysteriously expelled before graduation. She and Julian shared the bond of being scholarship students, and they'd started going out before Dusty was expelled. But a month ago Dusty had made the mistake of introducing Julian to her fellow sales associate in her new job. The fellow sales associate had been Claire

Satterfield. Now Dusty's usually cheery face was mournful and her cornflower-blue eyes pleading.

"Hi, Goldy," she said in her singsong voice. "Where's Julian?"

"Busy. Dusty, do you know Frances Markasian? Frances works in Aspen Meadow, at the *Journal*. Frances is a friend of mine," I said. I did not add *sort of a friend. Not a friend I would ever call when I had to confide something.* They nodded at each other.

"You work for Mignon, Dusty?" Frances asked in such an innocent voice that it was clear to me she already knew precisely what Dusty's job was.

"Don't say anything," I warned Dusty as I covered up the food trays. "Frances thinks she's the premier investigative reporter in our little burg."

The shorn quality of Dusty's Dreamsicle-colored hair made her look younger than eighteen. In fact, I always thought she resembled a plump Peter Pan. "Wow! I mean, you don't look like a reporter. You must be successful. I saw that St. John's suit in Lord & Taylor. It looks great on you. Really! *Great.*"

Frances shot me a spiteful look and announced she wanted a couple of brownies. Dusty said yes please, she wouldn't mind a couple herself. I doled the baked goods out, then asked if they could help me get my equipment into the boxes. Thankfully, the nightclub staff was responsible for cleaning the tables and washing the dishes. The cosmetics crowd thinned out. When they'd swiftly polished off their brownies, Frances, in her usual trying-unsuccessfully-to-be-delicate manner, pumped Dusty for information about Mignon's animal-testing practices as they helped me pack. Dusty shrugged. Frances reflected, frowning, as she rinsed and wrapped the steamer. Then she cleared her throat and asked how security was at Prince & Grogan. Dusty folded up the last box, said she didn't know much about security, and moved off.

Frances, disappointed, hoisted up a box and tottered on the sling-back shoes. "Did that girl flunk verbal skills, or what? Do saleswomen talk just about what they sell?" Now it was my turn to feign ignorance. She went on: "I really shouldn't help you, Goldy, but I need a cigarette. The antismoking cops in this mall will throw me in handcuffs if I light up anywhere but in the garage. You blew my cover. I can't walk in these damn heels. And I'm going to wreck this frigging expensive dress if I carry this box anywhere. A couple of your brownies aren't worth the aggravation —"

"Sorry about that, Frances," I interrupted.

78

"You are such a dear. Not only that, but you're the only person I know who uses the phrase 'blew my cover.' And anyway, I'll bet you got the paper to pay for your outfit and your lunch. What did you tell the Mignon cosmetics people, that you were from *Cosmopolitan?*"

"*Vogue.*"

"Fabulous."

We lifted our boxes and walked out to the garage. The temperature had risen. Heat seemed to shimmer above the pavement. Three hours had passed since the accident, and everything appeared back to normal. There was no sign of either the demonstrators or the police. In another attempt at nonchalance, Frances glanced furtively in all directions. If she thought I was going to tell her anything about the day's tragic events, she was very mistaken.

"How's married life treating you?" she asked mildly after she'd pushed her box into my van. I noticed someone had inexpertly applied bright red polish to her stubby, much-gnawed fingernails. Part of her cover, no doubt.

"Just great," I told her.

Frances nodded without interest and unceremoniously unzipped her dress from the collar to the chest and pulled a squashed pack of cigarettes out of her bra. She leaned against the van, lit up, and inhaled greedily, then grinned at me as she blew out smoke rings. I asked, "So how do you cover demonstrators outside a building from inside, when you're at a banquet? And why were you asking about security? The security guys were all out here."

"Oh, they were, were they?"

"Frances, don't jive me."

"And you, Goldy, are the only one I know who'd use the phrase 'don't jive me.' " She drew lavishly on the cigarette. "That department store has a lot of problems," she said with an arched eyebrow. She blew out smoke, stuck the cigarette back between her lips, and used both hands to rezip her dress. "Or haven't you heard?" When I shook my head, she shrugged. "I've heard some rumors. You know, got to follow everything up, check everything out. Let's just say I thought the cosmetics place was a good place to start."

I decided to ponder that in silence.

When she'd finished her smoke we walked back to the nightclub, picked up the last batch of boxes, and took them to the van. We chatted about the heat and how we would never in a million years spend the money Mignon was asking for all that night cream, day cream, outside- and inside- and in-between cream. Once the boxes were stacked and secured, I hopped behind the steering wheel, turned on the motor, and thanked Frances again for helping me. As I drove away, I watched her oddly stylish silhouette in my rearview mirror. Just checking out rumors, my feijoada. A new dress, high-heeled shoes, nail polish, and no cigarette for two hours of banquet and pre-sentation? Lucky for me, I knew when she *was* jiving me.

Sometimes I think my van returns to Aspen Meadow by rote. And it's a good thing too, since I was in no shape to be analytical about anything, least of all driving. I rolled down the windows and filled my lungs with hot air. It wasn't much of a relief after the putrid-smelling warmth of the mall garage. Heat shuddered off the windows and pressed down on the van's roof. My elbow burned the second I acciden-tally rested it on the fiery chrome. When I started out in the catering business, most of my jobs had been in Aspen Meadow. So of course I hadn't bothered to get air-condition-ing in my vehicle. Occasionally, like today, I regretted making that small saving.

The van wheezed up westbound Interstate 70 and soon the sultry wind flooding the car cooled. Thirty minutes later I pulled over to take a few deep breaths under a pylon of what Aspen Meadow folks call the Ooh-Ah Bridge, nicknamed for its spectacular panoramic view of the Continental Divide. A small herd of buffalo grazed in a fenced meadow near the bridge. I stared dejectedly at them and felt a fresh surge of remorse. Why hadn't I accompanied Claire to her vehicle? Why hadn't I insisted Julian go with her? No, that wouldn't have been a good idea. In his lovestruck state of mind, Julian could have been hit as well. But a contingent of the sheriff's department had been stationed nearby. Why hadn't I insisted a policeman walk with Claire? Why?

Afternoon clouds billowed above the horizon like mutant cauliflower. Below them, the sweep of mountains were deeply shadowed in purple. My ears started to buzz. *Tom would be calling.* Three dark, stolid-looking buffalo eyed me, blinked, and then shuffled away. I had a sudden memory of Julian reeling out of control as his eyes fluttered shut. *Julian was in shock.* Next to the road, delicate bluebell blossoms bent in the mountain breeze. *Claire, lovely violet-eyed Claire, was dead.*

I drove home. I needed to be in my own place, needed a cold beverage, needed most of all to reconnect with my family and friends. When I came through the back door, the place felt empty and unusually stuffy. Irritation snaked up my spine. Because of the security system I'd been forced to install to keep my periodically violent ex-husband at bay, the windows stayed shut — and therefore wired — in my absence. I'd been tempted to disable the system once I was married to a formidable, gun-toting policeman. But Tom promptly vetoed that idea. *You never know when he might turn up,* he warned. *I can't always be around.* But it was okay now, I'd protested. The Jerk wouldn't dare bother me with a policeman in residence. Although he was ridiculously vain about being a doctor, my ex-husband was basically a coward. *You haven't seen ex-husband jealousy the way I've seen it,* Tom replied flatly. *Believe me, you don't want to* was the unspoken end of that warning.

Anyway, I'd given up trying to convince Tom to let me disable the system about two weeks after we were married this spring. Back then, during a typically frigid and snowy April in Aspen Meadow, I hadn't thought we'd have a summer with record-shattering heat. But now it was July, and June had been the hottest since the state started keeping weather statistics in the late 1800s. Coming into the old house when it had been clamped up tight in our absence, I felt like Gretel being forced into the oven by the witch.

I opened the windows downstairs, then threw the upstairs windows open and allowed the afternoon breeze off Aspen Meadow Lake, a half-mile away, to drift in. Combined with the lilting notes of jazz saxophone coming from down the street, the fresh air felt heavenly. The music came from the Routts' place. Dusty's grandfather played the instrument to placate Dusty's little brother, Colin, who was born prematurely at the beginning of April, before the Habitat house had been finished. Dusty's mother hadn't done too well hanging on to men; I'd heard both Dusty's father and the father of the infant had taken hikes.

Mesmerized by the music, I crossed to the windows looking out on the street and gazed at the Routts' place. To build the dwelling, the local Habitat for Humanity had relied on funds and workers from our parish, St. Luke's Episcopal Church. The house was a simple two-story affair with inexpensive wood paneling, a tiny deck, and a room with jalousie windows off the right side. Church workers had repeatedly graded the driveway during Aspen Meadow's muddy spring. The yard was covered with freshly excavated dirt. Red clay over the septic tank was as raw as a wound. Along the sidewalk, a stand of purple fireweed had somehow survived the construction. Unlike several of our neighbors, I'd welcomed the Routts, even if they were poor. I'd enjoyed being the church person assigned with coordinating two weeks of dinners sent in during the move and unpacking. Although I'd never met the grandfather, Dusty and her mother, Sally, had been profoundly thankful. I liked them. And at the moment I was even jealous of them: The saxophone music was coming out of open windows, something *I* could have only when I was home.

Maybe Tom would agree to keeping the upper-story windows ajar, at least for the summer. Even if I regretted marrying the Jerk, shouldn't I be able at least to get a summer breeze? My ex was a wimpy, jealous, temper-tantrum thrower who had given me black eyes more times than I cared to remember. But of one thing I was sure — John Richard Korman would never scale an exterior wall to get in a window.

Downstairs, the saxophone music was louder. I flopped into a wingchair and listened to the music, taking care not to look at the couch where Julian and Claire had embraced only a few hours before. Where was Arch? I checked the kitchen, where a note in his handwriting was taped on my computer screen: *Todd and I came back & now we're doing tie-dying back at his house, just like they did in the sixties. Back around 5. Have fun today, Mom.*

Arch, the most serious thirteen-year-old on the planet, always hoped I had fun. It was good he wasn't here. I didn't want him asking forty-five questions about Julian or Claire before I had any information. Besides, with his new activity, Arch was well occupied. At his age, my son developed enthusiasms on a bi-annual basis, and I had learned to go with whatever was the current wave. This had not always been the case. When he'd become involved in role-playing games two years ago, I was convinced one of us was going to end up institutionalized. When he finally abandoned constructing paper dungeons and fictional dragons, he and his friend Todd Druckman had switched to elaborate trivia quizzes. For months, Guinness books of records had spilled off every available shelf. Although Arch's ability to spout interesting facts still had not positively affected his school performance, the trivia obsession had eventually lost its lure when Todd had refused to answer one more question about Evel Knievel. Then Arch had renewed his interest in magic. He'd been intensely serious about magic all last summer. But the magic phase had been quickly followed by a C. S. Lewis phase, complete with a handmade model of the *Dawn Treader*.

Now Arch was fascinated by the sixties. Posters of Eugene McCarthy and Malcolm X decorated his bedroom. The walls reverberated with the sound of the Beatles and Rolling Stones. My general attitude toward these hobby-passions was that as long as they were neither extravagantly expensive nor physically dangerous, they were okay. At least he wasn't into gangs.

Still, I sighed. I suddenly missed him intensely, and Tom, and Julian. And I didn't even mind solitude as much as I minded a lack of information. Why didn't somebody call to tell me how Julian was? I took a deep breath to steady myself.

Loneliness frequently brought my ex-husband to mind. I remembered the many nights I'd waited for him. Most of the time, instead of being in the delivery room with a mother-to-be, he'd been with a waitress, or a nurse, or someone he'd just met. . . . Marla, who'd stayed married to John Richard Korman six years less than I, told me she'd timed the trip home from the hospital to thirty-eight minutes. Anything over that, and she knew she might as well go to bed.

Speaking of Marla, she should be showing up any moment. I filled the espresso machine with coffee and water. Because Marla was plugged into every gossip network in Furman County, she heard news at the speed of sound. If it was bad news, she heard it at the speed of light. What had happened to Claire was extra-bad news, though. Incredibly, my door-bell and telephone remained resolutely silent. I poured the dark espresso over ice cubes and milk, then dialed Marla's number. No answer.

I downed the iced latte and told myself I had plenty to do; I could call her later. After an hour of schlepping food and dirty pans into the house, washing and putting equipment away, I called the hospital to check on Julian. Who was I, the operator wanted to know, next of kin, wife, what? A guardian? I said hope-fully. A legal guardian? she asked. Well, no. Then no information could be released. Thanks loads.

I dialed Julian's adoptive parents in Utah, told them briefly what had happened, and promised to keep them posted. Was Julian going to be all right? they wanted to know. Yes, I assured them. I told them Southwest Hospital had refused to give me any infor-mation about Julian's condition and that they'd be better off phoning the hospital di-rectly. Was he serious about this girl? his mother asked. My voice broke when I an-swered that he had seemed to be very serious about Claire. Next I called Tom at his desk and got his voice mail. I tried Marla again. Nothing.

Cook, my inner voice said. *Get ahead on as-signments.* I consulted my calendar. Oh yes, the damn mall food fair. At the moment, I never wanted to see the mall again. But work was work. A Taste of Furman County was part of a big Fourth of July celebration the new mall owners had put together to lure people to shop over the long weekend rather than follow the more traditional pursuits of baseball and picnics. The benefit for Playhouse Southwest, at forty dollars a pop, looked as if it was going to make outrageous money. The fair would occupy the open-air top level of the mall garage. I'd taken the health department's required course on the subject of serving food away from one's established place of business, which was all I ever did anyway. Now all I had to do was prepare all the food.

I checked my watch: Wednesday, July 1, just before four in the afternoon. Claire's death would surely be on the local news tonight and in the papers tomorrow. And speaking of journalism, nothing in this world would convince me that Frances Markasian was at the Mignon Cosmetics banquet for her health. Or for her beauty, for that matter. So what had she been looking for? I resolved to get going on the food. Then I'd give Tom another buzz.

I looked over the menu I'd planned for the opening day of the fair: baby back ribs with homemade barbecue sauce, steamed sugar snap peas with fresh strawberries vinaigrette,

Vanilla-Frosted
Fudge Cookies

¾ cup all-purpose flour
½ cup unsweetened cocoa powder
1 teaspoon baking powder
¼ teaspoon salt
¼ cup canola oil
1 cup sugar
1½ teaspoons vanilla extract
4 egg whites, unbeaten
2 cups confectioners' sugar
2–3 tablespoons skim milk,
    approximately
additional unsweetened cocoa powder

Preheat the oven to 350°. Spray a large nonstick cookie sheet with vegetable oil spray.

Sift the flour, cocoa, baking powder, and salt together; set aside. Mix together the oil, sugar, 1 teaspoon of the vanilla, and the egg whites until well combined. Stir in the flour mixture. Chill one hour. Using a ½-tablespoon measure, scoop the dough onto the cookie sheet, leaving 2 inches between cookies. Bake for 8 to 10 minutes or until the cookies are puffed and cooked through. Do not overcook.

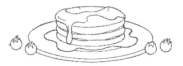

Transfer the cookies to a rack and cool completely. Mix together the confectioners' sugar, skim milk, and remaining ½ teaspoon vanilla until pasty. Add skim milk if necessary. Spread a small amount of vanilla frosting on each cookie. Put the cookies back on the rack, dust lightly with cocoa powder, and allow the frosting to dry.

Makes 4 dozen cookies

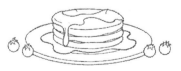

homemade bread, and vanilla-frosted fudge cookies. The barbecue sauce needed to simmer for hours before being slathered over the ribs. People can't resist spare ribs, I reflected as thin, fragrant slices of onion fell from my knife. Ribs smelled great when they were cooking, and, like potato chips, one was never enough. When I added the onion to the simmering vinegar, tomato, and lemon of the sauce, a delectable scent perfumed my kitchen, and I began to relax. Needless to say, my newfound peace was interrupted by a jangling phone.

"You never tell me a damn thing," Frances Markasian barked into the receiver. "I don't know why you think we're friends. I *especially* can't understand why I helped you with those damned heavy boxes! Women can get hernias, you know." I heard the striking of a match in the background, then a noisy inhalation. "You knew what went down at the mall this morning. And I had to wait to hear from the sheriff's department's public information office! The hell with you!" I could imagine Frances sitting at the edge of her ragged canvas-covered swivel chair next to her paper-strewn desk, chugging Jolt cola and working her way through the second of her three daily packs of cigarettes. Frances believed if she acted enough like a hotshot journalist, maybe

92

she'd become one.

"The hell with me? That's what you're call-ing to tell me? You're always saying," I said as I stirred the aromatic sauce, "that you're the journalist and I'm the cook. What did you want me to tell you?"

"Let's start with what you know about Claire Satterfield. Were you in the garage when she was hit?"

I cradled the phone against my shoulder and slid the heavy, meaty slabs of pork into the oven. "C'mon, Frances, I'm already married to a cop. The last thing I need is for *you* to start acting like one."

She took a drag and blew into the phone. "Uh-huh. And did you know your boarder-assistant guy, Julian Teller, was only the *latest* in Ms. Satterfield's list of male conquests?"

"No, I didn't." And I certainly hoped Julian didn't either. On an ordinary day I would have enjoyed sparring with Frances. Sometimes she was as good a source of information as Marla. But today was not ordinary, and I found her questions and insinuations annoying in the ex-treme. "Who told you Claire had other male conquests?"

"May I please speak to Julian?" Frances in-quired sweetly.

"He's in the hospital. He went into shock when he heard about Claire. Some people,"

I added harshly, "have *normal* human emotions in response to death."

"Oh, damn!" she exclaimed. "I'm going to have to clean up my desk, because it looks as if my heart just bled all over it. So what's Investigator Schulz saying about the" — she cleared her throat — "accident? Anything quotable?"

"Why don't you call the sheriff's department and find out? Then maybe you can tell Investigator Schulz why you were down at the Mignon banquet today. Incognito. All dressed up. Exactly what rumors have you heard about the department store?"

"Cut the tripe, caterer. I'm on assignment, which should be obvious to you, even though it's been a lot of years since you did that major in psychology. You think it was easy zipping myself into that dress? And the so-called banquet was like some kind of punishment. Diet food makes me gag. I have to eat too much of it, and that makes me feel like a bear foraging for winter. How many tomatoes can one individual consume? But the brownies were terrific." She chuckled. Like we were such good pals. Like she had told me everything she knew and now I was supposed to do the same for her.

I took a deep breath. "You know, Frances, you *did* ask me if I knew about the department store's problems. Since I assume you mean Prince & Grogan, and since I was working for their Mignon people today, I'd like to know what kind of problems would bring you down to the mall all the way from Aspen Meadow. That's all."

"Uh-huh. Miss Nosy Caterer. A sales associate at Prince & Grogan gets splattered all over the parking lot and you ask me what kind of problems the department store is having."

"Don't talk like that about Claire. It's disgusting."

"Oh-ho! So it's *Claire* now. You did know her. In fact, you were there in the garage when someone smacked into her. Yes? Spill all, Goldy."

"Tell me why you were at the banquet in disguise. What's the problem with the department store?"

Frances took another drag and seemed to consider. "Let me get my pen."

Doggone it. "No, Frances, don't act as if we can trade information, for heaven's sake," I said to empty air. If anything got into the newspaper, Tom was going to be a tad upset.

Frances came back to the phone and rustled her materials about. "You knew the dead girl," she prompted.

"You already know she was Julian Teller's girlfriend," I replied impatiently. "And you also know I can't talk to you until Tom —"

"Ah-*ha.* 'Wife of homicide investigator asks newspaper about department store scandals. Declines comment on witnessing murder of store employee.' Your husband the investigator is gonna love it."

"What do you mean, *murder?* So help me —"

"Do you know anything about those demonstrators?" she demanded.

"Of course I don't," I replied, struggling to sound calm. Frances had the annoying ability to make me feel constantly off balance.

"Did they get in the way of the catering? Were they near the area where the girl was hit? Or can't you talk about that either?"

"What makes you think that —" I waved my hand in the empty kitchen, unable even to articulate the thought.

"What makes me think that Claire was run down?" she finished.

"Yes."

"Things I've heard."

"Gosh, Frances, more rumors? Maybe I should have Tom come over and talk to you."

"Great idea. We could have lunch and chat about the Bill of Rights. You could cook. That is, if you didn't throw vegetables around beforehand."

"Frances, don't."

"The way I heard it, the fellow you threw

the red peppers on was an activist by the name of Shaman Krill."

"Why, did he talk to you? All he did was yell at me."

"That name, Shaman Krill," she said thoughtfully. "Think it's short for something? Maybe it's an alias. We're talking about a real short guy here? Dark curly hair pulled back in a ponytail? Gold earring? Sort of a cross between a leprechaun and a terrorist? Think he was one of Claire's boyfriends? How long had Satterfield been going with this Julian guy?"

"How do you know Claire was involved with other men?" I countered. "Why did you say Julian was the latest in her batch of conquests?"

"First you tell me something, Goldy. Did you ever get something for nothing? Listen — I'll come visit you at the food fair, okay? Maybe then you'll be ready to have a *real* chat."

Before I could retort, she hung up. She wasn't going to share anything she knew with me until I gave her information. And if I did that, I could just imagine the wrath of Investigator Tom Schulz. Still, he'd be interested to hear about bullying activist Shaman Krill, if he hadn't already. Maybe you had to have a weird name to get into Spare the Hares. I slowly swished the spoon through the pot of dark barbecue sauce. There were two things Frances had been digging for: Had I known Claire was involved with other men? And who was Shaman Krill? I wondered if the two questions were related.

But that was speculation. I returned to my culinary duties to chop, boil, and beat my frustration away. I gathered cocoa powder, flour, sugar, and egg whites, and got out the recipe for the fudge cookies. The dark, delicious cookies had been one of two great inventions in my search for a lowfat chocolate torte. The other had been a lowfat chocolate soufflé that had worked not in the oven but on top of the stove. I sifted the cocoa, flour, baking powder, and salt and beat egg whites, then stirred oil, sugar, and vanilla. After combining all the ingredients, I put the cookie batter away to chill. I had just retrieved the ingredients for icing when the doorbell rang. Oh good, I thought: Marla. Finally.

I looked through the peephole prepared to see my big-bodied, big-hearted friend triumphantly holding up the bags of gourmet goodies she always brought to ease tense or troubling situations. But anticipatory delight quickly froze to dread. The Jerk's distorted mug grinned broadly into the peephole's circular eye.

"Let me in, Goldy," he bellowed. "I have to talk to you!"

Fear opened a hollow in my stomach. In the years since the divorce, my ex-husband had rarely demanded to talk to me. Looking for Arch, he either barged in angrily — pre-security system — or waited sullenly for our son on the doorstep. But this afternoon Arch was doing tie-dying with Todd. I looked out at John Richard, trying to decide what to do. He drew back in a dramatic gesture from the door and held his arms out. He was wearing Bermuda shorts, Polo shirt, Top-Siders without socks — the very portrait of a rich guy.

"I've got news," he shouted, pressing his face in again at the peephole. "Bad news! You want to hear it or not?" He added snidely, "It concerns somebody you care about a lot!"

I really did not want to see him. The day had been awful enough. And yet here he was, doing a typical power-trip, teasing with the possibility of bad news. I hesitated. The security system was disarmed. I could go out on the porch to talk to him. All I had to do was unlock the dead bolt and walk out the door. But when I started to fumble with the bolt, the phone rang in the kitchen. Darn it all, anyway. I dashed for the kitchen.

"Goldilocks' Catering —" I began breathlessly. The Jerk was banging on the front door.

99

There was a smart *thwack* of wood against metal. I heard the Jerk curse loudly. "Goldilocks' Catering," I repeated, "Where Everything —"

"It's me," Tom interrupted. "I'm at the hospital."

"Boo!" said John Richard Korman as he walked up behind me. His breath smelled of whiskey. I shrieked and dropped the phone.

"Who's that?" said Tom. Coming from the dropped phone, his voice was distant but clearly alarmed. "Goldy? Are you there?"

I stared furiously at my ex-husband, who gave me a wide-eyed mocking leer in return. Involuntarily, I glanced around for my wooden knifeblock. John Richard followed my gaze and wagged one finger at me. He moved in the direction of the knifeblock, scooped it up, and cradled it and its protruding black handles as he moved into the dining room. Goose bumps pimpled my arms. By the time John Richard walked empty-handed back into the kitchen, I'd managed to pick up the dangling receiver. "It's . . . John Richard, and Arch isn't home, but John Richard says that there's bad —"

"For crying out loud, Goldy, what the hell is he doing there?" Tom hollered. "Get him out! Now!"

I closed my eyes so I wouldn't see the Jerk's

100

furious expression. "Tell me how Julian is," I said firmly into the receiver. "Then I will."

"I'm not calling about Julian —" Tom began.

"Hey, Gol-dy-y!" the Jerk said calmly. Nastily. "He's not calling about Juli-a-n. He's at the hospital and he's calling about somebody *else*."

"This is bad news —" Tom began again.

John Richard grabbed the receiver out of my hand and slammed it down in its cradle. I closed my fists and glared at him.

"Listen to me, goddammit!" Dr. John Richard Korman shouted in my face. "Marla's had a heart attack!"

5

"A what?"

"Are you deaf?" He lowered his voice, sat down at the kitchen table, and assumed his all-knowing tone. The mood-switch was both predictable and frightening. "She was trying to jog her lard-assed self around the lake. She got home, didn't feel well, and called her g.p. He hadn't seen her in five years, of course, so when she described her symptoms, he sent in some paramedics, and they called for the Flight-for-Life copter." The phone on the counter rang again. The muscles in John Richard's face locked in anger. I knew the look. Now he was just a time bomb. He sat at the kitchen table and said too calmly, "I would like to talk to you without interruption."

My throat constricted with the old fear. My palms itched to answer the insistent rings. But I knew better than to defy the Jerk. As the phone continued to ring, John Richard made no move to answer it. He crossed his legs. Ever smooth, ever urbane. But I was watching. He said, "You won't get in to see her without me."

102

"That's not true," I said, trying to sound unruffled. "Look, you've been drinking." It didn't take much to set John Richard off. Two ounces of scotch was enough to ignite him for at least four hours. "Why don't you just —"

"Are you interested in Marla or not?" His eyes blazed and he tightened the formidable muscles in his arms. "I mean, I *thought* she was your best friend."

The phone rang and rang. I didn't take my eyes off John Richard. "Have you seen her?"

"No, no, I was waiting to take *you* down," he said with mock sweetness. John Richard leaned forward. A hard pain knotted in my chest. "Whether you like it or not, Miss Piss, as an ex-husband, I *am* a relative." The phone shrilled. Tears pricked my eyes. I hated to be so paralyzed with fear. *Marla. Forty-five years old. A heart attack.* The Jerk, unheeding, talked. "You, as the friend who fed her all the cholesterol-filled crap that blocked her arteries, are *not* a relative. Friends might not be able to get into the Coronary Care Unit whenever they want. Relatives *can.* Are you with me so far? So if you want to see Marla at the hospital, *I'm* going to have to go in with you. Am I getting through to you?"

Any moment, I thought. Any moment and this man who worked out with the fanaticism of an Olympic athlete could take hold of one of my wrists and shatter it against the table with such force that I wouldn't be able to knead bread for a year. I kept my eyes on his maniacally composed face and picked up the receiver. "I'm okay," I said without my customary greeting. On the other end, Tom noisily let out air, a sound somewhere between a sigh and a groan. "Thanks for calling back, Tom. He's just leaving."

"Just leaving?" Tom yelled. "You mean he's still there? I'm staying on this phone until he's out of that house and that door is locked and bolted. Turn that security system back on. If you can't do that, get out. Understand? Goldy? You listening? I can get the 911 operator to call your neighbor. Have a department car there in ten minutes."

I turned to my ex-husband. "Please go," I said firmly. "Now. He's going to send in the authorities. They'll be here in ten minutes."

Dr. John Richard Korman leapt to his feet, grabbed the box of cocoa I'd used for the cookies and flung it against the wall. I screamed as brown powder exploded everywhere. John Richard dusted his hands and gave me a look: *Now why did you make that necessary?*

"Get out," I said evenly. "Leave. Nine and a half minutes, and you're in a lot of trouble." He'd thrown something because he was thwarted. I wouldn't go to the hospital with him, and I had paid.

The Jerk assumed an attitude of nonchalance and shrugged. Then, without another word, he withdrew from the kitchen and sauntered his Bermuda-shorted self through the front door. I followed, pressed the bolt into place and armed the system, then ran back to the phone.

"Miss G.?" I broke out in a sweat from the relief of hearing Tom's old term of endearment. "Will you please talk to me?"

"He's gone," I said breathlessly. "Can you tell me where, I mean, how long ago did she . . . how is she?" I remembered all too vividly Marla's sad history, that her father had died from a heart attack when she was very young.

"She's okay. In the Coronary Care Unit at Southwest Hospital. She had a mild heart attack this morning either before or after jogging around Aspen Meadow Lake. Since when is she a jogger?"

"Since never," I replied angrily, "and she's on some weird lemon-and-rice diet —"

"Not anymore, she isn't. You coming down here or what? I probably won't be able to stay. The investigation of the death over in the mall garage is getting under way."

I replied that I was on my way and that he shouldn't wait for me. I scribbled a note to Arch: *Back by dinner.* How was I going to tell Arch what had happened to Julian or Marla? He adored them both. Stepping out the back door, I glanced around to make sure the Jerk wasn't lurking in the bushes. That would have been typical of him. I also checked the van's rear area. It was empty. I locked the doors, gunned the engine, and let the speedometer needle quiver past seventy as I raced back to Denver. I wished I didn't know as much as I did about the statistics of heart disease running in families.

My best-friendship with Marla had blossomed out of the bitterness of being divorced from the same horrid man. I shook my head and thought of the cloud of brown cocoa powder erupting as it hit the wall. To get emotional control over his cruelty, Marla and I alternately reviled and ridiculed John Richard. But through the years, the relationship between Marla and me had deepened beyond our mutual crisis. We'd formed a discussion group called Amour Anonymous, for women addicted to their relationships. I zipped past Westside Mall and headed for the parking lot at Southwest Hospital.

Our Amour Anonymous meetings had been alternately heartfelt and hilarious. And when the group petered out, as those kinds of groups tend to do, Marla and I remained steadfast to each other with daily phone calls and long talks over shared meals. Moreover, Marla's generosity with her considerable wealth meant not only that she was one of my best clients, but that she also referred me to all her rich friends. The people in Marla's address book had provided an endless stream of assignments for Goldilocks' Catering, including Babs Braithwaite of the upcoming Independence Day party.

My hands clutched the steering wheel. If the Jerk was right and they wouldn't admit me to the CCU, I was going to have to come up with some way to talk my way in. Just thinking of John Richard made my flesh crawl. How dare he break into my house and blame my cooking for what had happened to Marla? Of course, that kind of behavior was nothing new for him. John Richard Korman, whose mother had been a hard-core alcoholic, frequently had just enough whiskey to release the enraged demon that lived inside.

But there was some truth in what he said. Marla was indeed a large-bodied woman. She ate with gusto, then dieted remorsefully, never for very long or to much effect. Eventually she always resumed her passionate affair with chocolate chip cookies and cream-filled cakes. But what worried me more than her erratic eating habits was her phobia concerning doctors and hospitals. I wasn't surprised to hear that she hadn't seen her general practitioner for years.

I pulled the van into the hospital lot. Southwest Hospital was a subsidiary of a Denver chain of medical facilities. When Westside Mall was in the process of being refurbished, fund-raising and construction began on the new hospital. There was another irony: For all her disdain for doctors, Marla had been one of the most generous donors to Southwest Hospital's building fund.

Inside the hospital, I followed yellow-painted footprints and then blue ones until I came to the automatic doors of the Coronary Care Unit entrance on the fourth floor. A red-haired receptionist wrinkled her brow at me.

"Name of patient?"

I tried to look both innocent and deeply bereaved. "Marla Korman," I replied.

"She can see visitors only the first ten minutes of each hour, and that's just past. You'll have to wait an hour."

I said quickly, "She's my sister. Surely I can see her?"

"And you are . . ."

"Goldy Korman."

She consulted a clipboard, then gave me a smug smile. "Is that so? When we asked her about next of kin, she didn't list you."

108

"She'd just had a heart attack," I said with an enormous effort at *long-suffering* bereavement. "What do you expect? I really need to see her. I'm worried sick."

"I'll have to see some ID."

Think. I rummaged through my purse and brought out my sorry-looking fake-leather wallet with its wad of credit card receipts and expired grocery coupons.

"ID?" the receptionist repeated serenely.

Wildly, I wondered how I'd talk myself out of this one. Then I had an inspiration. Well, of course. My fingers deftly pulled out a dog-eared card. Good old Uncle Sam! I handed the nurse my old Social Security card.

"Goldy Korman," she read, then shot me a suspicious look. "Don't you have a driver's license or something?"

I bristled. "If my sister dies while you're doing the Nazi documentation routine, you'll never work in a hospital in this state again."

The receptionist snapped the Social Security card with my old married name onto her clipboard and said to wait, she'd be right back. Well, excuse me, after notifying the federal government of the name change to go with my social security number, I had tried to get a new card. I had called the Social Security Administration numerous times after my divorce, when I'd resumed my maiden name.

109

Their line was always busy. Then I'd called them thirty more times this spring, five years after the divorce, when I remarried and assumed the surname Schulz. Again I'd written to them about the name change. All I wanted was a new card. The line was still busy. If people died listening to that bureaucracy's busy signal, did their survivors still get benefits?

The red-haired receptionist swished back out. Apparently my old ID had passed muster, because she led me wordlessly through the double doors of the CCU. Curtained cubicles lined two walls, with a nurses' station at the center. I tried desperately to summon inner fortitude. Marla would need all the positive thoughts I could send her way. I was handed over to a nurse, who motioned me forward.

On a bed at the end of the row of cubicles, Marla seemed to be asleep. Wires and tubes appeared to be attached to every extremity. Monitors clustered around her.

"Ten minutes," said the nurse firmly. "Don't excite her."

I took Marla's hand, trying not to brush the IV attached to it. She didn't move. Her complexion was its normal peaches-and-cream color, but her frizzy brown hair, usually held in gold and silver barrettes, was matted against the pillow beneath her head.

I rubbed her hand gently.

Her eyes opened in slits. It took her a moment to focus. Then, softly, she groaned. To my delight her plump hand gave mine the slightest squeeze.

"Don't exert yourself," I whispered. "Everything's going to be fine."

She moaned again, then whispered fiercely, "I am perfectly okay, if I could just convince these idiots of that fact."

I ignored this. "You're going to be just fine. By the way, in case anybody asks, I'm your sister."

She appeared puzzled, then said, "I'm trying to tell you, there's been some mistake. I had *indigestion*. That's *all*." Denial, I knew, is common among heart attack victims, so I said nothing. "Goldy," she exclaimed, "don't you believe me? This whole thing is a misunderstanding. I woke up feeling just a little under the weather, and you know how damn hot it's been." She twisted in the bed, trying to get comfortable. "So I went for a jog around the lake. I started to feel much better. Nice and cool. Refreshed. Of course, I wasn't going very fast. I was even thinking you and I could go out for lunch if you weren't busy. And then I remembered you were doing that cosmetics lunch, which I had decided to skip because I felt so fat."

"It's okay," I said soothingly. "Please, don't upset yourself."

"Don't act as if I'm *dying*, okay?" Her pretty face contorted with anger. Once more she tried to heave herself up but decided against it, and sagged back against the pillow. "It doesn't help. You know what my worst fear was when I heard the siren bringing those damn medics? That they would check my driver's license. They'd know the weight I put down there was a lie. All these years, whenever I hear a siren, that's what I think. I could just imagine some cop hollering, 'Leave your vehicle and get on these portable scales! Marla Korman, you're under arrest!'"

"Marla —"

"So let me finish telling you what happened. Before the paramedics came. I drove home real slowly from the lake. But at home I started to feel bad again — cold sweat, you know, like the flu. So I took aspirin and Mylanta, lots of both, and then I took a shower." Her voice collapsed into a sigh. "Finally I called Dr. Hodges and he about had a conniption fit, probably because I hadn't called him in ages. The man is a fanatic. He jumped to the conclusion that something was wrong. Those paramedics came roaring over, and before you knew it I was in this damn helicopter!" Tears slid down her cheeks. "I kept trying to tell them, I'm just *woozy*. I mean, how would you feel if you had your eardrums breaking with the *whump whump* sound of rotary blades?" The effort of talking seemed to exhaust her, but she plowed on. "And the sight of paramedics staring down at you? 'Excuse me, ma'am, *whump whump* you've *whump whump* had a heart attack'? I said, 'Oh yeah? What's that I hear beating?' "

"Marla. Please."

She wagged a finger absent of her customary flashing rings. "If they don't let me out of here, they've seen their last donation from me, I can tell you that. That's what I told the ER doc when I got here. He *completely* ignored me. 'Look me up on your list of benefactors!' I shouted at him. The guy acted deaf! I said, 'Better ask your superiors how much Marla Korman gave this hospital last year! You don't want to be responsible when those donations dry up!' "

"Marla, for crying out loud. There must be ways they can tell whether you've had a heart attack. There's your EKG —"

Her eyes closed. "It's a mistake, Goldy. Leave it to the medical profession to screw things up. What *is* going to give me a heart attack is thinking about all the piles of dough I've given this hospital."

"But you know it's better to be cautious —"

I started to protest, but she would have none of it and shook her head. The CCU nurse signaled my ten minutes were up. Reluctantly, I released Marla's hand and checked her chart. Dr. Lyle Gordon, cardiologist, and I were going to have a chat. After a quick kiss on Marla's plump cheek, I backed away from the cubicle.

When I returned to the reception desk and asked where I could find Dr. Gordon, the red-haired woman glowered, then shrugged. Very calmly, I told her I wanted to have Dr. Gordon paged. *Now,* please. Twenty minutes later, a chunky fellow wearing thick glasses and a white lab coat pushed through the doors of the CCU waiting room. Lyle Gordon had a high premature fluff of gray hair that did not conceal a bald spot.

"Don't I know you?" he asked, squinting at me. "Aren't you . . . or weren't you . . . married to — ?"

I tried to look horrified at the idea. Dr. Gordon scowled suspiciously. "I'm Marla Korman's sister," I told him. "Could we talk?"

He led the way and we sat in a corner grouping of uncomfortable beige sofas.

"Okay, does your mother know about this yet?" he began.

I had a quick image not of Marla's mother, but of my own mother, Mildred Hollingwood Bear. Perhaps she would be at an Episcopal

Church Women's luncheon, or a New Jersey garden club brunch, when she was told that her daughter, the divorced-but-remarried caterer, had been arrested for impersonating the sister of her ex-husband's other ex-wife . . .

"Well, no —"

"Your sister said your mother was in Europe and that finding her would be tough," Dr. Gordon said politely, nudging his glasses up his nose with his forefinger. "Father deceased by heart attack at the age of forty-eight. Will you be able to find your mother?"

"Er, probably." *Maybe, perhaps, hopefully,* I added mentally. I imagined a lie detector needle etching out mountains and valleys of truth and deception.

"Any other family history of heart disease?"

"Not that I know of."

Dr. Gordon adjusted his glasses again and succeeded in smearing his fingerprints on their thick lenses. "Your sister's had a mild heart attack. She's only forty-five. And unfortunately, she's —"

"She seems to think she *hasn't* had a heart attack."

"Excuse me. Her first EKG indicated she was having extra heartbeats, one of the warning signals. We also saw her STs were way up —"

"STs?"

115

He sighed. "A portion of the electrocardio-
gram that shows the recovery of the heart between contractions is abnormal. If the STs are
up, a person's having a heart attack, okay?
The paramedics called in the copter, put her
on oxygen, put nitroglycerin under her
tongue. It's a blood vessel dilator."

"Yes . . . I do know about nitroglycerin."
I also knew that if the vessels could be dilated
close enough to the beginning of an attack,
blood could get to the heart and prevent damage, sometimes even abort the attack. I said
tentatively, "Maybe —"

"We think that the nitroglycerin actually
thwarted a more severe attack. Her blood tests
have come back, her enzymes are up, so no
matter what she says now, she *was* having a
heart attack. Do you believe me?"

Blood rang in my ears. I felt despair closing
in and weakness taking over. "Yeah, sure. Just
. . . could you tell me if she's going to be
all right? What's next?"

"She's scheduled for an angiogram first
thing tomorrow morning. It depends on what
that tells us about blockage. If an artery is
badly blocked, we'll probably schedule an
atherectomy for the afternoon. Do you know
what that is?"

I said dully, "Roto-rooter through the arteries." But not for Marla. Please, not for my

best friend. I tried not to think about catheters.

Gordon quirked his gray eyebrows at me, then continued: "Has she been under the care of a physician? She gave the name of a general practitioner in Aspen Meadow. We called him: He said he hadn't seen her in five years. That's why her phone call to him came as such a warning signal."

"Marla hates doctors."

"She claims she's a hospital benefactor."

"My sister is superstitious, Dr. Gordon. She thinks if she gives a lot of money to a hospital, she'll never actually have to spend any time in one."

"And she's not married."

It was sort of a question. If an unknown sister turns up, a spouse may be next. "Not married," I said curtly.

"Well, then, I need to tell you this. As I said before, her blood tests show she's had what looks like a very minor heart attack. If all goes well tomorrow, and barring any complications, I think we'll be able to discharge her in three or four days. If the attack had been more severe, we would have to keep her in the hospital for a week or more. But when she does go home, she's going to have to have care."

"No sweat. My sister has lots of — er — *we* have lots of money. I'll get a private nurse.

Just tell me what her prognosis is."

"She needs to change her lifestyle. Her cholesterol was at 340. That *must* be reduced. Then she has a good chance. We've got nutrition people who can help her. There's a cardiac rehab program here at the hospital that she can get into. If she's so inclined, that is. And she better become so inclined if she values her life." His tone was grim.

"Okay. Thanks. Can I see her again now?"

"Not for long. Are there any other relatives I should know about?"

Without missing a beat, I replied, "Our nephew might be in. His name is Julian Teller."

"Is this your son?"

"No, the son of . . . another sister. Julian is nineteen. Actually, he's here in the hospital. I think."

"Looking for his aunt?"

"No, being treated. Could you check for me? Please? It's so much easier for a doctor to get information than the rest of us peons."

Dr. Gordon disappeared for a few moments, then sat back heavily on the beige cushions. "Julian Teller was treated for shock and released about an hour ago. Shock brought on by hearing about his aunt Marla?"

"No, something else. Another family tragedy."

The doctor gave me a strained, sympathetic smile. "Your family is having quite a day, Ms. Korman." He shifted impatiently in the chair. *Other patients are waiting,* his movement said. "It would be good for your sister if you could visit as much as possible. Good vibes, touchy-feely, all that helps."

"Don't worry, I'll be here every day." I wrote my phone number on a piece of paper. "Please call me if anything unusual develops with her situation. Will you be checking on her every day?"

He wrinkled his face in incredulity. "Of course." He looked at me unblinkingly through his spectacles that were so thick they reminded me of old Coke bottle bottoms. "She may get very depressed. It's a common response to heart attack. Even if we can bring her back to health, she's going to need you to give her courage and support. Are you going to be able to help with that?"

It was my turn to give him an incredulous look. I pressed my lips together and nodded.

6

The second time I saw Marla that afternoon she slept through the whole ten minutes of my visit. Her chest rose and fell weakly inside the drab blue hospital gown that was nothing like her customary flamboyant outfits. I closed her hand lightly so as not to disturb her. Her lips, ordinarily lush with lipstick, were dry and cracked, and her breathing seemed uneven. I had seen a young woman dead that morning. Now more than anything I wanted to hold on to this friend who was closer to me than any sister could have been.

I resolved to call our church as soon as I got home. Marla was both popular and active at St. Luke's. She chaired the annual Episcopal Church Women's jewelry raffle and animated the monthly vestry meetings with her irrepressible brassiness and wit. If I didn't let the parish know what was going on, I'd be the recipient of some very unchristian phone calls. I also needed to find out about arranging for a private nurse to come in as soon as the hospital discharged Marla.

I tried to make more mental lists but ended up driving home in a stupor. When the tires crunched over the gravel driveway, I was thankful to see that Tom had squeezed his Chrysler into our detached garage next to Julian's Range Rover. Arch bounded in my direction as soon as I came through the security system. He was sporting the result of his afternoon of tie-dying: a T-shirt big enough for a quarterback and a pair of knee-length shorts streaked with vivid orange and purple splotches. I didn't care what he looked like. I swept him into my arms and twirled him around in a circle. When, breathless, I let go of him, he stepped back, astonished.

"Hey, Mom! Get real! What's going on? I mean, what's happening?" He pushed his glasses up his nose and eyed me. From his puzzled but happy response, I guessed Tom had not yet told Arch about the events of the morning. "Where've you been?" he continued suspiciously. "Tom brought Julian home but he's lying down. Everybody around here is out of it. But look." He stepped back dramatically and held out his thin arms. "Is my outfit cool or what?" A proud smile broke out over Arch's freckled face as he waited for my assessment. I was not about to tell this just-turned-thirteen-year-old that the spotted, too-large outfit hung from his bony shoulders and small torso like something salvaged from a large person's clothesline.

"It is cool," I agreed emphatically. "Really. You look absolutely, positively great."

He turned his mouth down in an exaggerated frown. "Mom? You're not tripped out or anything, are you?"

"Do you know what being tripped out means?"

Arch scratched his belly under the shirt. "Forgetful? That's what they used to say, 'I can't remember anything, man, I was tripped out —' "

"Look, I'm fine. I'm only in my thirties, remember, and I was just a kid during the period you're talking about. Where's Tom?"

"Cooking. I told him to fix something groovy from the sixties and he said the only groovy food he knew was hash brownies. That's disgusting! How can you put corned beef hash in brownies?"

It was going to be a tiresome hobby. When I entered the kitchen, Tom was bent so intently over a recipe that I repressed the greeting on my lips. The walls had been cleaned of the cocoa powder thrown by the Jerk, and lump crabmeat glistened invitingly on the countertop next to a tall green bottle of white wine. A seasoned crêpier waited next to a wide sauté pan, where butter for a sauce sizzled in a slow, circuitous melt. Tom relished cooking even more than gardening. I happily let him do both. I'd take crêpes stuffed with crabmeat in white wine sauce any day. Especially when it was made by somebody else.

As I watched, Tom leaned over the crabmeat and methodically nabbed and tossed bits of shell and cartilage. I felt a surge of pleasure. It was not only that I now lived in a household where people vied to prepare the food. Nor was it, because of the day's events, that I'd developed a sudden appreciation for life. This unsettling joy surfaced because I still didn't know why I'd been so reluctant to marry the man who now stood in what used to be my domain and was now *our* kitchen.

I watched the butter dissolve into a golden pool. Of course, my hesitancy stemmed from all that bad history of my first marriage. After I'd left the Jerk I'd come to relish those years of single motherhood and solitude. Except for the celibacy, which I kept telling myself I'd get used to, being single constituted the perfect life for me, I'd decided. Until Tom.

Nevertheless, transition from my fiercely maintained aloneness to daily companionship did have its glitches. There had been the financial questions. Years ago, the divorce settlement from Dr. John Richard Korman had paid for the expensive retrofit of my kitchen for commercial food service, and I couldn't leave it and still maintain my business. So Tom had moved in with Arch, Julian, and me, and found a renter for his cabin in a remote mountain area. He insisted on putting the rent money into a vacation fund for the four of us. Of course, as a self-employed woman with the only catering business in town, I'd forgotten what the word *vacation* meant.

These and other material aspects we'd been able to work out fairly well. Our biggest problem was anxiety. Tom worried about me and I returned the favor. Tom had seen some of the damage done by John Richard Korman before our split. He knew my left thumb didn't bend properly because John Richard had broken it in three places with a hammer. Tom had examined the hutch glass I'd never replaced after John Richard had shattered it in one of his rampages, and the buffet permanently dented from the Jerk's repeated kicking when I'd been hiding behind it. After Tom moved in, one of his first acts was to replace the hutch glass and sand and refinish the buffet's dents.

My apprehension over the dangers of his job were legion. Whenever I heard over the radio of a shooting, whenever a midnight phone call brought him out of our warm bed, whenever that midnight phone call meant that before he left he was cinching the Velcro bands around his white bulletproof vest, my heart ached with fear. My anxiety had not been eased when a murderer had kidnapped Tom for four days this spring, just as we were about to be married. He scoffed and said that had been a bizarre event. He hadn't even believed it himself.

Nor did Tom and I quite know how to talk to each other about our work. Tom claimed he enjoyed discussing investigations with me as long as I wouldn't get upset. Or worse, tell anybody what he or I had uncovered. To me, Tom always appeared either in control: when he was surrounded by his team in an investigation, or in relaxed good humor, when we were together and he was telling me about bloodstain patterns or check-kiting. I, on the other hand, did not relish rehashing the trials of cooking for, serving to, and cleaning up after the rich and shameless. Occasionally I would regale him with stories about the Thai guest at a reception for two hundred who'd insisted on giving me his recipe for whole baked fish — in Thai, or about the drunk Polo Club host who fell off his horse before eating one bite of the vegetarian shish kebabs.

Reflecting on all this, I'd failed to notice that Tom had stopped cooking and was staring at the cupboard above the kitchen counter, his face twisted with pain.

"Tom! What is it?"

Startled, he dropped the shell bits he was holding. I apologized and helped him wipe them off the floor. By the time he straightened up, he had assumed his normal end-of-the-day relaxed look. Still, I was taken aback. In the two months that we'd been married, I'd never seen him look agonized. Until now. Despite his disclaimers to the contrary, the job did take its toll, after all.

He forced a wide grin. "Hey there, Miss G."

"What's wrong?"

"No more than usual." He rinsed his hands and dried them on a dish towel. "Julian's okay, he just needs to rest. I think he's asleep. Did you get in to see Marla?"

I hugged him briefly and murmured that I had. Which reminded me. I phoned the St. Luke's answering machine and left a brief message about Marla's condition, then left another message for a woman in the parish who had once hired a private nurse. Did she have any recommendations? I asked her tape. Then I washed my hands and glanced at the recipe before retrieving some fresh garlic. Alas, the Jerk had carried off my knives somewhere.

"Marla was very angry. Claimed she hadn't had a heart attack," I commented over my shoulder as I looked around the dining room for my knifeblock. This seldom-used space was a monument to my former life as a doctor's wife. It looked like a furniture store. I'd bought the solid cherry buffet, hutch, and dining room suite right after my first wedding. Then I'd feverishly crocheted an enormous tablecloth and undertaken the tiresome needlepointing of floral covers for the chair seats. I should have been taking a karate class. Better yet, shooting lessons. I hefted up the knifeblock from the table and brought it back to the kitchen.

"I'm guessing Marla will be home at the beginning of next week," I told Tom as I sniffed a clove of garlic. The garlic was fresh and juicy; its pungent smell filled the air. I told Tom what the cardiologist had told me about Marla's condition and her upcoming angiogram and potential atherectomy. "I'm going to go in and see her every day," I added defiantly as I minced. But of course Tom wouldn't be jealous if I made a daily visit to a friend. I shook my head and reached for another clove of garlic. Old reactions died harder than I thought.

Tom turned back to his recipe card and abruptly changed the subject. "How did Korman get through the security system?"

"Look, it was a fluke . . . I was in the middle of undoing the dead bolt, and the phone rang, and he hollered that there was some bad news . . . and before I knew it, he was right beside me . . . I just wasn't careful."

"Are you all right?" He glanced up from the recipe card, his mouth in a thin line.

When I said I was, he frowned disbelievingly.

"Sorry," I amended, "it won't happen again." And there went my summer breeze through the unsecured upstairs windows, I thought. "What did the hospital say about Julian? Is there any special treatment?"

He dropped ingredients into the melted butter. The delectable scent of crabmeat and garlic rose from the pan. "He just needs to rest. We probably shouldn't talk about the accident around him. Not just yet, anyway, although we'll have to eventually." He reached for a wooden spoon and stirred in flour to make a roux.

"Why not talk to him about it? And why will you have to eventually?"

Tom exhaled deeply. "Goldy, he looked god-awful coming home from the hospital. I just don't want to upset him anymore. He cried off and on all the way up the interstate. I don't think I've ever seen that kid in tears."

"Maybe if he talks about it he'll feel better."

Tom stopped stirring and gave me a half-grin. "Well, Miss Psych Major, I know that's true. But we've got a lot of unknowns right now, and I'm not sure Julian should hear about them just yet."

"Unknowns?"

He whisked broth into the sauce, set it to simmer, and then trundled over to the walk-in refrigerator. A moment later he emerged with two bottles of carbonated apple cider, one of Arch's favorites. He opened a bottle and poured us each a glass full of spritzy gold bubbles. The icy drink was heavenly after the heat of the day.

Tom said, "This mess with Claire Satterfield looks real bad. I'm going to be tied up with it for the foreseeable future."

"But I thought the state patrol handled traffic accidents —"

"It wasn't an accident," he said curtly. He drained his glass. His deep green eyes regarded me grimly. "The patrolman and I saw *acceleration* marks on the garage floor. They're very different from *deceleration* marks. That's what you get when somebody's trying to stop."

"You mean you can — wait! Acceleration? Somebody saw her? Somebody saw her and . . . sped up? Oh, my Lord —"

He nodded. "And our one eyewitness," he said, "or the one person who *thinks* he might be an eyewitness, observed a dark green truck veer out of the garage." He stood up to check on his sauce. "We found an eighty-seven green Ford pickup parked by the outside entrance of Prince & Grogan. Stolen. Dented on the grille where it could have hit someone. Coroner's office will match that up with impact marks on the victim."

I said weakly, "Impact marks? You mean bruises? And wasn't there any blood on the grille?"

"The body doesn't have time to bruise." I closed my eyes. "Sometimes there's blood on the vehicle, sometimes there isn't," he went on. "This time there wasn't. The only blood was on the garage floor, from when her head hit the pavement. Unfortunately, there's not a single discernible hair or fingerprint inside the truck. At least so far. Our guys are working on it. We're grasping for anything." He paused. "But here's something. You were the closest person that we know of to the scene of the crime. Relatively near the body, you found that flower."

"You don't think —"

"I have no idea, it's probably nothing. But every now and then you get a hunch. When a flower so perfectly fresh is found by the scene of what we're now realizing was a homicide, we have to get it analyzed. So I took a picture of it and sent it to the American Rose Association."

"Sheesh, that *is* grasping for straws. What do you mean, our guys are working on the truck?"

He measured out white wine and stirred it into the bubbling crabmeat mixture. "As I said, we're now treating Miss Satterfield's death as a homicide. State patrol's out, we're in." His big body sighed. "So. Now all we have to do is figure out who would want to kill her. That's why I'm going to have to talk to Julian as soon as he's feeling a little better. The team's working on the evidence too. We need to figure out who could smash into her like that and then leave. Without being seen. We're thinking the perp either had another car right there, or went right back inside the mall."

"I don't believe somebody could do that without *anybody* seeing."

"Believe it. People usually are just minding their own business." He swirled Parmesan cheese into the sauce. "Poor Julian."

"What about those demonstrators? Think this could be something they'd do out of spite against Mignon Cosmetics? Because Claire worked for them?"

"At this point, nothing can be ruled out. We're getting the demonstrators' names and addresses. The usual drill."

My glass was long empty. I needed something else to do with my hands. So I set about assembling ingredients for a fruit cup — luscious, ripe cantaloupes, strawberries, grapes, bananas. I chopped and sliced and arranged the fruit in concentric circles, trying to bring a similar order to this chaos of news.

At length I poured myself another glass of cider and said, "Remember the guy I dumped the vegetables on?"

Tom's smile was enormous: back to his old self. "One of your better moments, Miss G. What about him?"

"And remember Frances Markasian?"

"Goldy, how could anyone forget a reporter who looks like a Caucasian Bob Marley and dresses like a class in salvage?"

I told Tom that Frances seemed to have ferreted out the activist to interview him and that his name was Shaman Krill. Not only had Frances somehow learned that Julian was only the most recent of Claire's many boyfriends, but she also seemed, like Tom and the state troopers, to believe Claire's death was no accident. Tom turned the stove off, held up one hand, and dug out his trusty spiral notebook.

"Other boyfriends. Thinks Claire was run down. How'd she come to these conclusions, did she say? Maybe I should give her a ring."

"Right, and get an earful about her First Amendment right to protect her sources. Then she'd never tell me a thing. You should have seen her: I hardly recognized her this morning, all decked out in an expensive new dress and tame hairstyle."

He snorted with disgust. "Why was she at the Mignon banquet? Since when is southeast Furman County the beat of an Aspen Meadow reporter?"

I shrugged and sipped cider. "She said she'd heard rumors about Prince & Grogan having problems. How that translates into attending a cosmetics lunch I don't know. And please, don't ask what kind of rumors, because I already asked her and she's not saying. But I'm going down there day after tomorrow for the food fair, and tomorrow I need to pick up my check from the Mignon people —"

"Oh, Goldy, no —"

"I'm just going to ask —"

"Okay, ask." He reached over and took both of my hands in his.

"You know I think you have a great mind for these investigations. That's why I like to talk to you about them. I *want* your ideas."

"Sure."

He kissed my cheek. "I do, doggone it. You love to talk to people and they love to talk to you. Great. You have insights. Also great. I just don't want you getting into danger."

"You act as if I'm trying to take over your

job or something."

He laughed. "Are you?" Then he answered his own question. "Of course you're not. Take catering. I help you chop, right? Sometimes you even give me a little scoop to measure out cookie batter. Small jobs. Helpful jobs. 'Cuz that's all you'll trust me with, right? I don't tell you what to serve or who to serve it to. Correct me if I'm wrong here. Because you're the caterer and I'm the cop."

"Please, Tom. Let me help Julian by asking around. He loved Claire so much."

He frowned, then held up a warning finger. "Okay. On two conditions. You don't go into situations that you know are going to be dangerous. And two, if I tell you to back off, you do."

"I thought you said your work wasn't dangerous —"

"It isn't when *I'm* doing it. It could be for you."

I set out the forks, knives, and plates before replying. Then I said calmly, "Okay. But I'm telling you, Tom, I'm going to help Julian. Frances Markasian and I are friends, remember. Or at least sometimes we act as if we are. I have an idea where she might have found out some of these things." I told him that I'd chatted with Dusty Routt, the Mignon sales associate, at the banquet. I'd even introduced her to Frances. After hearing about Claire's death, Frances would have felt no qualms about contacting Dusty for information.

"Routt, Routt, that name is familiar. R-o-u-t-t? There was a big bank job done in the early fifties here in Colorado by a guy named Routt. How old is this Dusty?"

"Julian's age. She lives down the street with her mother, little brother, and grandfather. Maybe the grandfather is a bank robber, although in our little town, that's just the kind of news folks love to spread, and I haven't heard a thing. Not only that, but our church helped build the house they're in. A bank robber doesn't sound like the kind of person they like to have living in houses built with charity money and sweat equity. But . . . don't you remember my telling you Julian had dated Dusty a couple of times? Then she was expelled from Elk Park Prep, and they sort of broke up. At a party on Memorial Day, she was the one who introduced him to Claire."

"Let me get this straight." Tom was scribbling in his notebook. "This Dusty . . . Routt works for the cosmetics people and used to go out with Julian? When Julian met Claire, Dusty had already been dumped? Why was Dusty expelled, do you know?"

I pursed my lips. "Nope. Julian was always too embarrassed to ask her. You know how that school is, it was all kept very hush-hush."

"Another fact the local gossip network seems to have missed," he observed. "And Frances mentioned Claire Satterfield, former boyfriends, and the guy you trashed with roasted vegetables in the mall garage, all in the same breath? Like she thinks there's a connection?" He looked at his notebook and considered. "Sounds like somebody's doing a lot of speculating."

I ignored this. "I'm just saying the rumor is, there seem to have been former boyfriends. Would Shaman Krill have had enough time to get back up to the garage and his precious demonstrators if he'd been driving the truck that hit Claire?"

Tom stood up and ladled a spoonful of crêpe batter into the hot pan. It emitted a delicious hiss. "Don't know yet. We're going to have to pace it out, time it. Are you going to call Arch to eat or should I? Think he should hear us talking about the investigation? Think he'd feel bored? Left out?"

"Talking about the investigation? Boring? You don't know Arch." I could well imagine a police-band radio becoming the next craze. When I called to the TV room that dinner was ready, Arch pleaded loudly that he was watching a rerun of Antonioni's *Blow-Up* and could we just save him some on a plate?

"It's a real complicated film," he yelled helpfully.

Before I could say anything, Tom called back that that would be fine. I murmured that the crêpes might toughen with microwave reheating, but he shrugged my worries away.

"What about Julian?" I asked.

"What about me?" said Julian from the doorway. He slumped into a kitchen chair. He still wore his serving outfit, and his face was gray with exhaustion. I had not heard his customary footsteps on the stairs. "This looks good," he said in a tired voice as he regarded the fruit tray. "And before you ask, I'm okay."

I tossed a salad while Tom filled the crêpes and put them in the oven. While I poured more cider, Tom said, "Julian? How much of our conversation did you hear?"

Julian's face reddened. "Oh, probably most of it."

"Then I need your help," Tom said matter-of-factly. "If you know the worst already and you're not going to pass out on us, then maybe you can answer some questions."

"I don't know the worst already," Julian shot back fiercely. He glared at Tom. "The worst I know is that she's dead and we don't know who did it, okay? That's the worst so far. What else is there?"

Tom continued calmly. "Do you know if

Claire had other boyfriends?"

"Yeah, she had some. I don't know who they were. But she was here on a twelve-month visa, do you think she was just going to spend all day behind the Mignon counter and then go back to her apartment and sit around?"

"Julian, please." I set a glass of cider in front of him. He ignored it.

"Well, do you think I knew her every move? I mean, come on!"

"Do you know any former boyfriends who were jealous of your relationship?" Tom asked.

"No."

"Do you know anyone who could have thought of Claire as an enemy?"

Julian rubbed his brow so hard I feared he might bruise his skin. "Look," he said finally, "I just know they were investigating shop-lifting at the store."

"Did she report any shoplifters?" Tom asked. He wasn't writing. "No," said Julian with a sigh. "I don't think so."

"What about these other men? Anybody shady that you knew about?"

"Claire just told me she'd seen other guys. But she also said she had admirers. Male admirers," he added dejectedly.

"Who?"

"Oh, Tom, I don't know." Julian gestured helplessly. His bleached hair caught the light, and he looked suddenly childlike. "She used to laugh when she told me men were always after her. She said she was glad to have a glass counter between herself and them. One time she teased me and said she'd managed to get rid of the guy who pestered her most. But she was so pretty, I guess you'd have to expect . . ." He didn't finish the thought. "And as for being bothered, well, sometimes she thought somebody was playing weird practical jokes on her at the counter —"

"Like what?"

"Like getting into her stuff, I don't know . . . she just said some of her stuff was missing, that's all."

"Did she say that she suspected anybody?"

"No!" Julian snapped, and Tom backed off.

The oven buzzer went off and I took out the crêpes. I requested that we put off the discussion of the investigation. Endless talk about crime can put a damper on the appetite. And we hadn't even told Julian about Marla yet.

The crabmeat in wine sauce was succulent, wrapped inside the thin, tender pancakes. But Julian, who occasionally ate shellfish as part of his not-strictly-vegetarian diet, consumed next to nothing. He had gone from furious to sullen. Over dinner I broke the news to him about Marla. I tried to make it sound as light as possible, with a good prognosis and quick recovery.

Julian's mood went back to anger. "What can we do? Is she going to need us to help her when she gets out? I thought heart attacks only happened to *old* people."

I felt a wash of relief that he did not react with either a fit of despair or more shock. "Yes, we'll all have to help. You especially, Julian, you know how much she adores you. And she's not old."

I shifted the topic to business. While Tom had a second helping of crêpes, Julian and I pushed our plates away and did the final planning for catered events coming in the next three days. Despite the crises breaking all around, or maybe because of them, Julian seemed desperate to be preoccupied with food service. Maybe it was a way of reasserting control. Day after tomorrow he would do a Chamber of Commerce brunch, and we talked about preparing lamb with nectarine chutney and avocado salad. He even asked earnestly if he should be taking notes. I said no; the menu, supplies needed, cooking and serving times were all in the kitchen computer. I wanted to embrace him in his pain. But I had learned from Arch that hugging teenage boys is a precarious enterprise.

When we had finished eating, Julian made a pitcher of iced espresso, a drink we'd all taken to imbibing after dinner in the unusual heat. Since I'd had latte as soon as I got home from the banquet, more caffeine would surely wire me for the night. But worry about Marla and the events of the day ought to guarantee insomnia anyway, I reasoned. I set aside a covered dish for Arch, and took the brownies and peach cobblers that I'd stashed for the banquet out to the front porch.

I loved our porch, although the only time you could use it in Colorado was the summer and early fall. Mercifully, the evening air had cooled. Savory barbecue smoke drifted through the neighborhood. As soon as Tom and I were sitting in the old redwood chairs he'd brought from his cabin, baby Colin Routt started to wail again from down the street.

"Poor kid," Tom commented. "I just read an article about preemies. They have a hard life, all the way through."

"Especially when they're born at under one pound and their dad takes off for parts unknown," I said.

Dusty Routt appeared in the tiny dirt-covered yard holding her little brother, or, more correctly, half brother, on her shoulder. She was jiggling the infant up and down, but the motion failed to comfort him. Then the mellow notes of jazz saxophone again floated out of the house's screened porch, and the tiny baby was immediately quiet.

"Music therapy," Tom and I said in unison, and then laughed. When Julian appeared with crystal glasses filled with espresso and ice, we thanked him and sat listening to the jazz filtering through the dusky air. I sipped the cold, dark stuff and waited for one of them to speak.

Julian popped a brownie into his mouth and pushed off on the porch swing. After a moment he addressed Tom and me.

"She was under a lot of pressure."

"What kind?" asked Tom without missing a beat, as if we had not stopped talking about Claire twenty minutes earlier. Wisely, he didn't reach for his notebook.

Julian shrugged. "Pressure to sell. That was the main thing. You know, Prince & Grogan carries Mignon exclusively in Colorado. Not only that, but the Mignon counter is the only million-dollar cosmetics counter in the state. If the saleswomen don't sell there, they get fired." He grimaced.

"Pressure to sell," repeated Tom.

Julian sighed. "They live off those commissions. *Lived.*"

"Julian," I said, "don't —"

He waved this away. "Plus what I men-

142

tioned. You know — pressure to watch for shoplifters." His tone was resigned. "There was a lot of theft there. It was a big problem in the store. Credit card fraud, employee theft, shoplifting, you name it. Claire introduced me to the guy who was in charge of security. Nick Gentileschi. He was okay, I guess. She was helping him with something."

"What?" Tom said, too sharply, I thought. "Helping the security guy with what? The shoplifting investigation?"

"I don't know!" Julian cried. "If I don't even know the identity of this admirer who wasn't bothering her anymore, how do you think I know what she was doing with security?"

Arch made one of his sudden appearances, probably lured by the sound of raised voices.

"Hey, guys! What's going on? *Blow-Up* was too weird and complicated, I didn't like it. Is that pancakes on my plate out there? Neat. I put them in the microwave."

I nodded and held up one finger: I'd be there in a minute.

"She was afraid," Julian said tonelessly, as if he were speaking from a distant asteroid.

"Who —" Arch began.

I gave him a warning look and shook my head: *Say nothing.* Arch crossed his arms and waited for an explanation, which he didn't get.

"Afraid of what?" Tom asked Julian gently.

"Just yesterday she told me she thought she was being followed," Julian replied wearily. "But she said she wasn't sure. Oh, God, why didn't I tell you? I just thought it was some stupid thing, like the unexplained stuff at the counter."

"Wait," I said. "Wait." I thought back through the muddle of the day. Claire, her Peugeot, the helicopter. When I'd swerved the van into the right lane, I'd barely missed a pickup truck. Then when I'd looked again . . . the pickup had fallen back several car lengths. "Someone might have been following us on I-70 this morning. In a pickup," I said miserably.

"Make?" asked Tom mildly. "Color? Did you see the driver?"

"No," I said helplessly. "No . . . I don't remember any of that. Maybe I'm just being paranoid."

Julian was holding his head in his hands.

"Big J.," said Tom, "why don't we go inside —"

Julian's head jerked up. "There's a part of you that's always alone," he blurted out. "People always have secrets, and you know they have secrets, but maybe they don't want to tell you because they're afraid of your re-action, or maybe they don't want to tell you

144

because they don't want to burden you. She didn't want to be a burden to me. And I didn't want to trouble you with it."

Tom and I exchanged a look. Inside the house, the microwave buzzer went off. My instinct told me Arch and I should leave Tom and Julian alone. Perhaps without an audience Julian would feel more inclined to talk to Tom.

"Let's go," I said to Arch.

"Why can't I eat out here?" Arch asked, perplexed. But he obeyed.

"Mom?" he asked when we were back in the kitchen. He held up his plate precariously. "Should I eat now or not?"

"Sure, hon, they just need to be alone for a while."

He took a mouthful of crêpe and said, "So what's going on with Julian? Who was afraid and what's the big secret?"

I told him Julian's friend Claire had been killed in a hit-and-run accident. His eyes opened wide behind his glasses. "Do they know who hit her?"

I told him they did not but that Tom was working on it. "Arch, something else. Hon, Marla had a mild heart attack jogging around Aspen Meadow Lake today. She's at Southwest Hospital but should be out in —"

Before I could finish, Arch whacked his chair back and bolted from the table.

"Arch, wait! She's going to be okay!"

I bounded up the stairs after him. By the time I got to his and Julian's room, Arch was lying facedown on the upper level of the bunk. I put my hand on the back of the awful tie-dyed T-shirt, but he shook me off.

"Just go away, Mom!"

"They can treat a mild heart attack —"

"I'm not upset about *Marla*. I mean, I *am* upset about Marla. Of course I am. It's only that . . . Look, just leave, okay?"

I didn't move. "Claire, then? You didn't really know her, although I know you worry about Julian —"

He shot upright suddenly, his brown hair askew, his face pale with rage. "Why are you *so* nosy? Why do you have to know about *everything?*"

"Sorry, hon," I said, and meant it. When he dropped back down on the mattress without saying more, I asked, "Want the curtains closed?" He didn't answer and I backtracked toward the door.

"Wait." His voice was muffled by the pillow. Slowly he sat up. He looked at the wall with his fifth-grade drawings of wildflowers, made during an intensely lonely period, the painful time before Tom came into our lives and well before Julian became Arch's personal hero. "Could you close the door, Mom?"

I did as directed. Arch gave me a fierce, guilty look.

"I wanted Claire to leave," he said harshly. "I hated her."

"Why? You met her only once —"

"So? Julian was always *with* her or *thinking* about her or on the *telephone* with her, or *something*. We never had any fun anymore. I wanted her to go back to Australia." He faced the drawings again. "Now I'm being punished for wanting her gone."

I hate feeling so helpless. "I may not know much, Arch, but that doesn't sound like the way punishment works." He shook his head and refused to look at me. I went on. "Claire's death wasn't just a terrible accident. Somebody ran her down on purpose."

He was silent, his eyes on his drawings, his face expressionless. Then he muttered, "I still feel bad."

"Then help Julian over the next few days, especially when I go down to work the food fair. He'll need your company now more than ever."

He hesitated, then said in a resigned voice, "Yeah, okay." After a moment he asked, "Do you think Julian will ever find another girlfriend? I mean, sort of the way you found Tom after things didn't work out with Dad?"

It was so tempting to give him an easy an-

147

swer. I said softly, "Arch, I don't know."

He shook his head mournfully. "Okay, Mom," my son said finally, "it's not helping to talk to you. Would you please just leave?"

7

Storms ripped through the mountains that night. Thunder boomed overhead, echoed down Cottonwood Creek, and seemed to shake the walls of our home. I woke and saw lightning flicker across our bedroom. The flashes were so constant that it was difficult to tell when one ended and another began. Rain pelted the roof and washed noisily down the gutters. I slipped out of bed to close our bedroom curtains, and found myself mesmerized by the storm. Torrents of muddy water gushed around the vehicles parked on our street, including a pickup truck blocking the end of our driveway.

As a lightning flash faded, I hesitated. Did a light turn on and then quickly off in the pickup? I narrowed my eyes. The storm slapped rain against the window. It was an unfamiliar truck; I didn't recognize it as belonging to one of our neighbors. But people had summer guests all the time, especially in Colorado, where we were usually spared the heat that afflicts the rest of the country. In the midst of the storm's violence, the truck was dark and still. I stared through the slashes of raindrops and decided the light was something I'd imagined.

A wave of water spewed up over the curb and surged toward Aspen Meadow's Main Street. This summer gullywasher would dump tons of mud and gravel on Aspen Meadow's paved roads. It would leave in its wake deltas of stone and a river of caked dirt. Driving after one of these torrents is invariably slow and treacherous. I sighed and wondered if Alicia, my supplier, would be able to get her truck up the street, to park anywhere close to the house in the morning. Especially if the pickup was still blocking the driveway.

When the tempest seemed to be abating, I glanced at the digital clock. But the clock face was dark. The storm had probably taken the electricity out. I fell into bed next to Tom's warm and inviting body. Incredibly, he had slumbered sonorously through it all. But when I inadvertently woke him by touching his foot, we had a deliciously stormy half-hour to ourselves.

With the power out, the usual artificial reminders of morning — ringing alarms, the aroma of fresh-brewed coffee — were absent. Luckily, Tom seems to possess an internal clock. I dimly registered his departure when watery morning sunshine slanted through the bedroom windows. During a homicide investigation, he always leaves at sunup for the investigative team's strategy meetings, and returns home late. He phoned after a few hours, when I was moving slowly through the end of my yoga routine. He wanted to make sure I was okay, and that I knew the electricity was off. Yes, he'd been able to back out of the driveway, he said when I asked about the pickup, but I should be careful to avoid the mud on Main Street. I caught sight of my own short-statured, disheveled-haired, stupid-happy reflection in the mirror when I hung up. Living with someone who tried to take care of *me* still brought unexpected pleasure.

Thursday, July 2, my kitchen calendar informed me, was a preparation day for the events ahead — the food fair and the Chamber of Commerce brunch on Friday, the Braithwaites' party on Saturday. Thinking of the Braithwaites, I groaned. Babs had been as snooty at the Mignon banquet as she'd been after she'd rear-ended Julian in her Mercedes and claimed it was his fault. But her personality wasn't about to stop me from making a splendid profit on the seated dinner she and her husband were giving for July Fourth. The two of them threw this celebrated annual party on their manicured five acres atop Aspen Knoll, the high point of the Aspen Meadow country club area. Supposedly the knoll had the best view of the fireworks over Aspen Meadow Lake. Perhaps if the guests plowed through their curry early enough, I'd even see part of the display. On second thought, with Julian's participation now uncertain, I might have to clean up until dawn.

I checked my watch: eight-forty. Alicia should arrive with seafood, meats, and produce around nine. The power came back while I was wondering about the best time to visit Marla. With her angiogram scheduled for first thing, perhaps I could visit in the early afternoon . . . then stop at Prince & Grogan to get the second half of my check, final payment for the banquet . . . that is, if Tom didn't object to my presence there. . . .

The phone rang. It was Tom again. "Look, Goldy, I'm sorry about last night —"

"What about it? It got kind of fun around four A.M. Of course, I couldn't see the time . . ."

"Well, I've just been thinking about it." He paused. "Look, Goldy," he said seriously, "you *know* I want you to . . . think about this case. It always helps to have your input."

"Think about the case," I repeated.

"You know I respect your intellect."

"Uh-huh. My intellect. My charming personality. And my cooking, don't forget that."

"Be serious. Fabulous cooking, charming

152

personality, and a *great* intellect."

"Gee, Tom. I wish you'd been one of my professors. *Great* intellect. La-de-da."

"All kidding aside — I just don't want you to interfere, get yourself in a compromising position. Believe it or not, Miss G., there is a difference. For example, you should ignore a demonstrator. Not dump vegetables on him."

I glanced into the walk-in for ingredients that would make a show-stopping bread for the food fair. "Okay, no more vegetable-dumping. Promise. How'd your meeting go? Speaking of the Spare the Hares people, have you found out anything? Did Shaman Krill complain about me?"

"The strategy meeting took two hours. And how can I find out about demonstrators when I'm making conciliatory phone calls to my wife?"

"Just answer the question, cop."

"The guy didn't make a formal complaint. And nobody from that mall is being overly helpful. Sometimes your prime suspect is always around, bending over backward to give you advice and guidance. That's when you have to expect to be deceived." He made a grumbling noise. I could imagine him considering his cup of bitter sheriff's department coffee. "So are you and I okay?"

"Of course."

He grunted. "Julian up yet?"

"I was about to check on him. Aren't you always telling me how the first forty-eight hours of a homicide investigation are the most profitable? I'm making bread. We're fine. Tom, please, I can't bear not to know why someone would do that to Claire Satterfield. Go investigate."

As I tiptoed up the stairs to the boys' room, his words echoed in my ear. *I've just been thinking about it . . . I'm sorry . . . don't want your interference.* The many, many wrinkles of two single lives, of separate ways of communicating, were taking a while to smooth out. Every aspect of our entwined experiences was under scrutiny. Even the way we referred to possessions was a challenge, I thought as I caught my reflection in one of the old-but-not-antique mirrors that Tom had collected over the years. He'd hung them just last week on the wall above the stairway. *Tom's* pictures, *my* stairway. *His* stove, *my* refrigerator, *his* deck furniture, *my* bed, *his* car, *my* house. Now I was learning to say *our, our, our.* I side-stepped Scout the cat, curled into a furry ball on one of the steps, and gazed into a mirror. A short, slightly plump, thirty-two-year-old woman with curly blond hair and brown eyes looked back. *Our mirrors. Our life.* Goodness, even *our cat.*

I eased the boys' bedroom door open. Arch's slow, regular breathing from the top bunk indicated he was still asleep. There was no noise from Julian's bed. In the morning, his muscular limbs usually sprawled from under the covers on the lower bunk. But at the moment the navy-blue bedspread covered his inert form from head to foot. I hoped he was asleep. Somehow, though, I doubted it.

I tiptoed back to the kitchen and contemplated the egg yolks I'd been accumulating in the refrigerator. They were left over from my preparation of lowfat recipes that invariably required egg *whites*. I'd have even more yolks to deal with when I got going on the vanilla-frosted fudge cookies. The yolks, though, what could I do with the yolks? I mentally tasted a cake or rolls enriched with yolks, then hit on the idea that the yolks could be the mainstay of a light, sweet, Sally Lunn-type bread for the fair. I hummed to myself as I made a yeast starter, chopped fresh pecans, and measured sun-dried cranberries. When a large chunk of butter was dissolving into golden globules in a pan of milk, I peeled thin curls of flavorful zest from juicy oranges, then spooned out flour from a copper canister Tom had brought from his cabin.

I had learned a great deal about Tom, I reflected as my mixer began its slow route

WHAT-TO-DO-WITH-
ALL-THE-EGG-YOLKS
BREAD

2 ½ teaspoons (1 ¼-ounce
    envelope) active dry yeast
¼ cup sugar
¼ cup warm water
¾ cup skim milk
¼ cup butter, melted
½ cup canola oil
1 tablespoon chopped orange zest
1 teaspoon salt
4 egg yolks, lightly beaten
3½ to 4 cups all-purpose flour
¾ cup sun-dried cranberries
1 cup chopped pecans

Butter a 10-inch tube pan; set aside. In
a large mixing bowl, combine the yeast,
one teaspoon of the sugar, and warm
water. Set aside for 10 minutes. Combine
the milk, butter, oil, zest, remainder of
the sugar, and salt, and stir into the yeast
mixture. Add the egg yolks, stirring well.
Add the flour ½ cup at a time, stirring
well after each addition to incorporate the
flour thoroughly. Knead 5 to 10 minutes,
until the dough is smooth, elastic, and

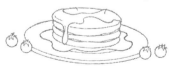

satiny. Knead in the cranberries and pecans. Put the dough back in the bowl, cover the bowl, and let the dough rise at room temperature until it is doubled in bulk. Using a wooden spoon, beat down the risen dough for about a minute.

Place the dough into the buttered tube pan and allow it to rise at room temperature until it is doubled in bulk.

Preheat the oven to 375°. Bake the bread for 45 to 50 minutes or until it is dark golden brown and sounds hollow when tapped. Place on a rack to cool or serve warm. Once cooled, the bread is also excellent sliced and toasted.

Makes 1 large loaf

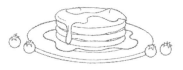

through the warm liquids. For example, I'd discovered that he preferred saving money to spending it, except when he could lavish exorbitant sums on antiques. I didn't understand the point of antiques — why would you pay more for something used and old? He'd proudly showed me his cherry sideboard and announced, "Hepplewhite, 1800 to 1850." I'd almost passed out when I learned what he'd paid for that hunk of wood. He'd bought it before we were married, though, and had vowed to purchase no more "goodies," as he called them, until we could figure out what to do with the stockpile of possessions we were now trying to cram into one house.

In terms of money, though, these days Tom took great pleasure in setting aside funds for Arch and Julian, whom he referred to as the kids, the guys, the boys. *Our* boys. And he didn't want any more children, he said when I asked. Two were enough. Which was fine by me. But now *our* two boys had college funds, savings funds, Christmas funds. All generously supplemented by Tom, who took a childlike pleasure in giving.

I set aside new egg whites for the fudge cookies, then mixed the butter, milk, and egg yolks into the yeast starter. I stirred flour into the rich, flaxen-colored mixture until it was thick. Once I started to knead the dough, I thought back to the second phone call from Tom this morning. He did/did not want me involved in the investigation. He wanted me to think about it. He wanted me to be willing to back off once I'd brought my *great intellect* to bear. I *had* helped him before, when an attempted poisoning closed down my catering business, then again when Julian's mother was involved in some bizarre crimes, and again when Arch's and Julian's school was the scene of homicides. When Tom was kidnapped this spring and our local parish had been turned upside down by crime, I had thrown myself into the investigation with every ounce of my will. Sometimes the sheriff's department welcomed my involvement; occasionally, they did not. At least Tom asked for my opinion, even respected it, I thought with a wry smile. He had always treated me as a resource. But unknown to him, I was very sensitive about the issue of offering my thoughts.

My vulnerability came from interaction with Husband Number One. Dr. John Richard Korman not only disliked hearing any of my opinions on things medical, he resented my occasional input. In one case, expressing my ideas had backfired so appallingly that I'd never ventured another word about his work.

I pushed the bread dough out, folded it over, pushed it out, and recalled the freckled face and wiry red hair of Nashville-born Heather Maclanahan O'Leary. She and her husband had been newcomers some years ago to Aspen Meadow and St. Luke's Episcopal Church. Heather had become pregnant with her first child almost immediately after arriving in Colorado. But in her first trimester she was so debilitated by anemia and homesickness for Tennessee that the parish had started to send in meals, coordinated daily by yours truly.

John Richard was Heather's obstetrician. He worried aloud about the fact that her red blood cell count didn't seem to be improving even with standard doses of iron. I brought the O'Learys their first supper — a cold roast beef and spinach salad with Dijon vinaigrette that I secretly thought of as my Ironman Special. Heather had been so happy to see me, so grateful to have a new friend, she'd insisted I stay for tea. When our teacups were empty, she showed me the nursery her husband was painting, then she proudly pointed to the framed pictures of the Maclanahan and O'Leary clans. She was going to hang this pictorial album around the baby's crib, so that the newest O'Leary would grow up with what Heather called "ancestor appreciation." I'd acted more interested than I really was, until one photograph caught my attention.

"Who's that?" I pointed to an old, formally

composed photograph of a couple. A very pale man — an Irishman? — stood behind a dark-haired, dark-complected woman.

"Oh," said Heather with a small laugh, "that's Grandfather Maclanahan and Grandma Margaretta. He was an importer and had to travel to Italy every so often. He met Margaretta on a trip to Rimini, and fell in love with her because of her great Tortellini Della Panna. Whoever heard of an Irishman smitten by pasta?"

I stared at the picture with a prickly feeling. In those days, before I had a catering enterprise to keep me busy, I spent hours reading magazines. Friends said I was like a walking *Reader's Digest*, especially when it came to food and medicine. When Heather was telling me about her grandmother Margaretta Sanese Maclanahan, I remembered an obscure article on genetic diseases similar to sickle cell anemia. I offhandedly asked Heather if she'd ever been tested for thalassemia, a blood disorder common among people from Mediterranean countries. She looked puzzled and said no. That night I mentioned to John Richard the possibility that Heather could be a carrier of this genetic blood disease. As a carrier rather than an actual thalassemic, Heather's disorder might have manifested itself only in pregnancy. With a genetic irregularity of that kind,

Heather and her husband should both be tested, I said, in case the infant would have full-blown thalassemia.

Well. John Richard hooted. He scoffed. He laughed until the tears ran down his handsome cheeks. *Where did you go to medical school?* he wanted to know. Then he even called one of his buddies to cackle, *Listen to the little wife's diagnosis.*

The dénouement wasn't pretty. John Richard refused Heather's request to be tested for thalassemia. She went to an ob-gyn in Denver who did the blood analysis — a very simple one, as it turned out — and confirmed the diagnosis. *My* diagnosis. Heather's husband was tested — he did not carry the gene. The new doc pumped lots more iron into Heather than she'd been getting, she began to feel better, and she gave birth to a normal baby girl.

I was rewarded with a black eye.

I set the dough aside to rest. Here I was, years later, understandably ambivalent about sharing my ideas. Unfortunately, with my personality, once somebody presented me with a problem, I felt duty bound to jump in and help solve it. Arch sometimes resented this fiercely, of course, and I had painfully learned to let him take care of his own messes. Whether Julian felt the same way, I was not sure.

I kneaded the cranberries and nuts into the silky dough, gathered the whole thing up, and nestled it into a buttered bowl. Time to have some espresso and put the past aside.

As the coffee machine was heating up, Arch appeared in the kitchen with Scout draped over his shoulders. Once the dark liquid began its noisy spurt into shot glasses, Scout leapt to the kitchen floor.

"Jeez, Mom! You scared him!"

I steadied the shot glasses under the machine's twin spurts. "It's not as if he hasn't heard this machine a thousand times before."

Arch watched the ten-second process in silence. After I stopped the flow of water, I poured the espresso into a small cup.

"Gosh!" he exclaimed. "All that noise, and that's all you get?"

I sipped the strong coffee and let this pass. "Is Julian up yet?"

Arch knelt on the kitchen floor and tried to attract the cat. Scout, however, wanted a fresh bag of cat food. This he indicated by standing resolutely next to his bowl, which held only undesirable, four-hour-old food. Receiving no response in the meal department, Scout sauntered across the floor and rolled onto his back. Arch enthusiastically rubbed his stomach.

"Julian's crying," Arch announced without looking at me.

"Did he talk to you? Is he still in bed?"

"Still in bed. Under the covers. Didn't want me to stay." Scout curled his paws and stretched to his maximum length to prolong Arch's ministrations. "He said for you *not* to bring him any food. He wants to be left alone today, and he'll do all the cooking for the Chamber of Commerce brunch tomorrow morning."

Well, that was just great. But not unexpected. "How about you, kiddo? Want some breakfast?"

He looked around the kitchen, but nothing caught his fancy. "No, thanks. Who are you cooking for?"

"The food fair and the Braithwaites."

Arch pulled a long face. "Mrs. Barf-mate! That cow."

"Nice talk about a rich client, Arch."

"With Mrs. Barf-mate's driving, you're lucky I'm still alive."

Arch had been in the back seat when the accident occurred, and he was not about to let anyone forget it. He maintained to this day that Julian had put on his turn signal and slowed properly, even though Claire was giggling and cavorting around in the front seat and Julian couldn't remember what he'd been doing. But it was Mrs. Braithwaite, Arch

164

claimed, who was the bad driver. My son had insisted he had whiplash and post-traumatic stress syndrome, and we should sue Mrs. Braithwaite for bad driving. Unfortunately, the police had sided with Mrs. B.

"Well," said Arch in a resigned tone, "I guess Julian and I aren't going to the Aspen Meadow Animal Hospital today. He promised, but he probably forgot. They let you hold the rats there," he added brightly. "Big black and white rats."

"I'm sorry, Arch. I'd take you, but I have a ton of cooking to do, and I need to go see Marla."

Arch lifted the towel from the rising bread, peered in, and poked the dough with his finger. "How is she?"

"Don't know yet."

He sighed. "Maybe Todd's dad could take us to the animal hospital. Their rats don't bite there, they've trained them —"

"Arch, please."

"I didn't say I wanted to *have* a rat, I just want to *hold* one."

"Give Julian a little slack, hon. And me too, while you're at it."

"I am, I am, but can't we get another pet? If you don't like rats, can we talk about ferrets? Tom likes them," he said with a hopeful smile.

I punched down the bread dough, divided

it, and reshaped it in ring pans. "We have a cat. Please don't bring Tom into this."

Arch frowned and reconsidered his strategy. "I guess I better go check on Julian. Should I take him some coffee? That doesn't really count as food, does it?"

"Sure, take him some. If he doesn't want it, come on back." I fixed a latte the way Julian liked it, with lots of cream and sugar. Arch disappeared just as Alicia knocked on my door. While she lugged in boxes of Portobello mushrooms and fresh herbs, I called the Coronary Care Unit of Southwest Hospital. Someone at the nurses' station crisply informed me that Marla Korman had not yet been taken for her angiogram, and that the patient could not come to the phone. Marvelous. By the time Alicia had finished unloading the supplies, Arch had returned, dressed for the day in his tie-dyed shirt and torn jeans.

"Julian's drinking the coffee and says thanks. I'm going to Todd's. There's nothing to do around here."

"Does Julian want —"

Arch pulled his mouth to one side and nudged his glasses up his nose. "He says he'll come down when he wants to be with people." Seeing my disappointed face, Arch patted my shoulder. "He'll be okay. You know Julian. He's had a hard life, but he always manages

166

to come through. All right, I'm leaving. It's been real, Mom." And with that, Arch strode out the front door clutching a bag of audiocassettes.

Feeling helpless, I started on the fudge cookies. As I sifted dark brown cocoa powder over a white mountain of flour, I kept running the previous twenty-four hours through my mind. If only I had not accepted the assignment for the banquet. Would that have helped? Why had Claire even recommended me to her employers? I beat egg whites with canola oil and measured aromatic Mexican vanilla into the batter. *Julian's had a hard life.* No kidding. His adoptive parents were far away, and now the young woman he'd fallen head-over-heels for was dead.

The bread loaves came out of the oven golden-brown, studded with cranberries and nuts, and filling the kitchen with their rich scent. I placed the loaves on racks to cool and called the hospital again. Marla still hadn't gone for her angiogram and could not come to the phone. I banged the receiver down and wondered how many people had heart attacks waiting in hospitals to *be* treated.

I spooned even half-spheres of the cookie batter onto tin sheets and popped them into the oven. Ten minutes later, the fudge cookies emerged as perfect dark brown discs that smelled divine. I inhaled the life-giving smell of chocolate and quickly transferred the cookies to racks. While they were cooling, I got started washing the pile of dirtied bowls and pans. I was thinking black thoughts about Southwest Hospital, when Arch returned.

I said, "*Now* what?" and immediately regretted it. Arch's face was crestfallen.

"I just . . . wasn't in the mood for playing with Todd. I think I should go down to the hospital with you to see Marla."

I gathered him in for a hug, which, being thirteen, he didn't return. "It's okay, hon. I don't know what's going on with Marla, and I don't know who they'll let see her. If you stay here with Julian, that would be the best thing. Why don't you try to take him some warm cookies and cold milk?"

"He's not five years old, Mom. And he said no food."

"Well then, take him another cup of coffee." Not five years old. This was true. So at the last minute I poured an ounce of Tom's VSOP cognac into Julian's second latte. Julian was nineteen, in fact, but he wasn't going to be driving anywhere today, and it was my — *our* — house, and I thought the kid needed a drink.

Arch steadied the cup, took a whiff, said "Blech," and left the kitchen. Five minutes later he returned, just as I was mixing skim milk into powdered sugar to make a vanilla glaze for the fudge cookies. "Okay. Julian took the coffee and he's out of bed. He's just kind of staring out the window and saying, 'She was so beautiful, she was so perfect,' and junky stuff like that." He shrugged. "He didn't want me to stay, though."

"Want to help me cook?"

"Sure." He washed his hands, watched what I was doing, then meticulously began to spread thin layers of white icing over the dark cookies. As I sat beside him icing my own pile of cookies, I knew better than to ask what he was thinking, and why he had decided to come home from Todd's.

"So," Arch said at length, "d'you think Julian liked Claire so much because she was beautiful or because she was, you know, a good person?"

I considered the icing on one cookie. "I have no idea. Probably both."

"I don't think anyone will ever love me because of my looks."

I iced my last cookie and put down my spatula. "Arch, you *are* good-looking."

He rolled his eyes, then bent his wrist to ease his glasses back up his nose so he wouldn't have to let go of his spatula. "You're my mom. You're supposed to say that."

Without looking at him, I started to sprinkle cocoa powder over the first row of iced cookies. The dark chocolate cookies with their pale icing and cocoa dusting looked beautiful. My son, the most precious person to me in the world, thought he was ugly. *What's wrong with this picture?*

"Arch, I don't care what anyone says, you *are* attractive."

"Uh-huh. Remember the Valentine's Day dance I went to at Elk Park Prep this year? My first and last dance at that school?"

"But I told you, when you're older you should try again —"

He waved his spatula for me to be quiet. "There was an artist there. The school hired him for, like, entertainment. An artist who makes people look like cartoon characters, you know? What's that called?"

I sighed. "A caricaturist?"

"Yeah. He drew caricatures of all the kids. Instead of dancing, we stood around watching him work. He gave each person's . . . caricature . . . titles like Class Hero, Class Brains, Class Beauty. He would exaggerate each kid's appearance, so that they would be flattered, you know?"

I nodded, unsure of where this was going.

"So then he did me. He exaggerated how thick my glasses are, how dark my freckles are, the way my chin goes in and my hair sticks out. He wrote in big letters at the bottom Class Nerd. Everybody laughed. So please don't tell me I'm good-looking, when *you* know and *I* know and *everybody else* knows that I'm not."

"Oh, for heaven's sake, sometimes the people at that school just make my flesh crawl —"

"Don't worry, Mom, the guy, the artist, apologized when the dance was over. Everybody was gone by then, but he did say he was sorry. The dance would have been awful without that happening anyway." He waved his spatula dismissively. "Looks like all the cookies are done."

I took his spatula and mine and placed them in the sink. Embarrassed by his revelation, Arch stood up to leave.

"Wait, hon, please. Sit down. I want to tell you something."

The air outside was heating up, and with all the cooking, the kitchen was even hotter. Arch threw himself into one of the kitchen chairs while I poured us both some lemonade.

"You know I lived in New Jersey during most of my growing-up years."

"Mom, so what? What does that have to do with anything?"

"Have you ever seen the famous Miss America pageant? It's held in New Jersey. In Atlantic City. When I was growing up, we used to watch it on television. The neighborhood kids, I mean. It seemed like it was our pageant because it was held in our state."

Arch sipped lemonade. "I think that pageant is stupid. Todd and I always watch horror movies when it's on."

"Listen. When I was fourteen, I was the oldest girl in our group of neighborhood kids. That year, I remember, we all watched the pageant and ate lemon Popsicles. At one point the announcer said this and that about the contestants, what they had to do to enter, blah, blah, and that young women had to be eighteen. So one of the kids in our little group piped up, 'Gosh, Goldy, you've just got four years to go!' "

Arch furrowed his brow. "So is that supposed to make me feel better about being called a nerd? That your friends wanted you to enter the Miss America contest?"

I reached out for his hand, but he pulled it away. "You don't understand. *All* the eyes of my friends turned to me. Expectantly. I wasn't long-legged and skinny and I never would be. But that's the problem. Whoever said girls should be expected to be in beauty contests? *Why* should anyone expect it? And that's what I'm trying to say. They called you a nerd. Whether or not you believed it, you

172

accepted it. What I realized at age fourteen is that everybody was counting on me to *want* to be in a beauty contest. But it was a contest that I had no intention of ever, ever entering." I took a deep breath. "The problem is, if you're a woman, and maybe if you're a man too, when you get to be a teenager, it seems as if your whole life is going to be absorbed by a long series of stupid beauty contests, and I'm not just talking about Miss America. I'm talking about the way people judge you when you walk down the street. Or walk into a class. Or go to the gym. And the only solution is to say, 'I'm not going to play this game! I quit the beauty contest! Now and forever!' "

Arch waited to see if I had finished what I was going to say. He took a careful sip of his lemonade. Then he said, "May I go check on Julian now?"

I exhaled, suddenly exhausted. "Sure. I'm going to see Marla."

"Okay. I'll let you know if Julian comes out of the bedroom." He paused, then said, "I don't think he's crying because Claire was so beautiful. I think he's just feeling really empty."

"Yes, Arch. I'm sure you're right."

Feeling disoriented and exhausted by my diatribe, I gathered up my purse and keys. That was when Arch did something that sur-

173

prised me. He walked over and gave me a hug.

At the hospital, a new receptionist referred me to the CCU nurses' station.

"We don't know when your sister will be back, Miss Korman," a nurse informed me. "They just wheeled her down to the cath lab."

"Will the angiogram take more than an hour?" I asked.

"It shouldn't, but you never know."

The thought of waiting in that hospital for an indeterminate amount of time seemed unbearable. I looked at the clock: three-thirty. *Courage,* I said to myself. *She's your best friend, and you're going to be there for her.*

"Thank you. I'll be back in an hour."

I still had to get my check from Prince & Grogan, so I drove over to the mall. A larger group of demonstrators was massed at the outside entrance to the department store than had been the previous day. Because of the accident, I doubted the police would let them back into the garage that day to wave their signs at the other entrance. Afraid that Shaman Krill might catch sight of me, I parked the van at the edge of a nearby bank parking lot. As soon as I got out of the car, I could hear the hoots and chants of the activists. Most of them were wearing white sweatsuits. As I came closer,

I could see the chanting white-clad group wore blindfolds.

Hip, hop! I can't see!
Hip, hop! Wha'ja do to me?

Scores of hand-held placards denouncing Mignon Cosmetics' animal-testing practices bounced up and down above the crowd. I looked around helplessly for a way to get into the store that did not involve trying to slip past crowd-restraining sawhorses. A thin stream of shoppers was headed for a nearby pasta place. I followed.

Once inside the mall, I ran up a chrome and polished granite staircase and entered Prince & Grogan on the second level. Bright lights and mellow piano music — coming not from speakers but from a real piano player in the center of the store — took me off guard. After a moment of attempting to get oriented, I saw a far-off neon sign. OFFICES. Someone there, presumably, would have my check.

I negotiated a labyrinth of sparkling crystal and china displays, blaring audio equipment, whirring small appliances, and large, blank-faced mirrors. These were not like Tom's quasi-antique mirrors with their charming, wavy glass. These were oversize, glaring department store looking-glasses, the kind the ad maven surely had in mind when he said, *Make a woman insecure enough and you can sell her anything.* I closed my eyes. I didn't want to see myself in my denim skirt, white T-shirt, and sneakers; I just wanted to find the department store office.

Eventually, I was successful. The Prince & Grogan personnel, security, billing, credit, and customer service departments were grouped together in a section of the second floor that was still being renovated. After several misdirections I finally ended up sitting in a tiny office across from a straight-haired woman named Lisa, who claimed she handled accounts payable. Lisa shuffled through papers and files with no luck, however, and went off mumbling about finding someone from security.

While she was gone I looked around her office, which was in desperate need of the upcoming paint job. The interior walls of the old Montgomery Ward had been covered with a mind-numbing aquamarine pigment. On the far wall of the office, paler squares indicated spots where framed recognition of merit awards, maybe even family photos, had once hung. Next to them, also painted aquamarine, was what looked like a medicine cabinet or key box. On the floor, computer print-outs were neatly stacked two feet high. Then by the wall closest to me was a gray set of file cabinets. My fingers itched to open the cabinet and look up Satterfield, Claire. But with my luck, not only would the drawer be locked, but Lisa of accounts payable would sashay back in while my hand was still on the handle.

Lisa did indeed sashay back in, and luckily my hands were placed innocently in my lap.

"The head of security has your check, and his office is locked. Nick's out dealing with some insurance investigators today, and was wondering if you could come back tomorrow."

I wanted to growl something unappreciative, such as *Why doesn't the bonehead just mail it to me?* but I was coming back to the mall the next morning for the food fair. Besides, after a few years of running my small business, I was becoming somewhat cynical. Promises of checks coming in the mail all too frequently meant *We might mail this when we get to it. Then again, we might not.*

I checked my watch again: three forty-five. I still felt repulsed by the idea of going back to the hospital to wait, so I made the instantaneous decision to go down to the Mignon counter. Just briefly, just to see if Dusty and Harriet and maybe even Tom were there. I had Julian grieving at home. Perhaps if I returned with something to tell him . . .

Before I knew it I was on the down escalator. As I descended I could see both Harriet and Dusty on the floor below. Harriet was talking to a hunchbacked woman whose white hair was piled elaborately on her head. One of Harriet's hands held a bottle, the other tapped the bottle's shiny gold top.

"And what's that one called?" I heard the older woman ask as I neared them.

"Tangerine Tide," confided Harriet smugly. "It's coordinated with Raspberry Dunes and Apricot Sunset —"

I imagined a beach full of fruit.

"— and it's *exactly* the hue the designers are using for the fashion colors of late summer. We sell so much of it, we can't keep it in stock!"

"Well, then!" said the white-haired woman decisively. "I'll take some!"

Dusty was lifting the long, heavy pages of what looked like a ledger. A handsome, balding customer had approached the counter and was picking up bottle after bottle and appraising each one. Dusty, shaking her head over the pages, seemed not to see him. She did catch a glimpse of me, however, and came scuttling over. Her forest-green uniform barely swathed her ample tummy. Her orange-gold hair was somewhat wilder than usual, and her eyes were bloodshot.

"Goldy, did you hear about Claire?" Her voice was raw. I figured she'd been crying for quite some time.

"I did. I'm sorry. You all must be devastated."

She took a shuddery breath. "We are. How's Julian doing?"

"Not well. I'm trying to convince him to take some time off."

She said, "*We* have to work. Do you believe that? So, the cameras are watching. Are you interested in something? What kind of problems are you experiencing with your face?" she asked brightly.

"What cameras? Can I look around? Will you show me?"

"I can't now," she replied softly. She brought out a slender white tube with a gold top. "This is Timeless Skin." She squinted at me. "This will do wonders for those dark circles under your eyes. Why don't you let me do a free makeover?"

"Er, thanks, but not now. I was thinking that *sleep* would do wonders for my dark circles."

"Well," Dusty said, scrutinizing my face, "how about some Ageless Beauty/Endless Appeal night cream for when you're getting all that extra sleep? What kind of skin regimen are you using for your face?"

"No regimen." I gestured at the stacks of glistening bottles arrayed on the glass countertop. "Nothing, really. I don't want to buy anything, Dusty. I just wanted to check on you. Because of Claire."

She shook her head. "We have a new line of —" she began.

The man at the counter cleared his throat loudly; Dusty glanced nervously at him.

"Go help him," I pleaded. "I'm really just looking."

"Okay," Dusty said with a hasty look back at the ledger book. "But I doubt *he's* going to buy anything."

I moved away from the blushes and scanned a pyramid of Carefree Color lipsticks. Cherry-blossom Cheesecake. Fudge Soufflé. Rosehips Revolution. The person who named Mignon lipsticks must have been a dessert caterer.

Dusty greeted the balding customer and nodded knowingly. She became animated, or pretended to be animated, when he started to talk. Tall, mid-fortyish, good-looking, he was the kind of fellow I saw at high-society catered events all the time. I squinted: Maybe I'd even seen this guy at some catered event in the Aspen Meadow Country Club area. He picked up bottle after bottle and examined it, asking questions the whole time, as if the shape of the container were more important than what was in it. Then he put down the bottle, leaned in to Dusty, and said something. She reared back and replied. Their conversation appeared to be veering toward an argument.

"Don't act ignorant, Reggie," Dusty said loudly to her customer. "We saw you. You are going to get into so much trouble!"

I touched the tops of the lipstick tubes. Trouble? What kind of trouble? Who saw him? Saw him doing what? I peered at a display of blushes near Reggie, and then moved toward it as if I'd finally discovered what I'd come for.

Reggie, whoever he was, waved off Dusty's concern and pointed to a large white bottle. "So what are your sales projections on the new moisturizer?" he asked. Farther down the counter, Harriet Wells gave Dusty and her inquisitive customer a disapproving glance.

I picked up one blush after another — Sensuosity, Valentine Kiss, Lustful Gaze. No thanks. I peeked sideways: Dusty and Reggie were standing with several trays of mascara between them. *Yes, I was eavesdropping,* I could imagine myself admitting later to Tom. I wanted to hear what Dusty had to say to Reggie, the guy who was going to get into trouble.

"I noticed they changed the packaging for

the compacts," Reggie was observing.

"Yuppies don't want white," Dusty informed him airily. "White reminds them of old ladies. So Mignon changed it to navy-blue and gold and we've sold a zillion of them."

"Don't use the word *zillion,* Dusty, it's not specific. And I can't imagine that *you* were selling lots of them. You said you were behind the last couple of months."

"Don't be a prick, Reggie, or I'll tell the world the truth."

"You wouldn't do that. Now, listen," he went on, "just tell me if they've set their sales goals for this new line they introduced yesterday, before all hell broke loose."

"Yes, of course they have, you know they always set goals. Twenty-three hundred a week for the full-time people."

Reggie considered this. "What did they send you to advertise them?"

Harriet had finished with the white-haired woman and was heading back toward the center of the counter. For the first time, I realized that although she was short, the way she held herself revealed she was either a former model or dancer. Instead of coming to me, however, Harriet walked straight up to Dusty and her male customer, Reggie-the-troublemaker.

"Mr. Hotchkiss," Harriet said with a tiny, wicked smile, "are you actually going to buy something today?"

"Buzz off, Harriet," Reggie Hotchkiss said loudly. "Look." He gestured in my direction. "You've got a customer. You can't keep up those hefty sales numbers if you ignore a customer, now, can you?"

Harriet lifted her chin and walked past him to me. Like Dusty, her face sagged with fatigue, but she did not look quite as disheveled. "Ah, Goldy. The caterer. You heard, I suppose . . . ?"

I nodded.

"So tragic. That girl had a future in cosmetics, she was a natural. We're all going to miss —" Her voice broke, and she stopped to reassert control. Her large blue eyes appealed to me. "Is your boy all right? It must have been a terrible shock for him."

My watch said 4:05. "Yes, thanks. Julian is my helper and he's fine. But I have a friend in the hospital, and she's quite ill. I'll . . . see you tomorrow."

"Then why are you —"

But I waved and hightailed it out of the store, past the demonstrators, through all the cars, and to my van. Revving my vehicle over to the hospital, I was obsessed with wondering who Reggie was and why he was going to get into trouble for being seen. Reggie Hotchkiss, Reggie Hotchkiss.

Oh yes, how could I forget? He did indeed live in Aspen Meadow. His family owned a prosperous Denver-based company: Hotchkiss Skin and Hair.

8

When the orderlies finally wheeled Marla back up from having her angiogram, she looked completely transformed. Her complexion was wan, and her usual animation had disintegrated into grogginess. I waited while the nurse hooked her back up to her monitors. By the time I came into the cubicle, Marla, a large, raucously funny person whom I always thought of as being in full bloom, appeared completely deflated.

She caught sight of me and groaned. "I feel gross. I look gross. My back's killing me. You gotta get me out of here, Goldy."

"I'm trying, believe me —"

Dr. Lyle Gordon walked into the cubicle and checked Marla's IV. He was wearing a white lab coat over his scrubs. His gray fluff of hair stood up straight on his head. "Ah, the patient's sister. Did she tell you?"

I said, "Tell me what?"

His eyebrows pinched inward. "We had an emergency operation this morning and had to delay her procedure. Your sister's angiogram showed blockage at the mid-right coronary. So we're going ahead with the atherectomy."

He turned to Marla. "But it's too late today, unfortunately. We'll need to wait until tomorrow."

"Oh my God," groaned Marla. She eyed her cardiologist with as much fierceness as she could muster. "You mean, I'm going to have to go all night with this . . . this thing sticking into my groin —"

"It's called a catheter," said Lyle Gordon patiently, patting the sheet. "Ms. Korman. We're going to get through this —"

"Oh yeah?" Marla interrupted. "Who's *we*, white man?"

"Ms. Korman —"

Marla snapped, "Shut *up!*"

Dr. Lyle Gordon clenched his teeth and straightened his shoulders. Then he addressed me, enunciating each phrase: "I need. A surgeon. On standby. Tomorrow. I can't get a surgeon to be on standby *until* tomorrow. And we need the surgeon in case something goes wrong. Worst case, we'll have a surgical suite ready if the catheter perforates the heart or tears the artery or she has another heart attack —"

"As God. Is my. *Witness*," Marla growled from her bed, "I am never giving this hospital another —"

"Help me out here, would you please?" Dr. Lyle Gordon begged me.

I said, "Sure," and he abruptly left the cubicle. "Marla, look," I said lightly, pointing to a potted coral begonia on her nightstand, "someone's sent you flowers."

She skewed her glance sideways at the perky blossoms, then turned away. "I don't care."

I opened the card and could not hide my astonishment. "They're from the general. 'Hoping for a speedy recovery.' I thought your brother-in-law was in jail for possessing explosives."

"He is in jail, but Bo has friends everywhere." Marla closed her eyes.

I put my hand on her shoulder. "They're going to kick me out of here any minute. Please tell me what I can do for you."

"I'll give you a hundred thousand dollars to help me escape."

"Marla —"

"You'd have to cater birdwatchers' picnics for three years to make that kind of dough."

"And your second choice is . . ."

She sighed such a deep, depressed sigh that I briefly considered trying to break her out. "Okay, Goldy." She seemed suddenly tired, as if she'd given up. "Get somebody to bring me some lingerie and my mail. Some folks have been calling, and I guess Tony's coming in tomorrow." Tony was her on-again, off-again boyfriend. "I don't know what the hell the hospital's done with my stuff. The spare house key is in a key box under my dryer vent."

"Okay. Anything else?"

"My life is over. I'll never eat another éclair. They'll put me in a wheelchair to go around Aspen Meadow Lake. . . ."

"Your life, sister, is just beginning. Buck up, now, I'm going to learn how to cook lowfat, and we'll walk around the lake together —"

Before we could pursue this healthy vision further, Marla drifted off to sleep. I kept my hand on her shoulder until the ten minutes were over.

Then I zipped out to a pay phone, put a call in to Tom, and reached his voice mail. I told him about Reggie Hotchkiss, proprietor of what could be a rival company to Mignon, and about Reggie's conversation with Dusty Routt. I told Tom that I missed him and hoped we'd see him tonight.

At home I fixed grilled cheese sandwiches for Arch and me, at his request. When he asked about Marla, I put my gooey sandwich down and decided against finishing it. I took a salad and bowl of soup upstairs, but Julian said through his door that he didn't want anything, thanks. Finally, Arch and I sat in the backyard and watched rippled pink clouds slowly change color as the sun drifted toward the mountains.

"Did you talk to Tom on the phone, Mom? Has he found out anything yet?"

"Haven't talked to him. He'll be home late."

"Seems as if he's always working when you most want to talk to him," Arch observed. "During an investigation, I mean."

"I know." I'd been thinking the same thing myself.

A gentle breeze bowed the stems on the nearby columbines. Close by in the neighborhood, someone was cooking steak on a grill. The succulent smell filled the air and reminded me I had the food fair to start in the morning.

"Todd and I are going out tomorrow afternoon to look for 33 rpm records," Arch announced. "Unless Julian needs me. Do you think he will?"

"Hard to tell."

The doorbell rang. It was Todd, wanting to see if Arch could walk into town for ice cream. After I gave my permission, however, Arch hesitated. "Are you okay, Mom? You seem . . . sad. Is it because of Marla?" When I nodded, he said, "I know she's your best friend."

"Thanks for asking. As soon as she's out of the hospital, I'll feel a lot better."

"How about if I bring you back a pint of mint chocolate chip?"

"You're sweet, but no. I just want to work in the kitchen, get my mind off things."

And work in the kitchen I did. The second batch of ribs needed to be precooked and cooled, then chilled overnight before being reheated at the fair the next morning. I lifted the thick, meaty slabs and arranged them on racks in the oven. Soon the rich scent of roasting pork wafted through the house, and I went upstairs and opened the windows for air. Poor little Colin Routt started wailing when a motorcycle roared by. Within moments, though, someone started playing the jazz saxophone, and the baby quieted. I wished we could all have our jangled nerves calmed so easily.

I glanced up and down the street, looking for the pickup truck that had been blocking our driveway the evening before. The pickups along the curb all looked alike. I found this to be true even when they were zooming past me down the highway. In Colorado, the only difference I could distinguish between moving pickup trucks was how many dogs were trying to keep their balance in the back of each one.

Arch trudged home at nine and headed straight for bed. At one A.M. I set the alarm for six and fell between the sheets. Poor Tom, I thought as I drifted off. Such a long workday.

A sudden blast of noise brought me to full consciousness. I sprang out of bed and irrationally checked the closet. Tom's bulletproof vest was still there. I crossed to the window. A flash of lightning and rumble of thunder heralded another nighttime storm. That would account for the noise. I fell back into bed and wondered how long it would take to get used to being married to a policeman.

I listened to rain pelt the roof and wished I could fall asleep. Tom came in later, finally, and nestled comfortably beside me. The nights are too short, I was foggily aware of thinking as sleep finally claimed me. And the days are too long.

I awoke in a sudden sweat. The bedroom was flooded with light. The radio alarm had not blared some forgettably peppy tune, because the doggone power was out again. This time Tom had departed without my realizing it. His terse note on the mirror read: *No news on investigation. We're checking Hotchkiss. I called SW hospital. Glad Marla's recovering. T.* I wondered if he'd had a nice chat with Dr. Lyle Gordon.

I buttoned myself into my chef's jacket, zipped up a black skirt, and checked on a still-sleeping Arch. After a frantic search I located my watch and dully realized that I had less than forty minutes to put together the ribs and other goodies for the food fair. If I was not set up down at the mall by nine-forty, I would miss the county health inspector's visit to my booth and risk being expelled from the whole event. And then what would I do with three hundred individual portions of ribs, salad, bread, and cookies? Not something I wanted to think about.

On so little sleep, facing such hurried preparation without the ability to brew a caffeinated drink was truly the punishment of the damned. When I scurried into the kitchen, Julian was chopping fervently for the Chamber of Commerce brunch. Neat piles of raisins, grated gingerroot, and plump slices of nectarine indicated he was starting with the chutney. His hair was wet from his shower and he was wearing pristine black pants, a white shirt, and a freshly bleached and ironed apron. But his happy expression of two mornings before was gone. Grieving took different forms, and I trusted Julian to tell us if he needed help. On the other hand, the kid could be as stubborn as a mountain goat.

"I don't know how I'm supposed to cook without power," he announced ferociously as he whacked the spice cabinet open. "I called Public Service, and they said it would be at least an hour before electricity was restored. What is the matter with these people?"

His anger dissolved my resolution not to pry. "Tell me how you're doing," I said.

He faced me, clenching two glass spice jars. His skin was gray, his eyes bloodshot. He had cut himself shaving and a corner of tissue stuck to his cheekbone. "How do you *think* I'm doing?"

I said nothing.

He turned away. "I'm sorry. I know you care. I just . . . don't want to talk about what happened day before yesterday." He measured out cinnamon and added in a low voice, "I'm not ready."

"Look, Julian, I don't know if it's such a good idea for you to be doing this brunch today. Why don't you let me call somebody in to help? Maybe one of your classmates from Elk Park Prep could come over. It's just not that big a deal to get a temporary server."

"No, no," he said angrily as he measured ground cloves. "I've got the whole day mapped out. All I *need* is some fucking *electricity.*"

"It'll come back on just when I'm leaving," I told him as I opened the refrigerator. "It's called Murphy's Law of Food Preparation."

"Huh?"

"Oh, nothing." I got out the covered containers of ribs, salad, bread, and cookies. The walk-in refrigerator would stay cold for several hours if the door was not opened too often. Lucky for me the organizers of the fair were providing butane burners and grills for heating food. I couldn't imagine serving — much less eating — cold barbecued ribs at ten o'clock in the morning.

Julian set aside the spices and began to dice the onion. "Coronary Care Unit visiting hours are the first ten minutes of every hour," he continued in a clipped, controlled tone. "I'm going down when I finish the chamber shindig. Is the hospital staff going to give me a hard time? Should I tell them she's my aunt Marla? That sounds kind of funny, I've never called her that before. I mean, really, I've been on my own for quite a while."

"As long as you're there the first ten minutes, you'll be fine. I was there yesterday, and the receptionist guarding the doors to the CCU was like a female Doberman. But Marla's doctor's pretty nice, although she treats him terribly." Julian shook his head morosely. I continued. "The doc wants her to have as much emotional support from visitors as she can get. Why don't you come get me at the mall? My time at the food fair will be up by then, and we can go see her together."

He set aside the onion and washed his hands. "Okay. I have the chamber brunch, then cleanup, then drive down and pick you up at the food fair, then go see Marla. Does that sound okay? I wanted to take Arch with me, but he said he promised Todd they could go to a record swap this afternoon. The thunder woke us up last night, so we talked about his plans." His words were still coming out fast, much faster than usual. "Arch wanted to help me today too. But I said no. I asked him if I could help him find some sixties albums." Julian took a breath and poured sugar into a measuring cup. It cascaded over the top and he cursed softly. "I mean, I've been promising him all summer that I'd help him with his new hobby and I haven't done any of it. Plus I was going to take him to some veterinarian's office yesterday." He reached for the cider vinegar and measured it carefully. "Now I'll have lots of time. I guess. We can go to the animal hospital. I don't know much about sixties music, though, like Jimi Hendrix —" He broke off, slammed the bottle of vinegar on the counter, and clasped his arms around his shivering body.

"Julian, don't —" I put my arms around him. I couldn't bear to see someone so young in such pain. I murmured to him how sorry I was, that the whole situation was awful, to go ahead and cry all he wanted, that he should forget the damn chamber brunch. I'd order everything in from the Chinese place.

"If I just knew why," he sobbed into my shoulder. "If I just knew who would do this! God! What is the matter with the world?"

"I know. It's screwed up."

"I feel as if —" He choked on his words, then said, "Life is so stupid. It is just dumb, that's all. When something like this can happen and people just go on . . . Oh, what's the point?"

Again I replied that I didn't know. My heart felt painfully heavy. Would he please take a day off, I begged. But Julian merely shook his head, and said he was doing the brunch. Just could I stop talking about it, he asked me. He looked disconsolately around the kitchen and then began to arrange frozen rolls on a rack to thaw.

The phone rang. A woman from the church was volunteering to contact an excellent private nurse for Marla. I thanked her and said that would be wonderful. Would I be at the early service this Sunday to tell the parish how Marla was doing, she asked. I replied that I would.

When I hung up, I touched Julian's arm. "Will you call Tom today and check in occasionally? Please? I won't be near a phone, and I'm going to be a wreck worrying about you —"

"Sure, of course." He managed a mirthless

smile. "When we were talking during the storm, Arch told me — real serious, you know how he is — that he was going to stick to me like epoxy all morning while I was cooking. He swore he'd call an ambulance if I went into shock." Julian chuckled morbidly. I sighed. "So I told him to concentrate on the Mothers of Invention and I'd worry about the fathers of commerce. Tell you what, Goldy. I didn't want to mention that even if he finds some of those old LPs, he's never going to get hold of a system that'll play them."

"Who's fighting?" demanded a sleepy Arch. He stood in the doorway of the kitchen. "I heard you guys."

"Nobody," I assured him. This morning, my son was wearing an oversize black T-shirt that said GO PANTHERS! on it. Looking for memorabilia from the civil rights movement, Arch had been overjoyed to find the tattered thing at the Aspen Meadow secondhand store. I hadn't had the heart to tell him it was the booster uniform from the Idaho Springs High School football team.

He pushed his glasses up his nose. His straw-brown hair stuck out in all directions, like a game of pick-up sticks. "Don't you need to leave, Mom?"

"Yes, yes." But I didn't move.

Arch turned to Julian and frowned. "Okay,

here I am. Why don't you give me something to chop for the brunch you're doing?"

Julian said, "Why don't you sit down and have breakfast, Eldridge, and then I will."

Arch plopped into a kitchen chair, caught my eye, and gave me a nodding scowl: *Everything's going to be okay here,* his look said. Sometimes our clan felt like a pride of lions, everyone protective of everyone else. I scooped up the first chafing dish and walked outside.

With all their more harmful consequences, at least the storms had brought a welcome break in the weather. A breeze ruffled my chef's jacket. I hustled past Tom's garden. Cabbage butterflies and iridescent humming-birds flitted from red dianthus to purple Corsican violet. Aspen leaves that had stirred so languidly on their pale branches two days before now quivered, as if in anticipation of a change in season. In Aspen Meadow, fall usually begins in the middle of August, which was just six weeks away. In the distance, patches of brilliant sunlight on breeze-rippled Aspen Meadow Lake quilted the water with sparkles.

When I came back in, Arch was eating one of the cranberry-orange muffins Julian had made on Wednesday. I packed the food and the second chafer into the van. Julian insisted on hauling out the dry ice and the speed cart, where the cups of salad would stay cold. At the last moment I remembered the bleach water. The vat of bleach water is a necessary hygiene element for utensils when no running water is available. I packed the closed chlorine-smelling vat in last. With a coffee-deprivation headache percolating, I fervently hoped that one of the food fair booths would offer espresso, and plenty of it.

The van choked, coughed, and wheezed before moving unenthusiastically out of the driveway. An inch-thick spew of stones and gravel covered our road and Main Street. When I exited Interstate 70 and moved into the heavy stream of summer-in-the-suburbs traffic, my temperature gauge flickered upward ominously. The first surge of Denver's hot air filled the van, and I thought of Julian, with us for a year, part of the family. After his outburst in the kitchen, he had warned me brusquely to have something to eat before I started working. He'd said, You don't want to faint in that heat. I took a bite of one of the muffins he had placed on a napkin in the passenger seat. The tart cranberries and Grand Marnier combined for a heady taste. I remembered how energetically Julian had banged the tin into the oven before Claire arrived. And then his agonized questions from this morning echoed in my ear: *Who would do this? Why . . .*

I put on the turn signal to go back to Aspen Meadow. Turned it off. Turned it back on. *Leave him alone,* my inner voice warned. *If you do the chamber brunch, you'll only be saying you think he's incompetent.* Reluctantly, I turned off the ticker and resolved to stick with the day's plan. After all, the mall opened at eight for special sales in all the stores, and folks were going to come up to the food fair famished from shopping. At least, that was my hope.

"Hey, lady! Make up your mind! The light's gonna change!" came a shout from a convertible behind me.

When the light turned, I gritted my teeth and urged the van forward. I decided to concentrate on the morning ahead. But I had never done a food fair before, and the idea filled me with unhappy anticipation.

Booths at A Taste of Furman County were much sought after, although it was hard to figure out why. Great publicity, I guessed. The big beneficiary of the event was Playhouse Southwest. For the hundreds of servings the playhouse auxiliary told the food folks to provide each day, none of us was compensated. Visitors to the fair, though, paid forty bucks a pop to obtain the official bracelets that allowed them into the tent-festooned roof of the mall garage. The open air was necessary for ventilation, and the roof provided views of Denver's suburban sprawl to the east and the Front Range of the Rockies to the west. Once inside the roped-off area, tasters were promised that horror of horrors, *all you can eat,* which to food people translates as *until we run out.* There had been so much demand for booths from local restaurateurs, chefs, and caterers who wanted to offer their wares, the organizers had even split up the serving times into two-hour shifts. I did not know whether potential clients would be likely to shop or eat during my daily slot from ten to noon. I certainly hoped that they'd stop by my booth, be enthralled and enchanted, and whip out their calendars — and checkbooks — to sign me up for all kinds of profitable new bookings. Otherwise, I was going to be very upset. Not to mention out about a thousand bucks' worth of supplies.

My van sputtered and slowed behind a line of traffic crawling toward the mall garage entrance. After a moment I saw what was once again causing the slowdown. At the side of the parking lot, by the elegant marble entrance to Prince & Grogan, a crowd of animal rights' demonstrators waved placards that read MIGNON COSMETICS BRING DEATH —

DEATH TO MIGNON COSMETICS! Shaman Krill, arms outstretched, hair wild, was leading the crowd in a chant that I couldn't quite make out. The row of cars stopped. I reached across and gingerly rolled down the passenger-side window.

"Death on your hands! Death on your face!"

A uniformed officer was directing traffic. The van crept forward. As I neared the shouting demonstrators, my hands became clammy on the steering wheel. Three parked sheriff's department vehicles seemed to indicate that the police weren't just there to head cars up the ramps.

"Death isn't pretty! Death's pretty gritty!"

Maybe there were other cops I couldn't see who were keeping an eye on the activists. Or perhaps the officers were there as part of the continuing investigation into Claire's murder. From the small crowd of people pushing through the nearby door to Foley's department store, it looked as if shoppers were avoiding the protest. This, undoubtedly, was the deterrent the demonstrators wanted, since Mignon was carried exclusively by Prince & Grogan.

"Food fair or shopping?" the policeman asked when my van was finally first in line.

"Food fair."

He pointed to the far right side of the ramp,

where a food service truck was lumbering up to the top level. When I slowly accelerated away from the cop, there was a thud on the side of the van, and then another. Frantically scanning the mirrors, I thought I must have been hit by a car backing up, when Shaman Krill's face leered at the partly open passenger-side window.

"Hey! Caterer! Going to throw any more food around today? What're you serving, slaughtered cow?"

I leaned on the horn with one hand and rolled down the driver-side window with the other.

"Help!" I yelled. "Help, help!"

The policeman hustled over. By the time I could tell him one of the demonstrators had harassed me, Shaman Krill had disappeared. Even when I stopped the van and hopped out to look where he'd gone, I couldn't see the activist's dark, bobbing head in the crowd. The policeman asked if I wanted to file a report. I said no. I quickly told him that Investigator Tom Schulz was my husband, and that I'd tell *him* all about it, but that at the moment I was late to set up for the food fair. The officer reluctantly let me go, with the admonition to be careful.

I climbed back in the driver's seat and pressed firmly on the accelerator. The van whizzed up the ramp of the parking garage. Yellow police ribbons around the place where Claire died came into view. I averted my eyes.

I pulled into a parking space, pinned on my official Food-Fair Server badge, and glanced at my watch. Eight-thirty. A little over an hour remained to get everything set up on the roof before the inspector showed up with his trusty little thermometer to see if my hot food was hot enough and my cold food sufficiently chilly. The diagram of food fair booths showed my booth was next to the stairway up from the second-floor garage entrance to Prince & Grogan. A stream of weight-wielding walkers impeded my schlepping the first load of boxes to the elevator, but I finally made it. Within thirty minutes I had wheeled, carted, and hauled my stuff into place. I put out my ads with sample menus and price lists, fired up the butane burner, and waited for the grills to heat. And then, oh, then, I thanked the patron saints of cappuccino that right across from the spot allocated to Goldilocks' Catering was a booth with the sign PETE'S ESPRESSO BAR.

I slapped the first batch of ribs on the grill and dashed across the makeshift aisle to the deliciously appetizing smell. With more success than I would have thought possible, Pete had been running a coffee place at Westside

Mall since the shopping center had been refurbished. He'd taken it upon himself to run a wonderfully inventive promotional campaign, including taking nighttime orders for hot coffee drinks delivered first thing in the morning to nearby businesses. He called it Federal Espresso. Today, Pete, a thirtyish, dark-haired fellow who had managed both to transport and get a power source for an enormous steam-driven Rancilio machine, was wearing a T-shirt that said NEED COFFEE DELIVERED? USE ESPRESSO MALE. He instantly recognized the symptoms of latte-deprivation and fixed me a tall one with three shots. I sipped it gratefully while looking eastward off the garage roof. A beautiful old neighborhood called Aqua Bella was not half a mile away, and the rooftops of the large, older homes were just visible — the turrets of a pale Victorian, the chimneys of an Edwardian. It wasn't as good as looking at the lake and the mountains with my morning coffee, but it was okay.

"Gorgeous, isn't it?" said a dreamy voice. "Wouldn't you just love to live over there?" Dusty Routt sighed gustily. "Someday. When I get out of this place," she added bitterly.

"I like Aspen Meadow, actually," I replied. Dusty looked better than the day before — calmer, more in control. For which I was grateful. "Denver's too crowded," I added.

"How are you doing? Better?"

"Well, I . . . how's Julian?"

"Not so hot."

She sighed again. "I guess I'm doing better. I'm just getting some coffee before I go work," she said apologetically, and turned to Pete. She shook the food fair bracelet past the cuff of her dark green Mignon uniform to show him. "I'll take two chocolate-dipped biscotti to go with the latte." She picked up one of the pamphlets Pete was offering, *The History and Science of Coffee.* "Better make that three biscotti," she said. She wrinkled her nose and gave me the pamphlet when Pete handed across her drink and pile of cookies. While Pete tried to sell her some Sumatra Blend, I read that according to legend, coffee provided mental alertness, a cure for catarrh, an antidote for hemlock, and a lessening of the symptoms of narcolepsy. I could have used some narcolepsy last night. I tossed the pamphlet into a trash can. Dusty politely refused Pete's offer for a discount on the Sumatra, picked up her breakfast, and said in a confidential tone, "You know, Goldy, I really shouldn't be doing this food fair. I mean, forty bucks, and the mall workers don't even get a discount! But the bracelet's good all day . . . maybe I'll have something nutritious during my break. I just need to get a little sugar in my system before I go out there and sell, sell, sell."

I sipped Pete's marvelous latte and glanced at the ribs. They were now sending up savory swirls of smoke. "That's okay. Julian already told me about what cosmetics folks eat."

A look of worry crossed Dusty's pretty, chubby face. "But . . . did he come with you? Is he okay? They called all the reps last night to tell us about the police investigation. . . ." She faltered. This morning, Dusty's short, orange-blond hair was coiffed in a spill of stiff waves framing her cherub-cheeked face. Although I knew she was only eighteen, her heavy matte makeup, dark-lined eyes, too-rosy streaks of blush, and prominent blue eyeshadow made her look much older. Lack of sleep and worry lines didn't help. Not to mention dealing with the news that one of your colleagues had been killed.

"What did they say to the reps?" I asked.

"I have to get back," she said abruptly. "Come with me? I'd like to talk to you, since we didn't really have a chance yesterday. And it seems as if we never get to when we're in the neighborhood. You're always cooking or going off somewhere, and I have Colin to take care of, since Mom never feels very well. . . ."

I glanced at my watch again: nine-twenty.

There was still no sign of the goateed health inspector, and I did want to get the second half of my banquet payment from Mignon before things got too busy. . . . Nodding to Dusty, I quickly removed the juicy ribs from the grill and drafted a food fair volunteer to guard my supplies for twenty minutes. Then I picked up my coffee and walked with Dusty to Prince & Grogan.

"How is your mother, Dusty? I haven't seen her for a while."

Dusty snorted. "Heartbroken."

"Heartbroken?" I repeated. "Why?"

"Well," said Dusty as she finished her first cookie. "First she fell in love with my dad, had me, and then he left. They never got married, and of course I never knew him. So good old Mom worked hard as a secretary to raise me, and then, not too long ago, she got a chance to have a house, finally, through Habitat for Humanity. And what did she do? Fell in love with the plumber. The plumber working on the Habitat house! She was thirty-eight, he was twenty-five, but never mind! That woman, my dear mother, is gorgeous, she's passionate, she has no idea of the meaning of birth control. So the plumber got her pregnant with Colin, and it's bye-bye Aspen Meadow Plumbing Service! I heard from somebody that he drove his little pipe-filled pickup truck to the Western Slope, where he could start all over, donating his services to charity." Through a bite of biscotti, she mumbled, "At a discount."

"I'm sorry." Actually, I knew the details of this particular story from Marla. Strikingly stunning Sally Routt, Dusty's mother, a single mother with an aging father and a teenage daughter, had become involved with the young, plain-looking town plumber. Had Sally hoped he would marry her when she became pregnant? Who knew? I never saw Sally Routt when she was expecting, because she'd gone into seclusion, and then reportedly suffered through a difficult, premature childbirth. The plumber, with his sad round face and round eyes behind glass-rimmed spectacles, had departed Aspen Meadow at night, leaving behind accounts receivable and one emotional debt unpaid.

"Don't tell the people at your church, okay?" Dusty pleaded, suddenly conscience-stricken. "Heartbroken or not, Mom's living in fear that she'll lose the house on, like, moral grounds."

It was all I could do not to laugh. For Dusty to think that her mother's sad tale had not flowed through our parish with the speed of water through broken pipes was painfully naive. On the other hand, nobody in town seemed to know why Dusty had been expelled from Elk Park Prep, so maybe you could keep some secrets in Aspen Meadow. But at least the Routts were managing to keep a part of their bad news under wraps. "Well," I said, "are you recovering from hearing about Claire's death? How did you finally hear about what happened, anyway?"

"Recovering? How can you recover from that? Nick Gentileschi, head of security, called everybody Wednesday night to tell us the bad news." She shuddered, then daintily bit into another cookie. "You might have seen Nick day before yesterday? He was outside in the garage with the guys from Mignon, when they were watching for those stupid demonstrators. He was, like, crying and all on the phone," she went on. "Nick really thought a lot of Claire. Everybody did, actually. You could talk to her, and she was so enthusiastic about the products. . . . Anyway, he said it was a hit-and-run and they were going to step up the security police patrols of the parking garage, to look for careless drivers. I'm thinking, like, it's a little late for that. You know?"

I thought of Julian sobbing in my arms. Maybe Nick Gentileschi and I could have a little chat. After I got my check, of course.

"Dusty?" I said suddenly. "Do you want to have lunch?"

To my dismay, she became embarrassed. We were standing awkwardly in the mall hallway outside the Prince & Grogan entrance. "You want to have lunch with *me?* Why? You mean as part of the food fair?"

"Sure. I have a friend in the hospital across the street —" This wasn't coming out right. *And I need to pass the time before visiting hours? And I want to know what's really going on at that cosmetics counter? What kind of problems does the department store have, exactly?* No, those explanations wouldn't wash. "I have a friend in the hospital across the street, and she loves fattening food but can't have any." I stopped to think. How much cash did I have? For all my worry about money, I carried little beyond a single credit card and an emergency hundred-dollar bill. Dusty was looking at me with raised, perfectly plucked eyebrows. Her eyeshadow this morning gleamed like the hummingbirds in Tom's garden.

"You're going to *eat* for your friend?" she asked. "That is radical, I've never heard of being sympathetic like that, I'm like, *totally* blown away —"

"No, that's not exactly it." We walked inside. "Here's what I was thinking," I said. "You could sell me something that I can take to my friend. Hand cream, lipstick, makeup, I don't care. Then we can go around and sam-

211

ple the food fair. Twelve-fifteen? I'll pick you up?"

"Actually," she said in a low, hesitant voice, "no, I can't do it. If that's okay. I'm behind on my sales for the last two months, so I've been asking to work through the noon hour. That's when most of the women shop. You know, they're on their lunch hours. Or businessmen visit us then, for their wives' birthdays, and they want to buy perfume or something. . . . Why don't you come in and get your stuff when you finish at the fair?" She swallowed the last bit of cookie and attempted a cheerful grin. "But I need to go now."

We had arrived at the long, brightly lit Mignon counter. It faced the store entrance, prime shopping space that Mignon used to good advantage with sparkling mirrors, gilt decorations, and several video screens. I promised Dusty I'd see her later, then stood transfixed in front of the video screens. In my hurry yesterday, I had not stopped to watch the short films. The first showed impossibly thin twenty-year-old women frolicking beside a fountain. Gaping at them were what looked like well-built Italian movie stars posing as construction workers. Another video showed people clapping wildly as skinny models sashayed down runways wearing dresses that dripped long strands of beads. They were not the kind of outfits I could wear to the grocery store. But it was the third film that made me groan aloud. A lovely young woman knelt by the flat tire on her car just as an impossibly gorgeous guy drove up in his white convertible. Within five seconds she was driving off in the convertible with the fellow. *With Mignon makeup,* the video implied, *you can even save on Triple-A dues!*

Harriet Wells appeared and gave me a huge smile. The head sales associate wore her green smock and diamond-cluster earrings, and as usual her spun-gold hair was done up in an impeccable twist. "The caterer again!" she exclaimed. "Nick Gentileschi was looking for you, something about your check. Want me to see if he's in his office?"

I nodded. "That would be great, thanks."

She drew out a foil-wrapped package from underneath the counter. "My spice muffins. Why don't you try one and tell me what you think is in it?" She treated me to another sparkling grin. "Free perfume sample if you guess correctly. I'll be right back." And with that, she turned on her high heels and moved to the phone by the cash register.

The foil crinkled in my hand. I didn't really care about perfume samples, but I was a sucker for a bet on my tasting abilities. The muffins were tiny and golden, and flecked with something brown. I took a bite and then another: crunchy, with zucchini and cinnamon. Delicious. As I calculated what it would take to reproduce them — honey for the sweetener, large, ripe, extra-juicy zucchini, filberts chopped fine . . . I had the uncomfortable feeling that I was being watched.

I glanced around to the shoe department. A tall man with wild, white-blond hair had been looking at sale espadrilles. Now he was staring at me with his mouth open. Maybe it was against the rules to eat muffins inside the store. I swallowed the last bite, straightened up, and pretended to be studying the face cream display that cried: *You deserve to be retextured!* There was a tipped mirror a little farther down the counter. I moseyed over and acted preoccupied with my reflection.

Harriet's smile was icy when she returned to me. "The head of security is occupied and can't look for your check at the moment. He wanted to know if you could come back later?"

Occupied doing what, I wondered. Clearly Harriet was also upset that the head of security was unavailable.

I said that was fine, thanked Harriet, and told her her muffin was made with zucchini, filberts, and cinnamon. She laughed her high

tinkling laugh and rewarded me with two perfume samples: One was called Foreplay and
the other was Lies. I never wanted the samples, I just wanted the muffin. Oh, well.

Back at the food fair, I tossed the samples
into the same trash can where I'd thrown
Pete's pamphlet and hustled back to my booth.
The volunteer was happy to be relieved. I put
the first batch of ribs back on the grill, readied
the second batch, and lit the Sterno for the
chafers. As promised, another of the fair vol-
unteers brought hot water for the bain-marie,
the water bath for the chafing dish. This was
so that as soon as the first batch of ribs was
done, I could move the meat into a heated
serving area. And none too soon, as the health
inspector showed up just slightly later than
scheduled. He impassively surveyed the
spread and plunked his trusty thermometer
first into the pile of cooked ribs, then the salad
being kept cold in the speed cart. He wiped
the thermometer meticulously each time, giving a little nod. He asked to see the bleach
water and I showed it to him. Then he nodded
approvingly, refused a cookie, and moved on
to the next booth.

Within moments the first batch of visitors
shaking their little food fair bracelets appeared
on our line of booths. The mall walkers, who
had clustered, giggling, around Pete's coffee

machine, descended on my booth as if they hadn't eaten in a month. The ribs bubbled invitingly in the barbecue sauce, and I transferred two at a time from the chafer to small paper plates next to the cups of strawberry-sugar snap pea salad, slices of cranberry bread, and piles of frosted fudge cookies. Cries of "Oh, no, I'm supposed to buy a bathing suit today" did not remotely allay appetites. Thank goodness. Hunger makes the best sauce, my two-hundred-fifty-pound fourth-grade teacher had once said, and it seemed she was right.

For the next two hours I was so busy filling plates, cooking ribs, and chatting with shoppers about how Goldilocks' Catering could turn their next party into an *event* that I barely noticed anything outside my own food space. At eleven fifty-five, however, the two co-owners of Upcountry Barbecue showed up to claim my booth, and I was forced to take stock.

"Aw, no, Roger," exclaimed one, "she's got barbecue too! This is gonna *ruin* us!"

"I don't see any Rocky Mountain oysters," replied Roger with a smirk. "You gal-cooks just don't have the guts to serve real western food. Ain't that right?"

I grinned at Roger and his partner. "I know the women who frequent this mall will love the sliced reproductive organ of buffalo. Especially if you roast 'em, put 'em on croissants, and tell the gals *exactly* what you're serving. Ain't that right, boys?"

Roger and partner exchanged a rueful glance. They'd forgotten the damn croissants.

My food was gone. A hundred fifty portions in two morning hours wasn't bad, I figured, and I'd given out over a hundred menus and price lists. The grills and speed cart would be cleaned by the food fair staff and stay locked in place, so I had only one box of supplies to take down to the van. Once the box was stashed, I leaned against the closed van doors. Sudden inactivity made me realize just how hot and exhausted I was. I'd get my check, chat with Dusty, reconnoiter with Julian, visit Marla, then go home and crash. At least that was what I planned as I hauled myself up and walked down toward the entrance to Prince & Grogan. Before I could get there, however, I stopped and shuddered.

Maybe I have too active an imagination. Maybe I watch too many movie reruns with Arch. But seeing people — or even those boys in the film version of *Lord of the Flies* — wearing war paint just sends fear ripping through my bloodstream. People can hide their basest selves behind a veneer of fierce black and white stripes. Transformed, they can claim not to be responsible for what they do. I didn't know whether I was willing to be the victim of irresponsible aggression as I now stood facing at least sixty war-painted demonstrators jostling each other and their signs in back of police sawhorses by the Prince & Grogan entrance.

"When you buy, rabbits die!" they shouted at the few customers brave enough to scuttle timidly past the sawhorses and into the store.

Worse, there wasn't a policeman in sight. But then a woman strode confidently to the store entrance. Oh, Lord. The woman entering through the highly polished doors thirty paces in front of me was Frances Markasian.

She had told me on the phone she was coming to see me at the mall food fair. She hadn't shown up. And yet here she was, going into Prince & Grogan.

My check could wait. I swallowed hard and decided to follow Frances. When I came to the sawhorses, the demonstrators surged forward and screeched.

"Are you dying for mascara?"

"Do you care that innocent animals are tortured for your makeup?"

One waved a sign directly in front of my face: DIE FOR BEAUTY! it proclaimed, with a photograph of a pile of dead rabbits. I felt my face turning red, but I concentrated on getting through the doors on the track of the

Mountain Journal's premier investigative reporter.

Someone's elbow jostled me and my ears rang from the shouted insults, but moments later, I was safely inside. I scanned the opulent store interior. Frances Markasian had made a detour into accessories and was fingering the various leathers of expensive handbags. Once again she was, as my parents would say, all dolled up. This time she sported a scarlet dress with a flared skirt, scarlet heels, and scarlet scarf twisted in some remarkably woven way through her mass of black hair. I quickly paralleled her step as she minced past a table display of wallets and headed for the far side of the Mignon counter. I slithered into the shoe department that faced that side of the cosmetics counter. Frances had spied on me so many times that I felt no compunction about seeing what she was up to this time. It had even become something of a game between us. Whatever today's game was, the fact that it required two disguises in three days made it extremely interesting.

"I'm here because I need help with my face," I heard Frances inform Harriet Wells. Dusty was waiting on a man I vaguely recognized — the tall blond fellow I'd seen in the shoe department that morning. Maybe he was an undercover cop.

Harriet looked at Frances and frowned. "What would you say is the skin problem you'd like to correct the most?" she asked politely.

Out in the aisle between the cosmetics counter and the shoe department, a five-tiered display of plastic boxes filled with a navy-blue and gold display of Mignon lipsticks, soaps, toners, and creams offered a hiding place. I ducked behind it.

Within moments, Harriet's voice rose slightly. She was trying to sell Frances some concealer, and Frances was making such uncharacteristically enthusiastic responses that I ducked around the plastic box holding the Fudge Mousse lipstick and Nectarine Desire blush for a better view. From there, I could watch Harriet without her seeing me, since all her attention was focused on Frances, who was whining, "But I just want to look *younger*." Uh-huh.

"This is Rejuvenation, the newest product to come out of Mignon's European labs." Harriet delicately gripped the pale, ribbed cylindrical bottle. "It has biochromes in it, and just look at what it's done for *my* skin." She lifted her free palm like a fan toward her superbly painted face. "I'm sixty-two," she declared with a sunny smile. "Rejuvenation will take two decades off your face."

"Sixty-two?" Frances echoed with loud incredulity as she shifted uncomfortably in the red spike heels. "I would have sworn you weren't a day over fifty-five!"

A tiny frown appeared between Harriet's eyebrows, then swiftly disappeared. I myself wouldn't have put Harriet's age over fifty.

"The biochromes penetrate to the *deepest* layer of the skin. They actually *stop* the aging process," Harriet announced proudly.

"Is that right? How much for a big bottle of that?" Frances asked brightly.

"Well," mused Harriet, "you need all the preparations to do the complete job. It's like the four basic food groups. First we start with the pre-cleanser. . . ." Here she frowned at Frances and shook her head. "Here, you hold the Rejuvenation while I look for the right cleanser for your skin." She handed the bottle to Frances, who turned it, held it out at arm's length, and grimaced. Harriet groped beneath the counter. When she reemerged, she gave Frances's face a swift, shrewd assessment. "It really does look as if you have quite a bit of damage to your skin. Did your dermatologist send you?" When Frances shook her head, Harriet asserted, "You could certainly benefit from one of our rejuvenating cleansers . . ." and then she chided and explained and piled creams and cosmetics on the counter until

Frances's tab was, by my reckoning, well over four hundred dollars.

I leaned in closer to Harriet and Frances, but was stunned to be interrupted in my eavesdropping by a stocky fellow who edged in beside me and asked: "What are they saying?" He smiled at me as if this were some kind of joke only the two of us were in on. He had dark brown hair and short, stubby fingers that he drummed on his knees as he crouched next to me.

"I don't know what you're talking about," I replied huffily, and straightened up.

"Is that your boyfriend?" he asked as if he hadn't heard my answer. His accent was flat and midwestern. His arms seemed too short for his body when he gestured knowingly in the direction of the tall blond man with Dusty.

"He is *not* my boyfriend. Would you *please* go away?"

He opened his eyes wide, as if I'd refused to laugh at his joke. Then he touched the badge on my white jacket. "Are you really a chef? I mean, you're wearing one of those coats. Is your restaurant here in the mall?"

"As a matter of fact, it is. Two of my co-workers are right nearby." Maybe I could frighten this guy away with the threat of numbers.

"Really?" He looked around. "They won't

222

mind if I talk to their boss, will they? How long have you been here?"

"Look, mister, please, please, please go away —"

But the guy raised a thick brown eyebrow and didn't move. Emboldened by my ability to be convincingly dishonest at the hospital, I improvised wildly. "Actually, I work for the department store. You might have read about the accident we had in the mall garage day before yesterday?" He pursed his lips and nodded sympathetically. "That blond fellow over there is an undercover cop who's questioning a suspect, and I'm supposed to pay attention . . . so can you please leave so I can do my job?"

He ran his hands over one of the plastic boxes stacked in front of us. "This is so much more interesting than shopping for my niece's birthday."

"Are you listening to me? At the moment I'm doing something extremely important and confidential," I said desperately. When he looked skeptical, I hissed: "Look buster, what I'm trying to tell you is I — work — for — store — security."

"No kidding?"

"No kidding."

He took me gently by the arm and said, "We need to have a talk."

"Get your fingers off me," I said fiercely, unwilling to give up my hiding spot without a protest. "Let go, or I will pull so hard that I'll drag you right out of the store with me! And the whole time I'll be yelling so loud, the security SWAT team will come running!"

The guy grinned. His grip on my arm tightened almost imperceptibly. "We need to have a talk real bad."

That did it. "Security!" I shrieked, and began to wriggle. I had a brief glimpse of Frances, Harriet, Dusty, and the blond guy gaping as I twisted and flailed and tried to shake the man's arm off me. In my thrashing, I fell against the piled boxes. The clear containers with all their lipsticks, creams, toners, and soaps tumbled. My tormentor braced his legs and continued to imprison me in a viselike grip.

"Security!" I screamed. I thrashed and felt my hose rip. "Help!" I called again. Why wasn't anyone helping me? "Somebody from security come *now!*"

The man leaned down. "Lady, I'm here," he said.

9

I've had humiliating escalator rides in my day. The afternoon of a banquet for Brunswick sales reps, I lost control of an oversize box of bowling-ball-size handmade chocolates. I shrieked in futile warning as chocolate globes pelted the escalator steps and ten fur-coated women went sprawling: a strike. Another time, two-year-old Arch threw up all over me and several nearby teenage boys. The boys were extremely unsympathetic. This in spite of the fact that at Arch's age they had probably also overindulged in hot dogs and milk shakes.

Unquestionably, though, this was the most humiliating escalator ride of my life. This stocky, brown-haired guy — this lackey who mumbled that his name was Stan White — was presumably taking me to Nick Gentileschi, head of security at Prince & Grogan. Once we were on the escalator, Stan released my arm and quickly stepped behind my back. It was obviously a practiced maneuver, the kind a policeman or a security guy makes when he thinks his perp might bolt. I can't say I wasn't considering it.

I tried to ignore all the staring people. They

were below us, they were above us, they were pointing from the descending escalator paralleling ours. The usual high, excited hum of shoppers chatting about what they had bought or what they needed to buy ceased as the onlookers swiftly took in our little twosome — the cowering woman in the chef's jacket with a rent-a-cop parked right behind her. It was a particular challenge to ignore a gaping Frances Markasian. You could see the mental wheels whirring to compose a headline: *Caught Caterer Cringes! Wife of Homicide Investigator Apprehended after Struggle by Fudge Mousse lip gloss.*

"You are making a huge mistake —" I began to say.

Stan White shook his head regretfully. "Lady, if I had a nickel for every time I've heard that line. . . ."

Well, this was just great. The steps moved inexorably upward, past the top of the Mignon counter with its display of shiny white bags stuffed with pink tissue paper, past the elephantine Chinese-style planters sprouting fake palm trees. Just don't let any clients see me, I prayed fervently.

No such luck. A large woman was leaning over the railing next to the escalator at the second floor landing, just above the cosmetics counter. When she straightened up, my heart sank to new depths. The *last* person I wanted to see at this moment was Babs Meredith Braithwaite. Even so, I might have avoided her if she hadn't inched over so that the security guy and I collided with her on our rough arrival at the second floor. We stared at each other. Babs's rust-colored suit trimmed with white was somewhat rumpled; her white blouse was hanging out. Her rust skirt slanted crookedly above her brown and white spectator pumps, as if the skirt were unzipped. Nor was her hair as meticulously poufed as it had been two days before. Today it looked like a windblown bird's nest. She was clutching her purse, which was open, as if it had been hastily snatched up. She was panting. She looked as if she had just shoplifted a diamond brooch, when all she'd been doing was spying on the Mignon counter, or so I assumed. The nefarious possibility that I could sic Stan the Security Man on *her* occurred to me.

"There's somebody back there," Babs whispered in a trembly voice to Stan and me. Her hand rose toward the racks of gaily colored bathing suits. She added urgently, "Please help me." She looked the security guy up and down. "Do you work for the store?"

"Yes," said Stan curtly. "I'm with security."

"There's somebody back there!" Her

227

cheeks were aflame, and it wasn't blush giving the color. I tried to look around Babs's wide body. Somebody back where?

Stan White touched my upper arm gently to guide me away from Babs and oncoming traffic spilling from the escalator. When I didn't move, he put his hands on his hips and set his mouth in a stern frown.

Babs whimpered, "Aren't you going to help me?"

Stan cleared his throat and pointed at me. "Are you with this woman?" he asked Babs. Confused, she shook her head. Stan concluded, firmly, "Then you'll have to find a salesperson. I can't help it if there's nobody back there."

"But," Babs said frantically, grabbing his arm, "there's *somebody* back there in the dressing room. You've got to come and help me."

Stan White perked up. This interested him. "Is it a man?" he asked. "In the women's dressing room?"

"It's somebody behind the mirror," insisted Babs. "I heard him cough." Reluctantly, she released Stan's arm.

"Lady, please." The security fellow shook his head. "We haven't done that kind of surveillance for years. It's against the law."

Babs clutched her purse. Her vivid cheeks shook with rage. "But, I'm trying to tell you

. . . ! Somebody must have broken in behind the mirrors! Aren't you going to do anything? What kind of security guard are you anyway?"

Stan bristled. "Okay, look. I have to do something else first. Then I'll check the dressing room, all right? Please, we need to go."

"Go where?" she demanded shrilly. "What are you doing with this woman?"

"What we're doing doesn't fall under the Freedom of Information Act, lady."

Babs Braithwaite pressed her lips together. "This . . ." She looked at me. What was I, exactly? "This . . . *woman* is going to be catering an important function for us this weekend. She's also operating a booth at our Playhouse Southwest benefit, and we can't have her —"

"When's your party?" the security fellow asked amiably as he made a no-nonsense gesture to me to walk forward in the direction of the department store offices.

"Why, why —" babbled Babs as she hustled along beside us, past the Japanese china decorated to look like English bone, "— tomorrow," she finished breathlessly. She slapped her purse down imperiously on a table displaying Waterford crystal. An extremely large and undoubtedly expensive vase teetered, then, miraculously, straightened.

"It's Friday," Stan said wearily, without

giving Babs so much as a glance. "I promise not to detain her more than twenty-four hours."

"But . . . this department store! What is going *on* —" Babs wailed, while I thought, *Twenty-four hours? I don't think so.*

Stan White nudged me through a door that said SECURITY and slammed it with a satisfactory thwack on Babs Braithwaite's indignant face. A large, imposing man sat behind a large, imposing desk. I felt like the bad kid brought before the principal. Or, since the man who stared at me with such authoritative disdain seemed to be enthroned, make that a disobedient subject tossed in front of the king. From the scowl of the seated man, it was clear he was the one who decided whether the subject was thrown to the lions or was released to work again in the fields of the sovereign.

Stan White discreetly disappeared through a side door. I sat down and eyed the plaque on the desk: NICHOLAS R. GENTILESCHI, DIRECTOR OF SECURITY. Then I took in the man himself. Fiftyish, Nick Gentileschi had a face whose extraordinary pallor was set off by flat jet-black eyes. His dark, receding hair was slicked to one side, except for an errant strand that flopped rakishly over his high-domed forehead. If his suit cost more than fifty dollars, he'd been cheated.

"Sit," he commanded, gesturing to a wooden chair. Without protest, I obeyed. When Gentileschi said nothing further, I glanced around his windowless office. Like the other still-to-be-refurbished Prince & Grogan offices, the paint on these walls was a disintegrating aquamarine. The department store seemed to care about its appearance everywhere but in its offices, as if prospective employees and would-be criminals weren't worth the trouble of a lovely décor. On one wall someone had mounted a white-framed painting with a plaque underneath: PRINCE & GROGAN, ALBUQUERQUE. The style of the flagship store was Southwestern via Wonderland. The picture showed a multistoried pink stucco building complete with soaring columns, multistoried glass, and a bulging, gilded entrance. A Pueblo Indian wouldn't have recognized it as indigenous architecture, that was for sure.

"I didn't take anything, as you can see," I said defensively. "I was just looking around." I rubbed my arm. "Please call the police," I told Nick Gentileschi firmly. I wasn't really hurt. Nevertheless, I wanted to act miffed. I knew security people feared lawsuits like the plague. Maybe I should tell him Babs's story too, about somebody lurking behind the mirror in the women's dressing room. Then again, maybe not. I didn't want to confuse him. With an optimism I was far from feeling, I said, "I'm hoping we can get this all straightened out."

Nick Gentileschi raised his thin eyebrows and tapped a pencil on top of a camera on his desk. Vaguely I wondered if a hidden video camera had somehow monitored my not-so-surreptitious surveillance of the cosmetics counter. "The police?" Gentileschi's voice grated like sandpaper. He dropped the pencil and began to jingle the keyring hanging from his belt. Then he turned his boxy, pale face sorrowfully toward the picture of the Albuquerque store. "She wants me to call the police." He grinned, revealing oversize, horselike teeth. "Now, that's one I haven't heard. You haven't stolen anything yet? You want to be cleared before things get worse? Or you have a friend at the sheriff's department?"

"Please, Mr. Gentileschi." Acting patient and sweet sometimes worked. I'd give it a whirl. "I know who you are, and Claire Satterfield was a friend of mine —"

The thin eyebrows lifted. "Is that right? A friend of yours? You ever go to her apartment for a party? Where did she live exactly . . . ?"

I sighed. "I didn't go to any parties, and

I don't know where she lived, somewhere in Denver —" The heck with this. I wondered if I could remember my lawyer's phone number off the top of my head.

"Now, that's an interesting friendship when you don't know where someone lives. Claire was a party girl. Didja know that? Or didn't you discuss that either in your . . . friendship?" He sneered the last word. My skin prickled.

"Who do you think you are, the FBI?" I said angrily. "Are you going to make a call or not?"

He opened a desk drawer, got out a form, and then carefully selected a pen. His gleaming black eyes regarded me greedily. "What's your name and occupation?"

I told him, and he took notes. Then he shifted his weight, smoothed his Grecian-Formula-16 hair with the palm of his hand, and said, "Now, you listen to me, Goldy Schulz, the supposed good friend of Claire Satterfield. We have our ways of knowing what's going on in this store. I know what you were trying to do. I just need to know the reasons. If your answers aren't satisfactory, I'll call the cops myself."

"I can assure you my reasons won't be satisfactory, since *I* don't even know what they were."

He blinked impassively and, pen poised over his form, waited for me to say more. When I did not, he sighed, put down the pen, picked up the telephone, and raised one eyebrow, as if he were calling my bluff. "Who should I call at the sheriff's department? Another *friend?*"

"Homicide Investigator Tom Schulz."

"I know Schulz. Do you know Schulz? I suppose you're going to tell me you're his sister or something."

I chose not to answer. He wouldn't believe me anyway.

But to my relief he dialed the sheriff's department. After a few preliminary murmurings, he managed, thank heaven, to get through to Tom. I watched with no small amount of satisfaction as the security chief's features quickly registered first smugness (*"Caught her acting suspicious by the cosmetics counter"*), then discomfort (*"No, she didn't touch any of the goods"*), and finally embarrassment (*"No, she didn't hurt anybody or take anything"*). But the moment of discomfort passed just as quickly, and Gentileschi confirmed an appointment to meet with Tom later that afternoon. Then he thrust the phone across the desk at me. "He wants to talk to you," he said glumly.

When I took the receiver, I could hear Tom

humming a dirgelike tune.

I said, "The great intellect —"

He was not amused. "Look, I said *not* like hitting the demonstrator. That means *not* like being picked up for suspicious activity by department store security."

"This is *not* my fault," I said in a low voice. After all, I was just trying to learn something to help Julian. No matter what the security people said about my presence, I had not caused trouble in the store. "I wasn't doing anything."

"Goldy, please remember, we're trying to *work* with this guy."

"I wish you the very best of luck in that particular enterprise," I said crisply. "Listen, Tom, did you check out that other person I asked you about?" When Gentileschi leaned over just slightly to catch what I was saying, I turned in the wooden chair.

"Double oh seven, what would I do without you? Okay, Miss G. We're already looking into Hotchkiss. He has a record and he runs a cosmetics place. But I will definitely tell the guys to ream his behind. And don't worry about Nick, he's an old friend of ours. Watch out though, he's got a reputation with women."

I turned back to look at the polyester-clad, dyed-haired man across the desk from me.

"Must say, Tom, I find that *extremely* hard to believe."

He chuckled. "Okay, look. I don't know when I'm going to have another chance to talk to you while you're down there. And I've been hard to reach —"

"No kidding."

"But there is something you can do. Somebody I need you to talk to, a friend of yours. You think Dusty Routt is the one who might have hinted to Frances Markasian this Krill character was one of Claire's old boyfriends? He swore to us he didn't know Claire. Maybe Markasian was baiting you with an idea of hers, see if you'd bite."

"I'm seeing Dusty at lunchtime, once I get out of prison." I tried to give Nick Gentileschi a prim look. He smirked.

"Well, the organization called People for the Ethical Treatment of Animals hasn't heard of Shaman Krill. And neither has the National Anti-Vivisection Society. Hell, even the SPCA swears they don't have a member named Krill. I don't know how long he's been an animal rights activist, but he hasn't been one long enough to earn him any kind of reputation. Our guys went to bring him in for more questioning, but he'd taken off from his demonstration buddies, and he wasn't at his apartment. And by the way, none of the demonstrators belong to any of those organizations. The legitimate organizations think Spare the Hares is some kind of wacko splinter group. Anyway. If you think Frances got the idea Krill was Claire's boyfriend from this Mignon sales associate named Dusty Routt, I'd sure like to hear about it."

"Why don't your guys just ask her?"

"We've already talked to Dusty Routt. At length. She swears she's never heard of Shaman Krill. So either she's lying or your friend Markasian got the info from somebody else, or got it wrong about who the boyfriend was. And speaking of your friend Markasian —"

"You know *that* person in question is never going to tell me a thing. She'll protect her sources to the grave."

"Frances Markasian? Not tell a thing to my Goldy? Never." Tom chuckled again. "Feed her some doughnuts or something. You know, the way they loosen folks' tongues by slipping 'em a few drinks? How about a little sodium pentathol in your chocolate truffle cheesecake?"

I told him I'd do my best and hung up. Truth Serum tiramisù was not in my repertoire, but never mind.

"Well, Mrs. Schulz," said Nick Gentileschi with that equine grin that made my skin crawl. "Whadya know? Seems you were just the person I was looking for." Then, without a hint of apology for the fiasco of my in-store "bust" and "interrogation," he shuffled through an untidy stack of papers next to the camera and retrieved a check. After scanning it, he handed it over: the balance due Goldilocks' Catering on the Mignon banquet. I stuffed it in my skirt pocket. Gentileschi went on with, "Sorry we didn't get it to you sooner. Personnel gave it to me when we heard your assistant went to the hospital. As you know, we're in the middle of a major crime investigation here. An unexplained death doesn't help the accounts get paid."

I fingered the check in my pocket. There was something slimy, something Uriah Heepish, about Nick Gentileschi that made me increasingly uneasy. He'd gone straight from badgering and prejudging me to acting as if we were pals. Still, it would be better to have the man on my side than not. And Tom said I should cooperate. "I wasn't lying when I came up here," I confessed. "I don't know why I was listening to what was going on at the counter, except that my assistant, the fellow who went to the hospital, is practically a member of our family. He is — *was* — Claire's boyfriend. He's devastated by her death, and I'm trying to help."

Nick Gentileschi crossed his arms and wriggled in his chair. "We all cared about Claire, you can count on that. She was a good girl. We've stepped up security in the parking lot. Since it looks like foul play, we're going to help the police in any way we can."

I said innocently, "Yes, my husband referred to that. I certainly hope you are doing everything to help the case." I rubbed my arm again. "Everything relevant, that is."

He glanced at the picture of the home office again, clearly trying to decide what to tell me. He didn't know how to balance secrecy with my irritation over being falsely arrested. There was an ego thing involved too. He was dying to show me what a big shot he was. I guess Albuquerque sent back good vibes, because he said, "Know what our biggest problem is, Mrs. Schulz?"

I shook my head sympathetically.

"Lawsuits." Bingo. He exhaled and moved around in his chair, making it squeak. "If Claire Satterfield's parents decide to sue because they think we have lax security in our parking lot, this store and this mall could go down the tubes all over again." He raised his chin and added proudly, "I've been in this place a long time. Served as security chief when it was Ward's. And believe me, being unemployed for four years was not something I want to repeat."

I hadn't been a psych major for nothing. In good Carl Rogers fashion, I said, "Not something you want to repeat."

Abruptly, Nick Gentileschi stood up and braced himself against his desk. He looked at me for a moment and I squirmed. Then he announced, "We're analyzing all the films of her sales, seeing if anyone suspicious turns up too often. But you figure" — he held out his large hands too close to my face and ticked off his points on his fingers — "someone had to know when she was going to be in the parking garage, that she was going to be there at all. . . ."

Uncomfortable with his stare and his sudden closeness, I stood up too, and inched backward. "Figuring out Claire's whereabouts wouldn't have been too hard. Especially given that the banquet attracted so many high-rolling customers. Not to mention a few demonstrators."

"Let me tell you what the problem is," he said suddenly.

Another problem. I took up refuge against one of the smudged aquamarine walls. "Go ahead."

"We're not careful enough in this store," he said matter-of-factly. "Yeah, we have security. But we're not warning employees about people who come in with an ulterior motive. Take that guy you were talking to Schulz about."

I raised my eyebrows innocently, and he grinned. He said, "The one with the record and his own cosmetics place? His name's Reggie Hotchkiss. He's around us all the time. I mean, why? What's the big deal with our cosmetics counter? Guy went to jail in seventy for burning his draft card, destroying federal property. Convicted of trying to break into the CIA. He's into makeup now because his mommy founded a cosmetics company. Now that he's in his forties, Mr. Hotchkiss is suddenly interested in making money. Uh-huh. The guy's *spying* on us, I say. That's what I told Schulz. Could be more there, that's what we're going to discuss later," he concluded grimly, "*after* I escort you out of the store." He strode to the door and opened it.

"But . . . I don't want to leave the store just now. What do you mean by 'more there'?"

He wagged a finger at me. "Remember Martha Mitchell? Maybe you're too young. She wanted to get too involved in her husband's business too. A guy can't be Attorney General and tend to a wife who's always meddling."

"A guy can't be Attorney General if he's intent on breaking the law," I said sweetly.

Gentileschi's features hardened. "Mrs. Schulz, let's go."

As we walked back through the china department, I took a new tack. "I hope you told my husband the details of Hotchkiss's record, if he didn't know already."

"You bet."

"So tell me," I continued, "how are you going to analyze these films you were talking about? I mean, where are your cameras?"

He gave me a look that told me I'd lost any tactical advantage I'd had. He wagged a finger at me and said, "I don't think so."

"Oh, come on." We started our descent on the escalator. "I'm just wondering how you saw me. I mean, technology must have changed the way you do things over the years."

Nick Gentileschi puffed out his chest. "Things haven't changed that much, I can tell you that." He raised one of those eyebrows. "And we're talking some years." He gestured to a protruding area that framed the entrance to the store just inside the doors. The three-sided frame, which looked like a walled-in deck that had been painted the same color as the store walls, was about six feet wide and deep all the way around — up one side of the entrance, spanning the top of the door, and coming down the other side of the entrance. It faced the Mignon counter. About five feet up the horizontal section of the frame, a large vent extended the length of the front. "I can't tell you how the cameras work, but I can tell you how we *used* to do most of our security. See that boxed-in area across from the Mignon counter? They decided not to get rid of it when they renovated the store." I nodded and studied the large, protruding structure as we descended the escalator. I had never even noticed it before. "It's called a blind," Gentileschi went on. "We used to sit up there."

"A blind?" I repeated.

"Yeah, we'd sit in the blind. Like a duck blind, you know? The place where the hunters sit to watch for the ducks. You can see out, but whoever is hunted can't see in. Anyway, we'd look out through those vents to see what was going on in the store. We'd watch people. Say a woman picks something up, maybe a bottle of perfume. She wants to steal it but she isn't sure. She hawks all around. . . ." He slitted his eyes and looked from side to side in imitation. "That's hawking. She could spend ten minutes trying to make up her mind whether she's gonna swipe it." He chuckled. "So say she finally doesn't lift it. That would really piss us off. So we'd squirt her with Windex. Right through that vent on the blind!"

"Why, Nick," I said demurely, "I never

imagined a security guy could get away with that kind of behavior."

We had reached the first floor. His warm, moist hand shook mine briefly. "You'd be surprised," he said. He winked roguishly.

And on that happy note, he headed off for men's suits.

"Gosh, what *happened* to you?" exclaimed Dusty when I returned to the Mignon counter. She was picking up the last of the plastic boxes and arranging them on a cart. "What were you *doing?*"

Harriet Wells, who was waiting on a black woman, tilted her head and smiled to acknowledge my return. Dusty and Harriet must have known I wasn't stealing anything. Why didn't they speak up in my defense when they saw Stan White leading me away? Maybe they were taught not to trust anyone. Given what had been happening around this mall lately, perhaps they were spooked by anyone acting odd in their domain.

"I wasn't doing anything," I told Dusty, "except trying to see if you were free. But you were talking to some guy." I gave her a naive, questioning look. "A tall blond guy? I mean, you looked as if you were *very* involved with him."

She laughed and waved this away. "Harriet did put me down to work through lunch. So if you come over and let me do your face, you can buy something for your sick friend and we can talk, all at the same time. Then if another customer comes along, if you don't mind, I can wait on him or her, and then get right back to you."

I was hungry but said that was fine, helped her stack the last of the plastic boxes on the cart, then asked if I could use the phone by the counter. She told me to go ahead, she'd be right back. Then she wheeled the cart away. I called Southwest Hospital and asked if Marla Korman had had her atherectomy yet. Someone at the nurses' station reported that Marla had not gone yet, and they did not know when she would be going. Typical.

I meandered over to the counter and listened to Harriet tell her customer that, believe it or not, she, Harriet Wells, had just had her sixty-fifth birthday, and just look at what Rejuvenation cream had done for her skin. The black woman put a ninety-dollar bottle of the stuff on her credit card.

"Here we are," said Dusty brightly. She nipped behind the counter, flipped through a file box, and retrieved a card.

As she was writing my name at the top, I slid onto one of the high stools on my side of the counter and said, "Tell me where the cameras are."

Startled, she looked up at me and giggled. Her cheeks colored. She gestured toward a silver half-globe protruding from the ceiling above the shoe department. "That's like, a one-way mirror. The camera sees out but you can't see in. It has pan, it has zoom, and it's watching us all the time. See, check this out." She ducked behind the counter and came up with a Prince & Grogan bag in one hand and three miniature jars of pink stuff in the other. "These are free samples of Rejuvenation, the new cream Mignon is pushing. I'm allowed to give three samples to each person, which includes me. And of course, it includes you. Anything more than that is considered employee stealing and I'll be out on my behind. Now, you can bet they're zooming in on me." She nodded at the silver half-globe and held up the three jars before putting them in the bag. "Okay," she said with a laugh, "now you've got your free stuff that ordinarily costs ninety bucks a bottle. Let's take a look at your face. Would you describe your skin as oily?"

Actually, I told her I wouldn't describe my skin as anything besides normal, because I just didn't pay that much attention to it. She frowned, and I remembered that when I was a doctor's wife, I'd worried about my complexion endlessly, and bought all kinds of stuff. I guess it was some kind of sublimation for worry about what was going on in the rest of my life. *Your skin is under relentless attack,* the ads screamed, *and you have to fight back.* No kidding. Needless to say, the gumption I'd eventually developed hadn't come from a bottle. In the money-scrimping years that followed my divorce, the only thing I used on my face was sunscreen. As far as makeup went, I hadn't missed a thing. And certainly the last thing I wanted to go back to was my endless trips to the counters of La Prairie, Lancôme, and Estée Lauder, seeking the best concealer to cover my black eyes and bruised cheeks, looking for someone who hadn't waited on me before, hadn't seen the damage the Jerk liked to inflict.

"Goldy? Hello? You in there? What kind of cleanser are you using now?"

Pulled back to reality, I replied that I used soap.

"Soap?" echoed Dusty incredulously. "Real soap? Soap-soap?" When I nodded, she persisted, "What brand of soap-soap?"

"Whatever's on sale at the grocery store."

Dusty couldn't help it, she put her hand on her chest and began to giggle. "That must be how you got to be friends with Frances Markasian! You know, that reporter you introduced me to?"

"The woman in red who was here earlier,

right? The one I introduced you to yesterday?"

"Yeah, spending lots of money, I couldn't believe it. She sure has changed her tune. Maybe she has a new boyfriend. Did you see that article she wrote on cosmetics for the *Mountain Journal*? I went home and looked it up, to see if it was the same person. I swear, she must be the queen of the skinflints. She wrote that people should just use Cetaphil, witch hazel, and drugstore moisturizer. Can you imagine?"

"I must have missed that issue. When was it?"

Before she could reply, Harriet, who had been writing in the large ledger, closed it with a firm slap and came over.

"I remember one time," she said in her honeylike voice, certainly not a voice I would associate with someone in her late sixties, "when we had a widow come in. She was fairly young, and all she'd ever used was drugstore makeup." She shook her head at me beneficently, as if to say, *You see, being a soap-user isn't the stupidest thing we've ever seen here.* "That poor woman . . . it just brings tears to my eyes to remember." I looked at Harriet's eyes. They were wet, all right. "Of course, her skin was a mess — too dry in one place, too oily in another. Her foundation didn't match her skin tone, she wore bright green eyeshadow, and her cheeks were so caked with blush, she looked like she had scarlet fever. I sold her our complete line. She had the insurance money, you see, and she could do whatever she wanted. A thousand dollars' worth of cosmetics I sold to that woman, and she was so happy! In less than an hour." She reached for a tissue and dabbed at her eyes.

"I'll bet you just loved that, Harriet," Dusty commented.

Harriet ignored this. "Oh, it was wonderful," she said to me. "Really touching, what I did for that woman. She looked beautiful when she walked out of here. She looked perfect."

Down the counter, a woman began to try out the perfume testers. She was wearing what looked to be some kind of designer sundress with big black squiggles on a white background. Below her elaborately streaked and curled hair, gold necklaces dripped around her neck and a gold bracelet with bells tinkled when she shook her wrist with each new perfume sample. Dusty put down her pen and moved toward her. Catapulted out of a post-green-eyeshadow reverie, Harriet took two quick steps in Dusty's direction, put a hand on her shoulder, and snapped a loud "Excuse *me!*" before pushing past her to be the first one to stand in front of the Woman with Bucks.

"Whoa," I said when Dusty returned, crestfallen. "What was that all about?"

"Don't worry," said Dusty bitterly. "I have Harriet's pump prints all up my back. And I'm the one who has to worry about the sales figures." She gestured to the big blue volume in which Harriet had been writing. "Every time I look at the ledger book, I break out in a sweat."

"Does she walk over everybody that way?"

"If you're in her way," murmured Dusty as she held up a bottle of foundation to my cheek to see if it matched my skin tone. Shaking her head, she clinked the bottle back into its drawer and picked out another. "You know this Rejuvenation we're selling?" I nodded. She continued. "Our sales goal on it is twenty-three hundred dollars a month per sales associate." She pointed to the ledger. "Today's the third of July and Harriet has already sold two thousand dollars of the stuff *this month*. That's what, eighteen total hours of sales time? Incredible. Of course, she says the most awful things to customers." Dusty's smile was wicked. "Claire and I figured Harriet must be at least eighty by the end of the day, since she gets older each minute when she's trying to sell anti-aging cream."

I unscrewed the lid on a jar of thick cream, then used the little plastic applicator to spread a dollop of the viscous, sweet-smelling stuff on the back of my hand. I said mildly, "Was Harriet jealous of Claire?"

The wicked smile on Dusty's lips traveled to her eyes. "Claire had one client, a man who's a weird-genius kind of guy, who spent a lot of money. You mentioned him, he was here before — a thin, tall blond man? Anyway, never mind that it was his wife's money, this guy spent it like crazy, buying stuff for his wife, I guess, but always only from Claire. He wouldn't even buy a tube of lipstick from one of the rest of us. He'd hang around here like a loyal dog, waiting until her shift. And you know how Claire was. She'd flirt and bat her eyes and just have the best old time. Or maybe you never saw her do that. . . . Hold still, I'm going to use this cleanser on you."

I sat motionless while Dusty used two cotton balls to spread luscious-smelling cream over my cheeks. It felt divine. If my stomach hadn't been growling, I would have been certain I was in heaven.

"Anyway," she went on, "Claire would just make this guy feel like a million dollars. 'You're not really goin' to buy that too! Y'goin' t'be broke!' " Dusty's imitation of Claire's Australian accent was dead-on. "So.

Pretty soon the wife, who spends a lot of money here herself, comes in *with* her husband to see why her husband's developed such an enthusiastic interest in cosmetics all of a sudden."

"When was all this going on?" I asked, trying to keep still as Dusty smeared lime-scented toner over my face. I slid my glance sideways to see if Harriet was having any luck with Mrs. Got-Rocks in the black and white dress.

"Watch out!" Dusty cried sharply.

Startled, I fell off the stool where I was perched. "Huh? I was just looking to see how Harriet was doing."

"I don't want to get this stuff in your eye! You don't know what could happen!"

Dusty had become so suddenly flustered that I sat back slowly on the stool and opened my eyes wide. "I'm fine. Look. I love the feel of this stuff you put on me —"

Dusty took a deep breath and began to write on my ticket, or whatever it was. When I asked her what she was doing, she informed me that this was my client card. She'd record everything she sold me so that next time she could just look it up when I came in and needed new blush or whatever.

"I have to tell you honestly, Dusty, I don't think there's much chance that I'll be spending a lot of time or money here. . . ."

"Okay, close your eyes and *keep* them closed. I'm going to do your moisturizer." She didn't seem to hear me.

I obeyed. "So what happened with this man and his wife and Claire?"

Dusty finished with the moisturizer and began to dab on something else. From the position of her fingers, I guessed it was concealer. I didn't dare open my eyes though, for fear of another eruption.

"I think Claire and the man had an affair. He was, like, smitten. I mean, the guy seemed crazed. *Obsessed*. I do know they broke up later, because she told me. But he still came around — you know, hanging back where he figured we wouldn't see him. He would skulk through Shoes, watching her. I mean, who could miss him? He's so tall, and that blond-ish-white hair makes him look kind of young and real cute. Okay, now I'm doing your foundation." More scented stuff was liberally spread over my face. Pat, pat, pat. "Never tug or pull on your face," Dusty warned sternly. "That's what causes premature loosening of the skin around the eyes."

Noted. Keeping my eyes closed, I inquired, "So what happened to the skulking guy? Why was he here this morning?"

"Well, I don't know about this morning, because he was just asking a bunch of disgusting questions, like what had happened to Claire's body and stuff like that. Okay, I'm doing your eyes. Hold still."

While Dusty worked on my eyelids, I was reminded of those X-ray technicians who tell you to hold still and not breathe. Then they go behind a foot-thick wall and zap you. What happens if you breathe? Do you go radioactive, or do you just screw up the X ray?

"All right," said Dusty. "Now *blush*."

It took me a second to realize that wasn't a command. "Can I move? What happened to the guy?"

"Don't talk or I won't get this on straight. Well. As far as the affair goes, a while back the guy's wife started coming in just to ask if her husband had been here. I mean, you talk about screwed *up*. You can look in the mirror now."

I did as ordered. I looked different, that was for sure. No more smudges under my eyes from lack of sleep; lots of radiant cheek tone that made me look either acutely embarrassed or much more physically active than would be justified by a short daily regimen of yoga. Most prominent and startling were the black eyeliner and brown eyeshadow. I no longer looked like a caterer; I resembled an Egyptian queen. Make that a *promiscuous* Egyptian queen.

"Wow, Dusty," I gushed. "You're amazing! This guy who was watching Claire . . . What was his name, do you remember?"

Dusty batted her eyes at me and then held them open wide. I had the uncomfortable feeling that she was vamping me. But the eye movements were apparently some kind of universal signal of what she wanted me to do. She needed to apply my mascara. When I obeyed, she continued. "His *name* was Charles Braithwaite. Don't you know the Braithwaites? Our bio class went over to his lab once on a field trip. Look up now, and hold still."

"Yes, I know them," I said carefully. "Babs Braithwaite invaded my life a few weeks ago, and it hasn't been pleasant." In fact, I thought with a shiver, Babs was making me feel distinctly uneasy, the way she kept interjecting her presence into Julian's and my life.

Dusty said, "The Braithwaites are, like, mega-rich. I mean, they live in this huge place in the country club. But I guess Charles Braithwaite fell in love with Claire. Like the bumper sticker, you know? *Scientists do it unexpectedly.* Okay, look out, I'm going to do your lipstick." She giggled. "Nectarine Climax. How do you like having that on your lips?"

"Sounds . . . intriguing. You went on a field trip to Braithwaite's lab? What did he do in the lab?" My head was spinning.

Dusty dotted my lips with a Q-Tip loaded with what resembled cooked pumpkin. She spread it all around, then ordered me to blot. Only when she'd put the cap back on Nectarine Climax did she answer, "Oh, you know, he has that big greenhouse. Haven't you seen it? I never wrote up my report on the trip because I . . . left the school. But anyway. Last I heard, Charles was working on roses or something."

10

I looked in the mirror. Nefertiti blinked back. My eyes, dark-lined and shadowed the color of burnt toast, had a hard time concealing astonishment. *Roses or something. Experimenting. The way you experiment to produce a blue rose, like the one I'd found on the garage floor near where Claire was hit?* I furrowed my newly powdered brow, squinted at the smorgasbord of brightly packaged products lined up on the shiny counter, and asked Dusty to sell me some hand cream for my friend in the hospital. While I dug through my wallet looking for the emergency hundred-dollar bill, she picked out a jar for eighty bucks. Twenty dollars wasn't going to get me too far in an emergency.

"Please, Dusty," I begged, "don't you have something less expensive?"

She shrugged, as if I were about to make the biggest mistake of my life. "The smallest jar is sixty."

"I'll take it." While she rummaged below the counter for the sixty-dollar size, I asked nonchalantly, "What about a guy named Shaman Krill? Did Claire go out with anybody by that name, before or after her fling with Charles B.?"

Dusty plunked a shiny box down on the counter. "Shaman Krill? Never heard of him. What does he look like?"

I handed her the hundred-dollar bill. "He's an animal rights' activist with a dark ponytail, gold earring, short stature, and big attitude. Sound familiar?"

She wrinkled her nose. "Are you kidding? He sounds disgusting. I never saw anybody like that. And Claire would *never* have gone out with some weirdo." She pressed buttons on the cash-register terminal to ring up my purchase, lifted the jar and the receipt — for the cameras, I guessed — and gave me the bag.

"Thanks, Dusty."

She tilted her head and gave me a sweet smile. "Come back soon. It's fun to have somebody to talk to."

Time to leave the store, time to find Julian, time to go see Marla. Time to see if I could get my friend-who'd-just-had-a-heart-attack to smile at my freshly minted face. And yet something was holding me back. I couldn't go just yet, and besides, Julian was still doing the chamber brunch. The paper bag crackled in my hand as I surveyed the store, the store that twinkled with bright lights and glittering décor and mirrors I hated to look in. *Mirrors.* I looked up to the second story. Not an hour ago I had seen Babs Braithwaite leaning half-dressed over the escalator and claiming *somebody was back there.* Nick had talked about surveillance from the blinds-that-were-like-duck-blinds. Claire had been helping Nick; Claire thought she was being watched. Now *Babs* thought *she* was being watched. I dashed up the moving steps. Back *where? Behind the dressing room mirrors?* Was there somebody back there?

On the second floor, I knew better than to look up to locate the camera or glance back and forth to check on the presence of security people, called "hawking" by Nick Gentileschi. That would alert them to my attentions, and I certainly didn't want to have them watching me again. *Even a paranoid has real enemies,* Henry Kissinger was reputed to have said. I lifted a hanger with a hot-pink and yellow bikini and headed confidently in the direction of the dressing room.

In the recessed entry, a short hallway to the right led to the mirrored rooms. I walked along the row of dressing rooms. One was occupied by a woman trying on a suit while attempting to calm her recalcitrant toddler. The rest were empty. Was this just more evidence of Babs acting hysterical? She'd seemed so convinced that someone was watching her. And not just a camera either. But where could you watch someone from?

At the end of the hallway of dressing rooms was one of those expensive imitation rubber plants and a rack of bathing suits apparently waiting to be returned to the sales floor. Behind the rack and almost invisible because it was painted the same color as the walls was a door. Without hesitation I dropped the suit, pulled the rack out of the way, and tried the door handle: locked. Now, where would Nick Gentileschi, that cliché of a dime-store cop, put the spare key, if there was such a thing?

I thought back to my visit to his office. He had been wearing a keyring. But there had to be more than one key. Where would the department store keep a key to an area behind the ladies' dressing room?

Wait. I had seen something the day before, when I was trying to find the right person with my check. There had been a key box on the aquamarine office wall belonging to Lisa, the lady perplexed by the notion of accounts payable. I veered off toward the offices. What would Tom say if he knew I intended to filch a key? Well, I would see if I could get the key and find out what Babs was talking about with *somebody back there*. Then I would worry about Tom.

The store offices were virtually deserted, probably because of the food fair. To the one young woman in accounts receivable, I asked knowledgeably, "Is Lisa here? I talked to her yesterday about accounts payable." I touched my Food Fair badge, as if that made me official. "She told me to come back today."

The young woman shrugged. "You can check her office."

Well, now, I would just do that. I knocked and walked into Lisa's office. She was gone. Hallelujah. I stuck my head out and announced to the young woman, "She's not here. I'm just going to leave her a note."

The woman shrugged. Instead of writing a note, of course, I stepped over the pile of computer print-outs, crossed to the key box, and pulled on it. It wasn't locked, but one corner was painted closed. I needed something like a blade to cut through the aquamarine muck. Lisa's desk yielded a nail file and I levered it in. My next tug brought the cabinet open and I stared at what must have been forty keys, of which only about half were labeled with ancient, corroded masking tape. I scanned them. In barely visible ball-point pen, one scrap of tape said, SECOND FLOOR — LADIES' DRESSING ROOM. My fingers closed around the key and I slipped it into my shirt pocket. Thanks, Lisa.

Not wanting to attract the attention of the cameras, I walked calmly back to the dressing room. I moved the plant out of the way, fumbled with the lock, and then pushed into the blackness of the space beyond the door. The odors of dust, concrete, and cardboard containers were almost overwhelming. I slipped the key back into my pocket and groped along the wall for a light. There was no way I was going into this area, whatever it was, and risk breaking my neck tripping over a box of lingerie. Eureka. My hand closed on a switch. When dim fluorescent light flooded the room, I saw that I stood in a huge, tall rectangle. Stripped of all the cameras, concealed piping, lighting, and other electrical wiring of the main store, this ceiling went up what looked like two full stories, past enormous steel shelves and a metal ladder going up to the roof. There was a door on the left. It couldn't lead to the dressing rooms. I turned. The dressing rooms should be located on the right beyond the back wall where I stood.

Boxes, plastic bags full of merchandise, and carts impeded my progress as I advanced parallel to the wall. My feet scraped across the concrete. My uniform was getting filthy from all the dust I was kicking up. But I was rewarded. Two boxes had been moved haphazardly — and hastily, it appeared — to make a narrow pathway to a door in the wall. I wiggled through and tried the door: it was open. On the other side was a very dimly lit passageway that appeared to be horseshoe-shaped. I tiptoed along and gasped. I was behind one-way mirrors. In front of me, a thin woman was trying on a pink bikini. I felt myself blush. I held my breath, averted my eyes from the mirrors, and walked quickly around the U-shape. Along both rows of mirrors, there were chairs, a half-empty paper coffee cup, and several crumpled fast-food wrappers. If there had been someone here earlier, he or she was gone now.

A plump woman appeared behind the revealing mirrors, her arms loaded with swim suits. In the dressing room beside her, the thin woman, now clad in the pink bikini, swiveled her hips and frowningly scrutinized her cleavage. I beat a hasty retreat. Pushing past the clutter of the storage space, I closed the door behind me. Then I hightailed it out of the store grasping my bag with its jar of cream for Marla. Tom would, no doubt, be extremely interested to know that the security/peeping-tom area was accessible. He'd also be intrigued by what Dusty had told me of Claire, the infatuated Charles Braithwaite, and Braithwaite's horticultural experimentation. But frustration ruled as I rushed along the mall looking for an available pay phone. The kiosks were full. Waiting lines for every pay phone snaked in front of the boutiques. I cursed under my breath; my stomach growled in response. Half past one with no lunch and two small muffins for breakfast — typical meal schedule for a caterer. I decided to zip up to the food fair for my share of the free samples, then find Julian and hurry over to the Coronary Care Unit to see Marla. I'd call Tom from the hospital.

Out on the roof, a refreshing breeze stirred the air. A nearby bank thermometer announced a digital neon temperature that blinked from eighty-one to eighty-two and back again. I scanned the rows of booths, trying to decide where to indulge my hunger. Despite the maze of roads, fast-food spots, and housing developments spreading as far as the foot of the mountains, here on the roof the food tents, flowers, streamers, and music had transformed the expanse of concrete into a completely credible fair. Marvelous scents mingled and wafted through the air. So did laughter, happy voices, and a band playing jazz. As I stood underneath the flapping Playhouse Southwest banner, I smiled and took a deep breath of the delectable aromas: pizza, barbecue, coffee . . . and something else.

Cigarette smoke? No. I looked around. Yes.

Perched on a small raised platform on a roof adjoining the parking structure, and utterly heedless of the dirty looks she was attracting, Frances Markasian, eyes closed, face set in bliss, was relaxing and indulging in her nicotine habit. Her chin tilted skyward while her mouth opened and closed like a guppy's. Unlike a fish, however, Frances was blowing perfect smoke rings. Her dark mass of curly hair lay wild and undone over her shoulders. Her red heels and bags of cosmetic purchases lay scattered in disarray on the concrete. To cool off, or maybe just to catch a few rays, she had pulled the flouncy red skirt up to reveal knobby knees and calf-high stockings. I wondered where she'd stashed the smokes this time.

I skirted the garage wall, hopped onto the adjoining roof, and walked up to Frances. I was quite sure being where we were was illegal, but that had never stopped Frances before. I cleared my throat. She opened one eye, then both. "Don't tell me. Bathsheba as a chef."

"Don't tell *me*," I replied evenly. "Bob Woodward as Elizabeth Taylor. In a Marlboro ad. No, wait. Doing the roof scene from *Mary Poppins*. Except you don't look like Julie Andrews, either."

She blew a smoke ring and gestured for me

to have a seat. The two-foot-square platform contained litter that could only be hers: an M&M bag, a Snickers wrapper, an empty can of Jolt cola. Of course, Frances was too much of a skinflint to spring for a ticket to the food fair. Which made her enthusiastic cream/rouge/lipstick/concealer/foundation/mascara shopping spree this morning all the more intriguing. I brushed her wrapper-debris into a small pile on the asphalt roof and sat.

She took another greedy drag on her cigarette, then blew a thin stream of smoke upward. "So where's your escort? He was kind of cute for a rent-a-thug. What'd he catch you doing anyway?"

When I opened my mouth to reply, my stomach howled in protest. I ignored it and said, "Nothing. Security's just suspicious, that's all."

She lifted one eyebrow. "Suspicious of a caterer?"

"Maybe they were suspicious of the wrong person," I countered. "Look, Frances, I've seen your duct-taped sneakers and second-hand clothes. I know you're a tightwad and proud of it. I even heard you wrote an article on what a ripoff all makeup is. For someone with your thrifty bent, you sure bought a lot of cosmetics today." I watched for her reaction, but behind the unaccustomed makeup, she was stone-faced. "Isn't it about time you told me what you're doing with Mignon?" I pressed. I was getting light-headed from hunger, but I was weary of Frances's evasions. "Why the sudden interest in cosmetics at a Denver department store, when your beat is Aspen Meadow, forty miles away?"

She smiled, leaned over, and picked up one of the red shoes to crush out her butt. "You keep asking me that," she said, then smiled slyly.

If I didn't eat soon, I was going to pass out. I tried to think. Frances didn't care about Claire as a person, and she certainly couldn't be convinced to have any sympathy for a grieving Julian. I needed another angle.

"Okay, Frances, here's the deal," I announced grittily. Caterers could be just as tough as small-town reporters. "To you, this whole thing is a story. What kind, I don't know. But my assistant, Julian Teller, wants to know what happened to his girlfriend. He *needs* to know what happened to his girlfriend. And *I* need to know, because Julian Teller is like family, not to mention that he's running my catering business right now. The guy is having a very hard time. He's simply not going to be able to function until we get this cleared up." *If then,* I added mentally. Over at the food fair, a group of teenagers in T-shirts,

267

ragged shorts, and scruffy high-top shoes shuffled along devouring pizza. They stopped by the open tent where the jazz band was finishing up its set. I took a deep breath, which was unwise: The aroma of the pizza sauce, garlic, and melted cheese made me dizzy with hunger. "So. If you don't tell me what you're up to, I'm going to march right into the Prince & Grogan offices and tell them who you are and where you're from. Then, in case there's no action, I'm going to get on the phone with every Mignon executive in Albuquerque —"

"Tell me, Goldy," Frances interrupted blithely, "do you ever listen to jazz?"

"Jazz? Of course I do. So what?"

"Y'ever heard of Ray Charles?"

"Frances, what on earth is the matter with you?"

"Ask a simple question, you get a simple answer."

Frances was losing her grip. Perhaps it was the lethal combination of Marlboros and M&Ms. Then again, maybe she was trying to be clever by pulling her usual routine. She invariably changed the subject to get away from whatever she didn't want to discuss.

"Tell me what you're doing with Mignon," I demanded fiercely.

"Investigative reporting. That's it, I swear."

"I don't think an atheist can swear," I snapped. "It doesn't mean anything." When she chuckled, I insisted, "What kind of investigative reporting?"

She sighed and reached for the Prince & Grogan bags at her feet. "Your husband isn't the only one with medical training. I did a year of med school before turning to journalism —"

"Excuse me, but that's the *ex*-husband."

"Sorry." Her mournful look was accentuated by the heavy makeup Harriet Wells had applied around her eyes. Here we were, I reflected, two normally unadorned women who'd been outwardly transformed to look like a couple of hookers — and just so we could get information. "By the way, Goldy, I was wondering something." Frances lit another cigarette. "Did you hear that your *ex*-husband beat up his new girlfriend last night? She called the cops and we picked it up at the *Journal,* on the police band. Seems she slid his Jeep into a ditch during the storm, where it stuck in the mud. The doc got really pissed. She's across the street in the hospital with broken ribs and bruised arms."

An image of this poor, pained woman, a new girlfriend I wasn't aware of, floated up in my mind. The Jerk had always been able to find fresh female companionship. When a current girlfriend didn't work out, or ended up in a problematic place like the hospital, he would quickly find a replacement. I thought about Arch. Although he knew why I'd divorced his father, Arch had never witnessed the violence that had destroyed my marriage. If his classmates at Elk Park Prep heard about this incident from a tabloid-type article by Frances in the *Mountain Journal*, which I wouldn't put past her . . .

I demanded, "Are you going to run a story about it in the paper?"

Frances took a deep drag. "Nah. The publisher's wife is pregnant and John Richard is her doctor. The wife wants the publisher to hold off on running any story until she delivers."

A headache nagged behind my eyes. "Look, Frances, John Richard's not my problem anymore. What's the deal with the department store? I have to go get something to eat, and then I need to go visit a friend in the hospital."

She pretended to look puzzled. "Not the girlfriend —"

"Frances! What are you up to?"

She set her face in steely anger and tossed her butt in an arc across the roof. "I'm investigating the false claims of Mignon Cosmetics to make women look younger. Period."

I was incredulous, partly at Frances's own

naiveté. "You're kidding. That's it?" She frowned and nodded. "Was Claire Satterfield helping you?" I asked.

"I didn't even know who Claire Satterfield was before the accident," Frances replied. Her tone indicated that she sure wished she *had* known Claire. Just think of all the information a Mignon sales associate could have provided. . . .

"But why did you bother to find out she'd had other boyfriends? Why do you think she was deliberately run down?"

"Background, Goldy, background. The claims are what's news."

"But for heaven's sake, those claims are *not news*. This so-called story has been in books, newspapers, magazines, on radio and television. Haven't you read any Naomi Wolf? Get real."

"What are you talking about?" she said bitterly. She blew smoke out her nostrils. "I beg to differ."

"Look, Frances," I said. "In their hearts, women know all this outrageously expensive goop doesn't make them look younger. But the cosmetics people try to guilt-trip every female in the country into feeling they have to do *something* to take care of themselves. Otherwise, these companies want women to believe, they'll grow old and ugly. They'll never have money, a husband, a white picket fence, a lover, a fur coat, a station wagon, and somebody to drive away with when you get a flat tire. That's the name of the cosmetics game."

She glared at me and held the cigarette aloft. "Foucault-Reiser is the parent company of Mignon. F-R has been experimenting with cosmetics for thirty years. And experimenting in ways you would not believe," she added darkly.

In my mind's eye, I saw heaps of rabbit carcasses. Hard to take on an empty stomach. "Well, I guess I sort of would —"

Heedless, Frances went on: "Foucault-Reiser launched the hideously expensive Mignon line five years ago, with all kinds of wild claims, fancy packaging, and questionable products. *Control the destiny of your face.* Like hell. Large pink plastic jars of cream didn't sell, so Mignon switched to dark green glass jars with gold lids, the kinds of containers you imagine once held royal jewels and medieval potions. The message was: *This is magic stuff.* Sales took off."

I nodded and remembered eons ago, when Arch asked if he could have one of my empty perfume jars for a Dungeons and Dragons prop.

Frances reached into her bag and pulled out

a bottle of makeup. "Nobody wants a jar of mud — otherwise known as foundation — with a little white plastic top." She wrenched the shiny cover off the lid, revealing — sure enough — a white plastic top. "But they put a tall gold top over the white plastic so that consumers will think they're getting something of infinite value. And then there's perfume . . ."

I groaned, ready to admit she had a story. But she was on a roll.

Frances made a face. " 'I need something really sexy,' I told that woman with the French twist. She sold me Ardor." Frances brandished a heart-shaped bottle of perfume. "Funny, she sold Ardor to my neighbor for her eighty-year-old mother, whose sexiest social engagement is when her garden club plants bulbs. And the same sales associate, Harriet, told the daughter of the head of the *Journal* advertising department that Ardor was just the right perfume for a girl to start wearing to school. She's *twelve*, Goldy. Sales of Ardor, as you might imagine, have taken off. And speaking of sales, if their associates don't keep up their quotas, they're fired. Kaput. So these same sales associates, of which your Claire S. was one, make claims to customers that get more and more bizarre. More and more *outlandish*. No one has challenged Mignon, and I'm going to be the one who does it."

"Oh yeah? And just how're you going to do that?"

She rustled around in one of her bags and held up a small rectangular box. It was covered with navy-blue satiny paper crossed with thin gold and silver stripes. "Mignon Gentle Deep-cleansing Soap with Natural Grains. Twenty bucks. It's soap, period, with about a dime's worth of ingredients, including" — she peered at the label — "ah-ha, oatmeal! But it'll chap your skin if you use too much of it. Did you hear what that Harriet Wells said to me?" She glared at me indignantly. " 'Cleans deeply but gently into the pores. Restores the original state of your skin!' " Frances grunted. "Crap. Soap robs the skin of lipids. Use it as much as old Harriet says to, and you'll have a nice red face."

"Don't you think people know — ?"

"No, I don't think people know anything, I think people believe what they're told." She reached into the bag again, then held up a tall rectangular box covered with the same elaborate decoration. "Magic Pore-closing Toner? Forty-five bucks? To do what? They swear it *tones* the pores. As if your skin cells were muscles, ha. You want an astringent, try witch hazel. If you *need* anything at all. Oh, and did you happen to notice this fall they're going to be adding Mediterranean Sea Kelp to their Magic Pore-closing Toner? Link any cosmetic with something European, and it's a sure sell. And this!" She thrust a squat jar of cream at me. "Did you hear all the baloney that Harriet-woman was feeding me about how she was sixty-two and this moisturizer stuff stopped her aging process? This junk doesn't even have *sunscreen* in it! Hate to tell maybe-early-fifties Harriet, but that's the only thing that'll prevent wrinkles, and folks need to start using it when they're young or they're sunk. *Biochromes,* my ass. What the hell is a biochrome, I ask you?" Her black-striped eyes opened wide. "It was never mentioned in any biology class *I* ever took. Or in chemistry. Or physiology. Or dermatology, for that matter."

I clapped. "Yeah, yeah. They're going to run all this in the *Mountain Journal.* And the wife of your publisher is never going to wear makeup again. Is the *Journal* bankrolling you in this undercover operation?" I gestured to the red shoes, the bags of cosmetics, and her dress.

Before she could answer, however, I got that strange feeling I'd been having the last two days, the kind I used to get when the Jerk was following me in his Jeep after we were separated. I'd been having the feeling a lot lately: on the highway coming to the banquet when I'd veered in front of a pickup, just after the helicopter passed over; during the storm night before last, when I thought I saw the light go on in the pickup at the end of our driveway; even at the Mignon counter this morning. As I sat next to Frances, the feeling began again as a kind of prickling along the back of my neck. I looked up for the pizza-eating teenagers, but saw only a sudden movement toward one of the tents, the kind of thing you catch out of the corner of your eye.

"What is it?" Frances demanded, her senses ever acute to some emotional change in the person to whom she was talking. "Goldy, what's the matter?"

I looked around and saw absolutely nothing suspicious. This was what happened when you didn't get enough sleep, I told myself. Or enough food. You had hallucinations. A teenager with long, stringy brown hair hopped onto the store roof where we sat and approached us.

He said, "Uh, who's the caterer?"

I identified myself and the fellow said, "Somebody said to tell you there's a message for you over at your booth."

"From whom?" I demanded.

But he had turned his back. When I called out to him again, he shrugged without turning and loped back off into the food fair crowd.

"I'll go," Frances said firmly as she gathered up her glossily wrapped parcels. "It might be the rent-a-thug. I could vouch that you've been sitting here berating me for the last fifteen minutes. Besides, you need to eat your lunch."

I smiled at Frances's ill-disguised nosiness, at her sudden insincere concern about my need for nourishment. "Nah," I told her lightly, "it's probably the food fair people. Or maybe it's a new client. I'll be right back." But she ignored me.

We walked across the roof and maneuvered back onto the top of the parking garage. I told the money-takers that Frances was helping me, and didn't need a bracelet because she didn't eat normal food. They waved her through. The jazz band had gone on break. Their audience had dispersed and turned their ravenous attention back to the booths.

"Okay," I said, as if granting Frances permission for what she was going to do anyway. "Let me get just a quick bite to eat first, and then we'll see what the message is."

The crowd buoyed me along to the booth of a vegetarian Mexican restaurant. I chose a burrito stuffed with roasted peppers, tomatoes, and onions. It dripped with guacamole and melted cheddar, and sour cream oozed out of both sides when I took a bite. The American Heart Association definitely wouldn't approve. My mouth full, I thought of Marla and resolved to get really serious about lowfat cooking. Tomorrow.

"Enjoy," said Frances with a laugh. "Isn't this where your booth was?"

The booth had been abandoned early by the barbecue people. I guess "all you can eat" had been more than they could handle. They'd even pulled down the flaps on the tent, as if to say nobody was home.

Frances pulled up the flap and peered into the dark interior. I stepped up beside her and felt the hot, stuffy air inside. There was a plastic bag taped to the near table.

"There it is," said Frances as she stepped confidently forward. "Wait," I said. "Frances," I said again sharply, *"wait."* But I couldn't restrain her; one of my hands held the burrito, the other the tent flap.

There was a sudden movement. I heard the intake of breath that accompanies effort.

"Frances!" I shouted.

"Help!" she cried.

Stale air swished against my face. Something was coming at us. Because of my years with the Jerk, I had learned how to protect myself from a potential assault. The air — or maybe it was liquid, I realized — *whoosh*ed. I dropped the burrito and buckled forward.

"Duck!" I shouted to Frances.

A loud *sloosh* traveled through air. It was coming toward Frances and me. The smell was familiar . . . acrid.

It was a bucket of bleach water.

"Close your eyes!" I screamed to Frances. I shut mine tight, held my breath, and covered my face with my hands. The water cascaded over my doubled-over body in a hard, heavy slap. Cold liquid saturated my chef's jacket.

Someone pushed past me. One of the canvas tent flaps brushed my legs and I heard footsteps. But with the possibility of bleach anywhere nearby, I knew better than to open my eyes.

"Frances! Are you there? Keep your eyes shut, it's chlorine bleach!"

A stream of loud, inventive curses came from about a yard away. Yep — Frances was there.

"Back out of the tent," I ordered, ignoring her angry protests. "Follow my voice. Go slow." Still doubled-over, my hands covering my face, I treaded backward slowly. Soon, cooler air indicated I was outside the tent. I felt metal. Moving metal. A baby stroller.

"Help!" I cried. "I have bleach on me! Don't let any get on the baby!"

A woman screamed and the metal veered

away. I started to lose my balance. Voices erupted all around and within a few seconds I felt a large, gentle hand on my shoulder. An adult? A teenager? Whoever had assaulted us? The hand guided me sideways.

"Come on," a man's calm voice urged. "Let me get you a towel."

"I have a friend with me. She needs help too."

"The red dress?" asked the voice. "I'm holding her arm."

More colorful curses indicated this was true. I sighed.

Over the acrid stink of the bleach, the welcome aroma of coffee came close. The masculine voice attached to the hand on my shoulder asked someone for a couple of towels. A piece of cloth with the consistency of a dish towel was placed over my head and tucked around my ears. My sodden hair was being expertly wrapped, turban-style.

"Please," I said, "I need some plain water to rinse my face —"

"All right, stand back, everybody," came another male voice, a familiar one. It was Pete, the espresso man. "Goldy, I'm going to toss a pitcher of plain water in your face," he warned, up close. "It's not cold, not hot. Well, maybe a little cool. Just relax. Then I'm going to do the same for your friend."

A splash of liquid hit my face and neck. Another towel was thrust in my face and I vigorously scrubbed my cheeks, forehead, and eyes free of bleach and eye makeup. Frances yelped when the water gushed on her, but then she fell silent, no doubt engaged in the same drying activity.

I straightened and felt the cool bleach water trickle down inside my clothes. I opened my eyes, sure that my makeup had run together into one unholy mess. A sea of curious faces surrounded me. The one recognizable face was Pete's. The person guiding me had brought me to the front of Pete's espresso booth. Instead of wondering just what had happened in the tent, my first ridiculous thought was: How in the world did Pete get a booth for the whole four-hour time period, when I had to share mine with the barbecue folks?

"Goldy?" Pete's grin was benevolent. "Do you and your friend want some coffee with a couple of shots of brandy? How about a couple of dry sets of clothes? On the house."

Half the folks in the crowd laughed, as if the whole incident were some kind of stunt arranged by the fair people for the band's break. As I accepted Pete's offer of coffee, I searched faces for anyone familiar — malevolent or otherwise. But whoever had done this appeared to be long gone. At my side,

Frances was brusquely demanding to know what was going on, had anyone seen anything? Anyone seen someone rush out of the tent? Ignoring her, I waved at the person approaching us. It was Julian. The crowd, sensing that the entertainment was over, dispersed. Only a couple of stragglers remained. Maybe they were hoping the bleach bath would belatedly eat through our clothes or skin.

"Listen," said a deep voice from behind me. The first thing I noticed, looking up, was that his long-sleeved shirt was wet. My eyes traveled upward to the delicate features of his face, to the mop of frizzed, Warhol-type white-blond hair. I had seen this tall man that morning, that day, in Prince & Grogan.

It was Charles Braithwaite.

"I . . . I helped you," he faltered. The skin at the side of his earnest blue eyes crinkled with concern. He was in his thirties, maybe early forties, but because of his height and his extreme thinness, his age was difficult to determine. "I . . . I wrapped those towels around the two of you. But you need to rinse that stuff out of your hair, ladies. Either that or you're both going to look like skunks. Dark on both sides and a white stripe down the middle." His palm pressed his long, pale hair over to the side in a practiced gesture.

I groaned. "Oh, that's just great." I took

the cup of spiked coffee that Pete offered and wondered what Charles Braithwaite was doing first at Mignon, then at the food fair. Tom's words echoed in my ears: *Someone who's too helpful . . . someone who's always around . . .*

Frances demanded if Pete had seen anything. When he said no, she took a large swallow of her drink and said it was too hot. Did he have a phone, she wanted to know, she had to call her boss. Pete laughed. No phone. He handed us T-shirts and sweat pants that listed his location and all the curative powers of coffee. The man was an advertising genius. I turned back to my tall, blond savior. If that was what he was.

"Did you see what happened to us?" I asked. "Did you see anyone else come out of the tent?"

He shook his head. "I heard you," he replied. "Then the two of you stumbled out of the tent. I smelled the bleach, and then I came over . . ."

"Yes, thanks," I said lamely. He nodded. His light blue wrinkled rayon shirt, now streaked with liquid, fell unfashionably from his thin shoulders. He was wearing dark slacks and old-fashioned tie-up saddle shoes. His canoelike feet were at least a size fourteen.

Frances blew noisily on her coffee, then turned her attentions to the tall man. "What are you doing here?" she demanded abruptly.

Charles Braithwaite blushed to the roots of his filament-like hair. The saddle shoes began to inch away. "Well, as I was telling your friend . . . I was here because . . . well, let's see . . . I heard the two of you yelling —"

"What in the hell —" Julian began as he rushed up, puffing. He was still wearing his serving clothes from the morning. "Goldy? And you?" He looked quizzically at Frances. "From the newspaper? Why are you all wet? Why is your hair all wrapped — ? Dr. Braithwaite! What's going on . . . why are you here?"

I looked curiously at our tall, gangly rescuer, who again mumbled something along the lines that he had to go.

"Goldy, what happened to you?" Julian demanded. "Did you all fall into some water, or what?"

"We'll be at your place tomorrow, on the Fourth," I said to an increasingly uncomfortable Charles Braithwaite. "Maybe you could show me your greenhouse —"

"No. I can't show anyone," mumbled Dr. Charles Braithwaite, embarrassed. He brushed a shock of white hair out of his eyes. "You need to get some dry . . ." His long fingers gestured awkwardly in my direction.

Irritated, Julian hovered over me. "What

happened to you?" he asked again.

"Somebody threw a bucket of bleach water on us," I answered with resignation. "Whoever it was said there was a message at my booth. Frances was trying to help —"

Frances narrowed her eyes at Charles Braithwaite. Alarmed by the predatory assessment in them, the doctor began to sidle away. Unabashed, Frances caught him by his wet sleeve to halt his retreat. "Doc-tor Charles Braithwaite," she said in an accusing, parental tone. "Thanks for helping us, indeed. You were at the Mignon Cosmetics counter this morning. Now you're here. Just what kind of interest does a world-famous microbiologist have in a cosmetics company? Eh, Charlie-baby?" Holding Charles's sleeve with one hand and the wet turban on her head with the other, Frances glared ominously at her prey.

Being wet and disoriented can put one at a disadvantage. Not so Frances, whose crimson dress was already drying with a large orange stripe down its center. Over in the heart of the food fair, the jazz band returned from their break and began a blues riff. Charles Braithwaite glanced fearfully at me, then stared longingly in the direction of the jazz band, as if the soothing music could bail him out.

Julian, meanwhile, had followed our wet trail to the tent that had been my booth that morning and our attacker's hiding place this afternoon. He angrily whipped back the tent flaps and then quickly strode around the entire tent. At each corner he threw the flaps up, as if daring an intruder to be concealed there. At the back of the tent he stopped short. I shivered inside my cold, wet clothes and tried to ignore the fact that Frances was fiercely interrogating Charles Braithwaite concerning his interest in the mall and the food fair. *Here at the mall for no reason?* I wanted to say to him. *Looking for your blue rose, maybe? It's at the sheriff's department.* Julian came around the side of the tent holding a clear plastic bag with tape on it. He'd removed it from the table. Inside the plastic bag was a single sheet of paper. Julian ripped into the bag and offered me the contents.

It was one of those cryptic messages we used to send in school, where the words and letters are cut out of magazines or newspapers. This note said: GOLDILOCKS GO HOME. AND STAY THERE.

11

"Well, I better, ah . . . I need to be going," said Charles Braithwaite in a meek voice. He had somehow tugged free of Frances and was backing away. His wild, pale hair shone like a corona in the sunlight. "Glad to have been able to help. I have to meet somebody," he babbled as Frances made a step to follow him.

"I want to thank you again in person," I called after him. "Maybe tomorrow, at your place! Your Fourth of July party, you know? Remember?" He didn't respond, not even to wave, as he slunk swiftly away. I turned back to Julian, who was puzzling over the note. "Okay, kiddo," I said, "did you go with Dusty on some field trip to his place?"

"Oh, yeah. Don't you remember? It's awesome. But he's got a real hangup about security. He got all our names printed out on a list before we came in. Then he wanted to check our driver's licenses to make sure we were who we said we were, only not everybody had a license. And even though I think he believed we were who we said we were, Dr. Braithwaite still had covered some of his current experiments with tarpaulin before we came trooping through. It was a kick. Real secretive. You know, like he was the CIA or something."

"Did you see any roses? Experimental roses?"

"Oh, Goldy, he was doing all kinds of experiments. We just saw his equipment."

I said, "Hmm." Tom could take care of Charles Braithwaite and his experiments. I didn't know what to do about the note. My clothes were damp. My heart was still beating hard. If the mall security force was as distasteful as Prince & Grogan's, they wouldn't be much help. *Call Tom asap,* my inner voice warned. *If you don't let him know you've been attacked, he's going to be mightily upset.* "Listen, Julian, could you put the flaps down and let me go into the tent and change? I still need to see Marla today."

He obeyed in silence. Frances, hands on the hips of her wet dress, squinted thoughtfully at the departing Charles Braithwaite. Then she gathered up the clothes Pete had given her and slipped into the tent next to me. The flap thumped down into place.

"What do you suppose is going on?" she hissed as I removed my sticky chef's jacket.

"I have no idea." I peeled off my skirt and decided to keep my underwear on. It was only slightly damp. But my skirt surely resembled

288

one of Arch's tie-dying projects. My fingers grasped the dressing-room storage key; I slipped it into my splotched bra. I didn't even want to picture what bleach would do to my hair. My thoughts were on Charles Braithwaite. Why had he been up on the roof? Maybe there'd been a breach in his security. Had the blue rose been stolen from him? Why? And what possible connection could it — and Braithwaite — have with Claire's murder? I struggled into the clothes from Pete and rubbed my arms.

"I'll call you later," Frances said abruptly, "I need to go talk to our helper." She quickly gathered up her wet belongings and ducked out of the tent. I felt a surge of pity for Charles Braithwaite. But I envied Frances, too, as I was also desperate to know more about what the reclusive scientist was up to.

When I emerged from the tent wearing my new duds and shaking my damp hair, Julian was sitting on the concrete, looking depleted. Fairgoers gave him occasional curious glances. But most rushed around and past him, like stream water flowing around a rock.

"What is it?" I asked him. "Feeling sick?"

He didn't respond right away. Finally he looked at me. His face was patchy and covered with the familiar sheen of sweat produced by the exertion of cooking and serving. His eyes glittered with a wetness he wasn't about to acknowledge. "God, I don't know. I'm just so tired."

"I told you not to do that damn chamber brunch." I helped him up. "How'd it go, anyway?"

His voice was weary. "Fine. And that's not it." He brushed himself off and rubbed his knuckles, raw from too much washing, on his white caterer's shirt. "I called Tom, the way you said. He said that when they get here, Claire's parents are taking her body back to Australia. They're not even going to have a memorial service in Colorado."

"Julian, I'm sorry."

"It doesn't matter." His toneless voice wrenched my heart. "Something else. After the chamber brunch, Marla's nurse at the hospital called. She said they're moving Marla into a private room, and she was asking for her nightgowns and her mail, and would someone from her sister's family go get her stuff?" I cursed at myself for forgetting. "Anyway," Julian went on, "I said I was the nephew and I would. Marla told the nurse where the spare key was and so now everything is in my car. I thought I should bring it down. Since I was planning to come anyway."

Bless Julian. We picked up Marla's belongings from the Rover and I drove us to the hospital in the van. I checked the lobby's pay phones to call Tom. They were both in use. After some confusion at the reception desk, we found the right elevator and made our way to Marla's new private room. I clutched the jar of hand cream I'd bought at Prince & Grogan. Julian, his mouth pressed in a tight line, held a grocery sack full of bedclothes and mail. When we were on the right floor, I asked at the nurses' station when Marla was expected to be discharged. The on-duty nurse smiled and said probably tomorrow, and they certainly were going to miss her! I grinned back. Sure.

"Oh, I swear, finally!" Marla said when we entered the room. She was lying in bed, looking even more uncomfortable and depressed than the day before. Tony Royce, a thick-mustached equities analyst who was Marla's current boyfriend, sat on a ventilation unit next to a window. In a corner of the room sat a nurse, one I recognized from the Coronary Care Unit.

The nurse announced softly: "Two visitors, Miss Korman."

Marla said, "Tony, I need to see my family. Okay?"

Tony Royce appraised Julian and me the way you would cattle, then snorted. "They're not your family!" But he propelled himself off the ventilation unit anyway and sauntered toward the door. Because my income did not allow me to invest heavily in equities, Tony viewed me as being from a lower rung on the evolutionary ladder. I didn't much like him, either, but I kept that to myself. Usually, like now, I ignored him.

"How are you?" I asked Marla gently. "Did the atherectomy go okay?"

Marla raised a warning finger and whispered, "I guess so. It's over, that's the best part. Notice the private room and nurse?" I nodded. For the first time in three days, I saw a tiny, brief smile cross Marla's face. I guessed she'd finally convinced someone to look up her record of contributions to the hospital. I smiled too, but then noticed Tony Royce standing by the door. Since Tony had not been to the hospital since Marla had her attack, he was probably feeling as bereft as I had the first day. On the other hand, his relationship with Marla rested largely on the fact that she was one of his best clients. Maybe he was just being difficult.

"I'm sorry," the nurse said with more insistence, "the patient can't have more than two visitors."

I glanced at Julian. His eyes pleaded with mine. I relented. "Okay," I said. "Stay here and I'll walk out with Tony."

"Oh, thanks a lot," Tony said jokingly as I took him by the arm and propelled him out the door and into the hall.

"Come on, you've been with her today and we haven't," I told him. "Besides, I need to ask you a financial question."

"You? A financial question?" He looked at my borrowed outfit. "What, coffee futures? You're talking about a lot of money."

"What do you know about a company run by someone called Reggie Hotchkiss?"

"You mean Hotchkiss Skin & Hair?" When I nodded, he massaged his mustache with his index finger. "Not much. Why, Goldy? You interested in the stock? I'm not sure they're publicly owned."

"I'm interested in the company. Can't you just find out how they're doing? I'll pay you in cookies."

He snorted again and said he'd see what he could do. He gave another you've-got-to-be-kidding assessment of my damp hair and sweatsuit proclaiming the virtues of Pete's coffee.

Back in the private room, the drabber-than-yesterday's hospital gown and absence of her usual twinkling barrettes and jewelry made Marla's depressed visage seem even more washed out than during either of my previous visits.

"Do you . . . want me to stay?" Julian asked Marla when I returned. He hesitated, perched beside a turquoise chair of molded plastic. "I know you probably need to be with Goldy. I just . . . wanted to bring you your stuff. And see how you were doing."

The juxtaposition of *needing* to see one person and perhaps *wanting* to see another was not lost on Marla. "Stay," she said weakly. "I need as many friends as I can get, at this point. And the nurse says I can have longer visits now, anyway."

"Thirty minutes," came the calm admonition from the corner.

Marla held out her hand to Julian. "Here I am thinking of myself, and I understand you've had the worst news. I'm so sorry about Claire."

Julian took her hand and looked at it. His shoulders slumped.

"Thanks, Marla. I'm sorry too."

Eventually he let go of her hand and flopped into the chair. I asked her how she felt now that she'd survived the atherectomy. She told me to lean in close, then whispered that her groin and back were still killing her. Then she told us she'd talked to the private nurse arranged to start when she came home. The nurse would double as a driver, and this seemed to relieve her. I sat in Tony's place by the window. The ventilation unit blew chilled air out onto my calves. Outside the window, people of all ages in athletic gear walked and jogged around a paved track. They weren't patients, I wagered, but doctors, nurses, and administrators. In any event, it wasn't exactly the view I'd want if I'd just had a heart attack while running. I thought I could see Dr. Lyle Gordon lumbering through his laps. If Marla could have seen him, she would have made a joke about it. That was her way. But she was still flat in the bed, and every few minutes her mood seemed to sink a little lower. The three of us sat for a while, saying nothing.

"How's Arch?" Marla asked finally.

Julian and I fell over each other saying how great Arch was, wearing his Panthers shirt and doing tie-dying, and looking for old Beatles and Herman's Hermits records.

"I think I have some Eugene McCarthy buttons in my attic," Marla said feebly.

We all fell silent again, the brief spark in our conversation like a fire gone cold.

"Well, show me what you brought," Marla tried again.

Julian picked up the bag and delicately unloaded the articles and mail onto the foot of the bed. I picked up the bedclothes and folded them into reasonable clumps before stacking them on the bedstand within Marla's reach. Marla took the pile of mail from Julian and sorted through it without interest.

"Oh, boy, the doctor's not going to like this," she said, holding up a postcard. She read, "From my mother, postmarked Lucerne. 'Have found a perfectly wonderful couple to hang around with and will be going to their château for a month! I'll write again when I have their address.' " She tossed the postcard on the floor. "So much for Mom coming in to lend a hand."

"Jeez," said Julian, "can't you write to her General Delivery or something?"

"It's one thing if it's Bluff, Utah, Big J.," Marla told him affectionately. "It's another if it's the entire country of Switzerland. This couple probably latches on to Americans and brings them to their rented château to give them a big pitch and swindle them out of millions of dollars on some stock deal in Mexico. Wouldn't be the first time for dear Mom. I actually think she enjoys it."

She stared at another postcard. "I already told good old Lyle Gordon all he needs to know about our family history. I got the 'you-are-going-to-die-if-you-don't-change-your-ways' speech." She gave me a mournful look. "No more goodies from Goldy's kitchen." She sighed again and turned her face toward the window. "God, I'm better off dead."

"Don't worry," I said, too quickly. "I'm going to cook all lowfat food for you. And it'll be so delicious you won't be able to tell it's good for you."

She closed her eyes. "You hate cooking diet stuff."

"I'm going to learn to like it."

"Oh, to be thin!" Marla said with a hoarse laugh. "I may get there after all. The hard way."

"Don't," I said. Then my eyes fell on a FedEx package on the white hospital bedspread. "What's this? Want me to open it?" She nodded. I ripped it open and handed it to her.

After a moment, she grunted. "It's from Hotchkiss Skin & Hair. They always want to impress their customers with how they're getting you all the latest things. You know Reggie Hotchkiss, Goldy. Don't you? He was a big radical with the S.D.S. and got his picture in *Life* magazine ages ago. He went to jail for destroying federal property and dodging the draft and all that."

"Destroying federal property? What kind?"

"Oh, I don't know. Let me think." She took a deep breath. "Oh, yeah. After he burned his draft card and failed to break into the CIA, he tried to drive his mother's Bentley up the steps of the Lincoln Memorial, and hit a lamp-post en route. That was the picture that was in *Life*," she added. "Someone said it was all propaganda from the British car maker. You must have seen him around town, he goes to everything."

"The only time I saw Reggie Hotchkiss up close and personal, I was trying to eavesdrop on a conversation he was having with Dusty Routt about Mignon products. She said he was going to get into trouble."

Marla sputtered, "The guy's a genuine yuppie, Goldy. The last thing he would do is get into trouble when he's trying to take over his mother's cosmetics business." She frowned at me. "Haven't you ever had a facial at his place?"

I laughed. "No, can't say that I have. Haven't had the time, money, or inclination. Especially since I've been knee-deep in nonfat dips and chocolate tortes."

"And ducking bleach water," Julian interjected.

Marla ignored him and handed me a yellow piece of paper. "Well, here's a free coupon for the facial. You have to buy fifty bucks' worth of cosmetics from their fall line, though, so you might not want to use it. God knows

I won't be able to."

I glanced at the coupon, then flipped through the slick pamphlet from Hotchkiss. The glossy photographs were of boxes, bottles, and jars of soap, cream, toners, makeups of various shapes, sizes, colors. What confused me was how the printing underneath each photograph was imperfectly aligned with the products. It was as if the photos had been taken long before, and the descriptions added hastily, just before the pamphlet went out. . . .

Wait a minute. *Fall into Color with Hotchkiss Skin & Hair!* Hadn't I just had those very words printed at the top of a banquet menu? *Hotchkiss Magic Pore-closing Toner with Mediterranean Sea Kelp — tones skin as it closes pores! Hotchkiss Patented Extra Rich Nighttime Replacement Moisturizer with Goat Placenta — slows down the aging process scientifically! Ultra Gentle Eye Cream Smoother with Swiss Herbs — firms eye area with secret European formula! Hot Date Blush. Chocolate Mousse Lipstick.* Unbelievable. The words and descriptions were virtually the same. I thought again of Reggie Hotchkiss, the man with the persistent questions at the Mignon counter. But this mailer had gone out yesterday morning. My bet was that it had been hastily printed and FedEx'd the day after the Mignon banquet, when Mignon's latest products were unveiled.

He was there. He had been. What had Dusty said? *We saw you.* Maybe Claire had seen him too. Maybe she wasn't supposed to.

I tucked the coupon into the loaned sweatpants. I had to talk to Tom, the sooner the better. I scanned Marla's face, and saw that fatigue was finally triumphing over her desire — her *need* — to be with family. Julian and I made noises about leaving.

Eyes half-closed, she protested weakly. "Tony told me a friend of his played golf three days after he had a heart attack."

"Golf sucks," Julian observed.

The weak smile widened. Marla shifted her bulky body around under the sheets, trying to get comfortable. "Tony thinks I should go to this dinner party with him tomorrow in the club. Since I'm pressuring Gordon to bust me out tomorrow, it's a possibility. I can't imagine anything more depressing than being at home alone when all the fireworks go off, anyway."

"A party?" I said, confused. "A golf party?"

"Golf *parties* suck," Julian contributed.

Now Marla seemed to be having trouble breathing. But she inhaled and struggled onward anyway. The nurse in the corner looked up from her notes. The EKG machine did not seem to be registering any distress, however, so she stayed put. Marla went on. "No, no, at the Braithwaites' big estate, do you know them? She's quite the socialite and he's a —"

"Scientist," I said. "I know. Please don't talk about it. Marla, do you need the nurse to come over here?"

She pressed her dry lips together and shook her head. "Do you know the people having the party?"

"Yes, of course I know them. But I thought *you* knew them. I'm catering the dinner, for goodness' sake. And Babs Braithwaite said *you* recommended me." I thought back to Babs's chatter about Marla. I said, almost to myself, "So how did she hear about me if you didn't —"

"Oh, Goldy, for heaven's sake!" interjected Julian in a harsh whisper. "You've got ads. You're in the Yellow Pages! You're doing the food fair. Why does it matter how she heard about you?"

Marla had fallen asleep. Her chest rose and fell regularly. Julian and I tiptoed out of the hospital room and stopped in the hall.

I faced Julian suddenly. "I'll tell you why it matters. Babs Braithwaite lied."

He gave me a patronizing look. "This is the *Braithwaites* we're talking about? The scientist who's married to the woman who slammed into the Rover" — he demonstrated

301

by whacking his hands together — "when she said I didn't put on my turn signal? Which I did."

"The very same."

"Goldy, she's a *cow*. She'd lie about anything."

"That rich cow called me before she hit you, and said she'd heard so much about me from Marla. Why lie about that?"

"I don't know," he said, resigned. "Look, here's a pay phone. If you're going to call Tom, you'd better do it."

I got Tom's voice mail at the sheriff's department. Where was he? I asked the tape. I added he might want to keep checking into Hotchkiss Skin & Hair, that they seemed to be involved in some very obvious industrial espionage with Mignon, courtesy of Reggie Hotchkiss. Dusty Routt, I said, claimed there was no relationship between Claire and Shaman Krill. I also told Tom there was an observation area behind the mirrors in the ladies' dressing room on the Prince & Grogan second floor, and that he might want to check out the Braithwaites. And Charles Braithwaite, I said finally, was deeply involved with roses. Blue ones, maybe? Suddenly, I decided not to tell Tom about the bleach water or the threatening note. I knew he would get extremely upset. Julian gave me a curious glance, so I hung up and we took off for the mall garage to get the Range Rover.

But retrieving the Rover was not that easy. Neither of us could remember where he'd left his car. As we drove up and down and back again, Julian became increasingly agitated. It had been stolen, he insisted. We'll find it, I assured him. The garage was just very confusing. I began another circle of the levels of the packed parking structure. No Rover. Finally we decided to hunt on foot. I parked in the first available free spot. The parking space was by the shoe store's entrance where, unfortunately, the Spare the Hares! people were back in force.

The war-painted crowd was larger and louder. They surged forward each time someone started toward the doors. They were chanting another slogan that buzzed in my ears.

"Just walk quickly by them," I said under my breath to Julian, who had drawn in his chin and was staring at the chanting demonstrators. I absolutely hated walking by them. Every time I did, it seemed, something bad happened.

"What are they saying?" he asked.

"Hey, hey, Mignon Cosmetics! Get your hands off helpless rabbits!"

Julian said, "Far out, man," and kept on

walking. Kept on walking, that is, until Shaman Krill popped out from between two parked cars. The demonstrator was holding something long, furry and stiff in one hand. I didn't want to look at it. When I tried to move away, Shaman Krill shadowed me. When I tried to duck around him, he followed.

"Oh, no," I moaned. I wanted to look around for the police, but was afraid to take my eyes off Krill.

"What's going on here?" Julian demanded. Krill did not heed him. He fastened his wild-eyed, Charles Manson gaze on me and leered. His small, pointed teeth gleamed eerily. Something shifted in the dark eyes of the angry, taut man in front of me. He was gleeful. He knew he was in control. I, of course, had seen that look many times before, in the eyes of the Jerk.

"Hey!" shouted Krill in an exaggerated mockery of recognizing an old friend. "Food-fight lady! Look what I got! And this time your *pig* won't save you!" He yanked the rabbit carcass upward; I recoiled. "You're history!" he screeched as he tossed the carcass at me. I ducked for the second time that day. The carcass bounced off my back. "That oughta even things up a little!" Shaman laughed hysterically. "No luck from that rabbit's foot!"

"You're sick!" I shouted. I stood up, my fists clenched. "You're crazy!"

"You're arrested," said Tom Schulz happily as he grabbed Shaman's arms. "For assault."

12

Another policeman, a fellow named Boyd whom I knew well, snapped on the handcuffs. The dead rabbit, I noticed, lay by the front left Cadillac tire. I wondered if they would have to take it as evidence.

"Wow," said Julian, brightening. "That was cool. Talk about just in the nick of time, man, I'm impressed."

"So this is where you've been." I walked quickly over to Tom. "Why didn't you tell me you were staking out the garage to look for Krill?"

"Because we haven't been here that long —"

"Tom, I really need to talk to you. You wouldn't believe the things that have happened today —"

"Life-endangering things?" he queried, holding tight to a struggling Shaman Krill.

"You pig!" shouted Krill. "You idiot!"

"Well, not *exactly* —" I said.

"Look, Miss G., we just got a tip" — he aimed his remark at Krill — "from a *real* member of People for the Ethical Treatment of Animals that this guy was here. They call you the volunteer cheerleader," he told Krill.

He turned back to me. "Goldy, where'd you get those clothes?"

"Oh, it's a long story."

"It always is with you." He eyed Julian. "Is he okay?"

"Who can tell? Check your voice mail when you're finished with this guy."

"I'll finish *you!*" Krill yelled, but no one was listening.

Officer Boyd picked up the rabbit carcass with gloved hands and put it into a paper evidence bag, and then the three of them took off in a sheriff's department vehicle. Who, I wondered, was Shaman Krill really working for?

Two levels down, Julian and I finally found the Rover. Julian drove me back to my van and we arrived home in tandem around six o'clock. When we came through the door, the melancholy rhythm of "Sgt. Pepper's Lonely Hearts Club Band" reverberated down the stairs from Arch's room. When I called to him, he replied that he was testing a strobe light and would be there in a minute.

Trying to focus on things domestic in general and on dinner in particular, I opened the walk-in. Wrapped triangles of creamy Port Salut, tangy Brie, and crumbly Gorgonzola cheeses beckoned. Tom had made a sign that said *Ours!* with an arrow pointing to the shelf

below, to distinguish the extravagant purchases of foodstuffs he made for our newly
formed family. I could always count on that
shelf to bulge with the choicest berries and
other produce, the ripest cheeses, the most
expensive seafoods. I was trying to decide
from the *Ours!* shelf when Arch arrived in
the kitchen, still wearing the Panthers shirt.
He'd found a pair of round-framed sunglasses
and strap-up-the-legs sandals to go with the
shirt. He looked like a beachcomber.

"I'm hungry," he announced unceremoniously. "In fact, I'm going to *faint* if I don't
have some food." He lifted up the sunglasses
and glanced at my outfit, then at my face and
hair. "Gosh, Mom, you look weird. I know
you like coffee, but don't you want to advertise your business instead of Pete's?"

"Arch, please . . ."

"All right, all right. Just . . . when are we
going to eat? I mean, I don't want to be rude,
but it's been a hundred hours since lunchtime."

"Well, I was kind of thinking of taking a
shower first," I said hopefully.

Arch moved the sunglasses down his nose,
clutched his stomach, and made his eyeballs
bulge.

"Oh, stop," I grumbled. So much for the
shower. Marla was coming home the next day,

in any event, and if I was going to follow through on my promise to do some lowfat cooking for her, now was the time. "Dinner in forty-five minutes?" I asked brightly.

Arch looked around the empty kitchen. No food was started. The table was covered with advertisements for the fair. "What are you fixing?" he asked dubiously.

"Why don't you let me —" Julian began.

"Absolutely not," I broke in, "you're taking a break. I'm fixing pasta," I said noncommittally to Arch. Pasta was always a safe bet. What did I have on hand? Hard to remember, since Tom had taken it upon himself to buy so many goodies for us.

"What kind?" my son wanted to know.

"Arch —"

"Maybe you'd just better let me order in from the Chinese place."

"Hey, kiddo! What are you, the plumber's son who can't get his leaky sink fixed for a year? I'm going to cook dinner! I may be in professional food service, but I always fix the meals around here, don't I?"

"Well, not always —" he began, but when he saw my glowering expression, he fell silent.

Julian came to my rescue. "Come on, Arch, let's go listen to rock groups for a while." Julian tousled Arch's brown hair that stuck

out at various angles. Since it was summer-
time, I never told him to comb it. Worrying
about the prep school's dress and appearance
code didn't start until fall.

Arch pulled away. "You don't need to take
care of me, Julian. I'm okay."

"I'm not trying to take care of you. I really
want to listen to some tunes."

"But I can't on an empty stomach!" He narrowed his eyes at me, not to be dissuaded.
"What kind of pasta? Fettuccine?"

"Fettuccine Alfredo," I pledged. It was his
favorite. If I promised it, maybe he'd quit has-
sling me and allow me to cook. On the other
hand, how I would make a lowfat Alfredo —
a dish that ordinarily required a stick of melted
butter, two cups of heavy whipping cream,
and loads of Parmesan cheese — was beyond
my reckoning.

"I don't believe it," Arch replied stubbornly.

"That's what they said when Eugene Mc-
Carthy won the New Hampshire primary,"
Julian interjected.

Arch gaped at Julian in awe. "How'd you
know that?"

"You'd be surprised at what you can
pick up," Julian said mysteriously. "Take the
Vietnam protest, which had as one of its favorite slogans *Johnson Withdraw! Like Your*

I yelled, "Julian!"

Arch shrieked with laughter and scampered up the stairs.

"Gosh, Goldy," Julian said in his get-a-life tone of voice. "Don't you think Arch knows about sex? Sometimes I wonder about you."

Well, I thought as I desperately scanned my freezer for cholesterol-free fettuccine, sometimes I wondered about me too. Miraculously, I found a package of the right pasta. I started water to heat in the pasta pentola. The boys had turned off Sgt. Pepper, perhaps to discuss . . . well, I didn't want to think about it.

I opened the kitchen window. A late afternoon breeze floated in along with trilling notes from the saxophone at the Routts' place. I smiled. Here we were in rural Colorado, and yet it felt as if our house sat across the alley from a New York jazz club. I chopped some red onion, then washed and sliced slender, brilliant-green asparagus that I had found in a tight bundle on the *Ours!* shelf. When I'd drizzled a bit of olive oil over a head of garlic and set it to bake in the oven, I thought back on the events of the day. Applying logic, or trying to.

I'd gone into Prince & Grogan trying to find Claire's murderer. Tom had said it was all right to do some digging, as long as I didn't

LOWFAT FETTUCCINE ALFREDO WITH ASPARAGUS

2 tablespoons finely chopped red onion

2½ cups diagonally sliced asparagus with tight tips (tough ends of stalks removed)

1 teaspoon (about 2 cloves) mashed and chopped *baked* garlic (see note)

⅓ cup nonfat dry milk

1½ cups skim milk or more as needed

1½ tablespoons Wondra instant-blending flour

2 tablespoons light process cream cheese product (*not* nonfat)

⅔ cup grated Parmesan cheese

9 ounces cholesterol-free fettuccine

½ cup chopped arugula

Heat a medium-size nonstick sauté pan. Remove from the heat and spray with vegetable oil spray. Add the onion and sauté over medium heat until limp, about 5 or 10 minutes. Add the asparagus and the garlic, cover the pan, and turn off the heat. (The steam from the onion will cook the asparagus.)

In a large skillet, combine the dry milk and skim milk and whisk until blended.

Add the flour, stir, and cook over medium-high heat until thickened. In a small bowl, add 2 tablespoons of the hot sauce to the cream cheese and stir until smooth. Return this mixture to the hot sauce. Add the Parmesan and stir until melted. Keep hot. If the mixture becomes too thick, thin it out with small amounts of skim milk. The consistency should be like cream, not gravy.

Cook the fettuccine in boiling water according to the package directions until it is al dente; drain. Add the hot pasta and the garlic and the vegetables to the sauce in the skillet. Stir and cook over medium-low heat until heated through. Serve garnished with chopped arugula.

Serves 4

Note: To bake the garlic, preheat the oven to 350°. Place a whole head of garlic in a small baking pan. Drizzle one teaspoon of olive oil over the head of garlic; add ¼ cup water to the pan. Bake the garlic, loosely covered with aluminum foil, for 45 to 60 minutes or until the cloves are soft. The cloves will slip right out of their skins to be mashed, chopped, or served whole. The whole garlic cloves can be served as a side dish with any roast meat; the mashed garlic cloves are also delicious mixed with hot homemade mashed potatoes.

313

get into trouble. And I *had* gotten into trouble, or at least been busted by store security, doused with bleach water, and told to go home. But these weren't my fault, I rationalized.

Besides, I thought as I got out Wondra flour, I was determined to help Julian recover from Claire's death. *If I just knew why this happened,* he had cried so helplessly here in the kitchen. Claire's life had revolved around Mignon. So it seemed *logical* to look at what she herself had called "that cutthroat cosmetics counter."

And, I also rationalized as I measured, since I was a woman, like it or not I was more able to get gossipy-type information than Tom and his deputies at the sheriff's department ever would. The Mignon counter at Prince & Grogan, Westside Mall, was a place of high energy, high profit, high emotional stakes. I mean, where else could you go and be promised beauty and endless youth with such enthusiasm, conviction, and pain to your wallet? Where else did you have to watch for shoplifters, pretend to be decades older than your actual age, worry about spies from rival firms, and fend off wealthy pick-up artists in the form of weird scientists?

I poked wildly through one of my drawers until I found a grater. I'd been able to help Tom before in his investigations. Of course, he'd never particularly welcomed my involvement until it was all over. And no matter how much I maintained Julian needed my help in figuring out what happened, my protestations would fall on deaf ears.

Still. I'd heard Dusty say to Reggie Hotchkiss, *We saw you. You are going to get into so much trouble.* I'd been in that garage. I hadn't seen anybody except a crazy demonstrator. But I'd found a blue rose close to Claire's body. And that rose had perhaps been developed by Charles Braithwaite — the same Charles Braithwaite who, according to Dusty, had been infatuated by, and later broken up with, Claire Satterfield. And then there had been *Babs* Braithwaite, who had run into me at the top of the escalator, claiming that *somebody* was hiding in the women's dressing room. Only I hadn't found anybody in the dressing room. Except I'd unexpectedly encountered her husband again. This time Dr. Charlie had magically turned up on the roof. On the roof, that is, after Frances Markasian and I had been hit with an unhealthy dose of bleach water. I wondered if Charles Braithwaite would have had the courage to do that. He didn't strike me as the courageous type.

It was the bleach water, and the warning to go home, that made me realize I *had* to figure out what was going on with the murder of Claire Satterfield, no matter what Tom said. Instead of Frances Markasian being at my side when the chlorine came sailing through the air, it could have been Julian.

It could have been Arch.

Whoever had tried to warn me off would stop at nothing, it seemed. So I was in this thing until the bitter end.

With that decided, I grated the pungent Parmesan cheese into golden strands. Then I rummaged through my cabinets for something that would be like cream and decided on mixing nonfat dry milk into skim milk. It didn't sound as good as whipping cream, it certainly didn't look as good as whipping cream, and I wasn't sure if it would taste anything like that favorite — and marvelously fattening — ingredient of food service people. But the mixture didn't have any fat in it, so it was definitely worth a shot. For Marla. I also retrieved a package of lowfat cream cheese from my refrigerator — one of the remnants of the Mignon banquet vegetable dip saga — and decided to blend some of that into the sauce, for richness. Or simulated richness, I thought dutifully, as I slowly poured the dry milk mixture over the flour and began to whisk vigorously.

As I stirred I tried to reflect. What could I deduce from my latest visit to the mall? I was becoming quite an expert on that place: the location of the covered catwalk around the entrance, called a "blind" by the security people who liked to lurk there, the intricacies of hidden cameras trained and focused on customer transactions, the not-so-obsolete one-way mirrors. I glanced out my window. The pale leaves of the aspen trees in my backyard shuddered in the wind. The saxophone music lilting through the open windows made me think of Dusty — poor, eager, friendly Dusty, expelled from Elk Park Prep, losing a potential boyfriend in the form of Julian, losing another friend in the form of Claire, stepped on by ambitious fellow sales associate Harriet. And living in a house built by Habitat for Humanity, which was certainly a long way from the Aqua Bella mansion she'd yearned for aloud when we were sipping coffee on the mall's garage roof. But looking back on her exchange with Reggie Hotchkiss, it seemed to me that she'd been radiant, teasing, even flirtatious, before they'd argued. If it really was an argument, and not just more of a tease. In that relationship, Dusty was the sought-after one. Dusty was the one with information. Or so, perhaps, Reggie Hotchkiss had made it appear.

And then I thought of Harriet, perfectly coiffed, ambitious, keeping her distance from the inquisitive Reggie, even attempting to prevent Dusty from talking to him. Harriet had been working at that Mignon counter a lot longer than Dusty had, why didn't Reggie Hotchkiss ask *her* questions? Perhaps he had, or he'd tried to, yet she was loyal to the company. She certainly wouldn't want to jeopardize her commissions by telling secrets to the rival Hotchkiss Skin & Hair. Or would she?

And what about the Braithwaites? Charlie was obsessed by more than science, that much was clear. Had he dropped the improbably hued rose near Claire's body? Why was Babs hanging out — literally — above the cosmetics counter, when I was hauled away by Stan White, Nick Gentileschi's henchman? Did Babs know what was going on between Charlie and Claire, if anything?

I scooped out some of the thickened cream sauce into the dollops of cream cheese, whisked them together, then stirred the mixture back into the sauce. While this was heating I sautéed the red onion and then added the smashed cloves of baked garlic and the asparagus, covered the pan, and put it aside. The water was boiling. I dropped in the ribbons of pasta, decided to serve it with a salad of fresh raspberries and lightly steamed baby peas, and turned my attention to dessert.

If we were going to have pasta with vegetables, then we could handle a dark, rich dessert. I decided on the fudge soufflé that I'd stumbled upon in my attempt to make nonfat chocolate torte. When chocolate chips and skim milk were heating in the top of a double boiler, I beat egg whites with sugar, salt, and vanilla until they were fluffed and opaque. Then I swirled the chocolate and egg white mixtures together and put the resulting dark cloud of chocolate back in the double boiler to cook while we ate dinner. Next I stirred the shredded Parmesan into the fettuccine, vegetables, and sauce, heated this until the luscious-looking concoction was just bubbling, and called the boys. I looked at my watch: six forty-five. Amazing. Not that Arch would appreciate my culinary speed and skill, however.

I put a call in to Tom and again got his voice mail. I told him we were eating the most delectable goodies for dinner that he could possibly imagine, and the later he got home, the less likely it was that he would get some. Mean, I knew, but tactics were tactics.

And delectable the meal was. The cheesy, thickened cream sauce coated every delicate strand of fettuccine and crunchy bite of asparagus. The salad was light and refreshingly tart. Arch ate hungrily. Julian consumed

FUDGE SOUFFLÉ

½ cup unsweetened cocoa powder
½ cup confectioners' sugar
1 cup skim milk
⅓ cup semisweet chocolate chips
5 egg whites
¼ cup sugar
½ teaspoon vanilla extract
Lowfat whipped topping (optional)

Whisk the cocoa powder, confectioners' sugar, and milk in the top of a double boiler over boiling water until smooth. Add the chocolate chips and stir until the chips are melted. Stir and lower the heat to simmer.

In a large bowl, beat the egg whites until soft peaks form. Gradually add sugar and beat until stiff peaks form. Fold the vanilla and ½ cup of the chocolate mixture into the egg white mixture.

Bring the water in the bottom of the double boiler back to a boil. Stir the chocolate-egg white mixture into the chocolate mixture in the top of the double boiler. Using an electric beater or a whisk, beat this mixture for a minute or until it is well combined. Cover the double boiler and continue to cook over

boiling water for 25 to 30 minutes or until the soufflé is puffed and set. Serve with lowfat whipped topping, if desired.

Serves 4

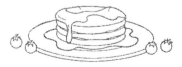

nearly nothing. When I asked if they wanted fudge soufflé for dessert, he merely shrugged. As I began to clear the dishes, I again suggested to Julian that he go to bed instead of trying to help clean up or work on the Braithwaites' party. He wouldn't be much help on the Fourth if he was too exhausted to do anything. To my surprise, he assented and trudged up to his bunk. Arch, ecstatic that he'd get a double portion of dessert, gleefully sneaked away with it to the television room.

Grateful for the quiet, I started to rinse dishes and place them in the dishwasher. It was half past eight. So much for Tom making it home for dinner. But as soon as I had that thought, the front-door latch popped.

Tom strode in, stood at the kitchen threshold, opened his arms, and said, "You look beautiful."

Hard to ignore my runaway, bleach-splotched hair, my face streaked with makeup, Pete's oversize *Virtues of Coffee* sweatsuit. "Is that a joke?"

He circled me in an enormous hug. "Never," he whispered in my ear. For the first time that day, I relaxed. But then I tensed, trying to think of how to explain my appearance.

"Some . . . bleach water spilled on me

today." It was sort of the truth. Half of the truth.

"Well, I wasn't going to ask. How's Marla?" His mouth close to my ear sent shivers down my spine.

"Surviving. Want to taste some of the lowfat food I'm teaching myself to cook for her? Want to hear how I got into trouble today?"

"Do I have to? I'd rather do something else," he murmured.

"Incorrigible."

"Beautiful."

"Later."

On that hopeful note, he reluctantly pulled away from me. I poured him a glass of red wine, started the fettuccine reheating, and asked if he'd listened to the voice mail.

"Oh, yes," he replied with a broad smile. "Yes, yes. And I listened to my other messages too. Had a little visit with the horticultural powers that be. Seems Charles Braithwaite, Ph.D., is in the process of getting the blue rose patented, which takes quite a while. One thing you have to do when you're patenting a flower? You name it." I put a plateful of the steaming pasta in front of him. He wound up a spoonful of the fettuccine and downed it. His bushy eyebrows arched upward. "Gosh, Goldy, this is delicious. Lowfat?"

"Don't act so surprised. What's Braithwaite

going to name the rose? And did you do any research on Hotchkiss?"

His green eyes twinkled. "Charles Braithwaite was naming his blue rose the *Claire Satterfield*."

"Good Lord!"

Arch stuck his head into the kitchen, waved to Tom, and announced he was going up to bed early. I must have looked stunned. At the beginning of July, Arch was rarely willing to hit the sack earlier than he did during the school year.

"But —" I began.

Arch pulled his mouth into a tight scowl. "I just don't want Julian to think I've abandoned him."

"I'm sure he doesn't think you've —"

But he was gone. I didn't go after him because the phone rang. It was Tony Royce. While Tom savored the fettuccine and polished off the salad, Tony informed me that Hotchkiss Skin & Hair was a privately held company that didn't have to report its profits and losses to shareholders, so the information he'd been able to get for me was sketchy.

"That's okay," I told him. My pencil was poised. "Sketchy is better than zilch."

"Hotchkiss Skin & Hair needs a face-lift, Goldy. We're talking *major* surgery."

"Skip the puns, Tony —"

But he was on a roll. "I mean," he persisted, "we're talking a company that puts a new *wrinkle* on financing!" I know Tony and Marla had fun together, and that she thought he was brilliant with money. But the substance of their relationship, I had to admit, I just didn't understand.

"And their financial status is . . . ?" I prodded.

"Who are you talking to?" Tom suddenly wanted to know.

"Just a sec, Tony." I covered the phone. "Marla's boyfriend. He's an equities analyst, and he looked into Hotchkiss Skin & Hair for me."

Tom was incredulous. "Doing the financial check on the company is *our* job. What are you doing?"

I said defensively, "I just happened to run into Tony at the hospital. I'll tell you all about it."

"You'd better."

"Okay, Tony," I said back into the phone, ignoring the expression on Tom's face, "what's their financial status?"

Tony Royce snorted. "Terrible, terrible. Hotchkiss has been giving facials for years, when women thought they needed them and would line up out the door to get one. But from a business standpoint, facials aren't exactly a big growth industry these days. They're labor-intensive. Which means expensive, and you can't do a huge markup on them. *And,* unless you've got a steady demand from the carriage trade to sustain your business, you're out of luck." He paused to sigh, taking deep satisfaction from being the man in the know. "But baby-boomer women . . . now, there's an interesting demographic group. The ones who have money mostly work outside the home, and they don't have time for facials. Or," he said with a chuckle, "no advertising genius has yet *convinced* these women that they *need* to have facials. So Mama Hotchkiss, sensing she needed to change with the times, decided to launch a new set of products designed for these very same baby-boomer women. It was called Renewal. Didja ever buy any Renewal, Goldy? I mean," he chuckled, "not that you need it or anything."

"Can't say that I made that purchase, Tony."

Another lugubrious sigh. "Neither did anybody else. Renewal flopped. Big-time. Mama Hotchkiss went to the bank for a loan. Nobody was biting, even when she offered free facials. Bankers don't like facials, Goldy. They prefer to look intimidating and ugly inside their expensive suits so that customers will bow down, scrape, and lick the floor."

Speaking of licking and scraping, I checked on the soufflé that I was trying to keep warm for Tom. It was still dark and puffed. I removed the double-boiler top from the heat. I'd found that working with food often helps when listening to arrogant people on the telephone.

"So," he persisted, "what do you think happened?"

"Renewal flopped, just as you said," I replied. "But the business didn't go under. So . . . if a cake I'd staked my reputation on flopped, and I didn't lose the business, I'd develop a cookie. Or a torte. You have to sell something."

"Take you out of that apron and put you in a banker's suit, Goldy."

High praise indeed, considering the source. "Thanks. So Hotchkiss started to look for new products? But they needed more money for that, so they went to some pal of yours."

"Hey. I know everyone in the Denver financial community, and I've lived here for only a little over a year."

"You're marvelous. Forget the cookies, I'm going to have to pay you in brownies."

Tony made a long *hmmm* noise. "So they got a loan to develop new products. Their business plan was drawn up by none other than —"

"Reggie Hotchkiss!" I concluded triumphantly.

"If you knew all this, why'd you ask me?" He sounded peeved.

"I didn't know any of it, Tony. You did sketchy for me, I just filled in the holes. How long does Hotchkiss Skin & Hair have to prove themselves?"

"They report to my banker friend next month. But he's been getting glowing reports from Reg. They've got a new line, they're guaranteed success. Everyone makes piles of money."

Yes, I knew all about their new line, it was fresh from Mignon Cosmetics. But I decided not to mention that to Tony. I asked him how and when I could deliver the promised brownies to him. He said he'd be at the Braithwaites' party tomorrow night, and hadn't a little bird told him I was catering that party? You bet, I said, and hung up.

I told Tom what I'd learned. He even took out his trusty spiral notebook and jotted down a few notes. Then, while he watched in amusement, I flipped through the phone book, located Hotchkiss Skin & Hair, and put in a call. Lucky for me, the corporate number had a tape saying if I wanted a facial or any one of their products, leave my name and number. Someone would get back to me just as soon as one of their skin-care staff became available.

I summoned a frantic voice. My newly discovered acting ability was going to get me into deep trouble one of these days, but right now I had to admit I was rather enjoying it. "This is Goldy Schulz calling, and I need a facial at your earliest convenience! I . . . I saw a brochure of your new product line and I want to buy everything. *Everything.* I need it! You have to understand, I'm desperate! I know you all are the ones who can help me!" I left my number and disconnected.

"Woman," Tom mused as he rinsed off his dish. "Sometimes I don't know what to think about you."

I ladled scoopfuls of hot fudge soufflé into bowls and spooned on lowfat whipped topping. I handed one to Tom. "I've told you all I know. Now, what did *you* find out about Hotchkiss? And what about Shaman Krill? What he's up to?"

Tom shook his head and took a bite. "Oh, God."

Oh, God, was right. The fudge soufflé was warm and rich, and melted on the tongue, just the way the thousand-calories-a-bite hot fudge sundaes did. Marla was going to love this. "Tom? What did you find out?"

He wrinkled his brow and dug into the

soufflé. "Hotchkiss is in trouble financially. Desperately needs to have success with his new line."

"If you knew all that, why didn't you tell me?"

"Because I have ways of investigating that don't involve sleazy characters like Tony Royce."

I sighed. "So you don't mind if I get a facial?"

" 'Course not. Just don't —"

"Get into trouble, I know." I felt guilty not telling him about the bleach water and the threatening note, but I knew he would halt my sleuthing around immediately if I 'fessed up. "There's a ton of fudge soufflé here," I warned him. "Both of the guys went to bed already, so I hope you'll eat more."

He gestured with his spoon. "Remember when you were living with the Farquhars, and you told me all about how chocolate was an aphrodisiac?" I nodded, and he picked up our bowls and put them in the sink. Then he pulled me up from my seat. It was so unexpected that I laughed. Maybe because he'd been gone so much lately, it felt as if we were going to be newlyweds forever. He kissed my cheek, then my other cheek, then my ear. "Isn't that what you told me? You're such a *great* caterer. To do all that research, I mean." He narrowed one eye and arched one of those bushy brows. "Tell you what, though, I've always thought of myself as a good cop."

"A *great* cop," I corrected him, and kissed him back.

"But I certainly," he said as he scooped me up easily into his arms, "never" — I squealed as he started to walk out of the kitchen — "ever," he said emphatically as he carried me up the stairs to our bedroom, "had this much *fun* doing police work in my entire life."

So much for second helpings.

13

Saturday morning, July 4, brought a very early call for Tom. His subsequent departure accompanied a mumbled farewell to me that I thought included words about bail. But I was still half-asleep, and registered only the loss of his body heat from our bed.

At half past five I gave up on slumber. Daylight had invaded our bedroom, and the morning concert of birds was in full swing. I was exhausted. I'd crept downstairs at midnight when I heard Julian talking on the phone. His tone had been the one he used with friends — confiding, pleading. *I can't stop thinking about her. When they take the body, it'll be like she's really dead. Why would someone do this?* I'd felt guilty listening in and tiptoed back upstairs. Now, with another food fair day looming and no relief in sight for Julian's pain, I felt as if it was all too much.

I pushed the window open, took a deep breath of cool, sweet air, and gazed at the bowl of ultra-blue Colorado sky. Stretching up to the horizon, vast expanses of pines covered the closest mountains like thick waves of forest-green needlepoint. Brilliant chartreuse groves of aspens in full leaf patched the deep green undulating over the hills. The air was extremely still. Aspen Meadow Lake offered a plate-glass reflection of the spruces and ponderosa pines lining its shore. With any luck, this weather would hold through the food fair and the fireworks at Aspen Meadow Lake.

I went through a slow yoga routine, fixed myself a cappuccino, and moved efficiently around the kitchen to assemble more ribs, salad, bread, and cookies. I caught sight of the bag that had held Marla's hand cream and realized it was finally Saturday. The day Marla was due home. Also the day Claire's parents were arriving from Australia to claim her body.

I sat at the kitchen table and tried to remember if Julian had told me what he was doing today. Had I failed him in not being around during this painful time? At least during the night he'd been seeking companionship by talking to someone on the phone. I sipped the last of the cold coffee, rinsed my cup, and caught sight of a note Julian had left under a refrigerator magnet. He had arranged to get together with some school buddies. Would I please, he wanted to know, leave him instructions for preparing the Braithwaites' Fourth of July party tonight? *I'll be home by ten A.M., and I want to learn how to do that turkey curry,* he wrote in his small, cramped script, *so don't just give me the easy stuff!* And then — *Did you find out anything about Claire? J.*

Grief tightened my throat. In two months Julian would be at Cornell. A year ago, he'd needed a place to live for his high school senior year, a salary for his work with the catering business, and a short course in food service before he began his official college studies in food science. But the tight family unit we'd developed since had come as a bonus, a surprise, a slice of what the theologians call *grace.* Now his departure loomed like a black hole. I punched buttons on my kitchen computer to bring up the menu for the Braithwaites. My mind mulled Julian's last plea: *Did you find out anything about Claire?* No, Julian. Nothing helpful. Nothing to answer your questions or to ease your pain. Nothing to explain why I — and by extension, my family — was being threatened. Yet.

Through an effort of pure will, I pushed the sadness aside. I wanted to help Julian patch his shattered young life back together. That would be my farewell present.

In the interim, it was time to work. My screen held the lowfat menu Babs Braithwaite had ordered: *Cucumber-Mint Soup, Barbecued Fruit Skewers, Turkey Curry with Raisin Rice and Condiments, Vegetable Slaw, Homemade Rolls, Frosted Fudge Cookies.* Honestly, lowfat food was beginning to dominate my life. The printer spat out the menu while I checked that we had all the ingredients for the curry and the cookies. I removed ground turkey from the freezer to thaw, then chopped onions and apples for the sauce. I scrawled a note to Julian that he could start by chopping the fruit for the barbecue skewers.

The phone rang and I gave my usual greeting: "Goldilocks' Catering, Where Everything Is Just Right!"

"Ah, may I speak with Miss Shulley?" The voice was high and extremely snooty. I figured it was a wrong number, but the caller plowed on to explain: "This is Hotchkiss Skin & Hair. Is Miss Shula available? She requested an urgent appointment for skin treatment and asked to order all the products from our catalogue. I was wondering how she planned to pay for her order."

My blood ran cold. I'd never even had a facial, and here I was, a not-well-to-do caterer ordering all kinds of hideously expensive products and making an appointment for a *treatment* — which the woman pronounced with the same kind of awe usually reserved for *electroshock therapy* — under false pretenses. The caller was bound to ask all kinds

of questions I was not prepared to answer —
*What is your skin type, or do you even know?
Is this your first visit? How many years of neglect
are we talking about?* I pressed my lips together
and wondered how much of a drain it was
going to be — from time, money, and emotional reserves — to find out exactly what
Reggie Hotchkiss was up to.

"This is *Mrs.* Schulz. I made the call. And
I have a coupon for the facial."

The voice became instantly ingratiating.
"Oh, Mrs. . . . Zult, we can take you at your
earliest convenience. There's no problem with
scheduling a skin treatment. And of course
we'll also provide you with all the products
you requested. How soon can you make it in
today, and do you plan to pay by check or
credit card?"

Why did she need to know this? Did they
have people stiff them for soap and moisturizer? "Ah . . . well, I live up in Aspen
Meadow —"

"In the country club area? Or in Flicker
Ridge?"

Needless to say, the answer to that question
was *neither of the above,* although I catered
in million-dollar homes in those areas quite
often. I imagined my interrogator with a pen
poised over the same kind of client card that
Dusty had filled out for me at Mignon. I said,

"How much . . . er . . . time should I allow?"

"Well, Mrs. . . . Shoop, that depends on what you would like us to do for you. What problems are you having with your skin?"

"Aah . . ." What problems, exactly? "My . . . er . . . face is in a state of crisis. I . . . don't feel as if I'm as attractive as I could be."

"Mrs. Chute," purred the smug voice, "that's why we're here! You'd best allow two hours for a facial and makeup application. That's not very long to undo several decades of abuse."

Decades of abuse sounded a bit extreme, but I said only, "Two hours? I can be there by one. How do I get there from Westside Mall?"

She explained where in the Aqua Bella neighborhood Hotchkiss Skin & Hair was located. I could drive or I could walk.

"And with the coupon," I said uneasily, "just how much more will it cost to undo several decades of . . . complexion problems?"

She told me. I said I'd put the whole thing on my credit card, hung up, then grabbed the counter to keep from fainting.

"Gosh, Mom." Arch entered the kitchen from the direction of the TV room. He pushed his glasses up his nose. "*Now* what?" Today's tie-dyed T-shirt was a symphony of bilious colors.

"Remember . . . when your soles separated

337

from your sneakers and I couldn't afford to buy you a new pair?'"

"Only dorks call them sneakers these days, Mom. But okay, sure. That was in November of sixth grade. You got me some new *athletic shoes* at Christmas. So?"

"I'm about to spend the cash equivalent of ten pairs of *athletic shoes.*"

Arch, being a literal fellow, looked at my feet. "Why'd you do that?"

" 'Cuz my face needs it."

He slowly raised his large brown eyes behind their tortoiseshell glasses from the floor to my face. "Am I missing something here?"

"Oh, Arch. I'm sorry. You went to bed early, and now you're up early. What you're missing is a nice breakfast. How about some?"

Unlike the previous day, he brightened. You never could tell with kids, when they would be hungry. But breakfast, unlike the world of beauty, was something we both understood. Since Marla was coming home in the late morning, I resolved to prepare a dish that I could take over and leave for the private nurse to heat up in Marla's kitchen. Something healthful that wasn't oatmeal. If I worked quickly, I'd still be able to set up for the food fair with time to spare. Watched by my ravenous son, I began to measure flour and whip yet more egg whites. Something beautiful and appealing to the eye and to the tongue. Something breakfast-y that would satisfy Marla's sweet tooth. Something that could be frozen and reheated without catastrophe.

Within moments I was dropping dollops of batter speckled with fruit cocktail on a non-stick cookie sheet, and feeling pretty smug. Arch transported the food for the fair out to the van, and by the time he was finished, a delicious pancake aroma swirled through the kitchen.

"Oh, I forgot to tell you," he said as he mixed Dutch cocoa powder with sugar to make hot chocolate. "Julian's gone to visit some friends. He left early. And Tom left early too. Tom said to tell you Krill is an actor. I thought krill lived in the ocean."

I said I wasn't exactly sure, but I thought Krill was just some weird guy who was very convincing *acting* like a weird guy. I brought out the cookie sheet with the fruit-cocktail pancakes. Arch *ooh*ed approvingly at the golden, puffed rounds. He heated maple syrup — a mail-order gift from his grandparents, who doted on him — while I put together a fresh strawberry sauce for Marla.

When his mouth was full, Arch said, "You m'berd's c'ming early f'me today?" When I glared, he swallowed and repeated: "You remember Dad's coming early for me today?

2 cups all-purpose flour
1 cup sugar
1 teaspoon baking soda
½ teaspoon salt
2 egg whites
1 16-ounce can juice-packed fruit
   cocktail, drained and juice reserved
maple syrup or chopped fresh strawberries macerated with a little sugar

Preheat the oven to 350°. Spray 2 non-stick cookie sheets with vegetable oil and set aside.

Sift the dry ingredients together and set aside. Beat the egg whites until frothy. Beat in the juice. Gradually add the dry mixture, stirring until well blended. Fold in the fruit cocktail.

Using an ⅛-cup (2-tablespoon) measure, scoop dollops of pancake batter onto the sprayed pans, leaving at least 2 inches between the pancakes. Bake for 10 to 15 minutes or until puffed and golden. Serve hot with maple syrup, fresh strawberries, peaches, or other fruit.

Serves 4

We're going over to his condo for the Fourth. I think Keystone puts on some fireworks. Now do you remember? Not as good as Aspen Meadow Lake, probably," he added, no doubt to console me.

"No," I said lightly, "I didn't remember. Thanks for reminding me. Are you packed?"

"Sort of. I still have to find my sparklers. Hey, Mom! These pancakes are awesome . . . I mean, *cool!* You should call them Killer Pancakes!" He shoveled in a few more mouthfuls. I looked out my kitchen window and found myself wishing for some of that soothing saxophone music. But at this hour, the only sound was the morning rush of traffic down Aspen Meadow's Main Street, topped by a louder, closer sputter of a foreign car coming down our road. The sound was familiar, and I knew it the way I knew the sound of the mailman's old grinding Subaru. But I couldn't place it. Then I did hear a familiar roar — the Jerk's Jeep. I sighed and headed for the front door to let him in before he staged some sort of stunt. He'd never touched me when Arch was present. On the other hand, when it came to my ex-husband, there was always a first time for most things bad.

I opened the door and he strode in angrily. He bellowed for Arch. He seemed loaded for bear, although I judged him to be sober. Of course, I'd been wrong about that before too.

"In the kitchen!" was Arch's fearful response.

"Don't mind me," I said as I started to close the front door, then thought better of it and left it ajar.

John Richard bent over Arch's plate which held only a half-pancake in a puddle of syrup. Then he slowly moved his eyes to stare into the half-full cup of hot chocolate. Arch, who had stopped eating, gave me a confused glance.

John Richard rasped, "Why do you eat that shit your mother gives you? You want to grow up fat and sick and have a heart attack like Marla?"

I said, "Get. Out." Why was he doing this? Did he secretly feel guilty himself about Marla having the heart attack? Unlikely.

"Gee, Dad," Arch interjected, "it's okay —"

A loud knocking made the front-door frame reverberate; a female "Hoo-hoo?" echoed down the hall. John Richard stood with his hands on his hips, unmoving, staring at my collection of cookbooks as if fascinated by their arrangement on the shelf. Arch ran out of the kitchen and up the stairs. He knew he had to get his stuff, and quickly, to avoid a scene.

"Hoo-hoo, Goldy, it's your partner in bleach!" came the voice again.

Frances Markasian peered into the foyer. She had reverted to her normal attire: black T-shirt, frayed blue jeans, duct-taped sneakers, voluminous black raincoat, and equally voluminous black purse. She looked like a skinny bat. "There you are!" she said. "Sorry to be here so early, but I was just trying to catch you before you went to the fair. Is that okay? Can we talk? Can I come in? I won't smoke."

I came out onto the front porch and gestured in the direction of the porch swing. "Let's just stay out here. I thought I heard your Fiat, I just wasn't used to hearing it so early in the morning."

Frances backed toward the swing, her head tilted as she appraised me. "Goldy, are you all right?"

I attempted a smile. "Let's just say I had an unexpected visitor early this morning."

"Who?"

"Frances, what exactly is it you want me to do for you?"

She drew out a Marlboro, held it up for my inspection, and I nodded. Much as I hated cigarettes, I knew Frances would get down to business more quickly if she had nicotine. She fished around in her purse for a lighter, brought one out along with a Jolt cola, lit the cig, popped the can top, inhaled, exhaled, and took a big swig from the can, all in a quick series of practiced motions.

"Okay," she said presently, "I need more Mignon cosmetics and I don't want them to get suspicious. So I was hoping you could get the stuff for me —"

"Oh, Frances, for heaven's sake, I have so much to do today —"

"— and I've checked with my editor, and he wants you to cater a big shower for his wife in two weeks, lots of guests, couples, a hundred people, name your price." She smiled broadly and took another drag.

I guess I could spare five or ten minutes. "Look, Frances. I can't spend a lot of time at that counter today. I have another appointment today, my friend is coming home from the hospital, and I have to cook for a big party tonight —"

"I know, I know, the Braithwaites'. But that's not until to*night,* and I was really hoping you could get this stuff for me to*day.*" I sighed. When did she think caterers did their preparations? The cigarette dangled from the side of her mouth as she rooted around in her purse again and finally pulled out a list along with a plastic zip bag. She unzipped the bag and fanned out its contents: three hundred-dollar bills. Then she started reading the list: "Magic Pore-closing Toner, thirteen ounce; Extra

Rich Nighttime Replacement Moisturizer, ten ounce; Ultra Gentle Eye Cream Firmer, ten ounce. . . .” She finished reading, inhaled, blew out a fat stream of smoke, then flicked her ashes over the side of the porch and handed me the money. She was probably the last person in the universe who would want to *buy* three hundred dollars’ worth of cosmetics. “Okay? Bring me the change — if there is any — and the receipt in the bag. I mean, not that I don’t trust you. But you know.”

“Sure, sure, Frances, whatever you want,” I replied, resigned. I’d long since found that it was easier just to give in to this most-persistent reporter.

Behind us, the screen door creaked open. A scowl darkened Frances’s face. She flicked her cigarette in the direction of the sidewalk and began to root around again in her purse.

“Goldy,” came John Richard’s angry voice, “would you mind leaving the kaffeeklatsch until later and getting your butt in here to look for . . . what the hell —”

His brow wrinkled and his dark eyes were fastened on Frances as if mesmerized. I followed his gaze back to Frances and saw she was pointing what looked like a hunting knife handle at John Richard’s solar plexus.

“Oh, Frances,” I snapped, “for heaven’s

sake, put that away. What kind of thing is that anyway —"

But she paid me no heed. "Get off of this porch," she said calmly to the Jerk. "This is a ballistic knife. The blade is projected from the handle by a spring-loaded device. John Richard Korman, I've just taken the safety off my ballistic knife. I am not in the mood for another baptism by bleach water —"

"Bitch!" the Jerk spat out in furious bewilderment. "I don't know who you are or what your problem is —"

The muscles in Frances's unmade-up face were steely. "Funny, I know who *you* are. And I know about Eileen Robinson, lying in Southwest Hospital with two broken ribs and a pair of bruised arms to match. *And* I know what happened to me yesterday in the company of Goldy, your not-amicably-divorced-from-you ex-wife. I was unprepared before, but that's over." She waved the knife handle. "I am not even slightly intimidated by you." Sunlight glinted off the weapon. "Move."

Arch whacked the screen door open. "Okay, Dad, I found my sparklers —" He careened into his immobile father. "What's . . ." Then he noticed Frances and her weapon. His eyes and mouth opened wide. His eyebrows rose. "Uh. Excuse me? Mom? Should I call 911?"

My ears were ringing with frustration. What

if Frances released the knife and it hit Arch? "No, no, don't call. Just go with your dad. Frances, put that knife away. Please. Now."

Frances did not flinch.

John Richard's face was a study in fury. He stuck out his chin and curled his hands into fists. "I don't know who you are, lady, but you're confused. Not only that, but you are breaking the law." She stared right back at him. "Do you have a permit to carry that? I doubt it. I doubt it very, very much." He started in the direction of the porch steps. Down he went, with Frances's ballistic knife following each step he took. As if to attract the attention of neighbors, the Jerk yelled, "You are menacing me, you bitch! Whoever the hell you are! Do you hear? I'm going to file a complaint."

Frances retorted calmly, equally loudly, "Be my guest!"

John Richard bounded into his Jeep, started it, and revved it deafeningly. Arch was still gaping at Frances, who had her eyes and weapon trained on the Jeep. "Does that knife have an explosive charge or a spring-loaded device?" he asked in a low whisper. Before Frances could answer, John Richard leaned on his horn. Arch scooped up his bag and sidled over to the porch steps. "Miss Markasian? I don't mean to be, like, judgmental, but I think maybe you should cut back on your caffeine. Don't hurt my dad, okay?" And with that, he sprinted to the Jeep.

Frances pressed her lips together, nudged the safety back in place, and dropped the big knife back in her bag. The Jeep roared away.

"Dammit, Frances, what in the hell do you think you're doing?"

She picked up her Jolt cola. "I told you. Knowing what I know about what happened to Eileen Robinson, and after that little incident on the roof, I swore I'd be ready the next time. That's it. So when you came out your door looking so upset, and then His Menacing Majesty appeared unexpectedly, there I was, a little girl scout, all prepared." She sighed. "You should get a weapon, Goldy. It really gives you a sense of power."

"No, thanks. When do you want to come back to pick up all these cosmetics I'm buying?"

"Later." And with that she hefted up her bag, for which I had a new and profound respect, hopped down the porch steps, and strode away. I looked up and down the curbs for her car. It wasn't parked on the street. And by the time I looked for Frances, she had disappeared.

Back in the house, I finished making the

Killer Pancakes and set them aside to cool. Then I sloshed together a new bucket of bleach water for the fair, carefully covered it, and hauled it out to the van. After packing the Killer Pancakes between layers of waxed paper in a plastic container, I got the spare key to Marla's house from where Julian had left it for me, and started out. Clouds were just beginning to float in from the westernmost mountains. Perhaps it wouldn't be a bright and cloudless day after all. The events of the morning certainly hadn't been very sunny.

By the time I'd let myself into Marla's house, stored the food in the refrigerator, and written a note to the nurse, the westernmost sky was gray with fast-moving, towering thunderheads. Although the rain usually arrived in the mountain towns several hours before it traveled eastward to Denver, even the possibility of being drenched inside a roof tent was unappealing in the extreme. My spirits sank.

The early-bird shopping special had ended Friday. As a result, very few walkers and eaters were lined up outside the mall's entrance. The Spare the Hares! people were nowhere in sight. I parked and hauled all my supplies up to the roof, where a small cluster of people was already beginning to gather. For the early morning musical entertainment today, the food fair organizers had hired a calliope player. The place sounded and felt like a half-empty merry-go-round.

I fired up the burners, set out the salad, bread, and cookies, and plopped the ribs on the grill, where they began to sizzle. That done, I survived the daily visit from the health inspector and started to serve the occasional guest. Pete, whose customers were equally sparse, brought me a triple-shot latte and my caterer's uniform, which his wife had washed and pressed. I showed my gratitude by loading him down with ribs and cookies.

"This is probably the best brunch I'll have this year," he said appreciatively. I toasted him with the paper coffee cup. He frowned. When I looked confused, he said, "When you hold that cup up, turn the logo out, okay? I need all the advertising I can get."

I obliged. After a very slow two hours, I packed up the leftovers, returned them to the van, and plucked Frances's list and money from my purse. I had an hour to shop and make it to nearby Hotchkiss Skin & Hair. With any luck, the visit to the cosmetics counter would take less than ten minutes.

There were hardly any shoppers inside the department store either. Dusty Routt wasn't at the Mignon counter. The only sales associate was Harriet Wells, and she was writing in the by-now-familiar large ledger.

"Hi-ho, remember me?" I called brightly as I approached.

Her look was glazed, then memories clicked into place and she said brightly, "The caterer!" She glanced from side to side and whispered, "Would you like another muffin? Tell me what you think is in this one. The store's so dead today, no one will notice. You look *starved*." Her laugh tinkled above all the crystal bottles of perfume and bright shelves of makeup.

I gratefully took a fragrant golden-brown muffin. I bit into it: The orange flecks turned out to be carrot and the spice ginger. I truthfully told her the muffin was wonderful and asked for the recipe, always the most sincere form of thanks. While we were talking about the virtues of using sorghum versus honey for sweetener, the ceiling — or something nearby — cracked. Actually, there was a loud cracking *sound*. I glanced up at the security blind but could see nothing.

"What in the world . . . ?" I demanded as Harriet offered me another muffin.

"Well, you know," she said with a wise smile, "there is a fault line that runs right through Golden. We may be in for an earthquake yet!"

I finished the muffin, licked my fingertips,

and brought out my list. As I started to tick off the items, Harriet's eyes gleamed.

"Wait, wait," she commanded me excitedly. "Let me get your client card. That's the only way we'll be able to keep track of all these products!"

I didn't want to enlighten her that all this stuff was for someone else. If I did, we would have to start a client card for Frances, or at least amend the one she had, and on and on. As Harriet expertly assembled the lovely glass jars filled with creams and lotions, the ceiling, or wall, or whatever it was, made another ominous creak.

"Goodness!" she said, and looked up. "Maybe there's a plumbing problem. Honestly!"

I handed over the money, feeling nervous, feeling that I wanted to get out of the store. But not quite yet. While she was making the change, I asked quickly, "So what do you think happened to Claire Satterfield?"

Harriet shook her head and sighed. "I think she was run down by a member of that horrible group. Those awful people saying" — she made a face — "spare the hares. They've bothered us before."

"Really? How?"

"Oh! They come in here and yell at us. They say, 'How can you sell cosmetics that are tested on poor, innocent animals?' They make a scene and drive the customers away. It's pathetic. Why don't they just go out into the wild with the animals if they love them so much? Why bother us?" She showed me the receipt and made a perfunctory gesture to show the products and receipt to the camera. Then she ducked down and brought out my bag. I tucked it in the zip bag with the change and turned to leave.

Crea-eak! Craa-a-ack! went the wall of the security blind.

"For heaven's sake!" exclaimed Harriet. We were standing not two feet away from each other. I felt another shiver of fear.

"You'd better call security," I said.

Security came. It came in the form of Nick Gentileschi. Above the store entrance, the security blind floor broke open with a splintering crash. Gentileschi's heavy body plummeted from overhead. *Oh my God*, I thought as his bulk in its dark polyester suit fell and fell. *Oh my God, please, no* . . . His body would have hit me if I hadn't jumped out of the way. Instead, his weight landed hard on the glass-and-chrome Mignon counter. Metal shattered, glass crumpled, shards flew. At the last moment I thought to cover my eyes. Harriet Wells leapt back and screamed. She kept screaming like a woman possessed. When I uncovered my eyes, glass was everywhere. Gentileschi's body had landed in an impossibly contorted position. I knew he was dead. In fact, from the stiffness of his body atop the shattered makeup counter, I guessed he'd been dead for several hours before his weight sent him tumbling out of the blind. A gaping hole above the store entrance was jagged with splintered wood. Inside the craggy hole was blackness. Harriet Wells screamed on.

"Oh, no, please," I said as I backed up, away from the mess. "Please let this not be happening. . . ."

Harriet's screams turned into a sirenlike screech for help. Curious customers sidled up to the scene, like filings to a magnet. I was about to turn away, when a flash of paper caught my eye. Something slipped out of Nick Gentileschi's pocket and rested next to the place where the linoleum met the plush gray carpeting.

The slip was actually two pieces of . . . what? I looked more closely. Photographs.

I leaned in and stared incredulously at two photographs taken at very close range. A large woman was half-naked, caught by the camera in the act of undressing. A dark skirt hung from the woman's ample hips. A dark-and-light jacket was draped on a wall hook behind her. The top of her body was completely exposed; her breasts hung pendulously as the camera caught her action of slipping off her bra.

Even slightly out of focus, the woman was recognizable. It was Babs Braithwaite.

14

I backed away from the photographs, the shattered counter, and the sight of Nick Gentileschi contorted above fluorescent-lit displays. From the corner of my eye I could see Stan White hurtling down the escalator. Shoppers, surprised and morbidly curious, gathered on both ends of the aisle. My feet inched backward until I hit the table filled with zircons. The boxes tumbled. I fell on top of them. I realized that the gasping I heard was coming from me. I closed my mouth, rolled over, and saw Stan White display his badge to the onlookers.

"I'm from department store security!" he bellowed. "Please clear the store. Do not use this exit!" And with that, Stan White turned away from the hesitantly departing crowd and gazed dispassionately at Nick Gentileschi's body. He felt for a pulse, then stepped into the aisle and loomed over me. In the background, I could hear Harriet sobbing.

"Are you all right?" he demanded.

"Yes," I burbled from the floor, "I think so." My hair was in my face and my skirt was tangled around my hips. I was having a hard time breathing.

"Did you see what happened?" When I nodded, Stan stabbed a stubby finger at me and barked, "Don't leave." He gulped and added, "Please."

Leaving me sprawled amid the fake gems and their velvet boxes, he darted over to the remaining group of gaping spectators. Grimly, he herded them away from the area leading to the counter. Then he pulled displays into the aisles to isolate the area around the shattered glass, the destroyed merchandise, and Nick Gentileschi's twisted corpse. I watched as he made call after call on the phone behind the cosmetics counter. Harriet sat on a low shelf, her knees to her chest, her back pressed against the cabinet that held the Frosted Cherries Jubilee lipsticks. She was whimpering uncontrollably. Her lovely, perfectly made-up face and manicured hands were streaked with blood from splinters of glass. Her blond twist of hair had fallen apart and hung in clumps and strands, like remnants of insulation.

I maneuvered myself behind the counter, carefully avoiding the mess, and asked if I could help. Her whimpers immediately turned to wails: "Twenty-eight years! Twenty-eight years in this business! And nothing, nothing has ever happened. Not like this. Why is this . . . why?" When I reached for some cotton balls to dab away the blood on her face, she made batting motions to get me away. "No, no, no!" she screamed. "Leave me alone! Go away!"

Fine, I thought, fine. Wait for the police, paramedics, whatever you want.

"Okay, please move back," said Stan White once he was off the phone. "Please move away from the counter." He scowled in my direction, apparently recognizing me for the first time. "You? What are you doing here again?"

"Nothing." I squeezed past the mess again, in no mood for explanations.

He made an awkward move in my direction, then looked confused. When he caught shoplifters in the store, he knew what to do. When he had a corpse to deal with, however, he was less sure. "Don't leave," he ordered me again. "The police are coming. They want to know if anyone saw . . . if there were any witnesses."

"I'm not going." I stood, shaking, on the lush carpet. I couldn't bear to look at Nick Gentileschi's corpse sprawled on the shattered Mignon counter. Nor could I listen to another moment of Harriet's abject weeping. Dizziness swept over me. An empty seat in the shoe department beckoned. I sat down uneasily, making sure that I faced away from Nick Gentileschi's body. The store's overhead speakers crackled and the gentle background music stopped mid-bar. A female voice announced that owing to an emergency, Prince & Grogan was now closed. Apparently Stan White had called the office with the intercom. All shoppers should depart in an orderly fashion, the calm voice went on soothingly, either through the exit that went into the parking lot or via the elevator located next to Lingerie. This would take them down to the parking lot exit.

I glanced at the wall display of pumps, espadrilles, and walking shoes, and thought vaguely that the police wouldn't want everyone dismissed. But the store had a reputation to uphold, and that reputation said the only excitement was in shopping. The dramatic loss of their security chief didn't qualify as a good retail experience.

It wasn't long before the Furman County Sheriff's Department arrived in force. Tom must have been tied up with another investigation, because the stern-looking team strode in without him. A victim advocate accompanied them. I stayed only long enough to give my name and phone number and the very sparse details of what I'd heard and seen. Cracking noises. A body falling. No one suspicious around. Yes, I'd known the deceased, but only in passing. When the investigating officers asked if I knew whether he had any enemies, I said they might want to look at the photos that had fallen out of his pocket. Why? The cops wanted to know. I told them the woman in the pictures had claimed someone was behind the mirror when she was trying on a bathing suit yesterday. The investigating team took their pictures, brushed fingerprint powder over every surface in sight, and sealed up the photos from Nick Gentileschi's pocket in evidence bags. They also strung up yellow police ribbons, assigned a smaller team to start on a search of the store in general and the security office in particular. The victim advocate asked if I needed help. I said I did not, but that I was fairly sure Harriet Wells needed quite a bit of it. A policeman stationed himself at each door. The store was now officially closed.

I looked at my watch: one-thirty. I should go home, I thought. Go home and cook. Forget this event, these people, this place. These people and their products are the farthest thing imaginable from what they say they offer. And what did they say they offered? Beauty. Freedom from stress. *Longevity*. What a joke.

I walked out the exit by the parking lot. Rain pelted down. I slumped onto the curb and again fought dizziness.

Frances Markasian should have come herself

to buy her cosmetics. If she had, she would have been the one to see Gentileschi tumble out of the blind and crash onto the glass. Thinking of Frances made my stomach turn over. She wouldn't be sitting on a curb feeling ill. She'd be back there asking questions and making a pest out of herself.

I was crying. When I tried to wipe my face, I realized that somehow, through the horror and confusion, I was still clutching the bag with Frances's Mignon purchases. The paper, damp and limp from the rain, rustled softly when I looked inside. Yes, there were her jars of stuff and a plastic bag of bills and loose change.

I started walking. I wasn't ready to go back to the van. I needed to move, to clear my head. All around, people trotted through the rain to their cars or to the heavy main doors to the mall. I looked into a Prince & Grogan plate-glass window. I didn't see the leggy mannequins clad in short black suits, but instead gaped at my bedraggled reflection. Standing there, watching my elongated, pained face, I thought about the body as it came falling down, down, down. What had Nick Gentileschi been doing up in the blind? Especially when department store security supposedly didn't use them anymore? Why were the pictures of Babs in his pocket? Did this have anything to do with Claire's murder?

The cars whooshed behind me on the wet thoroughfare. *Oh, Claire,* I found myself whispering, *I am so sorry. I am so sorry I can't figure this out for you. I am so sorry, Julian. It's just getting worse, instead of resolved.*

Like my van returning to Aspen Meadow by rote, I walked as if I had someplace to go. Where was I supposed to go? I couldn't remember. My shoes sloshed through puddles. Cold droplets continued to beat down all around. Kids pedaled past me on bikes. One yelled something like *Get inside, lady!* but I didn't acknowledge him. Forks of lightning flared in the distance. Thunder rumbled overhead. I walked on. I didn't care about the wet, didn't care that my caterer's outfit was getting soaked. If I got pneumonia, I thought absurdly, I could go to Marla's house and her nurse would take care of both of us. I walked down one street, then another. I saw Nick Gentileschi's body tumble from a great height. Again I heard the sickening crack as his weight hit the glass counter.

Finally, I stopped. Where was the store, exactly? Where was the hospital? The mall?

Where was *I*, exactly?

The houses, street, sidewalk, shrubs, and fences swam slowly into focus. I had arrived in the older neighborhood of Aqua Bella that

Dusty had pointed out so enviously when we were sipping our lattes on the mall's garage roof. Of course, "older" in Denver usually means "from the 1950s." Along the sidewalk where I stood, drenched and disoriented, a Frank Lloyd Wright-style redstone-and-brick ranch was flanked by a white Georgian two-story with pristine black shutters and a turreted blue and pink neo-Victorian mini-mansion. The Victorian was like a large feminine presence. No one had controlled the zoning along this street, unfortunately, and none of these lovely buildings was an actual domicile. A small sign at the end of the sidewalk to the ranch home indicated it was now the office for a trio of dentists. The Georgian was devoted to accounting.

A blue and pink picket fence primly separated the sidewalk from the lush green lawn in front of the Victorian. White wicker furniture brimming with blue and pink cushions dotted a spacious front porch. An elaborately lettered sign on the picket fence announced that the business was Hotchkiss Skin & Hair.

Behind a glass door intricately patterned with white metal, the blue front door to Hotchkiss opened. Behind the fence, the rain, and the glass, a silhouette appeared in the lighted doorway. The visage regarded me, then beckoned. It was the young, cheerful face of Dusty Routt.

I moved toward the Victorian house. Perhaps I had intended unconsciously to come here all along, since I had received the directions over the phone. But Dusty worked at Mignon, not at Hotchkiss. Hotchkiss was Mignon's *competitor*. Dusty held the glass door open as I stumbled inside.

"Goldy! Jeez, come in . . . you're, like, totally . . . Look at you! You're a wreck! I mean . . . I saw in the appointment book that you were coming, but . . . you're so late! What were you doing out in the rain? Where's your van? Why didn't you wear a raincoat?"

I found myself in a foyer decorated with pale pink carpeting, matte pink walls, small gold and crystal chandeliers, white leather and gilt wood French provincial chairs, and a long glass counter arrayed with cosmetic products. The place was so at odds with my drenched, wraithlike appearance that I let out a crazy cackle. Dusty stared. I couldn't tell her what I was thinking — that Hotchkiss Skin & Hair looked like an upscale whorehouse.

A pretty woman stood behind the reception desk. Her wide, pale face boasted dark streaks of brownish-pink blush. Her voice was as soft as her swirled nimbus of cocoa-colored hair and pink mohair sweater. She asked, "Are you ready for your appointment?"

I looked at Dusty. Out of her Mignon uniform and wearing a white shirt and green culottes, she looked younger — more her age. I said, "Nick Gentileschi . . ."

Dusty tilted her head. "What about Nick? Did he come with you? Is he here?" She glanced back toward the rain-swept sidewalk. "He wouldn't come here," she said, confused, "because he works at —"

I cleared my throat. "Nick's dead. There's been an accident at the store."

Dusty's carefully plucked eyebrows shot up. "Oh my God! Dead? Nick? It's not true. Is it?" When I nodded, she said, "I've gotta go. Oh . . . this is unbelievable —"

"You are Mrs. Schulz, then?" inquired the soft-voiced woman at the desk. The pink mohair materialized as a dress around a voluptuous body. "How did you say you were going to take care of your charges today?"

"Uh . . ." I fumbled with the slippery opening to my pocketbook. What charges? "I need a cab," I said uncertainly.

"We'll call one for you," Ms. Mohair assured me breathily. "We just need your credit card."

I guess it had been a long time since I'd taken a cab. I thought they took only cash. I handed her my Visa.

"What happened to Nick?" Dusty demanded.

I was suddenly aware of being wet and very cold. "I have no idea. Dusty? Could I get a . . . ?"

"A what?" she asked. "What happened to Nick?"

"I don't know." My teeth chattered. "One minute I was standing at the counter, the next he was crashing out of that blind above the store entrance —"

"The blind?" She was incredulous. "He fell out of the blind? What in the world was he doing up there?"

The woman with the soft voice reappeared with my credit card and a paper slip and I signed. For what, I wasn't quite sure. What had happened to Marla's coupon? "We can take you back now, Mrs. Schulz. Let's get you a dry robe," she said intimately, ignoring Dusty, "and put those damp things in our dryer. Shall we?"

It sounded good. In fact, it sounded wonderful.

"Gosh, Goldy," said Dusty, "are you sure you want to do your facial now anyway?"

"Oh, I . . ."

Competing voices invaded my brain. *I'm so sorry, Claire. I'm so sorry I couldn't figure anything out.*

366

I'd made this appointment with Hotchkiss Skin & Hair because I was trying to discover why and how Hotchkiss was copying or stealing from Mignon, and if the fierce competition between the cosmetics companies could extend to killing people. Behind the reception desk, I saw first one, then another woman scurry down a far hall. Both wore lab coats. But I felt unsteady. Stay here, where all was unknown? Or ask Dusty for a ride back to my van? Tom would certainly want to know what was going on. With sudden resolve, though, I decided to stay. I would manage, I would have this facial, I would call a cab. And I would tell Tom all about what had happened at the department store. But a question nagged. "Dusty," I said, "what in the world are you doing here?"

She pressed her lips together and relieved me of my purse and the paper bag. Then she leaned in close and whispered, "Reggie Hotchkiss wants to hire me. I mean, he's promised. We just had a meeting. You know, I just *have* to get away from Mignon. That place is crazy. Come on, I'll take your stuff back."

"Mrs. Schulz," said the soft-voiced woman, who had materialized once again at my side, "just look at what a mess you are." She took my arm with surprising firmness. A shiver

367

with a life of its own went through my wet clothes. What a mess, indeed.

Dusty said she'd bring my stuff to my room when I was in the robe. The pink-mohair lady led me down the hall, where she put me in a small chamber that had the antiseptic feel of a doctor's examination room. Instead of an examining table, however, the middle of the room boasted an enormous reclining chair. It was probably the throne where you got your facial. Large, imposing machines sat next to the chair. Ms. Mohair handed me a green hospital-type gown that tied in the front. She said in that soft, whispery voice, "Somebody will be with you momentarily." Then she was gone.

Ravel's *Bolero* was being piped incongruously into the professional-looking space. I stripped off my damp clothing and hung it on a hook, stepped gingerly across the black and white linoleum, and pulled a couple of paper towels from the dispenser over the sink. After what I'd seen fall from Nick Gentileschi's pocket, I was paranoid about my own shivery nakedness. Who was watching? Oddly, the room held no mirrors. I glanced up at the ceiling — no cameras that I could discern — then chided myself for being ridiculous. I cinched the warm hospital gown around my middle, patted my damp hair with

368

the paper towels, and took a deep breath.

Within moments a short, ponytailed woman of about twenty-five swished into the room. She was carrying a large plastic bag.

"These are yours," she announced. "Your friend had to leave. Your purse and department store bag are inside. They're wet."

She dropped the bag lightly by the wall and shoved her hands deep into the pockets of her white lab coat. She frowned as she assessed me. She wore little makeup over an acne-scarred face that was quite plain. I don't know why I found both of these physical aspects surprising. But her whole appearance, from the tightly pulled ponytail to her white stockings and white tied shoes said *technician* rather than *beauty queen*.

"Your hair is wet too," she observed. She strode efficiently to a cupboard, retrieved a warm, folded towel, and handed it to me. I thanked her and rubbed the towel over my scalp. "But you did not make an appointment for hair," she said with a slight, scolding shake of the head.

"This towel's fine. My hair is just . . ." Well, my hair. No amount of money lavished on it was going to change that unstylish mass of curls into anything. "Let's just start with the face today, okay?"

And start she did. While *Bolero* played in

the background, the white-coated woman, whose name was Lane — short, crisp, efficient, fitting her persona — told me we were beginning the process with a thorough cleansing. Her fingers energetically massaged thick, creamy stuff onto my face which she then wiped off with a warm, wet towel. This was followed by a fruity-smelling toner, which she applied in simultaneous swipes across the left and right sides of my face.

"Okay!" she said when the toner was turning my face into what felt like a dry Popsicle. "I'm going to start a list of all the products you should be using for your face. For starters, Wizard cleanser and pore-closing toner."

"Well, er, how much do they cost?"

She waved this away. "We can just put it on your card."

"I'm sorry, I need to know."

She consulted a sheet. "Thirty-six dollars for a ten-ounce bottle of cleanser." Impatient. "Forty dollars for a twelve-ounce bottle of toner."

I didn't mean to gasp, but I did anyway. I saw Arch going shoeless for the rest of his life. "But that's even more than Mignon! And I thought they were the most expensive."

Lane pursed her lips, then announced: "*We* are the most expensive. Do you want to improve your skin or not? We are the best. You'll see *real* results if you work with these products."

I mumbled something along the lines of "Okay."

Lane slapped down the pencil on her tray. "Let's go to the next step, then."

She turned on one of the imposing machines next to the chair. I became more nervous when she assured me that the machine was for brushing. Or, as I thought when Lane stroked my face with electric brushes attached to hoses that ran to the machine, it was sort of like getting a shoe polish for the face, minus the shoes *and* the polish.

When she was done, Lane gave me a disapproving, suspicious look and ordered me to close my eyes. Having learned my lesson from my Mignon makeover with Dusty, I closed my eyes without argument. Lane placed a wet cloth over my closed lids, levered the chair back, and turned on a rumbly machine that she told me was for steam.

"I'm taking your clothes to the dryer, and I'll be back in twenty minutes," she said. Her white nurse's shoes squeaked toward the door. "Relax."

Left to steam, my thoughts, and *Bolero*, I tried to unwind. I tried to think about what it was Maurice Ravel was setting to music. Unfortunately, all I could hear was the crash and thud of a vehicle hitting Claire, the shatter and crack as Nick Gentileschi fell out of the department store's blind.

When Lane returned, she whipped the cloth off my eyes, turned off the steam, and retrieved what looked like a small magnifying glass from her pocket. I recoiled. My face had never been examined at close range.

"I'm going to turn off the light," she declared bluntly, "and assess the amount of damage you've done over the years to your skin."

By the time I'd managed to stammer, "Do I have to?" the overhead light was off, a purplish light had winked on, and Lane's magnified eye was accompanied by *tsk-tsk* noises à la Sherlock Holmes. She flipped the lights back on, donned plastic gloves, and picked up a needle.

"Wait, wait." I sat up quickly. "I thought women came in to have facials because it was fun and relaxing. Sort of like having a massage."

"You're going to look so much better," she assured me. "We need to get rid of those blemishes." She brandished the needle.

"Please, no," I said feebly. "I have a real problem with . . . needles."

Lane's countenance was that of a nurse with an unpleasant but utterly necessary medication.

She said, "The receptionist reported you claimed you were terribly upset about your skin. *Now* you say you're unsure about buying products, and you don't want to have a facial. Are you certain you came in here really wanting to improve your appearance? Or is there some other reason you're here?"

Paranoia reared its unattractive head again, and I succumbed. "It's why I'm here," I said meekly, and slumped back in the chair.

Lane poked and I shrieked. Again I got the displeased-nurse routine. *Blemishes,* she said as she poked again. I felt blood drip down my forehead. Lane dabbed at it. She put down the needle and, with two plastic-gloved fingers, squeezed the skin on my nose with all her might. I screamed again. At least with a dentist you got anesthetic.

Lane sighed reprovingly and brought the gloved hands to her abdomen. "Are you going to let me finish my work or not?"

"Not," I said decisively, rubbing my poor, bent nose. The area above my nostrils felt as if it were on fire. My will — my entire desire in life — was now focused on getting out of Hotchkiss Skin & Hair.

"Do you just want your masque now?"

"Will it hurt?"

She rolled her eyes and sighed, then said, "No! Of course it won't hurt."

Lane had no credibility with me anymore. But I didn't think a masque could be too bad unless you let it dry and it became more like a theater mask. Or maybe the masque would get to be like those masks they use in horror flicks to suffocate people. . . . Lane tapped her foot. Yes, I told her, I was desperate for the masque. She swabbed on some more thick, creamy stuff, draped towels over my face, and left. Oh, thank you, God, I said as I pulled the towels away and rubbed the cream off. Thank you, thank you, thank you for giving me a chance to get out of here. I didn't want a masque, I didn't want a facial, I certainly didn't want any makeup.

I tiptoed over to my damp shoes and eased my feet inside. The rubber soles squished noisily as I headed for the door. I can't escape in this robe, I realized with dismay. But how in the world would I find the dryer where they'd put my clothes? I retrieved the big plastic bag, grabbed the sack with Frances's purchases, and put it in my purse, which I snapped shut. Clutching my purse, I peeked out in the hall. It was empty. I again thanked the Almighty and began to sneak past closed doors toward the back of the mansion. At each door I listened, but heard only silence, the buzz of the machines, or the low murmur of the facialists as they tortured other clients.

My whole problem, I thought as I moved from door to door down the hall, is that I am not a masochist. If I'd been a masochist, I would have endured all that pain for beauty. Then again, if I'd been a masochist, I would have stayed in my first marriage.

At the last closed door on the hall, I stopped. It was a wider door, the kind that usually goes to some kind of utility room. Inside a machine methodically whirred and thudded. A dryer.

I opened the door and whipped inside a tiny room that held what looked like a closet and a pantry covered with louvered doors. The door squeaked closed behind me. Shelves in the closet held neatly arrayed towels, uniforms, and large bottles of what I assumed to be cosmetic stuff. I creaked open the louvered doors and was rewarded with a washer and dryer. Above them and on each side were shelves filled with a much more haphazard assortment of stored items. These I ignored as I squeaked open the dryer door and reached in for my clothes. They were warm but still slightly damp.

Someone was coming. I nipped into the pantry and pinched my fingers closing the door. I don't know why I was so afraid of being discovered aborting the facial, but I think it had something to do with the needle. The person who had come in was humming. I eased in behind a couple of white lab coats. Something like animal fur brushed my neck. Through the louvers I could see the hummer reaching for the bottles on the shelves. The fur began to tickle my neck. Sweat broke out on my cheeks. The hummer tapped the closet door shut with her foot and strolled out.

I creaked the door back open and reached behind me to snatch the fur away from my neck before I sneezed. No luck. A tiny but powerful convulsion escaped my lips and left my eyes watering. That would teach me to walk for blocks in the rain. Cursing and sniffling, I stepped out of the pantry clutching the fur thing. Wait. It was a wig, sort of a frosted blond affair. I tossed it down on the dryer, retrieved my clothes, and quickly dressed. As I was about to leave the room, my eyes slewed over to the wig again. Hairpieces frightened me, by and large. They were too much like dead animals. But I had seen this wig before.

I picked it up and examined it. Who had been wearing this monstrosity? Where had I seen her? A memory began to resolve itself. Before the Mignon banquet. I'd seen someone in the garage. A woman, dressed in bright yellow. Yes, I could see her striding purposefully toward the door, then sticking her head out the service entrance and demanding to know what was going on when Tom and I were trying to tend to Julian.

Then I remembered something else: Claire frowning when she recognized someone at the banquet. My saying, *What?* And her frustration. Her saying: *Oh God.* And then Dusty, the next day, saying: *We saw you. We recognized you. Man, you are going to get into so much trouble.*

Yes, I had seen this wig. Slender, good-looking Reggie Hotchkiss had been wearing it when he sneaked into the Mignon Fall into Color Banquet. It was at that banquet that he'd probably picked up the ideas he needed for his autumn catalogue. I just didn't know what else he'd done there. Run down the very successful sales associate of a rival firm?

15

I tossed the wig back on the shelf. I slipped out the utility room door and saw illuminated red letters at the end of the hall: EXIT. Ten steps to freedom. No alarm went off as I pressed the door bar, landed on a concrete step, and inhaled cool, rain-dampened air. Here behind the Hotchkiss establishment, a ragtag lawn and overflowing rosebushes ran the length of the pink and blue picket fence. A rusty-hinged gate interrupted the fence between the brambles at the far end of the yard. Praying that I wasn't being observed, I walked across the wet grass, lifted the latch, and felt a rush of light-headed relief as I escaped into an alley.

Steam misted off the streets of the Aqua Bella neighborhood. Sunlight struggled to cut through the thickly humid air. To the west, clouds lifted along the foothills, leaving trails of creamy fog snaking between dark green hills. To get oriented in the Denver area, the key is to remember that the mountains are always to the west. The mall was situated between the Rockies and me, so I started off at a moderate westward jog down the sidewalk. I hopscotched over shiny patches of puddle. Behind me, I could almost imagine Lane's terse, businesslike voice screaming, *Stop that unmasqued woman!*

But I was in no mood for entanglements. I panted and bumbled along. How could I have walked this far? I touched my forehead. It was still bleeding. Someday, I thought, Marla and I would have a good laugh about my Hotchkiss makeover masquerade.

By the time I slipped behind the wheel of my van, I thought I was going to have a heart attack myself. As I drove back to Aspen Meadow, I inhaled deep yoga-exercise breaths. Claire Satterfield had been dead for three days. Nick Gentileschi had tumbled out of the blind today. His body hadn't even twitched when it landed.

How long had he been dead? And then there was Reggie Hotchkiss, who had spied at the Mignon banquet, under cover of wig. In addition to all that, tonight I was catering a chi-chi dinner for a couple up to their wealthy ears in the imbroglio: Claire's presumed lover, Dr. Charles Braithwaite, and Charlie's wife, Babs, the woman Nick Gentileschi had been covertly photographing in the Prince & Grogan fitting rooms.

How did I get myself into these situations? When my van chugged off the interstate at the Aspen Meadow exit, the rain clouds had cleared and left an immense bluer-than-blue sky. I passed the country club, where sunlight glinted off the roof of the Braithwaites' greenhouse at its high point on Aspen Knoll. It was from there that the guests would finish munching their fudge cookies and watch the Fourth of July fireworks display over Aspen Meadow Lake. Which would give me some time to do some snooping around in the infamous greenhouse.

I swung the van up to our house and saw that Julian had returned and left the Range Rover at a slight angle in the driveway. I parked in the one available spot on the street. When I hopped out, Sally Routt, Dusty's mother, was outside, pulling weeds. Her son Colin was on her back, snuggled into one of those corduroy baby-holders. I didn't see Dusty, which was probably just as well. I couldn't take any questioning on how the Hotchkiss facial had gone. Besides, I needed to phone Tom. I called a greeting to them, but Colin seemed fascinated by the mass of long-stemmed purple fireweed. Colin was so thin and tiny, it was hard to believe he was three months old. As he reached for a monarch butterfly on a fireweed stem, his little hand was dwarfed by the butterfly's dark, outstretched wings. Deprived of his target, his head of gleaming strawberry-blond hair bobbed in my direction. Poor, sweet child, born too early, to a family that could scarcely manage to take care of him. I felt my heart squeeze inside my chest.

When I came through the security system, I smelled simmering onions, cooked potatoes, and . . . cigarette smoke. The latter seemed to be drifting down from the second story. At least it's not hashish, I thought grimly as I took the stairs two at a time. In the spare bedroom at the front of the house, I found Julian sitting hunched over in the maple rocking chair I had used to rock Arch when he was an infant. Smoke curled from an unfiltered cigarette in his hands. His foot tapped the floor as he pushed back and forth. A small pile of ashes lay at his feet. He had not noticed me.

I said, "I'm back. What's going on?"

He didn't look around. His voice was morose, resigned. "Not much. I read your note and marinated the fruit. I cooked the potatoes and onions for the cucumber soup too." His face twisted. "Did you find out any — ?"

"Not yet. Actually, there's some more bad news." I sat down in the old love seat that now belonged to Scout the cat. "Want to hear it?"

"I guess."

"Nick Gentileschi died at the store. He

had an accident."

Julian's eyes opened in terror and disbelief. "What? The security guy? What happened? Does Tom know? What kind of accident?"

"Oh, Julian . . ." I sighed. "He fell out of one of those blinds. I don't know more than that. I was just about to go call Tom. Want to come down?"

He seemed suddenly aware of the cigarette he held and tapped ashes into his palm. "I'll be down in a little bit. Listen, Goldy, I'm sorry —"

"About what? I'm trying to help you —"

"It's just that I don't want you to get hurt."

"I'm not going to get hurt. Now, I know you probably don't want to talk about this, but do you think you're going to be up to helping me with the Braithwaites' party?"

His "Sure" was anything but. I walked pensively down to the kitchen. Before I could call Tom, the phone rang. It was Arch. He rarely called from the Keystone condo because the Jerk, who lavished money on himself, complained about any extra dollar Arch cost him. The only exception to this rule was on those rare occasions when John Richard had done something — failing to show up was one of his favorites — that made him feel guilty. When John Richard was hit by a rare attack of conscience, Arch would get loaded down with gifts he would never use. In fact, when my son came home from one of these week-ends toting a new mountain bike, skis, or Rollerblades, I knew there'd been trouble.

I gripped the phone and tried not to sound panicked. "What's wrong?"

"It's not about Dad, don't worry. He's asleep in the other room," he said in a low voice. "I think he had too much to drink at lunch. He's having a nap."

"Too much to — " I let out an exasperated breath. "Arch, do you need me to come and get you?"

"No, Mom, I'm cool. Please, don't get hysterical. We're going to walk to the fireworks up here."

"I am *not* hysterical," I said through clenched teeth.

"Listen, Mom. I'm just calling to see how Julian's doing."

I sighed and thought of the slumped figure in the upstairs bedroom. "Not too great."

"Did you find out anything about Claire? Has Marla gotten out of the hospital?"

"Arch, I just got home myself. I'll call you as soon as Tom figures out what's going on. And I was just about to call Marla."

"You know, I really do think Tom is great," Arch assured me. Except I didn't need to be reassured.

"Arch, *why* are you telling me this? You sound as if you're in some kind of trouble. Did Dad hurt you? Please tell me."

"Oh, *Mom.* You take everything so seriously. It's just that I didn't want Tom to think that I thought he was a pig or anything. I would never call him that."

"He knows."

"And I didn't get to say good-bye to him because he left so early, and then Frances Markasian was waving that knife around later, and well, you know."

"So everything is okay?"

"Yes, Mom! I was just sitting here thinking about Tom and Julian, and Marla, that's all."

"You're feeling lonely."

"Mom."

"Okay, okay."

He said he couldn't wait to see us Sunday afternoon. And no, he was not looking forward to the fireworks because Dad had met a new friend and they were taking her along. She was afraid of loud noises, though, so they might have to leave early. He sighed in disappointment and said, "Peace, Mom."

I hung up and banged my fist on the counter. If the new girlfriend didn't like loud noises, she'd better find herself a new guy to date.

I put in a call to Marla's house. The nurse

said she was sleeping, but yes, she'd seen the lowfat pancakes. How was her frame of mind? I asked. Depressed, the nurse replied without elaboration. When could I come over, I wanted to know. Tomorrow. Marla was resting today after the trip home from the hospital; no visitors, no excursions. So much for Tony's push to get her to the Braithwaites' party. I even had the feeling the nurse had dealt with Tony in very short order. I said I'd be over tomorrow. You'll have to make it in the afternoon, she announced before hanging up. I wished I could send that nurse out to deal with the Jerk.

I braced myself and punched the phone buttons again. If Tom wasn't there, what would I say to his voice mail? But he snagged it after less than one ring.

"Schulz."

"It's me. I was at Prince & Grogan when Gentileschi —"

"I heard. He was strangled in the box up there. They call it a blind, where the security guys used to sit."

"I know. Do they know who —"

"Negative. I'm going to be here late tonight working on this."

"I saw the photos in his pocket, Tom. They're of Babs Braithwaite."

He sighed. "Goldy, you didn't touch them, did you?"

"No, of course not."

"Did anybody besides you see them?"

I tried to remember: Who else was around? Stan White, the security man, had come down the escalator; Harriet Wells had been whimpering behind the counter. I'd been the only customer within close range. "I don't think so, maybe the other security guy saw them. I was there buying some stuff for Frances and . . . what was the deal with Gentileschi anyway? Did he always do that kind of thing? Spy on customers?"

Tom replied in a flat tone, "You should see the pictures we found at his house. Had a thing for large women. Not that they would like to hear what he was doing back there behind the mirrors."

"Did you ever get the message I left you, that Babs Braithwaite was certain she'd heard something back behind the dressing room mirror? It was when the security guy nabbed me for eavesdropping."

"Yeah, Miss G., I got your message. We've got one team investigating at the store now, and another questioning Mrs. Braithwaite and her husband. Dr. Braithwaite spent quite a bit of time and money in that department store, the assistant security guy tells us."

"Tom, do you remember that I'm catering

at their place tonight?"

"Uh, Miss Goldy? I don't think so. Get somebody else. The Braithwaites are suspects in a homicide. Maybe two homicides. I don't want you going in there and starting to snoop around. Let us do our work. *Please.* Also, and this is official now, you're off the case. Thanks for your help, but it's too dicey for you to do any more digging in this thing. It's gotten too dangerous."

"Oh come on, Tom. The Braithwaites are big wheels in the community. If I cancel, I'm sunk in my own hometown. Look, if either of the Braithwaites comes after me, I'll put a vat of cucumber-mint soup between us."

Tom muttered something unintelligible, but said nothing further. I remembered guiltily that I hadn't even told him about the bleach water and the threatening note. Tom said he had two other calls coming in at the same time, general counsel for Prince & Grogan was having a stroke on line one, and his team at the Braithwaites' house was clamoring to talk to him on line two. He'd get back to me.

With the police team crawling all over the Braithwaites' place, I wondered if Babs still would even want to hold her annual party. I put in a phone call to her. A policeman I knew answered, and after some delay, Babs came on the line.

"Yes?" She was obviously unhappy to be interrupted.

"I apologize for calling," I began, then stopped. What was I supposed to say? *But I was just wondering if the cops would be done before the party? And by the way, I didn't think those pictures did you justice?* "Er, I was just wondering what the schedule was for tonight. When you needed us to set up, you know."

Her voice became stiff with impatience. "Your contract says set up for food service, then food service, followed by packing up from nine or so until you're done. The guests will start arriving at seven. How long do you need to set up for twelve people?"

"No more than an hour —"

"I won't be able to supervise you. I'm having my hair and makeup done from five to six forty-five."

"Not to worry, we do a great job supervising ourselves."

She paused. "Will that boy be with you?" she asked curiously.

"My son? Or the nineteen-year-old fellow who helps me?"

"The teenager. The one who did all that damage to my car."

I felt as if I were suddenly under the interrogation light, like the NFL coach who gets grilled on how many injured players will be in the starting lineup. I assumed an indifferent tone. "Julian will be with me."

"How's he holding up?"

I was very interested to know why she cared. But I merely replied, "He's doing okay. Oh, Babs, by the way. My friend Marla says she didn't recommend my business to you. I mean, since you said that she did, I was just wondering who in fact did the recommending. Just out of curiosity. You know? I want to thank whoever it was."

Her voice rose irritably. "For heaven's sake, I can't remember who referred you to me!" She paused, then continued in an even higher tone: "Why, you're not having second thoughts about coming tonight, are you? Don't *tell* me you're not ready. I don't know who I'd get on such short notice!"

"Not to worry, Babs. We'll be there. Around six." Before she could start interrogating me again, I politely signed off and wished Arch could experience what it *really* meant to deal with someone hysterical.

I checked my watch: three o'clock. It was time to cook.

Like many wealthy clients, Babs Braithwaite wanted to host an extravagant catered dinner but did not want to pay much for it. "Can't you make it look and taste sumptuous without using all those expensive ingredients?" she had demanded. "Can't you cook without larding all the dishes with butter and cream? You know, the way caterers do?" As if she knew so much. Lowfat ingredients were usually more expensive and labor-intensive than traditional foods. In any event, after a lengthy discussion we had decided on a turkey curry served with raisin rice. Then Babs had loftily dismissed me with the announcement that since it was the Fourth, she would wear a red, white, and blue sari to go with the food. Everyone else was supposed to be decked out in red, white, and blue, she'd maintained in a resigned tone. I didn't protest. I had long ago quit trying to figure out wealthy clients' idiosyncrasies. At least she hadn't told *me* to wear a sari. Or demanded only red, white, and blue food.

I sautéed the turkey, drained it, then moved on to chop fragrant piles of onion and apple. When these were sizzling in a wide frying pan, I started the sauce. As the pungent scent of curry filled the kitchen, I began to feel the tension in my shoulders loosen. My hands stopped shaking as I drizzled in skim milk fortified once again with powdered nonfat milk. This silky concoction did indeed provide the rich, thick consistency of whipping cream without fat. I smiled and tasted the curry sauce. It was divine. Working with food is always healing. The ingredients, the smells, the flavors — the delight in experimenting and putting a meal together — all these bring joy, no matter what the circumstances. I had another spoonful of the hot, creamy curry sauce. Doggone, but it was good. I was going to have to try it out on Arch and Julian.

When I was halfway through grating the vegetables for the slaw, there was a loud banging on the front door. Again I looked at my watch: three-fifteen. It couldn't be either Tom or Arch. Alicia, my supplier, had made her visit and I had all the ingredients I needed. I turned off the blender and trudged to the door to peer through the peephole.

"No smoking," I warned Frances Markasian when I opened the door. "And no ballistic knives."

"Okay, okay!" She held up her large black purse as if for inspection. I waved it away. "Don't be so paranoid, Goldy, I just want —"

But I was already walking away from her. "I'm working, so you'll have to talk to me out in the kitchen."

She followed dutifully and took a seat in one of the oak chairs while I peered at my recipe for vegetable slaw. Swathed in her usual black trench coat, she waited until I'd finished grating the carrots, radishes, jicama, and cucumbers before asking, "Where's my stuff?"

TURKEY CURRY WITH
RAISIN RICE

1 pound ground turkey
1 cup chopped *unpeeled* apple
1 cup chopped onion
1½ tablespoons olive oil
2 tablespoons all-purpose flour
1 tablespoon curry powder
1 tablespoon beef bouillon granules
½ cup nonfat dry milk
2 cups skim milk

In a large sauté pan, sauté the turkey over medium-high heat, stirring frequently, until browned evenly. Drain the turkey on paper towels and set aside.

Spray a wide nonstick skillet with vegetable oil spray. Over medium heat, sauté the apple and onion, stirring frequently, until the onion is translucent. Set aside.

In another large skillet, heat the olive oil over low heat just until it is warm. Stir in the flour and curry powder. Heat and stir over medium-low heat until the flour begins to bubble. Combine the bouillon granules, dry milk, and skim milk; whisk until combined. (The bouillon granules will dissolve when they are heated in the sauce.) Gradually add the

milk mixture to the curry mixture, continuing to stir over medium-low heat until the mixture thickens. When the mixture is thick, add the turkey and the apple-onion mixture. Stir well and heat through. Serve over Raisin Rice.

Serves 4

Raisin Rice: In a large nonstick skillet, toast 1 cup of raw white rice over medium heat, stirring frequently, until most of the rice is brown. (Appearance may be mottled; this is desirable.) Add ½ cup raisins and 2¼ cups lowfat chicken stock (see page 396–97), bring the mixture to a boil, reduce the heat to low, cover the pan, and cook for 25 minutes or until the liquid is absorbed.

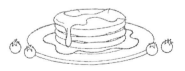

I took out plump, gorgeous scallions and began to slice them. "What stuff? I don't have any of your stuff!"

She rummaged through her bag for her pack of cigarettes, belatedly remembered she couldn't smoke, and impatiently rapped the cigarette package on the table. "Excuse me, Goldy, but I seem to remember giving you three crisp hundred-dollar bills and a list of cosmetics to buy? Did you get them or not?"

Patience, I ordered myself as I turned away from the mountains of slaw ingredients. I had cooking to do, and this journalist could make herself into a worse pest than the infamous mountain pine beetle. I dug through my sorry purse and found the still-damp bag full of the cosmetics Frances had ordered. When I handed it to her, she took it greedily and dumped the jars, bottles, and her change — bills and coins — out on my kitchen table.

I said loudly, "Gee, Goldy! Thanks *so much* for going out of your way to buy these cosmetics! Of course, I already know they aren't going to change my appearance one bit."

Frances ignored me, pawed through the items on the tabletop, then swept a handful of frizzed black hair out of her eyes and shot me a quizzical look. "Where's the receipt?"

"*What?*"

"Where's the receipt? *¿Entiendes inglés?* Did

you get a receipt for what you spent my money on or not?"

"Excuse me, Frances, but your change is all there. Give me a break! What do you need your receipt for?"

"Give *me* a break!" Her face was furious. "You're a businesswoman, you know the importance of a receipt! Without a receipt, this junk comes out of my pocket! Can't you do *anything* right?" Then, to my astonishment, she scooped up the cosmetics and money, stuffed them into the bag, and stomped angrily out of the room. My front door slammed resoundingly behind her.

I felt my mouth fall open in bewilderment. What was going on here? I looked at the chopped vegetables, the unfinished cucumber soup, and the pans of marinating fruit. My sane inner voice quietly urged me to forget about Frances and her tantrums and get on with the work of the day. After all, she had that spring-loaded knife in her purse.

But another, angrier inner voice demanded to know how Frances had known I was home. In fact, this was the second time I'd suspected she was spying on me. The first had been when she'd shown up just as the Jerk was leaving this morning. How had she known then that I hadn't left yet? How had she known this afternoon that I'd just returned home from the mall?

LOWFAT
CHICKEN STOCK

12⅓ cups canned chicken broth
  (2 49½-ounce cans)
1 large onion, chopped
1 carrot, chopped
3 to 3½ pounds chicken legs and
  thighs, skinned and all visible fat
  removed
12⅓ cups water (2 cans of water)
1 celery stalk with leaves
2 bay leaves
1 teaspoon dried thyme

Discard fat from the top of the cans of
chicken broth. Heat a very large stockpot. (If you do not have a very large
stockpot, you can divide the ingredients
and make the stock in two stockpots.)
Remove from the heat and spray twice
with vegetable oil spray. Toss in the
onion and carrot, lower the heat, and
cover the pot. Cook, stirring frequently,
over medium-high, add the chicken, and
cook until the chicken flesh is browned
on both sides, about 5 minutes. Pour in
the chicken broth and water, add the celery and bay leaves, and bring to a boil.
Boil for 5 minutes. As foam accumulates,

skim it off and discard. Lower the heat to simmer and add the thyme. Simmer, covered, for 2 hours. Add water as necessary to keep the chicken covered with liquid.

Remove the pot from the heat. Remove the chicken and allow to cool, then pick the meat from the bones and reserve for another use. Strain the stock and discard the vegetables and bay leaves. Cool to room temperature. Cover and refrigerate overnight. Lift any congealed fat from the stock and discard. Store for 2 or 3 days in the refrigerator or freeze for longer storage.

Makes 20 to 24 cups

I rushed outside and looked up and down the street: no dark Fiat, no Frances. I saw motion across the street. Frances's black coat was just visible moving beyond the stand of fireweed at the Routts' place. I darted after her. If it was Frances, what was she doing with the Routts? Was Dusty feeding Frances information? Given all that Dusty had told me, that didn't ring true. I had introduced them to each other at the Mignon banquet, for heaven's sake. Whatever Frances was involved in preceded that introduction, unless they were both lying. What was it Tom had told me? *In this business, expect to be deceived.*

As I came up the graded driveway, I saw the black-coated figure duck through a door at the side of the house. From the outside it looked like an old-fashioned porch with jalousie windows instead of screens. I'd always assumed the saxophone music had been wafting out of this room, because the slatted windows were the only ones on the Routts' house that faced the street. With some trepidation I started up the steps to this separate entrance. What would I say? *Uh, excuse me, just trying to be neighborly, but by the way, what's going on?*

The porch door was open. Frances stood next to a stout man whose white hair was brushed back in thin streaks. She was talking rapidly and intensely. Their backs were to me, and they were both oblivious of my presence. From the doorway I could see the porch room was simply furnished with a futon piled with unfashionably striped pillows, two mismatched chairs, and a table. On the table was an old rotary-dial telephone and a sax.

My attention was drawn to the older man listening intently to Frances. This, I assumed, was the grandfather I'd never seen. I tapped on the aluminum doorframe. Frances turned abruptly and fell silent.

"Excuse me?" I said politely. "May I come in?" Without waiting for a reply, I edged into the room. Through the jalousie windows on the other side of the small room, the roof of Frances's Fiat was just visible. So this was where she'd been parking. But who had told her when I was home? Maybe the grandfather was the one who'd been spying on my house. Uneasily, I asked, "Is Dusty home?" The man turned slightly in my direction, but not fully. "Are you Dusty's grandfather?" I asked politely. "I'm your neighbor, Goldy Schulz. Frances was just over at my house. . . ." I offered my hand. He ignored it.

Mr. Routt's face looked like a pie crust that had spilled over its edges. I looked at Frances for guidance, but her face had tightened in quiet fury at my appearance.

I said, "Mr. Routt?"

He turned large, watery blue eyes to me. There was no way this man had been spying on my house. He was blind.

16

"I'm sorry," I stammered. "Please forgive the intrusion," I added bitterly. I gave Frances the most withering glance I could muster. She assumed an indifferent demeanor and shrugged, as if to say, *You got yourself into this.*

"It's not her fault," said the old man. His voice cracked and wheezed, as if it were rusted from lack of use. "She was doing something for me. Please, Mrs. Schulz, don't be upset with Frances."

The three of us stood in the spare, dismal room for a moment without speaking. The man shifted from one foot to the other, as if he were trying to decide what to tell me.

"I'm John Routt, Mrs. Schulz," he said at last. His rumpled white shirt hung in soft folds, as if it had been washed and dried but not ironed. The shirt was slack over John Routt's chest, but a button strained to stay clasped over his copious stomach. His gray pants were as wrinkled as the shirt. I had the painful feeling that he did his own laundry.

"Forgive me," I said again, "I was just trying to find out why Frances here" — I glared at her — "always seems to be turning up only when she's certain I'm home." Then I remembered the truck outside my window during the storm. I added, "Or spying on me at night."

"I am not now, nor have I ever, been engaged in spying on you," Frances countered defensively. "I've got better things to do with my time."

"Mr. Routt," I said, "I don't know what's going on here or how you're involved." To Frances, I said acidly, "Do you want to come back to my house, Ms. Journalism? Tell me the real reason you went in disguise to Prince & Grogan? Or is department store intelligence not on the same level with spying on a caterer?"

Frances drew a cigarette out of her purse. She lit it and said, "Goldy, chill out. I'm working on a story. That's all you've ever needed to know." She blew smoke in my direction.

"Oh, really? Are you going to do a story on how the Prince & Grogan head of security was found dead this afternoon?"

This had the desired effect. Frances's body jerked. The cigarette dropped from her fingers.

"Nicholas Gentileschi?" John Routt said. "Dead?"

"Yes. Did you know him?"

John Routt was shaking his head. "No. No, I did not."

I said, "Well, then —"

His shoulders slumped. There was an uncomfortable silence. "You see, Mrs. Schulz," he said finally. "I was doing something for Frances and she was doing something for me."

"And what was that? I'm sorry, but this does affect our family . . . you see, my helper, Julian Teller, lost a dear friend —"

"I know," said John Routt. He absentmindedly patted his wrinkled pants. "Oh, Mrs. Schulz, the reason I hired Frances is that Nicholas Gentileschi suspected my granddaughter of theft. I'm sorry to hear he died, but I'm not surprised, with the people we're dealing with. Frances and I were trying to clear Dusty. That's why we needed the receipt. That's why Frances was asking you for it. Does that make sense? Dusty was being accused of not giving receipts, but our suspicion was that the *whole* place has a receipt problem."

"I'm sorry, I don't understand. I don't know what happened to the receipt. I saw it, but then Nick Gentileschi's body . . . the receipt is probably back at the store. And I still don't understand why you would need it."

John Routt said, "There has been some theft at the store. I was afraid Gentileschi suspected *I* was behind the thievery. You see, what you may not know is that I have a history with Foucault-Reiser Cosmetics."

I was suddenly aware of how much work I had to do before deadline time for the Braithwaites' party. What John Routt was saying confused me. Outside, raindrops began to fall.

I said, "What history? What theft?"

He invited me to sit down. When the three of us were settled in the sparsely decorated room, he smiled wryly. "Mrs. Schulz, did your husband serve in Vietnam?"

Taken off guard, I said, "Well, yes, as a matter of fact. That was before I knew him, though."

"And he came back and became a policeman," Mr. Routt said.

"He . . . finished his degree first, I think. Then he went into law enforcement."

Frances grunted, but John Routt held up an age-spotted hand. "When I got back from Korea in 'fifty-four, I was twenty-one. I tried to get into the police academy in —"

"Don't, John," Frances interrupted sharply. "Don't tell her where. No specifics. She doesn't need to know, for crying out loud! Goldy, I'm still trying to salvage a story here. If you don't mind, I'd like to keep you and your investigator husband out of this until it's published. Please at least let me do that."

John Routt shook his head. He continued, ". . . tried to get into the police academy . . . in the small town I was from. But there weren't any openings. No openings. There or anywhere else." He paused for a long time, his eyes closed. When he opened them he clucked his tongue. "Did you ever feel utterly worthless, Mrs. Schulz? As if everything that went wrong in your life was your fault?"

"Yes," I said evenly, "I have felt that way. For seven years, as a matter of fact."

"And what did you do to change things?" he asked. His watery eyes blinked as he waited for my answer.

"I got a divorce and started a catering business."

Again John Routt clucked. "I should have done that! My goodness. Actually, I didn't want a divorce, I just wanted a job. But there weren't any jobs." He sighed. "So I robbed a bank. More accurately, I drove the getaway car for a couple of buddies of mine."

The bank job. Tom had mentioned a famous bank robbery involving a man named Routt. His memory had been correct. Our neighbor was the same Routt. No wonder Sally Routt had told Dusty she was afraid of what the church helping to build their house might find out. "So if you were driving a getaway car, you . . . must have been able to —" I began.

405

Frances groaned.

"Yes," John Routt said softly. "I had my vision then. But I got caught and convicted for armed robbery. Eventually I ended up at the state penitentiary in —"

"John!" Frances interjected.

"I went to a state penitentiary," John Routt continued. "I was young," he said. "I was married. And so, Mrs. Schulz, when I was promised points in the time-off-for-good-behavior program, I took it." For the first time, his voice wavered. His head drooped forward. Frances and I sat very still as John Routt collected himself. "Catch was," he went on, "to get my time off, I had to volunteer for cosmetics testing from a company called Foucault-Reiser." He let out a self-deprecating cackle. "And here I am! The chemical the company used on me caused an infection in one eye. It spread to the other eye as quick as you could imagine. They don't use that chemical in cosmetics, thank the Lord. Because of me! I'm the reason your eyes don't burn when you smear your mascara."

"God help us," I said softly, appalled. I remembered Frances's cryptic answer to my demand to know what she was up to: *Did you ever hear of Ray Charles?*

Frances stood up. "John, you *don't* have to tell her all this. We'll get Mignon, one way or another. It is going to happen."

"Let me finish telling Mrs. Schulz what I'm going to tell her, will you, Frances? Please?"

She flopped back in her chair and rooted around for a cigarette.

John Routt shook his head and gestured with his large, trembling hands. Overhead, the rain beat down harder. "The warden was being paid by Foucault-Reiser, and he said if I told what had happened when their chemical ruined my eyes, I'd never get out of that place. Foucault-Reiser gave me some money, and I was released early. And before you ask, no, I didn't sue." When he shook his head, some strands of white hair came loose again. He patted them back into place. "Nobody but rich folks sued back then. I learned to play the saxophone. My wife, Jaylene, supported us by being a nurse. But when Jaylene died last year, I came to live with my daughter. Sally's had a hard life . . . connected up with two men who wouldn't marry her . . . well. Anyway, Sally's the one, Dusty's mother, that is, who read me the article Frances did on the high cost of cosmetics. That's why Frances is here. I called her. I told her I might have a big story for her newspaper." He chuckled. "She was doing it all for me, trying to get justice, trying to get a big story." His voice turned serious. "I didn't want my granddaughter to know. God only knows why she took a job with that same company. She knew what happened to me, but . . . I guess it's like the children of race car drivers, wanting to get involved in the same thing. . . ." He cackled sarcastically. "They must pay well. They've always paid well. But no matter what, I didn't want to get Dusty involved."

I could hear Dusty's voice as she applied eyeshadow to my lids: *Don't open your eyes! You don't know what could happen!* God only knew why she'd taken the job, indeed. I wondered where Dusty was.

Frances said, "John —"

"Frances, don't keep on. Mrs. Schulz?"

"Please call me Goldy."

"I just want to finish telling you, since you wanted to know why Frances was here. Last month, just after Frances and I started working together, Dusty told us they were targeting her for employee theft." He shook his head. "I thought, oh my Lord! They must know — Mignon, the parent company, Foucault-Reiser — someone must know I'm trying to get back at them! So they're targeting my granddaughter! They're trying to frame her with employee theft!"

Frances could no longer contain herself. "And then Claire Satterfield was run down," she interrupted. "For a while I even thought they were trying to get me."

I felt more bewildered than ever. "Who is *they?* And why spy on me?"

Frances Markasian shook her head at my profound ignorance. "First of all, Goldy," she said tartly, "no one is spying on you." She blew out smoke. "John has superdeveloped hearing. We knew you had the food fair this morning, and I didn't want to risk going into that store again so soon. So we had this idea that you could buy some stuff for us, and see if any of the other sales associates were neglecting to give receipts. That's probably all that happened to Dusty . . . she just forgot to give somebody a receipt! Anyway . . . John heard your van come back, that's how we knew you were home. That's it. *They* is Mignon Cosmetics, Goldy." She announced it the way a math teacher explains the end of a formula to a slow student. "It's all a conspiracy, don't you see?"

"No, I don't see."

Frances's voice became frustrated. "Mignon wanted to undermine John's story, so they cast suspicion on his granddaughter. When that didn't work, they killed Claire Satterfield, one of their top sales producers. And now they've killed the security guy. If John comes forward with his story, they'll be able to say, 'Ah-ha! This is the guy who's been causing all our problems, a convict undermining our company using hired killers!' Don't you get it?"

I'm not long on conspiracy theories. The JFK assassination still has me stumped. Watergate had seemed beyond belief, and it had actually been true. But Frances, I could tell, was not going to be dissuaded. And I wasn't going to argue with her. My kitchen was calling. I had cooking to do if the Braithwaites' guests were going to eat. Tom and the cops could separate the myth from the reality. I had just one last question.

"Frances, why were you so insistent about having the receipt?"

"Because Dusty's been in so much trouble —" John began.

"Because Dusty was convinced she was being framed," Frances rasped. "Claire said Gentileschi had been watching Dusty since the last inventory."

"Forgive me for being thick," I interrupted. "Why since the inventory?"

John waved Frances's objections away. He said, "It goes like this: A customer, say it's you" — he gestured with an open hand — "makes a large cash purchase. Say you buy . . . a scarf. The employee makes a big show of putting your receipt in the bag, but instead he palms it." He closed his hand. "Then the employee uses your receipt to do a cash refund

410

to himself. If you discover you don't have the receipt at the end of the day, you — the shopper — you say, oops, I musta lost it in all my shopping. And nobody's the wiser until inventory time six months later, when they find out a scarf's been shoplifted. Or at least, that's what they think."

"Oh, my," I said. "And had Prince & Grogan suffered a lot of loss?"

"Prince & Grogan just did their big inventory in June," Frances replied impatiently. "The store sharks were out to find out what had happened to thousands of dollars' worth of shoes, costume jewelry, lipstick, and perfume. That's probably why the security guy was so quick to come after you yesterday." Her eyes narrowed to knowing slits.

"But why would Harriet not give me —" I began.

Frances said, "I think Mignon has told Harriet Wells that Dusty is a potential problem to the company. Mignon could have told Harriet that when a big cash sale is made, put in Dusty's associate number. In other words, ring it up as if Dusty had made the sale. Then keep the receipt, and ring the return in as a cash refund, also to her associate number, so she looks guilty all the way around. And it's all computerized, so it looks official. I'm telling you, they're trying to frame her."

"That's quite a conspiracy, if you asked me."

"Exactly. If you'll pardon my saying so, it's the cosmetics company, stupid."

"Okey-doke," I said, rising. This time I didn't hold my hand out to John Routt, I just touched his forearm. "Thank you for telling me your whole story, Mr. Routt. Do you mind if I share it with my husband? He might want to come over and chat with you."

John Routt's voice caught in his throat. He seemed to sense I thought Frances's theory was baloney. Perhaps he even suspected that I'd lost the receipt, which was what I suspected myself. After a moment he said, "Do you think we still have a chance? Will people care what happened in the past? Now that all these other crimes are happening? I don't want Dusty to be hurt. She knows nothing of my dealings with Frances."

"But it was through Dusty that you found out Claire had had other boyfriends? And Frances suspected one of them was a good-looking animal-rights activist?" I asked him.

He hung his head. No wonder Frances had seemed to have so much information so early. Right from the beginning, she'd developed speculations — bizarre guesses, as it turned out — to go with Claire's being killed.

"Mrs. Schulz," said John Routt, "do you

think people will want to hear my story?"

"I hope so," I said delicately. "Frances won't give up," I added truthfully. "You can count on her. Good luck."

I excused myself and ran through the raindrops toward my house and my kitchen. Once I was safely ensconced in chopping a pile of mint leaves, I heard Frances's Fiat roar away.

"Where've you been?" Julian asked as he toasted the kernels for the raisin rice.

"At the Routts' place."

"You were gone a long time."

"I'm sorry. I'm working, I'm working."

In my absence, Julian had finished the slaw. I swirled yogurt and the freshly chopped mint into the soup, and we continued to work together in silence. We had a quiet teamwork in the kitchen that I would sorely miss when he went off to school. I reached for the ingredients for fudge cookies and wondered how much round-trip plane tickets cost from Denver to Ithaca.

"Are you okay?" Julian asked as he poured stock over the golden brown rice and it let out a delicious, steamy hiss.

"Oh, yes." What could have happened to that damn receipt? Had I ever had it? Had Harriet put it in the bag or handed it back to me with my change? But the change was in the bag. I'd never opened my wallet. "I

413

just . . . Julian, why was Dusty expelled from Elk Park Prep?"

"I really have no idea. You know, they were about to move into the Habitat House, and I guess her mom begged the school authorities to hush it up. I mean, since the Habitat House was sponsored by the church and all. They didn't want to look like the kind of people you wouldn't want to have in your law-abiding middle-class neighborhood, I guess."

Well, well. This undoubtedly was why I hadn't heard through the town grapevine that an ex-convict was living across the street. The Routts had managed to keep that quiet too. I asked, "Could Dusty have been expelled for stealing?"

He laughed. "Man, I doubt it. Right after she left, I had four CDs stolen from my locker. So if they threw Dusty out because they thought she was a thief, they didn't get the right person. Why do you care?"

"Oh, I don't know. She just seems so . . . needy or something. By the way, Arch called asking about you." Julian raised his eyebrows. "So what should I have told him? How are you, Julian?"

He sighed. "Functioning. Listen, we've still got two hours before we're due up at the Braithwaites' place. If you think you can finish the rice, I'd like to take some food over to

414

Marla's house. Lowfat, of course."

"Hey, I was born making fudge cookies and curry at the same time. But I should warn you — Marla's storm-trooper nurse may not let you see her."

He turned on our Jenn-Air grill and brought out some chicken breasts he'd marinated separately. "I don't really need to see her. I just want her to . . . start eating again. What is it you're always telling me?"

"When All Else Fails, Send in Food."

"Exactly." He laid the chicken pieces on the grill; they sputtered invitingly. I couldn't remember the last time I'd had a regular meal. A caterer's life. I stirred more of the cream alternative into the curry, took a final taste, and started in on the fudge cookies.

Julian started to tremble. When I looked over at him, he ran out of the kitchen and I finished the grilling. When he returned, his face splotchy, his eyes red, he said he didn't want to talk. If that was okay. I said it was fine, and helped him wrap up a dinner care package for Marla.

After he left, that angry inner voice nagged at me as I carefully sifted flour and cocoa powder. Claire Satterfield's death remained a bizarre, inescapable event. I whipped egg whites and added the dry ingredients, then stirred the whole concoction together. Tom wanted me out of the case. Sorry, Tom. Not when I must help Julian.

Before the store inventory, someone had been stealing from Mignon Cosmetics. One shoplifting theory was that employees palmed the merchandise receipts instead of giving them to customers, and then used the receipts later to get cash refunds. Who were the people there most often? Harriet, Claire, Dusty: All three knew the workings of the camera. But would they have dared to steal right in front of it? And of course there was Shaman Krill, who might have been involved in the thievery as part of his nasty campaign to destroy the cosmetics company. How could he get the receipts, if that indeed was how the shoplifting was done? If he shoplifted directly, then he might have been seen — or photographed — by Gentileschi or Stan White. Of course, if Nick Gentileschi had been unsavory enough to take surreptitious photos of Babs Braithwaite, there was no telling what other activities he could have been involved in. And then there was John Routt. He couldn't see to shoplift, so he was out, and Frances was up in the stratosphere with her conspiracy theories.

That left Reggie Hotchkiss. The man with the wig. He had spied on Mignon, and he'd shamelessly copied their promo campaign for fall products. Would he also have tried to sabotage them?

I dropped perfect rounds of shiny fudge batter onto a cookie sheet, set the cookie sheet into the oven, and stirred the curry. Maybe Reggie Hotchkiss would be at the Braithwaites' house tonight. Babs wanted to impress people, and the Hotchkiss Heir Apparent would be a perfect name for her guest list. I wondered who was doing her makeup.

I set aside the curry and rice to cool before Julian packed them into the van. Within half an hour he returned with the good news that although Marla was still asleep, the nurse had gratefully taken the dinner he'd brought and said his aunt had told her he was a brilliant cook. And yes, the nurse had said, Julian could come over tomorrow when I visited, as long as we didn't upset Marla.

"Who, us?" I said with a laugh as I started frosting the cooled fudge cookies.

Without being asked, Julian packed up the curry and rice, opened the door to the walk-in, and began hoisting boxes to go into the van. He said, "I'm the calmest person I know. Also the most depressed."

"Oh, Julian, what can I —"

"Nothing. And don't ask me again if I want to stay home, because the answer is no."

Resigned, I again decorated the vanilla-iced

417

fudge cookies by lightly dusting them with cocoa powder. While I took a quick shower, Julian finished packing the van. As we drove in silence to the Aspen Meadow Country Club area, I sneaked a glance at Julian's pale, exhausted face. I thought of all my friends who'd tried to fix me up with their single male neighbors, cousins, colleagues, coaches, and postal workers when I was divorced. Now, finally, I understood their impulse, because more than anything I wanted someone for Julian to find comfort from, as I had with Tom. But no friend can force that loving other person on you, I'd learned. If I hadn't stumbled into Tom in the course of my catering business, I'd probably still be the woman with a chip on her shoulder who refused to be comforted by anyone.

The stone entryway to the country club area had been draped with swathes of red, white, and blue fabric. I swung the van past an exuberant group of kids with sparklers and up toward Aspen Knoll.

"What was it exactly that Babs's parents did to earn their fortune?" Julian asked as we passed hillocks of elegant, showy landscaping that featured lush sprays of pampas grass, miniature aspens, iris of every conceivable hue, and masses and masses of pink and yellow perennials.

"Butter," I said.

"And here I thought all the money in this part of the country was tied up with oil."

I was still laughing when we pulled around to the back entrance of the colossal contemporary-style house. Neither Charles nor Babs was in sight. We didn't have any luck at the garage door, so we tried the front. A maid directed us to deck stairs that led to the side door to the kitchen. After we'd trekked up and down those stairs eleven times to unload our supplies, I began to wonder how much the Braithwaites had to pay someone to bring in the groceries. I also wondered about my boxes: They all said "Fourth of July party at the Braithwaites." I hadn't labeled the cartons, nor had I noticed that Julian had labeled them earlier. Well, he had to have taken them out of the refrigerator, so I knew they had to be right.

We were running slightly behind schedule, so the first order of business was to scope the place. The living room, where Julian and I would serve the soup and skewers as hors d'oeuvre, had a bar at the ready. It was an enormous room decorated in an Oriental style, which meant lots of heavy mahogany tables, silk screens, and low-slung silk-covered couches and chairs. Bowls of white and red peonies graced the mantelpiece and bar. The

419

maid had already set the dining room table for twelve. A lovely floral arrangement of red roses, white lilies, and blue gladiolas carried out the July Fourth theme for the evening. Each place also boasted a miniature American flag with the name of the guest engraved on its flagpole. We circled the table under the maid's watchful eye. I saw what I was hoping for. Mr. Reginald Hotchkiss was indeed one of the invited guests.

I sighed and tried to think of a strategy for asking him a few questions. Or for doing any sleuthing around this immense estate. When I was back in the kitchen, I looked out the window at Charles Braithwaite's greenhouse. With little actual cooking ahead, I'd surely have time to sneak down there while it was still light outside and look for a blue rose or two. The curry was done, all it needed was reheating. Ditto the rice. I knelt and opened the first carton, then stared at the contents. *My eyes aren't working*, I thought. *Something's wrong.* I leaned back on my heels, suddenly dizzy. What were the symptoms of heart attack? Indigestion, cold sweat, feeling light-headed. *This isn't happening*, I thought. *Maybe I'm going into cardiac arrest.*

I looked back inside the box. There was no curry. There was no raisin rice. There was no vegetable slaw. There were neatly packed

420

boxes of arborio rice, lowfat chicken broth, even several large bags of slightly thawed shrimp. And a note to me, in Tom Schulz's unmistakable scrawl. I opened it with trembling hands.

Dear Miss Goldy,

Sorry about this, but I really don't want you snooping at the Braithwaites' place tonight, and knowing you, that's precisely what you have in mind. You didn't tell me someone hit you with bleach water and wrote you a threatening note, Julian told me. You are in danger, dear wife. The only way to prevent you from getting into more trouble is to switch food on you so that you have to spend all your time cooking instead of sneaking around getting you — and me — into trouble. So: attached is my recipe for Shrimp Risotto. I had a Denver chef prepare all the ingredients for your menu. It perfectly meets Babs Braithwaite's requirement of being lowfat. And you can tell her it's even low-cost, since the shrimp is being donated by your local homicide investigator. She should be pleased as punch to be getting large shrimp for the price of ground turkey. And we'll all be pleased to eat turkey curry every day next week.

Don't be mad at Julian. I asked him to pick up the boxes and told him it was a nice surprise for you. I know you won't be pleased, because risotto is time-consuming and demands that the cook be there every second to attend to it. But that's what I want, Goldy. You doing your job and me doing mine. Don't be too mad at me. I'm just trying to think of both of us.

— Tom

"Brauuugh!" I hollered. Don't be too angry with him? I was going to kill him with my bare hands. "Julian!" I roared. "How the hell could you do this to me? How could you let him do this to me?"

"Let him do what?" Julian bounded over and picked up the note. As he was reading it, the maid appeared in the kitchen.

"The mistress would like to see the two of you when you have a minute," she announced.

Well, that was just great. I looked at all the food — the new food — that had to be prepared.

The maid cleared her throat. "The mistress —"

"Right now?" I demanded. "Does she have to see me this very minute?" I didn't have a speech ready yet.

"Yes," replied the maid. "First bedroom at the top of the stairs."

My stomach made an unexpected growl, no

422

doubt caused by hunger, apprehension at seeing "the mistress," and worry about preparing the accursed risotto. Julian, reading my mind, told me to go ahead. He'd read the recipe and start setting us up. No wonder he'd given me that guilty look at the house, and packed all the boxes so efficiently into the van while I was taking a shower.

"You and I are going to have a talk," I told him. "I won't be long." I marched out of the kitchen. I had my teeth clenched so tightly and was moving so fast, I failed to see that the next surface after the tiled kitchen floor was a slick green marble foyer. I avoided breaking my derrière by springing for the winding staircase. I landed facedown on the fourth stair up, and saw from very close range that the stairs were carpeted with a thick white wool weave, the kind you see either in ads or in houses without children. I stood up and walked more cautiously past two large silk screens showing carp floating in an ocean of gold. Again I felt my jaw clench with anger, and I averted my eyes. Carp made me think of bodies of water, and thinking of bodies of water made me think of shrimp, and thinking of shrimp in general and shrimp risotto in particular renewed a fury that was rapidly becoming volcanic. When I came to the top of the stairs, I took a deep breath and sat down

SHRIMP RISOTTO
WITH PORTOBELLO
MUSHROOMS

1 tablespoon dry sherry
1½ cups chopped portobello
   mushrooms
4 to 4½ cups lowfat chicken stock
   (see preceding recipe)
1 cup water
1 teaspoon Old Bay Seasoning
¾ pound (about 20 to 22) large "Easy-
   Peel" Shrimp
1 tablespoon olive oil
½ cup finely chopped onion
1 garlic clove, pressed
1¼ cups Arborio rice
1 teaspoon finely chopped fresh thyme
4 cups broccoli florets

Pour the sherry over the chopped mushrooms, stir, and set aside to marinate
while you prepare the risotto.

In a large saucepan, bring 1 cup of the
chicken stock, the water, and the Old Bay
Seasoning to a boil. Add the shrimp and
poach for 3 to 5 minutes or until just
pink. Remove and shell; set aside.

Heat 2 teaspoons of the olive oil in a heavy-bottomed skillet. Add the onion and sauté over medium heat for 2 to 5 minutes or until it is limp. Add the garlic and rice. Cook and stir for 1 minute or until the rice just begins to change color. Continuing to stir over medium-low heat, add the remaining chicken stock ⅔ cup at a time, stirring until the liquid is absorbed. Continue the process until the rice is tender and the mixture is creamy (this can take up to 30 minutes).

Heat the other teaspoon of olive oil in a small sauté pan and briefly sauté the marinated mushroom pieces over medium-high heat until they release their liquid. Remove from the heat.

Steam the broccoli for 5 to 6 minutes or until it is bright green and tender.

Stir the cooked shrimp, fresh thyme and mushrooms into the cooked risotto and stir over medium-low heat until heated through. Place the broccoli around the edge of a large platter. Fill the center with the risotto.

Serves 4 to 6

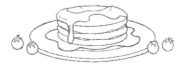

facing the upstairs hallway. *Relax,* I told my-self. *Think about something else. How much you love preparing labor-intensive Italian food, for example.*

When that didn't work, I took a few deep yoga breaths. *I should go see Babs,* I thought. *Maybe I can get her to tell me something I don't know about Claire. Or about Claire and her hus-band.*

But I wasn't ready. I let air out of my lungs and stared at two portraits hanging on the op-posite wall. The one on the left was of Babs, flatteringly painted with a somewhat slimmer face than the actuality. But the artist had been right on target with wide pink brushstrokes that had frozen Babs's girlish-insecure smile permanently into place. The other painting showed a bespectacled Charles looking somber and resigned, even a trifle defeated. Here, too, however, the painter had found the single fea-ture, that which spoke volumes about the personality he sought to capture. In the paint-ing, Charles's long, unruly pale hair said, *I want to be wild,* so that the effect he conveyed was a cross between a college professor and Harpo Marx.

From behind a door just down the hall I heard laughing and light rock music. I felt a surge of impatience. I had work to do. Oh, man, did I ever have work to do. But I had to go in and tell "the mistress" what was going on. My knuckles rapped on the cold white wood.

There was a giggled "Come on in!" and I pushed the door open with dread. Sometimes — especially in the summer, for reasons I did not understand — clients started the party early by beginning to indulge in alcoholic beverages long before their guests arrived. The results ranged from enthusiastically kissing someone else's spouse to falling into their own swimming pools.

I walked tentatively into the spacious boudoir. Suddenly I felt like Alice, miniaturized in Wonderland, except that I had landed not in water but in the middle of a giant wedding bouquet. Roses, roses, and more roses were everywhere; they filled every available space. White roses, red roses, pink roses, and yellow roses were bunched in vases, arranged in baskets, gathered into bowls that bedecked every shelf, bureau, and windowsill. Lush scent filled the air. It was unnerving.

I struggled for my bearings. In the midst of the bower, two figures were visible in front of a lighted bank of mirrors at the far end of the room. It took me a moment to realize that the seated person was Babs Braithwaite. With her hair full of rollers, her face covered with pasty-looking goo, and her large body swathed in a pink terry-cloth robe, she looked like a matronly alien in a science fiction movie. Standing next to her, an impeccably restored Harriet Wells wore a crisp white knee-length smock. Below the smock, her legs emerged long and ballerinalike. Harriet turned her sparkling smile on me and I saw a small bandage on her forehead. She sure didn't look like someone who was sixty-two, much less someone who'd been surprised earlier by a dead body tumbling down on the glass counter in front of her.

"Well, come on in!" Babs called gaily into the mirror. "Have one of Harriet's herb rolls! I don't suppose you'd better have any Asti Spumante though. Well, we've got juice. Lowcal!" Babs cried impatiently, "Well, come on, Goldy, we're not going to bite! Where's that young fellow who works for you?"

"Getting the food set up. Aah, there's something I need to talk to you —"

"Don't you think your assistant deserves a snack too?" Babs's speech was already slurred. When she talked, the facial paste moved up and down.

"Julian's fine," I assured her. "He really needs to work on getting things going. As do I, actually." Call me old-fashioned, but I didn't think it would be appropriate to bring Julian into a rose-filled boudoir where the partially clad hostess was halfway to being plastered, in more ways than one. If Julian was still intent on a career in food service, he'd have plenty of time to discover just how idiosyncratic clients could be. And just how idiosyncratic errant spouses could be.

"Well, you come on, then," said Babs, disgruntled. "This'll just take a minute. Have a little snack and come on over, I want to talk to you about tonight."

Babs allowed Harriet to start wiping off the pink goo. From my newfound knowledge, I recognized that it was a cosmetic masque. I strolled over to the silver teacart. The cart's top shelf held a globe vase of white and pink roses, a silver ice bucket containing a large green bottle set at a rakish angle, two tulip champagne glasses next to a stack of luncheon plates, a woven silver basket of puffed, delectable-looking rolls, and a silver plate piled with scoops of chèvre and pats of butter. My stomach growled in reproval, so to be sociable I reached for a plate, a roll, a dollop of chèvre, and one of those inviting pats of butter. When I pulled the roll apart, I was surprised to see it was speckled with bits of green.

"The rolls contain rosemary from my garden." Harriet shot a quick, shy smile in my direction. "You don't have to guess this time."

429

I took a bite. The soft, herb-flavored roll was feathery and light. "Out of this world," I told her.

Harriet nodded as she told Babs to close her eyes and relax. With her lids shut, Babs asked, "Did you know the police were here all afternoon, Goldy?"

"Aah," I said, and stalling, took another bite of my roll. Babs was a gossip who was always digging for nuggets, it seemed. I needed to be careful. Not only that, but how I would steer the conversation from the cops visiting to shrimp risotto was going to be tricky. "Seems to me I did hear about that. Harriet probably told you about the terrible thing that happened at the store."

"You're damn right she did," Babs said gruffly. "Don't you remember that day I told you somebody was back in the dressing room when I was changing into a bathing suit? I told you!" Tears trickled out over the remaining goop on her face. "I'm so embarrassed!"

Harriet patted her shoulder. "Don't upset yourself, it'll just make your nose red. Come now, dear." More patting. "Everything's going to be just fine."

I nibbled more roll and tried to think of what to say. *Well, I sure am glad I never bought a bathing suit there* would be kind of crass.

Babs sniffled mightily, grabbed the tissues

Harriet offered, and dabbed at her closed eyes. She said, "So how are the police doing in their investigation?"

"I really don't have a clue," I replied truthfully, "I've been too busy even to talk to my husband." *And when I do talk to him, it's not going to be about the investigation, you can be sure of that. It's going to be about what a pain-in-the-behind preparing shrimp risotto from scratch is. . . .*

Babs opened one eye. "Yes, I've been hearing from one of our guests just how busy you've been. That's why I was wondering if you were doing a little undercover work for the Furman County Sheriff's Department." The eye glared at me accusingly.

"Excuse me?"

Harriet's shoulders slumped in frustration as Babs slapped her hand away impatiently. "Reggie Hotchkiss is an important member of this community, Goldy," Babs said. "He's not someone you or I or anyone else can afford to alienate. If there's police work to be done, leave it to the police."

"I didn't alienate Hotchkiss," I said defensively. "I haven't even seen him today. And the last thing I would want to do, believe me, is get in the way of police work." And of course now, I wasn't going to have a chance to. "And Babs, I do need to talk to you about the menu —"

"Reggie called just an hour ago," Babs accused. She pointed a freshly manicured nail. "He said you'd gone to his boutique and pretended you wanted a facial, then went snooping all around and sneaked out when no one was looking!"

I finished the roll and put the empty plate down on the tray. "I had an appointment for a facial, which I kept. When the technician started poking me with a needle, I told her to stop and I left." All of this was technically true. "That's it. And I paid in advance, too, for a procedure they didn't even have to finish."

Babs leaned back and allowed Harriet to smoothe moisturizer on her cheeks and throat. "Look, Goldy, I'm just trying to calm things down before the party. You understand that, don't you? I used to be a client of Hotchkiss, but now I've gone over to Mignon, because Harriet just makes me look so much better. And I'm sure I'm not the only one. Reggie's green with envy, of course, and he's always been a big sponsor of our playhouse fund-raisers, so I have to keep a good relationship with him. Don't upset him, will you? You know he has such a temper."

"I won't upset him," I said acidly. "But I think he knows a lot more about Mignon

Cosmetics than he's revealing." Did I know Reggie had a temper? All I knew was that he was a pretty smooth industrial spy. Harriet stopped putting on Babs's makeup and gave me a very puzzled look, which I ignored. "Please, Babs," I blurted out. "There's something I have to tell you. My . . . er . . . shipment of ground turkey didn't come in. I substituted large, very expensive shrimp, and I'm absorbing the cost difference myself. I'll be making a risotto, and it's a very delicious —"

"I know what risotto is," she snapped. "I love it." She pondered my announcement for a moment, clearly glad she'd be getting prime shellfish for a ground-poultry price. "Fine, then, change the menu if you have to. I guess I'll have to find something to wear besides my sari."

"Well, I regret —"

"How's your assistant fellow doing?" she asked abruptly. Since this was the second time she'd asked about him, I grew wary.

"He's in the kitchen starting the —"

"I didn't ask *what* was he doing," Babs interrupted as Harriet dotted concealer under her eye. "I asked you *how* he was doing."

"He's doing fine," I said evenly.

"But I thought he was involved with that girl who was run over at the mall. Wasn't he? I'm sure I heard that somewhere."

"He was," I said, again careful. I wanted to protect Julian from Babs's tongue, and I was afraid we were getting into uncharted territory.

Babs lifted her chin for Harriet to dab green stuff on her reddish nose. After Harriet had rubbed the green in, her swift fingers deftly distributed foundation over Babs's face. Presto: The green disappeared and there were no more dark bags under Babs's eyes, no more red nose. Her face was a smooth, even tone. I was impressed.

Babs turned around again in her white leather chair. Her eyes didn't have any makeup on them yet, but they still bored into me. "Was Julian going steady with Claire Satterfield?" she asked icily.

"Going steady?" I asked. Now, there was a term I hadn't heard in a long time. "You mean, were they seeing each other to the exclusion of all others?"

"Whatever." Babs's voice was scathing. Her eyes never left my face.

"Yes, Babs, I think they were going steady. Now, if you'll pardon me, I do need to get back down to the kitchen if you want to have your party tonight."

Without another word Babs turned back to the mirror. Harriet gave me a quick sympathetic glance. Actually, I felt sorrier for her than she did for me. If it was up to me to make Babs Braithwaite beautiful on a regular basis, I'd find some new line of work.

17

Within twenty minutes, Harriet Wells had finished her makeup miracle and departed. While Julian busied himself shelling the shrimp — he dared not look at me — I stared at the menu Tom had written up and some Denver chef had assembled the ingredients for:

Fourth of July Ethnic Celebration
Cucumber Gazpacho
Grilled Focaccia with Garlic
Shrimp Risotto with Portobello Mushrooms
Caesar Salad
Vanilla-Frosted Fudge Cookies

Well, now, wasn't that nice. I noted that Tom had had the chef make a batch of the fudge cookies from my recipe. Maybe his hired cook used the kitchen down at the sheriff's department. I could imagine Tom insisting he had done the right thing. The bowl of dark red gazpacho, thick with chunks of cucumber, was snuggled next to nuggets of focaccia dough. Once I'd patted the dough out into satiny rounds, brushed them with olive oil, and inserted slivers of garlic at judicious intervals, Julian showed me where in the Braithwaites' three refrigerators he'd found spots to chill the other courses. The first kitchen cooler was devoted to food, the second to liquor, the third to flowers. While I was working on the focaccia, he'd sandwiched the gazpacho between bottles of Vouvray and wedged the salad underneath a bowl of roses. On the deck off the kitchen he had also lit off the gas grill without incident. Soon the focaccia loaves were sizzling merrily and sending up clouds of succulent smoke.

I looked out at Aspen Meadow Lake and wondered if Tom was feeling even remotely remorseful for sneaking around getting food switched on me. Despite my anger over what he'd done, I felt a pang from missing him on the holiday. Although I'd never thought the Fourth of July was very romantic, a little candlelit dinner around one A.M. would have been nice . . . once we'd had our argument about the food and the investigation and done some delicious making-up. Then I thought about Marla. I hoped she was resting comfortably, and not worrying about Tony Royce. And then there was Julian, who'd had great plans to take a nighttime picnic to the lake tonight after he'd helped me set up for the Braithwaites. He and Claire had planned to watch the fireworks together. I searched his face for a sign of what he was thinking, but he was inscrutable.

Now that we both knew the layout of the house and kitchen, we quickly discussed how we would orchestrate cooking and serving. When the guests began pulling up in their Porsches and Miatas, we were trying to remove the last focaccia loaf without burning our fingers. Suddenly, I saw Charles Braithwaite, his white-blond hair shimmering in the late afternoon sun as he trudged up from his greenhouse. His face was downcast. With no obvious enthusiasm he removed his gloves and headed for the living-room side of the house.

"Guess he's not really a party kind of guy," Julian observed.

I *tsk*ed. "With us catering his Fourth? Crazy. Look out, I need you to grab the other side of the platter so that the loaves don't go skittering off the deck." He did so and I added, "Gotta say, Big J., I think Charlie-baby is more than a little crazy, anyway."

"No, no, he's not," said Julian defensively as the tray of fragrant grilled loaves teetered between us, "he's a good guy. I told you the time he had our senior bio class over to look at how he does genetic engineering. It was cool. Like a spy mission." Julian smiled wryly through the plumes of garlic-scented barbecue smoke.

"Great." I looked back, but Charles had disappeared through a side door. The last thing I was going to do was mention to Julian that not only had Charlie been obsessed with secrecy; he'd gone mad over Claire Satterfield. "Better arrange the soup, we should be serving it in half an hour."

"O captain, my captain, wherefore art thou, *my* captain?" Julian said as he did as directed. I lifted the platters of bread and tried not to smile. He bowed in my direction and quaffed a pretend hat. Maybe he would recover. Maybe he was just acting.

I said, "Let's try to have fun in spite of Tom's stunt. We're still going to make a lot of money tonight."

"Then it's fun by definition," he said grimly.

When I came out to the living room with the loaves, the guests, all clad in some variation of red, white, and blue, were chatting amiably. Tony Royce, resplendent in a bright red shirt, navy bandanna, and white pants, had had the guts to invite another woman to replace Marla. His date was plump and fortyish, her bleached-blond hair held up in two perky pigtails. Her outfit matched Tony's. Although I didn't know her, something about her said *wealthy widow*. Too bad for Tony that his brownies were still in my walk-in refrigerator, along with the turkey curry. Reggie Hotchkiss, playing the part of casual cool rich guy, wore blue jeans and a shirt printed with a collage of the American flag. In my role as servant, I didn't dare tell Reg that his apparel came off as unpatriotic. But I couldn't have enlightened him anyway, as Reg made a great point of giving me his back when I offered him the platter of focaccia wedges. La-de-da, I thought. So much for sympathizing with the proletariat.

I did feel sorry for Charles Braithwaite, however, who had either forgotten or not cared to dress in the national colors mandated by his wife. Well, I thought the dress code was a pretty corny idea too. Charles didn't appear to have an opinion. With his long, lanky frame still completely clothed in khaki, he seemed oblivious. It was clear Charlie-baby would rather be in his greenhouse, or on safari with the French Foreign Legion — anywhere but here. By the time I reached him with the focaccia tray, he was slumped by a silk-draped corner window listening with a pained expression to Tony Royce's date. She was complaining about how impossible it was to grow orchids indoors in Colorado. *They just seem to know they're not in a rain forest,* she lamented. Charles groaned sadly, as if he'd give anything to be in the rain forest.

I whisked back out to the kitchen, added broth to the Arborio rice speckled with garlic and onion, stirred, and then helped Julian ladle chilled, chunky gazpacho into cold soup bowls. After sprinkling the soup with chopped scallions, I placed the bowls around the dining room table, then hustled back to the kitchen to add more broth to the risotto. I wiggled a spoon through the mixture, tossed home-made croutons for the salad in a mixture of olive oil and melted butter, stirred the risotto again, tossed the salad, and stirred more broth into the risotto. When Julian headed off to move the guests through the soup course, I stepped out on the deck to grill extra Portobello mushrooms and curse Tom Schulz. Forget the idea of making up over a romantic dinner. He'd have to pay for this little trick with a weekend at the Broadmoor.

In the fading light, the view of Aspen Meadow and the lake was even more spectacular than when we arrived. As the sun slipped rapidly behind the mountains to the west, a few rays backlit brilliant pink skeins of cloud. Darkness, and the fireworks, were just over an hour away. I flipped the large mushroom caps and allowed my eyes to rest on the gently sloping acreage around the house. Two paths led from the house to the lower grounds. About a hundred yards down,

Charles's greenhouse was separated from a small garden filled with lawn chairs by a split rail fence twined with rosebushes. It was these, I surmised, that must have provided the blooms for Babs's bedroom. Beyond the knoll, the roads coming into Aspen Meadow were already clogged with firework spectators from Denver.

Julian had cleared the soup bowls and finished arranging the salads when I returned with the mushrooms. He served the salads while I stirred the remaining ingredients into the steaming risotto. Plump shrimp were nestled invitingly between chunks of sherry-soaked Portobello mushrooms in the bed of luscious, creamy rice. Julian had steamed fresh broccoli to a bright green, and I artfully surrounded the risotto with the emerald-colored florets. Reggie Hotchkiss finally acknowledged my presence by giving me an angry, wide-eyed stare when I offered the platter. Of course, I was eager to tell him how much I disliked him, his procedures, and his silly outfit, but I kept my lips firmly sealed. When the guests had polished off the risotto and Julian had begun clearing the plates, I came out to the kitchen to get the fudge cookies. Unfortunately, Reggie Hotchkiss followed me.

I switched on the coffee urn and tried to ignore him as I reached for the cookie tin.

I didn't want to get upset on a festive occasion, especially a festive, *lucrative* occasion. *Let the mood fit the food,* we always say in the food business. But when Reggie marched up in his gaudy print shirt and edged between me and the dessert-plate platter, my mood turned decidedly dark.

"Would you *please* go back out to the dining room?" I said in a pained, sweet voice. I reached for the container of fudge cookies and arranged them decoratively on a separate piece of stoneware.

When I looked up, the brown hair around Reggie Hotchkiss's bald spot was trembling. His thin, good-looking face was filled with rage. "I'm not going anywhere until you tell me what you and your fascist-pig husband are doing investigating my place of business without a search warrant."

I leaned back, startled. A temptation arose to use language that certainly would never get Goldilocks' Catering invited back to the Braithwaites anytime soon. To keep my temper in check, I reached out for a fudge cookie, brought it to my mouth, and took a huge bite. The dark, velvety moistness melted over my tongue. I closed my eyes and chewed. It was better than a shot of tequila.

"Are you going to answer me," Reggie yelled, "or are you going to stuff your face?

What kind of damn caterer are you anyway?"

This eruption brought a furious, flushed Julian catapulting into the room. He slammed an uneven stack of plates down on the counter and hollered, "What in the *fucking* hell is going on out here?"

So much for future catering at the Braithwaites. I calmly swallowed the fudge cookie, squeezed past Reggie, and hoisted the platter of cookies. This I offered to Julian.

"Would you please," I asked with as much charm as possible, "take these goodies out to the guests? Mr. Hotchkiss wants to have a chat with me, and we're going to have to go outside, I'm afraid."

But Julian didn't take the tray. Instead, he addressed Reggie Hotchkiss: "You *touch* her, and I will beat your bald head to a pulp. Understand?" His sneakers squeaked on the tile floor as he grabbed the platter from me. "I'm going to be out on that deck in five minutes. Five minutes. Got it?"

Reggie Hotchkiss stared at the ceiling. He said, "Ah, but I do feel such a *bond* with the younger members of the working class."

Julian glared at him in disbelief, then pushed through the door to the dining room.

"Come on, Reg, you want to talk, let's make it snappy," I said as I led the way to the side deck.

The sun had set, and the sky, now violet, promised a perfect backdrop for fireworks. I sighed and wished fervently that Reggie were not there. Unfortunately, he placed his imposing self with its red, white, and blue shirt once again in front of my face.

"First," he said suddenly, holding up one index finger, "you call my place of business. You say" — and here he raised his voice to a falsetto that resembled nothing that had ever come out of my mouth — " 'oh, my, but I want to buy *all kinds* of stuff from your fall catalogue!' Then next" — voice back down, a second finger up — "you make an appointment under false pretenses —"

I'd suddenly had enough. "Don't you dare bully me," I said evenly. "I made an appointment. I kept it. I even paid for a job that didn't get finished. What's your complaint, anyway? I've got work to do and you're interrupting it."

"Oh, *I'm* interrupting *your* work, oh, *excuse* me." Reggie flailed his arms. "And what about all our new products that you wanted to order?"

"You mean all those products you *stole* from the fall line of Mignon Cosmetics? Those?"

His face colored in great red and white splotches that clashed with the loud shirt. "What?" he bellowed. "What?"

"Excuse *me*, Reg," I said, furious myself now, "I think you know quite well what I'm talking about. I catered that banquet for Mignon. You were there too, spying in your cute blond wig. You got your list of what you figured would be money-making Mignon products and you just copied them into your fall catalogue. Anybody with *half a brain* could see the plagiarism."

His face contorted with rage. Maybe I'd gone too far; maybe it took a *full* brain to figure the theft he'd committed. But he'd made me so angry with his accusations, I couldn't help it. And besides, I hadn't told him the cute blond wig had fallen on my head when I was escaping Lane, the needle-wielding facialist.

"You are in some kind of trouble," Reggie warned in an ominous voice. This time the index finger trembled when he pointed. "You have just dug yourself into a hole so deep, you'll never get out, lady. You —"

"Hey, you stupid fuck!" yelled Julian from the deck door. He strode angrily out onto the deck and squared off against Reggie's patriotically clad paunch. "What'd I tell you about not threatening her?"

"I know who you are too," Reggie raged at Julian, still wagging his finger. "You're the low-class creep that Claire Satterfield had finally decided was her one and only. Lucky you, boy. She went from robbing the grave to robbing the *cradle!*" The colors in his face were decidedly unhealthy.

"You better watch what you say," growled Julian, suddenly aware, as was I, that the rest of the guests had appeared on the other deck, their faces filled with curiosity about the disappearance of their fellow guest, their servers, and the resulting commotion.

Reggie held up his hands. "No competition from me, guy. I didn't want to sleep with her, I just wanted to hire her. That woman could sell cosmetics just by standing still. How was she in bed?"

That did it. Julian lunged forward. Reggie began to whack indiscriminately. I tried to step between them and caught the brunt of Julian's forceful, angry body on one side and Reggie's chest on the other.

From the middle of the male sandwich, I choked out, "Go inside, Julian! Please!"

He obeyed by whirling around and striding angrily back into the kitchen. Reggie Hotchkiss fell against the deck rail. Absent male support, I tottered on the deck planks. I caught my balance just a moment before my trajectory would have landed me on the grill. The pain from Julian's body crashing into mine was concentrated in my head. I rubbed my temples and tried to clear my brain.

When I looked up at Reggie Hotchkiss, he had recovered. Standing stock-still, he hissed, "I have been mistreated and misjudged, and I am not going to forget it."

"Fine."

He brushed imaginary dust off the American-flag shirt and made his final pronouncement in my direction. "In the classless society," he said as he headed for the deck stairs, "there will be no need for servants. *You* will be *obsolete*." He trod heavily down the wooden steps and headed for his Bentley, presumably not the same one he had driven up the steps of the Lincoln Memorial.

Everyone was staring. I asked lightly, "In the classless society, who does the cooking?"

Sensing that the excitement was over, the guests on the deck turned their attention back to Babs. Her perfectly made-up face was trembling with anger, but she managed to announce breathlessly that, goodness, time was marching on! Each guest was to carry a sparkler and a glass of sparkling wine down to the lower garden. Lawn chairs were set up there, she trilled on. Even as she spoke, the maid was moving across the yard lighting upright torches. The dark-haired woman Reggie Hotchkiss had come with volunteered to light the sparklers and pour the wine. Her high, laughing voice seemed to indicate that she minded not in the least that Reggie had deserted her.

But there was more abandonment going on. In the fading light, Charles Braithwaite skulked away from his guests, walking swiftly down the path toward his greenhouse. From the furtive, quick nature of his stride, it didn't look as if his purpose was to set up chairs, join in festivities, or have sparkling anything.

I took a deep breath of evening air and tried to remember what I still had to do. Babs was paying her maid to stay late and clean up, so all Julian and I faced was packing the pans and containers we had brought and schlepping them back down the deck stairs to the van. But cigarette smoke drifting upward from underneath the deck made me doubt Julian's commitment to the packing task.

"If a caterer is smoking next to the house," I announced downward into the deepening darkness, "that could get him into distinct trouble with the hostess, to the extent that a certain caterer and her capable assistant wouldn't get paid. We might not get paid anyway, after having a little squabble with a guest." I didn't tell him I needed help. If Julian wanted to unwind from his encounter with Reggie Hotchkiss, then that was fine by me, as long as he didn't get into any more arguments. Arch was in Keystone; Tom was working late; I had nothing to look forward to except an empty house and a rousing argument with Tom over switching my food. The later I got to it, the better.

The glowing butt of Julian's cigarette moved past one of the torches. I watched him turn not toward the garden, but in the direction of the greenhouse. After I'd brought our platters in from outside and come back out to check that the grill was off and the deck clear, I couldn't see him anymore, as the guests holding their champagne and their twinkling sparklers moved in a slow, loud knot down to the chairs.

The maid bustled about helping me clean pans. I checked my watch when all the catering supplies were in boxes: Nine forty-five. Julian had not returned. The fireworks would be starting soon. There was no sign of Charles Braithwaite either, but that didn't surprise me. I decided to wait ten more minutes out on the deck. It was not like Julian to be inconsiderate. On the other hand, he'd been so upset that he probably lost track of time.

There was a flash of light followed by a loud *peh-beh!* sound and a puff of gray smoke beside the lake. A white shot of light rocketed upward, paused, and then a shower of white lights sprayed down from the sky over Aspen

Meadow. The blossom of brilliance reflected gloriously in the smooth surface of the lake. The show had begun.

There was another boom and flash, and this time the shower of overhead glitter was emerald. In the few seconds of light, my eyes scanned the garden and the greenhouse. Julian's silhouette was briefly visible, along with the smoke from a cigarette. He was standing beside the rose-laden fence.

For heaven's sake, I wondered, what was he doing? An explosion-generated scream accompanied the next luminous fall of bits of light, and I felt a wave of unease. Impulsively, I headed toward the torchlit path. Maybe Julian was watching the fireworks and had forgotten about me completely. Maybe he was in one of his grieving-and-smoking spells and needed me to snap him out of it.

I made my way down the paved walk and learned to fix the path ahead by stopping at the torches, then waiting for the intermittent sprays of colored lights overhead. I knew I was getting close when the heady smell of roses and the laughter of Babs and her guests announced my proximity to the split-rail fence. I maneuvered around the fence and soon found myself at the edge of the greenhouse.

"Julian!" I whispered. "Where are you?"

"Over here!" came his called response after

a moment. "Come on around to the front!"

I followed his voice and tried to figure out where the front was. In a flash of pink and blue sparkles that reflected in the near side of the greenhouse panes, I saw that I was on the shorter wall. The door was probably somewhere along the longer one. When I came around to the length side of the greenhouse rectangle, I could make Julian out. He was standing beside a slightly open door.

"Julian! For heaven's sake! What are you doing?"

"Sorry if you've been waiting for me," he said when I was by his side. "I was thinking about that awful Hotchkiss guy . . . and smoking where Babs couldn't see me . . . and then I . . . well, I just got here. The door is open, and that worries me."

"You stayed down here in the dark, and left me to wonder what in the world had befallen you, and now you're worried about a door? So *what* about the damn door!"

Julian's earnest, boyish face and blunt-cut blond hair was suddenly revealed by a glistening shower of red, white, and blue. "Don't be upset," he pleaded. "It's just that Dr. Braithwaite . . . you don't understand, he would never leave this place open! Especially if he was going to be having guests who were strangers. The guy's a security nut about his experiments. I don't know where he is, but I think I should stay here and guard the place until he gets back. He's got a lot of stuff in there that's pretty dangerous."

I took a deep breath and tried to think. Really, Julian's loyalty to Charles Braithwaite was admirable. Misguided, but admirable.

"Okay look," I told him, "we can't stay here and wait for the host to show. Just close and lock the door. Please."

"No," said Julian stubbornly. "I owe it to Dr. Braithwaite at least to check if there's been any damage. Then we can call the police or something."

"Okay then," I said as amiably as possible. "Let's go inside and turn on the light, if there is one, and see if there's been any vandalism or whatever. Maybe there's a phone to call the main house or the police. Otherwise, we really need to go back up to the house."

"Okay, okay." Together, we moved up the concrete steps to the open door. "Actually," he added meekly, "I was kind of afraid to go in there alone."

Well, that was just peachy, I thought rather indignantly, as my hand felt along the inside of the Plexiglas. Did *a lot of stuff that's pretty dangerous* include woman-eating plants? I groped along the slick surface. My fingers brushed something cold and I instinctively recoiled. Then I realized it was a conduit leading to a light switch. Triumphantly, my fingers found the switch. I flipped on an overhead fluorescent fixture.

After the near darkness it took a moment to adjust to the light. Julian stepped forward and peered around the greenhouse, which really looked more like a lab than a place to raise flowers. Row upon row of tables was neatly piled with equipment that meant nothing to me. There were plants arranged on shelves too, a cornucopia of flora in all stages of development. But at least the place seemed orderly, and not as if someone had broken in and made a mess trying to steal, vandalize, or whatever it was Julian seemed so worried about.

"Looks pretty innocent," I commented as I moved toward one of the tables. "Maybe he just forgot to lock the door . . ."

"No, no, no, don't touch anything," Julian warned. He gestured at the space. "You're looking at a lab set up for molecular biology," he said with genuine awe. He pointed to two metal boxes on a near table. "Those are gel boxes for electrophoresis. That's the process for analyzing DNA. When our class visited, Mr. Braithwaite told us he was looking for an enzyme in plants that produces blue color. You know, because scientists hadn't had any luck at, like, splicing it into roses because the color receptors just weren't there."

I looked at the boxes, fascinated. So this was where he'd created the blue rose. In spite of the uneasy feeling that Julian and I didn't belong there, I found it astonishing that someone could put together this kind of complicated scientific setup in our little burg of Aspen Meadow. Of course, with enough money, you could probably analyze sunscreens in Antarctica.

"You just put the plant into the gel and look at it through the microscope?"

Julian shook his head. "No, no, first you have to grind it up." He pointed to a cylindrical tank that was three feet high and about three feet in diameter. "You have to put the flower petals into liquid nitrogen, which is what's in that vat. You grind the petals in there till they're like a fine powder, then you have to add a buffer —"

"Liquid nitrogen?" I interrupted. "Isn't that pretty cold stuff?"

He grinned. It was the first time I'd seen him amused since Claire's death. "Try minus one hundred ninety-six degrees. That cold enough for you? You wear latex gloves, Goldy." He pointed to some gloves tidily placed by a mortar and pestle next to the tank. "If you put your hands in there unprotected, they'd break off. Put your head in, and you'd be the headless horseman. Not to mention that the fumes would suffocate you."

I decided I'd had enough science lesson. "Okay Julian, thanks. Let's go back up to the house."

"But I haven't told you about the sequencing gel apparatus and the laminer air-flow hood! Not to mention the gene gun. That's really cool."

Cooler than minus 196 I couldn't imagine. "Gene gun? Can you shoot anybody with it?"

"Very funny." He moved to a table and picked up what looked like an elongated pistol. "You introduce your bit of DNA into the axillary buds of the flower you're experimenting with, and you pray like mad that you end up with your blue daffodil, or whatever it is —" He fell silent as his eyes rested on a cluster of flowering plants that I could just dimly see. They were grouped next to the vat of liquid nitrogen. "What the hell?" Julian peered in closely at the flowers. "He had these covered up last time . . . oh my God, it's a frigging *blue rose!*" He picked up a small pot and held it up to the light. I felt my heart stumble in my chest. I wanted to get out of there so badly. "Judas priest!" cried Julian. "Look at this, Goldy! I can't believe it! Do you know what this means?"

A whimper came from behind a shelf of books at the far end of the lab. Julian and I gaped at each other.

"Go away!" sobbed the voice. "Just leave!"

Julian carefully put the pot down with the others. "It's him," he stage-whispered to me.

The sobs grew louder. "Just go away! Leave me in peace!"

"Dr. Braithwaite," Julian said as he moved toward the shelves, "we were just worried about you, when the door was open —"

The entire shelf of books erupted at that moment as a growling Charles Braithwaite heaved them forward and emerged with his arms outstretched. Julian jumped back from the cascade of volumes. Sobbing, his arms raised, Charles Braithwaite had the aspect of a skinny, white-haired ogre. He growled at us, then screeched, "Go a-*way!* Leave!"

"Julian!" I yelled. "Let's get out of here!"

Julian didn't move.

"Why . . . won't . . . you . . . leave?" Charles Braithwaite bellowed. He stood with his thin legs apart, his long arms outstretched. "Nothing . . . means . . . *anything!*" Then, defeated, he stumbled through the fallen books and sank against one of the tables. In a much lower, more subdued voice, he murmured, "If you will just please go away, I won't turn you in for smoking as a minor."

The guy was losing it, that much was clear. First he was howling like a crazy person, then he was making calm pronouncements. I was sorely tempted to exit as bidden, but Julian stepped with determination over the piles of disheveled books.

"Dr. Braithwaite," he said calmly, "you're upset." Smart kid, I thought. Just keep your tone low. Smarter yet, I thought ruefully, get the heck out. Julian held out his hand. "Why don't you just come up with us —"

"No!" Charles Braithwaite roared, his white hair shaking wildly. "Leave me alone!"

"Come on, Julian," I implored from the entrance to the greenhouse. "Let's just —"

"I'm not doing it," Julian said in my direction, his voice sharp but still low. "We're not leaving without him. Look, Dr. Braithwaite, you don't have to —"

The white-haired man raised a mournful face to Julian. He raised his index finger, calm again in his bizarre way. He acted as if he were instructing Julian in an important point of molecular biology. "Claire Satterfield brought something into my life that I'd never had. So there's just one thing I want you to know before I die." Oh hell, I thought. "And that is," he continued, "that you did *not* cause the accident with my . . . *wife*." He spat out the word. "No. Babs was following you and

458

Claire because she thought *you* were bringing Claire to *me* for . . . an assignation. You didn't fail to signal, my *wife* was following too . . . closely. So there you are." He crossed his arms, QED.

"Claire?" asked Julian. "You . . . and . . ." He shook his head and seemed to make a decision. "It's okay, Dr. Braithwaite, it's . . . over." Julian looked around the lab, trying to assess, I thought, how Charles Braithwaite could fulfill what seemed to be his desire to do himself in. He picked up the pot he'd placed on the near table. "Come on, look! You've created a blue rose! You've got a lot to live for —"

"I wanted to give it to her," Charles said wistfully. Overhead, the finale firework showered red, white, and blue sparkles that absurdly lit the greenhouse with twinkling light, illuminating the tears on his stricken face. "To Claire. That's why I was in the mall garage that day. I wanted to give it to her as my parting gift. The flower named after her, because it was so beautiful. So rare." He looked at Julian and shrugged. "And then I — can you blame me? I heard that terrible sound, and I knew. You want to know the truth? I thought my wife had done it. Maybe she did! Maybe she hired somebody to do the hit-and-run." He stretched his arms to their full length. "And it was all Babs's fault I met Claire in the first place! She sent me in to pick up her damn stuff. And there was Claire, acting as if I were . . . as if I were the most wonderful . . ." He dropped his arms and shook his head vigorously, as if he'd just come to the realization of whatever it was he'd been concentrating on before he'd digressed. "Listen," he said abruptly, "I've thought this all through. Just leave me in peace, please. *Now,* all right?"

"Let's go talk about it up at the house!" Julian said brightly. "I mean really, Dr. Braithwaite, you're too young to die. You need to give it some more thought."

"No!" wailed Charles Braithwaite. "Go away!" He stepped agilely over the books, and to my shock, put both arms around the vat of liquid nitrogen. This was how he was going to kill himself. Using liquid nitrogen. We had to get out. Charles began to rock the tank. "Can't you hear?" he roared. "This is the end! Get out of the way!"

"Julian!" I shrieked.

But Julian ignored me. He stepped briskly over the pile of books and grabbed Charles Braithwaite's arm. The vat of liquid nitrogen continued to rock. Yanking hard, Julian pulled Charles away just as the top came off the tank.

"Get out!" Julian shouted to me as he

dragged a flailing Charles in my direction. "Go!"

I banged open the door. When I looked back, the tank teetered as the freezing chemical splashed over one side, emitting clouds of white smoke. Julian scrambled toward the exit, his arms firmly encircling Charles Braithwaite's chest. Charles, his white hair wild, kicked halfheartedly. But he was no match for young Julian's strength. The three of us bounded out of the greenhouse just as the vat crashed downward. I couldn't help it — I looked back again, just in time to see the liquid nitrogen spilling over and destroying the blue rose plants.

18

Our odd trio darted through the guests meandering up to the house. We turned deaf ears to "Oh my goodness, what's the matter with Charlie!" and "The fireworks must have really upset him!" and laughing exclamations of that ilk. In the kitchen I called 911 and told them who I was, where we were, and what was going on.

"Liquid nitrogen?" was the deputy's incredulous response. "Liquid *nitrogen?* Are you sure that's all it was? Were there any other chemicals? We're going to have to get the toxic waste team up there. Was this part of some wacko Fourth of July party?"

"No, no," I said. "Any chance you could put me through to Tom Schulz?"

The deputy stalled and kept asking me questions until I assured him I wasn't going to hang up, I just wanted to talk to Tom instead of him. He said he'd transfer me. Then he put me on hold.

I tapped my fingers on the kitchen counter and watched as Julian ministered to Charles Braithwaite. Using a low, quiet voice, Julian admonished Charles to lie relaxed on the spotless kitchen floor, and to breathe normally. Was he hurt, Julian wanted to know. When Charles shook his head, Julian asked him who he was and what was going on. Tears ran down Charles's thin face as he gave halting responses to Julian's steady questions. Then Julian patted his shoulders and checked his pulse and told him in a voice that rippled out like custard that everything was going to be all right.

Julian amazed me, really. He had proven himself to be singlemindedly ambitious in the schoolroom and the kitchen. He loved and hated with a ferocity that was frightening and occasionally explosive. But there were times like these when I was reminded he'd spent most of his life among the Navajo in Bluff, Utah. He had an uncanny ability to act the wise healer when it was needed. I watched him calmly checking Charles Braithwaite for shock. What had he said to Charles in the greenhouse? *You're too young to die.* Claire Satterfield had been much too young to die too. What was still unclear to me was whether Julian would be able to heal from that terrible loss. He was too young to have the loving part of himself die.

The deputy's voice crackled in my ear. "Tom Schulz isn't here." At that moment, the first wave of law-enforcement and fire vehicles pulled up, so I signed off.

Hours later, when the fireworks had ended and the moon had risen and the guests — including an angry Tony Royce, without his promised brownies — had finally left, when Babs Braithwaite had exploded in a fit of hysterics and Charles had been taken to the hospital for observation, when the toxic-waste team had realized only nitrogen — a fertilizer — had spilled, and Julian had decided to spend the night at a friend's, I drove the van home. The fireworks spectators had all departed, but in the moonlight I could see the enormous mess of trash they'd left on the golf course by the lake.

I came through the door just before two A.M. Tom, amazingly enough, was in the kitchen making chocolate ice cream. Waiting for me, and undoubtedly too wired from the investigation to sleep, he'd decided to concoct a Neapolitan ice cream torte, with a chocolate-cookie-crumb base and layers of homemade vanilla, fresh strawberry, and finally dark chocolate ice cream. Allowing thirty minutes per batch of ice cream, I figured he'd been at this for quite some time. The kitchen was a mess of cream containers, beaters, and bowls.

"It's not exactly the colors of the flag," he said ruefully when I peered into the bowl and raised my eyebrows. "But it's gonna be great.

464

I can't wait for you to try it. Where've you been anyway? I guess my little ruse didn't work."

"Little ruse? Little ruse? Is that what you call it?" I glared at him. He grinned widely. After a few seconds of trying to keep up my withering stare, I couldn't help myself. I burst out laughing. "And when did you have time to do all that menu planning, Mr. Investigator? I am never, *never* going to forgive you."

He grabbed me by the waist and swung me perilously close to the clutter of ice creams. "Oh, sure you're going to forgive me," he reassured me as I giggled wildly. "And I didn't have time to do the cooking. I faxed your recipes down to a chef from a restaurant near the sheriff's department, and paid *him* to get the ingredients together and make the cookies and the soup and the bread dough. It took *me* less than five minutes. Anyway, knowing you, the risotto didn't stop you, it just slowed you down. The fireworks were over a couple of hours ago. Was the party okay?"

He sat me down on a chair and I told him all about it. I assured him that Julian had been a champ and that Dr. Charles Braithwaite would survive, especially if he could get some intensive psychiatric help. I confessed to having a fight with Reggie Hotchkiss, and that Julian had been involved. Tom seemed worried — did I think Hotchkiss had thrown the bleach water and left the note? I said I had no idea. He asked if Reggie could know where Julian was tonight, and I told him Reggie had left long before Julian had decided to go to his friend's house.

"Think you'll ever cater for the Braithwaites again?" he asked.

"No. And I don't care either. I am kind of disappointed that they may be innocent in all this. I still don't trust either of them."

When I finished talking, Tom wordlessly cut me a wide wedge of the triple-layered torte. The chocolate ice cream was still soft over the more solid layers of strawberry and vanilla. Biting into the three delicious flavors and through the crunchy chocolate-cookie crust, I was reminded of childhood birthday parties in New Jersey, where Neapolitan ice cream and chocolate cake were the order of the day.

I told Tom, "This is the most delicious thing I have ever tasted in my entire life. But you know we shouldn't have it. We don't want to get into the kind of situation . . . like Marla."

Tom put his arms around me. "Everything in moderation, Miss G. Besides, you're too young to have a heart attack."

"Excuse me," I blubbered, "but I am not."

Too young. It seemed that phrase was cropping up a lot lately. I even remembered using it with Arch, when I'd told him he was too young to be using sixties language. . . .

I sat up straight. Wait a cotton-picking minute.

"Ah-ha!" said Tom. "She's changing her mind. She's going to have some Neapolitan ice cream after all —"

"Tom," I said urgently, "who did Shaman Krill say he worked for?"

"He didn't. I've been laboring on that guy day and night. He won't tell us jack."

"But he wasn't with the animal rights people, you know that. And he's an actor. How old would you say he was?"

"About as old as this Neapolitan ice cream is going to be by the time you eat it."

"Tom!"

"I forget. Twenty-seven, maybe."

"So he wasn't old enough to know any of that sixties lingo he was using with us like 'fascist pig' and 'capitalist imperialist' and all that."

"There are movies," Tom said dubiously. "Documentaries."

"And scripts," I said. To humor him, I had a bit of ice cream. He'd put fresh strawberries into the pink layer. It was like chilled, succulent essence of fruit. "You know who uses

467

that kind of language? For whom it's second nature, don't you?"

He cocked his head and lifted his eyebrows. "Nope. But I just know you're going to tell me."

"Reggie Hotchkiss. He knows the lingo. He paid for the demonstration, I'll bet, to disrupt Mignon. Shaman Krill is a Reggie Hotchkiss plant. Maybe Reggie ran Claire down himself. Oh, Lord, and I had a fight with him tonight. . . ."

Tom said, "The security for this house is airtight. And I have a forty-five, don't forget."

"You don't believe me. I'll bet you a thousand dollars Reggie has something to do with the murders at that department store."

Tom reached over and began to unbutton the top of my blouse. "Guess what? I get to sleep in tomorrow. No strategy meeting first thing. And why don't you bet something I *really* want?"

I shook my head. "You know what being newly married to you is like? It's like walking a marathon instead of running it. I hardly ever get to see you, so we're always in . . . what's it called? *The heady throes of romance.* At the rate we're going, we'll be newlyweds for the next ten years."

"So living with me is like stopping smoking and walking a marathon. What's a heady throe of romance?"

"Plus I can see you're just bowled over with my marvelous powers of deduction."

He kept unbuttoning. "As always."

"And I see catching a killer is the highest priority for you right now."

He let go of my blouse and reached for the phone. "I'll bet *you* a thousand dollars that I can put in a call to have Shaman Krill picked up faster than you can get those clothes off and meet me upstairs."

I didn't collect on his bet. I could have. When Tom reached the sheriff's department, they — true to form — put him on hold. I even had time for a shower.

Later, much later, I murmured, "I love you, love you, love you," into his ear and buried my nose in his short, sweet-smelling hair. For a night that had taken so many bizarre turns, this one was ending up pretty well. He pulled me in close. Pale moonlight filled our bedroom. I felt sleep fall as gently as the pink bursts of fireworks had scattered their lights over the lake.

When Sunday morning came, Tom was still sleeping soundly. I slipped out of bed with the idea that a hefty dose of caffeine was in order. But Scout the cat boldly rolled onto his back in front of the espresso machine and demanded attention. I rubbed his stomach as he writhed from side to side, demanding more! more! Eventually he decided he'd had enough affection and hopped off the counter, and I was able to load the machine with fresh beans and water. Soon dark strands of espresso hissed into the twin shot glasses and I poured them over milk and ice and stepped out onto the front porch.

The brilliant morning sky promised a return to hot weather. Geraniums and johnny-jump-ups in the porch pots moved in the breeze. A dog barked in the distance. Across the street, the Routts' house was silent: no Colin crying, no jazz saxophone. The morning of the fifth of July always felt odd. It was as if time had slipped around midnight during the fight for independence, and left the whole country to suffer a summer hangover.

I sipped my icy latte and wondered how Charles Braithwaite was doing. Julian had just gone through shock. He'd managed to recover fairly quickly. But Charles was older. Age usually dictated a longer recuperation from trauma. And speaking of recovering from trauma, Marla was due to greet the world again this afternoon. I checked my watch: seven-twenty.

When I finished the coffee I felt heavy-hearted and tired. I toyed with the idea of going back to bed. But before I could do so, the phone rang. I bolted for it so the ringing wouldn't wake up Tom. It was Officer Boyd from the sheriff's department.

"He's asleep," I whispered. "Can it wait?"

"Just tell him we got Krill," said Boyd. "Tom said it was your idea anyway, that the guy was a phony. Looks as if you were right, Goldy. Krill buckled when we asked him if his employer was Hotchkiss. He told us Hotchkiss hired him to be disruptive, even gave him a script. The lingo, the chants, the dead bunny — you name it."

"But did Krill drive the truck that killed Claire? Did he . . . have some connection to Gentileschi?"

"Not that he'll admit to. But don't worry," Boyd said in his laconic, confident manner. "He'll crack. Give it time. Tell Schulz when he wakes up that we'll have a confession in no time."

I hung up. I remembered my promise to give an update on Marla to the St. Luke's parishioners at the early service. Rather than wake Tom, I left him a note on the kitchen table that said Boyd was working on Krill and that he should call the department. As I quietly slid into a skirt and blouse, the key to Prince & Grogan storage caught my eye from where I'd left it on the bureau after removing it from my bra on Friday. I was, after all, going to

471

church, I reflected guiltily, and there was that bit about *thou shalt not steal.* I slid the key into my pocket. I would return the key. Eventually.

The sparse congregation at St. Luke's all looked droopy-eyed. The interim pastor, who was serving while a parish committee searched for a new rector after the loss of our last one, forgot to turn on the altar lights, but no one minded. We moved slowly through the prayers. Thankfully, there weren't any hymns. The choir, the organist, and our voices, were on vacation. When asked by the priest, I gave a very brief update on Marla's condition. During the intercessions, when we made special requests for intervention and healing, I tried to allow my mind to become blank. The excitement of the past few days would eventually fade. The spirit would return to its old rhythms. Into the blankness I summoned Marla's face. Then Charles Braithwaite's, then old Mr. Routt's. I prayed for Julian, for the repose of the souls of Claire and Nick.

Without warning, the parade of faces became muddled in my mind. The more I struggled to focus, the more curiosity insinuated itself, like Scout plopping between me and the espresso machine. *You're tired,* I told myself. *You've been through a lot.* I leaned back in the pew.

All around me parishioners continued to offer their supplications. I opened my eyes, then shut them. It didn't help. My mind was preoccupied with images, questions, memories that didn't connect. I remembered Arch repeating his science teacher's assertion that the memory was like a Rolodex. When you can't remember something, it's not that you don't have the information. You just can't access it. In my mind's eye I saw a vehicle following mine down to the mall the morning of the Mignon banquet. Saw again someone watching outside our house at night. Heard Shaman Krill shout sixties-style derision, saw him swing a dead rabbit at me. Viewed the pain on Mr. Routt's unseeing face. Felt the spray of glass as Nick Gentileschi's body hit the Mignon counter.

My muscles trembled with fatigue. The gentle susurration of prayer rose from the pews all around, and scraps of remembered conversation surfaced in my mind. About Claire: *That woman could sell cosmetics. . . .* From Nick: *We're reviewing the films.* From Frances Markasian: *They've got a security problem.* From Babs Braithwaite: *There's somebody back there.*

But the police had their man: Shaman Krill. Krill, or somebody else that Reggie Hotchkiss had hired, or maybe even Reggie himself, could have done it all. Claire was a fabulous saleswoman, so Reggie certainly had motivation to get rid of one of the competitor's best producers. Reggie further undermined Mignon's sales with his bogus Spare the Hares campaign. Covering all the bases, he also copied their products in his own catalogue.

Had Reggie covered all the bases with Nick Gentileschi, though? That was what didn't fit. Why would someone have to kill the security chief? Because of potentially embarrassing photographs? Because of something that had turned up on the films? What about the cash refund problem? Frances had said, *It's all computerized, so it looks official.* But what was official? I had seen stacks of computer print-outs in the department store office. Would they detail transactions, or would those be in the ledger?

Someone touched my shoulder; I opened my eyes.

"We're passing the peace," a woman told me. She had gray hair pulled back in a neat bun, crinkles around her eyes, and a worried smile. "Are you all right?"

"Fine, thank you." I stood quickly and shook her hand. "The peace of the Lord."

She smiled and squeezed my hand. "Peace."

Which was what Arch had said. And Reggie Hotchkiss, the plagiarizing pacifist.

With enormous effort I turned my attention back to the service and went through the communion portion of the liturgy. Afterward, the tired crowd engaged in halfhearted chat, and I nabbed a cup of church coffee. The stuff tasted like something you would lick off the inside of a twenty-year-old aluminum pot.

It was nine-fifteen. As I climbed into the van, the curious voices rocketing around in my brain began shooting off again. What could that camera above the Mignon counter record? What did the printouts and the ledger show? If Shaman Krill was under arrest, what harm could it do if I went down to the store and just looked around a little bit? If I could be there when Prince & Grogan opened, maybe I could snoop uninterrupted. If somebody like Stan White bothered me, I could use as my excuse the fact that I was looking for the receipt that Frances was so furious I'd lost.

I revved the van and took off for the mall. When I arrived, I realized that people were as reluctant to shop on the morning of July the fifth as they were to go to church. I felt foolish going into Prince & Grogan when the doors were finally unlocked. The place was virtually empty.

When I arrived at the department store offices, I announced to the woman behind the credit window: "I need to see Lisa in accounts payable. Is she in yet?"

"I don't know. You can check."

Lisa was not in. I rifled through the stacks of printouts on her office floor until I came to the one marked *Cosmetics*. I scanned each of the folded pages, but they yielded only columns of numbers, and then rows of numbers across from the columns under headings like YTD. Doggone it.

Determined, I picked up the accordion-folded sheaf, slipped the printout under my blouse, and headed out of Lisa's office. If I compared the printout to the ledger, maybe it would all make sense. Hugging the printout to my body, I rode down the escalator.

The Mignon counter looked as if a bomb blast had hit it. Tape held together the web of remaining glass. Plywood covered the bare spots. The broken blind was also haphazardly covered with strips of plywood. Harriet Wells, her blond hair frothed up in another of her twists, her Mignon uniform crisp, was tidying up. She looked up at me with a surprised, happy face.

"You're the last person I expected to see here!" she said with a high, tinkly laugh. She sat on her stool beside the counter and scowled. "This is always a slow morning."

I shifted the printout around and said, "Listen, Harriet, I'm looking for a receipt that

476

I might have dropped in here the other day, when Nick fell —" She tilted her head at me appraisingly, then closed her eyes and shuddered. "— anyway," I went on, "the purchase wasn't for me, it was for someone else, and now they're wanting the receipt, and blaming me that I lost it."

Before she could answer, a male customer came up to the far side of the counter and began to test perfumes. Harriet slid off her stool, came over to the counter and reached underneath for a Tupperware container of muffins.

"Are you hungry?" she asked with a bright smile.

My stomach reminded me that I had had quite a bit of caffeine and nothing substantial in the last three hours. "Of course. Especially for something you've baked."

"These are made with sour cream," she confessed as she took the top off the container. "But see if you can guess the other ingredient. You're so good at that."

I took a bite. Sour cream, though fattening, was a good ingredient for keeping things fresh. I even had a pound cake recipe that required that the finished cake be wrapped for twenty-four hours before being served. The muffin was buttery, rich, and delicious. It was flecked with tiny bits of green that tasted like mint.

"Can't tell what it is," I said, then looked down at the customer testing perfumes. It was Reggie Hotchkiss. My heart sank.

"Okay, Harriet," he crowed. "Tell me what was so important you had to see me on a Sunday morning."

"Look in the trash, if you want," Harriet said over her shoulder. "This shouldn't take long . . . I never tell Hotchkiss a thing. You can try in front of the counter too, although the cleaning crew's been in to vacuum up all the glass and . . . you know."

Did I ever. I scooted behind the counter and slipped the computer paper out of my blouse. What a relief. I just hoped Harriet hadn't seen it. When Reggie quizzed Harriet and sprayed one cologne on his right arm, the other on his left, I looked up at the security camera. From where it was positioned, it could take in the entire front of the counter, the cash register — at right angles to the counter — and the file cabinets and storage areas behind the counter.

Harriet was murmuring questions to Reggie, and he replied more expansively and loudly to each inquiry. Eventually he began to yak about perfume, citrus versus floral, pine versus patchouli. He seemed to be ignoring me, but I'd seen him do that before. I took another bite of muffin.

First things first. I put the computer paper beside the large blue ledger that I'd seen Dusty flipping through Thursday, the first day I'd visited the Mignon counter. Then I squinted at the file drawer. I remembered Dusty writing down all the information about my complexion and putting it on a client card. Would it be filed under my name or Dusty's? I took another careful bite of muffin and slid open the file drawer. *Routt. Satterfield. Wells.* Each file was jammed with the cards. Dusty had the least, Claire's file bulged, and Harriet had the most, which would make sense since she'd been working for Mignon the longest. I wondered if Dusty's was slender because she hadn't been working there as long as the others or because she was less successful. Or could it be because she'd been moving client cards over to Hotchkiss Skin & Hair?

Harriet looked around to see what I was doing. I held up the muffin with one hand, while making an enthusiastic okay sign with the other. She nodded, rolled her eyes in exasperation, and turned back to Reggie. He seemed to be enjoying making Harriet uncomfortable. I slid the file drawer closed and walked over to the trash receptacle. It was empty. My eye fell on the ledger and printout. I struggled with my conscience for thirty seconds, then opened the ledger first. If Claire was a top sales associate that Reggie was trying to get rid of, the proof should be in there, and be easier to read than the printout. Maybe they would subpoena the ledger at Reggie's trial.

I reached over and helped myself to another green-speckled muffin as I turned the ledger pages and tried to decipher them.

"Goldy!"

I looked around. Dusty was standing by the lipsticks looking disheveled and tired, but ready to work in her Mignon smock. "Why is Reggie Hotchkiss here on a Sunday morning, do you know? What are *you* doing here? My God, look at this mess."

I felt immediate guilt. What was I doing, anyway? "I'm just looking at this sales ledger. Show me what's what as compared to the printouts, will you? Did Claire have good sales?"

Dusty glanced down at Reggie and Harriet, then said, "Well, I guess so." She moved to the ledger. "She was getting there. Let's see." She flipped expertly through the ledger pages and then ran a gnawed fingernail across a row of columns. "April, I had eight hundred in sales, Claire had fifteen hundred twenty-two, Harriet had — whoa! three thousand and fifty." She flipped a page. "May, I didn't do so hot. Six-fifty. Claire had two thousand eighty and Harriet had twenty-five hundred. See? That's what happens when the weather's warm. People don't shop."

"Were you planning to take your clients over to Hotchkiss Skin & Hair?" I inquired.

Dusty put her finger to her lips and looked both ways. Harriet and Reggie were indeed watching us. "Shh! You want to get me into trouble?"

"Tell me this," I said in a very low tone. "Did you take the receipt out of my bag at Hotchkiss Skin & Hair while I was getting my facial?"

"Goldy! God! What's the matter with you? What receipt?"

I decided to cast the bait out one more time. "I'm sorry, I guess it's just because of your grandfather, and because you were expelled from Elk Park Prep. For stealing."

She colored deeply. "Ex-*cuse* me?"

"Well, why *were* you expelled from Elk Park Prep? Wasn't it for stealing?" I had a sudden, devastating thought. "Or because you were pregnant? With Colin?"

She turned around and closed the book with a dramatic thwack. "I'm like . . . who told you that?"

"Well, Julian wasn't sure. . . ."

Dusty rolled her made-up eyes dramatically. "It wasn't for stealing. And my *mother* was pregnant, not me. I told you, the woman does not know the meaning of birth control. I was expelled for *drinking*. I mean, Julian should know, he was there!"

"For *drinking?*"

"Yes — in that stupid bio class we had together. We had to do some dumb test about chlorophyll. We were putting sugar into grain alcohol and then placing strawberry leaves in the solution, and then we had to wait for something to happen, God knows what. I mean, it was *way* boring." She lifted her hands and shook them like a frustrated Italian shopkeeper. "So I figured, hey. We've got strawberries, we've got sugar, we've got booze. We've got daiquiris! So I . . . Goldy, what's wrong?"

What was wrong? My knees felt rubbery. My hands were trembling. Damn, but I must be more tired than I thought.

"Okay, look," I said impatiently. "Just show me how the printout compares to the ledger. Please," I added.

Dusty flipped the ledger back open and then shuffled the fingers of her free hand through the printout. When she came to the right pages, her pretty face wrinkled in puzzlement as she looked first at the ledger, then at the printout, then back at the ledger.

"Something's wrong here," she said, exasperated. "The printout has Claire's figures for June much lower than what she put in the ledger, because of some big returns —"

There was a sudden *pop*. I looked incredulously at the top of the sales ledger. It had been torn . . . it had been *shot*.

Dusty looked over her shoulder and grabbed me.

Pop! went another bullet, smack into the glass case containing makeup. The glass shattered and tan-colored stuff began to spill down the shelves. What in the . . . ?

"Move away from that book, Dusty," said Harriet's voice.

Holding me tight either to protect herself or me, Dusty let out a small shriek. Together, we stumbled backward. I couldn't see Reggie Hotchkiss.

Harriet was holding a small gun. She shot at my hand that had pulled the ledger down off the counter. I dropped the book and dived into the aisle.

"What the hell, Harriet!" Dusty crawled over to my side and glared at the other saleswoman. "What the *hell* is the matter with you? Put that down! We weren't *doing* anything. Go away!" she yelled at Reggie, who was advancing down the aisle. "Reggie, help! We've got a gun here!"

Reggie shouted something unintelligible and

ran toward the exit. I started to crab-walk sideways toward the entrance of the shoe department.

"You just *had* to know," said Harriet acidly as she came steadily toward me. "Questioning Nick. Sucking up to Dusty. Going after Reggie. You said *he* was the one who knew too much. That's why I told him to come here this morning. But it's you. And now you're getting into the printouts. Did you view the films, too?"

"Put the gun away, Harriet!" Dusty yelled. "Look out, Goldy!"

Harriet pivoted and strode toward Dusty. Again the little gun went *pop*.

"You bitch!" shouted Dusty. Crimson blossomed on the sleeve of her Mignon smock. "You shot my arm! God*damn* you!" Holding her arm, Dusty scrabbled toward Shoes.

I tried to move my legs, to get them underneath me. Harriet turned back and walked carefully in my direction. Why couldn't I move? Why did my hands and feet tingle? I knew foods . . . I knew poisons . . . *Something grown right near here.*

"Hemlock," I said as loudly as I could as she neared me once again. "You put hemlock in the muffins. You made them and were waiting to give them to Reggie after he blabbed about all he'd learned about Mignon. Only, he didn't know anything."

"Right," said Harriet, and fired again.

I thanked God she was a lousy shot when the bullet ripped through the upholstery of one of the seats in the shoe department. A deafening clang split the air. Someone — Dusty? — had tripped the fire alarm. Startled, Harriet whipped around, momentarily distracted, and I grunted ferociously and mustered every bit of strength to bring my legs underneath me. I was only five steps away from the escalator. With the few people left in the store now heading for the exits, I floundered toward the moving steps. Where was I going? My body was going numb. Was it the hemlock? Or had Harriet actually shot me? Where the hell was Security? It felt as if I were being taken over by Novocain. I'd figure out what to do if I could just get to the second floor. The steps moved. I tried to duck.

Harriet was whirling around, confused. Looking for me. I went lower on the steps, under the escalator's metal railing. Had she seen me? Hard to tell. I felt my heart beating as I thought hard. The sales figures: Harriet had been the leading sales associate, but Claire had been closing in fast on her, according to what Dusty had shown me in the ledger. Claire had reported her client cards had been stolen. I knew who had committed the theft. And maybe it was the theft of the client cards that Nick Gentileschi had seen on the tapes. Or perhaps he'd seen, on closeup, who it was that was carefully palming cash receipts and giving herself the stolen refunds, while charging the returns to other associates' numbers.

Half prone, I scrambled up the cold metal steps of the escalator, which seemed to be moving with preternatural slowness toward the second floor. Yes, Harriet knew the ins and outs of this business. She knew what Nick Gentileschi was up to behind the mirrors in the women's fitting room. She'd probably offered to trade her knowledge of his illegal activities for his silence and the photos of Babs. It wouldn't have been too hard for Harriet to convince Mr. Kinky Gentileschi that she was willing to have some kind of interesting encounter up in the blind. Hell, she'd probably offered to bribe him in the way he enjoyed best. Then she'd put the incriminating photos in his pocket, I wagered, to implicate the Braithwaites in his death.

"Goldy!" Harriet shouted. "I just want to talk to you!"

Yeah, sure. Like when she followed us down to the mall to see where Claire parked so that she could order her out to get something from her car. Like when she threw bleach water on me when I'd started snooping around. Or when she'd watched outside my house, so she could see if I headed down for the mall and the telltale printout sometime, maybe early in the morning, when she wasn't personally working at the cosmetics counter.

Finally I was at the top of the moving stairs. Not yet sure of how much muscular control I still had, I rolled wildly onto the floor and hit a china display. The whole thing toppled over with an ear-splitting crash. I cursed and hauled myself to my feet. I had an absurd vision of Socrates: How much time did hemlock take to kill someone? But I knew something the doomed philosopher hadn't. Thank God for Pete the espresso man's advertising. I'd learned the antidote for hemlock from his pamphlet. It was one of my favorite substances: coffee. And I'd had enough of it this morning — a four-shot latte and a big, strong cup after church — that the poison wasn't having the swift, lethal effect Harriet envisioned. I just needed more caffeine, and quick.

I could hear her heels *tap-tap-tap*ping up the escalator. I tottered recklessly through the bathing suit department. Harriet would be up here any moment with her little gun. I didn't have time to get to the exit. She'd see me and catch up. Damn, damn, damn. Then I noticed the dressing room. Hope bloomed. Could I still have the stolen key in my pocket?

I certainly hoped so.

Moving seemed a little easier at this point, and I had the absurd thought that perhaps hemlock was like heroin. If you kept propelling yourself around during an overdose, things might not end up so badly. I groped in my pocket, found the key, and fumbled to unlock the door to the storage room. I turned the handle and prayed. It opened. I careened into the darkness.

"Goldy!" came Harriet's voice again over the blare of the fire alarm. "Come out now!"

I wasn't in the mood to provide her with a better target. With renewed determination I wobbled in the direction that I hoped would lead to that other door, the one on the left that I now realized led to Nick Gentileschi's office. The space was not pitch-black. Light seeped downward from a distant skylight. I banged into the wall painfully, fell to my knees, and began to grope. I came to the moulding and then the door handle. I heard Harriet come into the darkness behind me. I turned the handle.

The door was locked.

"Goldy! Quit running! You just don't understand — I *had* to do what I did."

I felt the wall, wondering if Harriet had reloaded. My hand touched metal. Metal steps. I was confused. A metal staircase to what?

"I'm going to find a light!" Harriet warned, close, too close. "I'm going to turn it on!"

I scrambled up the steps. There had to be some exit up there at the top. And then I remembered Frances Markasian sitting on something — a raised box or platform that was just there, on top of the roof. Had it been the Prince & Grogan roof? Oh, please let that be it, I thought desperately. Some exit that they used for repairs. Please, anything. Up, up I climbed.

Thin fluorescent lights blinked once, then came on just as I reached the top step. Oh, Lord. The raised box was fastened with a schoolhouse lock. I glanced down. Harriet had the pistol pointed up at me.

She shouted, "Goldy, come down now!" Then she fired again.

The bullet ricocheted deafeningly off metal. I twisted the lock and pushed vertically with all my strength. The heavy door groaned. I was on the roof, I was out. The fair organizers were in the throes of breaking down the tents. Nearly everyone was gone. But I thanked the powers that be that Pete's Espresso Bar was the last tent standing. The King of Advertising wasn't going to be the first to leave, especially when volunteer crew members might want to buy coffee.

I ran awkwardly across the concrete and

fell at Pete's ankles.

"Espresso — straight — at least six shots — quick," I panted.

Pete switched on the machine and looked down. Today's T-shirt said I'M LEAN, MEAN, AND FULL OF CAFFEINE. "I swear, Goldy," he said. "I wish every customer was like you."

And then we heard a pistol shot.

It was over.

19

When Tom showed up with an investigative team at the department store, I was being discharged from the hospital across the street. I'd been given charcoal tablets, which I dutifully swallowed. The year before, I'd had an unpleasant encounter with the highly toxic — not aphrodisiac — substance known as Spanish fly, and I knew you had to get your system filtered, and quick. I wasn't going to have to stay in the hospital, the ER doc told me, but he repeatedly remarked how lucky it was I knew the antidote for hemlock and was able to get it so quickly. I couldn't agree more.

Tom scooped me up in his arms and hugged me long and hard. Julian had returned home and found Arch had already returned from Keystone. They'd called Tom on his cell phone and said they were on their way to see Marla.

"Sounds good to me," I said as I got into Tom's car.

He told me they'd found Harriet's body behind the security room door. Self-inflicted wound, but I knew that already. I didn't want

491

to hear the details.

"She couldn't stand the competition," Tom observed. "I guess Claire was just too successful for her to deal with. After all, Harriet had been Mignon's number-one salesperson for years, and now Claire was about to surpass her effortlessly. Surpass Harriet, that is, unless Harriet could relentlessly charge returns to her competitor's number. And I'll bet Harriet's cash-receipt scam is what Claire was helping Gentileschi with."

"You bet, huh?" I said. "Why don't you bet with something I really want?"

"Oh, woman," he said laughingly as we pulled into Marla's driveway, "you are going to regret those words."

Marla was walking very tentatively down the rock steps by the entryway to her house. Her skin was still sallow. She wore a brightly colored muumuu and her normally frizzy hair was pulled back into pigtails held with sparkling barrettes. The clothes and hair were courtesy of the nurse, no doubt. As she moved haltingly forward, Julian held one of her arms and Arch the other.

Four days ago, while I was preparing food, I'd reflected that beauty was in the eye of the beholder. It was something I'd always said, sort of offhand, the way the mind runs over a cliché without ever really examining its meaning. And yet if what was visually appealing did depend on what the beholder valued, who set the standards? How were the values determined?

In the past five days I'd seen and felt more pain than I cared to contemplate. John Routt had spent the best decades of his life blind. Nick Gentileschi's twisted desire to capture voluptuousness had gotten him killed. The Braithwaites' unhappiness with each other had led both to pursue goals of beauty that were unattainable, or easily destroyed. Reggie Hotchkiss had stolen and plotted and intimidated, trying to sell women expensive products that promised everything and did next to nothing. And Claire had been so gorgeous, so enthusiastic in her selling of overpriced, worthless goods, that it had gotten her killed.

Marla arrived at the bottom of the stone staircase. She let go of Arch and Julian and sank to rest on one of the steps. I rushed over.

"You're here!" she squawked. "I can't believe it." She held out her arms, and I scooted up and sat on a cold stone to embrace her. She murmured, "I feel like hell. And I look worse, I know."

"You look absolutely wonderful," I said, and meant it. "You look like heaven."

INDEX
TO THE
RECIPES

AUTHOR'S NOTE: All the recipes contain less than 30 percent fat. "What-to-Do-with-All-the-Egg-Yolks Bread," while technically "lowfat," is not low in cholesterol.

The employees of THORNDIKE PRESS hope you have enjoyed this Large Print book. All our Large Print books are designed for easy reading — and they're made to last.

Other Thorndike Large Print books are available at your library, through selected bookstores, or directly from us. Suggestions for books you would like to see in Large Print are always welcome.

For more information about current and upcoming titles, please call or mail your name and address to:

THORNDIKE PRESS
PO Box 159
Thorndike, Maine 04986
800/223-6121
207/948-2962

2 Routed 3.14 — 4.21
su 4.21
set 6 ha 4.23 (7)

Goldy Bear, 5